Property and Trust Law in Slovenia

Property and Trust Law in Slovenia

Second Edition

Jerca Kramberger Škerl
Ana Vlahek

This book was originally published as a monograph in the International Encyclopaedia of Laws/Property and Trust Law.

Founding Editor: Roger Blanpain
General Editor: Frank Hendrickx
Volume Editors: Alain Verbeke & Vincent Sagaert

Wolters Kluwer

Published by:
Kluwer Law International B.V.
PO Box 316
2400 AH Alphen aan den Rijn
The Netherlands
E-mail: international-sales@wolterskluwer.com
Website: lrus.wolterskluwer.com

Sold and distributed by:
Wolters Kluwer Legal & Regulatory U.S.
7201 McKinney Circle
Frederick, MD 21704
United States of America
Email: customer.service@wolterskluwer.com

ISBN 978-94-035-2740-6

e-Book: ISBN 978-94-035-2741-3
web-PDF: ISBN 978-94-035-2742-0

This title is available on www.kluwerlawonline.com

The Authors

Dr Jerca Kramberger Škerl is associate professor of civil and commercial law at the Faculty of Law of the University of Ljubljana. She obtained her bachelor's degree in law from this institution in 2002. She studied law and German language as a visiting student at the University of Tübingen, Germany. She continued her studies at the Faculty of Law of the University of Poitiers, France, where she gained a master's degree in private law in 2003. Since 2003, she has been employed at the Faculty of Law of the University of Ljubljana, Slovenia, first as a junior researcher and subsequently as teaching assistant and then university docent for civil and commercial law. Since 2012, she has also been employed as a researcher at the Institute for Comparative Law at the Faculty of Law in Ljubljana. She obtained a double PhD from the universities of Ljubljana and Poitiers in 2008, her thesis comprising a comparative study in the field of the recognition and enforcement of foreign judgments. She has published academic articles and has delivered papers at national and international conferences. Currently, she is teaching Civil Procedure, Private International Law and French Legal Language at the Faculty of Law in Ljubljana. She has been dealing with property and trust law within her research on comparative and private international law. Beside Slovenian, the author speaks English, French, German, Croatian, and Serbian.

Dr Jerca Kramberger Škerl is the author of the following chapters of this monograph: General Background, Part II, and Part V.

Dr Ana Vlahek is associate professor of civil and commercial law at the Faculty of Law of the University of Ljubljana, Slovenia. She obtained her bachelor's degree in law from the University of Ljubljana in 2003 and continued her education at University of Ljubljana with postgraduate studies in civil and commercial law including short-term research and education visits to Cambridge, Cologne, and Salzburg. In 2005, she was also an intern at UNCITRAL in Vienna. She obtained her PhD in 2009 by defending a thesis on derivative transfer of movables in the European legal environment. Since 2003, she has been employed at the Faculty of Law of the University of Ljubljana, first as teaching assistant, and subsequently as university professor. Since 2008, she has also been employed as a researcher at the Institute for Comparative Law at the Faculty of Law in Ljubljana. She has published several academic articles and has delivered papers at national and international conferences, her major interests being European law, competition law, property law, and contracts. She has been dealing with property law as a lecturer of property law at the Faculty of Law in Ljubljana and at the Faculty of Civil and Geodetic Engineering in Ljubljana, as well as within her PhD and other research. She is also a co-author of the Commentary on Slovenian Code of Property Law as well as of other property law related contributions and has in the last decade been actively involved in the symposia and other forums dealing with the challenges of regulation of property relations in Slovenia. Besides Slovenian, the author speaks English, German, Croatian, and Serbian, additionally she has working knowledge of French. Dr Ana Vlahek is the author of the following chapters of this monograph: Part I, Part III, and Part IV.

Table of Contents

List of Abbreviations

ABGB	Allgemeines Bürgerliches Gesetzbuch
AEDC	Act on Establishing Divided Co-ownership and on Determining the Land Belonging to a Building
BPLRA	Basic Property Law Relations Act
CESA	Claim Enforcement and Security Act
CO	Code of Obligations
CO with Commentary	Juhart/Plavšak (Eds), *Obligacijski zakonik s komentarjem* [Code of Obligations with Commentary], GV Založba, Ljubljana, 2003
CPA	Civil Procedure Act
CPL	Code of Property Law
CPL with Commentary 2016	Juhart et al., *Stvarnopravni zakonik (SPZ) s komentarjem* [Code of Property Law with Commentary], Uradni list RS, Pravna fakulteta v Ljubljani, Pravna fakulteta v Mariboru, Ljubljana 2016
CPL with Commentary 2004	Juhart et al., *Stvarnopravni zakonik s komentarjem* [Code of Property Law with Commentary], GV Založba, Ljubljana, 2004
FC	Family Code
FC with Commentary	Novak (Ed), *Komentar Družinskega zakonika* [Commentary of the Family Code], Uradni list, Ljubljana, 2019
FOIPCDA	Financial Operations, Insolvency Proceedings and Compulsory Dissolution Act
Ger.	German
HA	Housing Act
IA	Inheritance Act
Lat.	Latin
LRA	Land Registry Act
MFN	Most Favoured Nation
MFRA	Marriage and Family Relations Act

List of Abbreviations

NATO	North Atlantic Treaty Organization
NCCPA	Non-Contentious Civil Procedure Act
OECD	Organisation for Economic Co-operation and Development
OSCE	Organization for Security and Co-operation in Europe
Property Law	Juhart et al., *Stvarno pravo* [Property Law], GV Založba, Ljubljana, 2007
RS	Republic of Slovenia
Sl.	Slovenian
SPA	Spatial Planning Act
SRS	Socialist Republic of Slovenia
UN	United Nations Organization

General Introduction

§1. General Background on Slovenia

I. Geography

1. Slovenia is a central European country situated south of Austria, east of Italy, west of Hungary, and north of Croatia. It has an area of 20,273 km^2 and a population of approximately 2 million. Most of the country has a continental climate. The littoral zone by the Adriatic Sea (the Slovenian coast is about 50 km long) and the western part of the country share a milder sub-Mediterranean climate. The Alps stretch throughout the north-western part of the country and include the highest Slovenian mountain, Triglav, at 2,864 m. The two largest lakes, Bled and Bohinj, important Slovenian natural and tourist attractions, are situated in this region with an alpine climate. The eastern part of Slovenia shares the Pannonian plane with neighbouring Hungary. The south and south-western part of the country is dominated by the Karst (limestone) region, the location of some impressive Karst phenomena, such as the famous Škocjan (protected by UNESCO) and Postojna caves. Almost half of the country is covered by forests, making Slovenia one of the most forested European countries. Slovenia is also known for its vineyards, which stretch nearly throughout thc country. The capital of Slovenia is Ljubljana.

II. Cultural Situation in Slovenia

2. The population of Slovenia is of approximately 2 million. Slovenia's main ethnic group is Slovene (83%), and 95% of the population are Slovenian citizens.[1] Other nationalities living in the country are those from the former republics of Yugoslavia (Serbs, Croats, Bosnians, Macedonians, and Montenegrins), as well as Hungarians, Italians, Albanians, Roma, and others. Official minority status is recognized to the Hungarian and the Italian autochthon minorities, and their languages are the second official languages in their respective traditional areas of habitation. The Constitution also mentions the Roma population by providing that the law shall regulate the status and the special rights of this population living in Slovenia (Article 65). Slovenians adhere mostly (almost 60%) to the Roman Catholic

1. The exact number of the population in October 2019 is 2,094,060, see the Internet site of the Statistical Office of the Republic of Slovenija, https://www.stat.si/StatWeb/Field/Index/17.

Church, although many other religions are present in the country, as well as there being a relatively high percentage of atheists (10%).[2]

3. As Slovenians succeeded in gaining independence and forming their own national state only in 1991, the language has always been the most important element of the national identity. The first examples of texts in the old Slovenian language date to around 1000 AD (the so-called Freising Manuscripts). The first book in Slovenian was written and printed in 1550 by the Protestant reformer Primož Trubar (1508–1586), who is considered to be the 'father' of the Slovenian language. Baron Janez Vajkard Valvasor (1641–1693), also a member of the Royal Society of London, published the first encyclopaedia, dealing with Carniola (a large part of the territory of present day Slovenia) – *The Glory of the Duchy of Carniola* – in 1689. Between 1848 and 1918, in the era of the so-called Slovene National Awakening, numerous theatres and publishing houses, as well as political, financial, and cultural organizations, were founded. France Prešeren (1800–1849), considered the greatest Slovenian poet and also the author of the national anthem, *Zdravljica,* played an important role in that period, when Slovenian language was still not commonly used in the intellectual and artistic circles. Ivan Cankar (1876–1918), the central figure of the Slovenian modernist literature, is regarded as the greatest Slovenian writer and one of the most important Slovenian playwrights. Work by both has been translated into many foreign languages. Ever since the nineteenth century, the cultural life has continued to blossom in the territory of Slovenia with its innumerable professional and non-professional cultural institutions and many internationally renowned artists and scholars. World fame has been obtained, among others, by writer Boris Pahor, painter Zoran Mušič, philosopher Slavoj Žižek, and architects Jože Plečnik and Max Fabiani.

4. In 1997, Ljubljana hosted the European Month of Culture. In 2012, the European Capital of Culture title was shared by the Slovenian city of Maribor and the Portuguese city of Guimarães. Ljubljana also won the European Green Capital Award in 2016. The Partisan Hospital Franja, situated near the town of Idrija, was one of the sixteen sites to be awarded the European Heritage Label in 2014. Slovenian cities host numerous cultural events throughout the year, as for example the Ljubljana Festival featuring the highest level cultural events every summer since 1953, the Ljubljana Jazz Festival (since 1959), the intercultural Festival Lent held each summer in Maribor since 1986, and the Ljubljana International Film Festival since 1989.

5. The oldest of the Slovenian public universities is the University of Ljubljana, founded in 1919. About two-thirds of all students in Slovenia attend this university,[3] which comprises twenty-three faculties and three artistic academies. The Law Faculty of the University of Ljubljana had a total of 1,121 students in the year 2019/

2. All data was gathered by the Statistical Office of the Republic of Slovenia during the population census of 2002, www.stat.si/Popis2002/si/rezultati_slovenija_prebivalstvo_dz.htm.
3. The total number of 37,874 students were enrolled at the University of Ljubljana in the academic year 2018/19, http://www.uni-lj.si/university/university_in_numbers/.

2020. The other public universities are the University of Maribor, founded in north-eastern Slovenia in 1975, and the University of Primorska, founded in the coastal region in 2003. The first private university was established in Nova Gorica in 2006. Followed the University of Novo Mesto and the so-called New University, both in 2017. Law is taught at the universities of Ljubljana and Maribor and at the New University.

III. History and Political System

6. Historically, the territory of today's Slovenia had been part of many European countries before gaining independence in 1991. Slavic peoples first populated these lands in the sixth century AD. In the seventh and eighth centuries AD, the northern part of modern-day Slovenia belonged to the Slavic State of Carantania, which was later annexed to the Frankish empire. Since that time, Slovenian territory has been part of the Holy Roman Empire; the Habsburg Monarchy; the Illyrian Provinces; the Austrian Empire (and subsequently Austria-Hungary); the State of Slovenes, Croats, and Serbs; the Kingdom of Serbs, Croats, and Slovenes; the Kingdom of Yugoslavia; the Democratic Federal Yugoslavia (March 1945–November 1945); the Federal People's Republic of Yugoslavia (1945–1963) and of the Socialist Federal Republic of Yugoslavia (1963–1991). A large part of western Slovenia belonged to Italy between the two World Wars and was returned to Slovenia in 1947 and in 1975, when the final border between Slovenia and Italy was determined.

7. *After the Second World War* and up until its independence, Slovenia was one of the six constituent republics of the Socialist (until 1963, People's) Federal Republic of Yugoslavia. The official language in Slovenia was Slovene (as well as Italian and Hungarian in the areas of population of the respective minorities). The economic foundation of the new country was the state property, created mainly on the basis of different revolutionary measures, especially nationalization. The legislative competence was divided between the federation and the republics. Each republic had its own executive, legislative, and judiciary bodies. The overall competences of the republics were further reinforced by the amendments to the Yugoslav Constitution in 1971. Notwithstanding its socialist denomination, the political system in Yugoslavia was, at least from the major constitutional change in 1953, very different from that of the countries under Soviet domination (some describe the Yugoslav system as a 'milder version of socialism'[4]). This system was called 'self-management'. Yugoslavia was not a member of the Warsaw Treaty and played a leading role in the international organization of non-aligned nations, the Non-Aligned Movement, founded in 1955. These circumstances were reflected in the era of political and economic transition around the year 1990, which was a relatively

4. Galič, *International Encyclopaedia of Laws, Civil Procedure – Slovenia*, 13 (Wolters Kluwer 2008).

smaller change for Yugoslavia than for some other communist and socialist countries.[5] In fact, the majority of the legal texts adopted before independence could be applied in the new social order without many changes.

8. One sign of the approaching *independence*, as well as its necessary preconditions, were the amendments to the Slovenian Constitution adopted between 1989 and 1991, which reflected the growing demands for the democratization of the society as well as the wish for independence. The prefix 'socialist' was eradicated from the official name of the Republic in 1990. The national plebiscite on the question of independence was held on 23 December 1990. About 88.5% of the population with the right to vote voted for independence (and about 95% of those who actually voted, since voting in elections is not obligatory in Slovenia), which was declared on 25 June 1991. It was legitimated by the constitutional act adopted by the Slovene National Assembly, which was followed by the 'ten-day war' between the Yugoslav army, on one side, and the Slovenian armed forces, the so-called territorial defence, and the Slovenian police on the other. After the easing of the armed conflict, the Yugoslav army gradually left its positions in Slovenia, and thus also the factual conditions for establishing independence were met. From the independence until 2007, the Slovenian currency was the 'tolar'. In 2007, Slovenia adopted the common European currency, the Euro.

9. The Republic of Slovenia (RS) is a *democratic republic*. Its legal and political organization is determined by the Slovenian Constitution of 23 December 1991 (amended ten times to date). The biggest difference in relation to the former republic constitutions was the organization of the state. Instead of the principle of the unity of power, the new Constitution introduced the separation of powers. The formal head of state is the State President, who is, however, vested with mainly representative functions (the president currently in office is Mr Borut Pahor). The government, led by the Prime Minister, exercises the executive power. The legislative body consists first of the National Assembly, with ninety representatives elected directly at universal elections. The second house, the National Council of the RS, is the representative body for social, economic, professional, and local interests. It has forty members, who do not hold office professionally. An important role is given to the Constitutional Court (which was founded already by the Yugoslav Constitution of 1963), which evaluates the conformity of the acts of the National Assembly and other bodies responsible for creating law, with the Constitution, ratified international treaties, and the general principles of international law. It also decides on the petitions of individuals claiming violations of their human rights by the decisions of the state authorities (including judgments in civil matters). Despite

5. For more on the economic background of Slovenia, see Fatur & Podobnik & Vlahek, *International Encyclopaedia of Laws, Competition Law – Slovenia*, 20–23 (Kluwer Law International 2016); Fatur & Podobnik, *Slovenia/Commentary: SI/C*, in *Competition Law in Western Europe and the USA, Competition Law*, suppl. 412 (Hofhuis (ed.), Kluwer Law International 2018).

its denomination and some of its functions, the Constitutional Court does not belong to the general judiciary and is hierarchically not the highest court – this role belongs to the Supreme Court.[6]

10. Slovenia is divided into 212 *municipalities*. Those that include larger cities have the special status of 'city municipalities'. A municipality must have at least 5,000 inhabitants and exercise several functions delegated to it by the state,[7] including basic schooling (nine years), basic healthcare, etc. The Constitution also provides for a wider self-governing unit – the region (Article 143 of the Constitution). These have not yet been established, because consent has thus far not been reached as to the number of regions and the division of the territory.

11. Slovenia is a *member* of the European Union (EU) (since May 2004) as well as of the European Economic Area (since December 2005), the Eurozone (since January 2007), the Schengen area (since December 2007), the Organization for Security and Co-operation in Europe (OSCE) (since March 1992), the Council of Europe (since May 1993), the United Nations Organization (UN) (since May 1992), of the North Atlantic Treaty Organization (NATO) (since March 2004), and of the Organisation for Economic Co-operation and Development (OECD) (since July 2010), to name just some of the most important international organizations. The country was a non-permanent member of the Security Council of the UN in 1998 and 1999 and held the presidency thereof twice during this mandate. Slovenia presided over the Council of the EU from January until June 2008, over the OSCE in 2005, and over the Council of Europe from May until November 2009.

12. The Slovenian Constitution had to be amended in order to join the European Union and consequently adopt the European *acquis communautaire*. Paragraphs 1 and 2 of Article 3a of the Constitution (amendment adopted on 27 February 2003 in view of the accession of Slovenia to the European Union in 2004, entering into force on 7 March 2003)[8] thus provides:

> (1) Pursuant to a treaty ratified by the National Assembly by a two-thirds majority vote of all deputies, Slovenia may transfer the exercise of part of its sovereign rights to international organizations which are based on respect for human rights and fundamental freedoms, democracy, and the principles of the rule of law and may enter into a defensive alliance with states which are based on respect for these values.

6. Article 127 of the Constitution. Besides the Constitution, the organization, and the responsibilities of the Constitutional Court are regulated in Zakon o ustavnem sodišču [Constitutional Court Act], Official Gazette RS, No. 15/94, with further amendments.
7. For more details, see Zakon o lokalni samoupravi (ZLS) [Local Self-Government Act], Official Gazette RS, No. 72/93, with further amendments. Approximately half of Slovenian municipalities have less than 5,000 inhabitants (http://kjekajkakozakaj.blogspot.si/2013/06/seznam-obcin-v-sloveniji-po-velikosti.html), since this condition was introduced (without exceptions) only in 2010.
8. Official Gazette RS, No. 24/03.

(2) Before ratifying a treaty referred to in the preceding paragraph, the National Assembly may call a referendum. A proposal is passed in the referendum if a majority of those voting have cast valid votes in favour of the same. The National Assembly is bound by the result of such referendum. If such referendum has been held, a referendum regarding the law on the ratification of the treaty concerned may not be called.

§2. Legal Background on Slovenia

I. Legal Family and Tradition

13. Slovenia traditionally belongs to the *Romano-Germanic* (also referred to as the 'civil law') *legal family*. The legal tradition of the Austrian General Civil Code (the Allgemeines Bürgerliches Gesetzbuch, hereinafter 'ABGB') was long maintained, and modern laws were passed in the 1970s and 1980s. The main sources of law are thus the written laws adopted by the legislature. These are of an abstract nature; that is, they apply to an undefined number of subjects in an undefined number of cases. The case law of the Slovenian courts is an important interpretative instrument, but it is officially not a binding source of law.[9] According to the Courts Act,[10] Slovenian judges are bound by the Constitution, acts, and statutes, as well as by the general principles of international law and the ratified and published international treaties. The only case of binding decisions of the Slovenian courts are the 'legal opinions' and 'principled legal opinions' adopted at plenary sessions of the Supreme Court, which are formally binding on all the panels of the Supreme Court, but not on the lower courts.[11] Legal theory – that is, scientific articles and monographs – also have considerable influence on Slovenian law.

14. Slovenian civil law is strongly *linked to Austrian and German law*, although other influences and original solutions are common as well. The ABGB from 1811 (including the three amendments of 1914, 1915, and 1916) was applicable in Slovenia long after its territory parted from Austria after the First World War. In the regions that belonged to the Illyrian Provinces of Napoleon from 1809 to 1813 (where the French Civil Code of 1804 was briefly applicable), the ABGB came into force in 1815. It was translated into the Slovenian language in 1853. It was only in the 1970s that the Yugoslav legislature adopted new acts in the fields of the law of obligations (1978) and property law (1980). The Slovenian legislature adopted acts in the fields of family law (1976, on the basis of a Yugoslav Act of 1946) and the law of inheritance (1976, on the basis of a Yugoslav Inheritance Act of 1955). Due to the separation of legislative competences between the Yugoslav federation and

9. Besides a judge being able to adopt his or her own interpretation of legal rules, Art. 11/2 of the Courts Act of 1994 (Zakon o sodiščih (ZS) [Courts Act], Official Gazette RS, No. 19/94, with further amendments) provides that a judge is independent in applying the law also in relation to a court of higher instance that has already stated its opinion on the specific matter.
10. Courts Act cited in the previous footnote.
11. Article 111 in conjunction with Art. 11 of the Courts Act.

the republics, a complete civil code could not be adopted. Despite the full legislative competence of today's Slovenian National Assembly, there are still no official projects to create a civil code with its five traditional parts: general part, law of obligations, property law, family law, and the law of inheritance. Some provisions commonly found in the general part of civil codes are integrated into the *Code of Obligations* (CO) adopted in 2001.[12] The latter is mainly founded on the Obligations Act of 1978, which was considered a very modern act at the time and which brought many changes in comparison to the ABGB, because many other influences were taken into consideration, the most important being German and French law of obligations. This act started the era of monism in Slovenian civil law since it stated that its rules were applicable to commercial and non-commercial contracts. This tradition was followed by the CO, so there is no commercial code in Slovenia. The Slovenian *Code of Property Law* (Sl. *Stvarnopravni zakonik*, hereinafter 'CPL'),[13] was adopted in 2002. The *Family and Inheritance Acts* of the 1970s have been amended numerous times since Slovenian independence. In 2011, the Parliament adopted the new Family Code, which did not enter into force, as it was rejected in a referendum,[14] as was an amendment of the existent family law legislation passed in March 2015 which was to give the rights to same-sex couples to marry (at the time being, they only can register their partnership) and adopt children. It must however be noted that the Slovenian Supreme Court granted recognition of a foreign judgment on adoption of a child by a same-sex couple already in 2010[15] and that a partner in a same-sex couple can adopt biological children of his/her partner. The new Slovenian Family Code was finally adopted in 2017 and entered into force on 15 April 2019.[16] It does, however, not contain provisions on marriage and adoption by same-sex couples, the legal position of which is being gradually regulated by other acts and case law.

II. Relations and Hierarchy among the Sources of Law

15. As Slovenia is traditionally a civil law country, the most important sources of law are written and abstract legal texts. The highest internal legal source in Slovenia is the *Constitution* (Sl. *ustava*). The Constitution is directly applicable; nevertheless, its articles usually need elaboration by secondary legislation. The first level of secondary legislation are the *acts* (Sl. *zakoni*) adopted by the National

12. Obligacijski zakonik (OZ) [Code of Obligations], Official Gazette RS, No. 83/01, with further amendments. The CO entered into force on 1 Jan. 2002.
13. Stvarnopravni zakonik (SPZ) [Code of Property Law], Official Gazette RS, Nos 87/02 and 91/13. The CPL entered into force on 1 Jan. 2003.
14. For more detail concerning the development of Slovenian family law, see: Podobnik & Vlahek, *Chronology of Development of Private Law in Slovenia*, in *Private Law Reform*, 283 ff. (Lavický, Hurdík et al., Acta Universitatis Brunensis, Iuridica, Editio Scientia, No 501, Masaryk University 2014).
15. Decision No. II Ips 462/2009 of 28 Jan. 2010. For more detail, see J. Kramberger Škerl, *(Ne)razumevanje pridržka javnega reda in posvojitev s strani istospolnih partnerjev* [The (Non)Understanding of the Public Policy Defense and the Adoption by Same-Sex Partners], Pravna Praksa, Y. 29, No. 29/30, Supplement, pp. II-VII.
16. Družinski zakonik (DZ), Official Gazette RS, No. 15/17, with further amendments.

Assembly. All rights and obligations have to be determined either in such acts or in the Constitution, while executive *regulations* (Sl. *uredbe*) can only determine the implementation and enforcement of rights and obligations and cannot in principle create any new ones.

16. According to Article 8 of the Constitution, *international treaties* are hierarchically ranked between the Constitution and the acts of the National Assembly and apply directly, but only after their ratification by the latter. The *law of the European Union* has a special place in the hierarchy of the sources of law and applies in Slovenia in accordance with the general principles of EU law. Its position is determined by paragraphs 3 and 4 of Article 3.a of the Constitution, which provide:

> (3) Legal acts and decisions adopted within international organizations to which Slovenia has transferred the exercise of part of its sovereign rights shall be applied in Slovenia in accordance with the legal regulation of these organizations. (4) In procedures for the adoption of legal acts and decisions in international organizations to which Slovenia has transferred the exercise of part of its sovereign rights, the Government shall promptly inform the National Assembly of proposals for such acts and decisions as well as of its own activities. The National Assembly may adopt positions thereon, which the Government shall take into consideration in its activities. The relationship between the National Assembly and the Government arising from this paragraph shall be regulated in detail by a law adopted by a two-thirds majority vote of deputies present.

17. According to Article 3 of the Courts Act, a judge must apply the Constitution and legislative acts, as well as, according to the Constitution, the *general principles of international law* and ratified and published international treaties. In civil cases, *analogy* is also permitted:

> [i]f a civil case cannot be solved on the grounds of the legislation in force, the judge applies the legislation regulating similar cases. If the solution is still legally doubtful, the judge decides on the grounds of the *general principles of the national legal order*. In doing this, the judge acts according to the *legal tradition* and the confirmed findings of the *legal science*.[17]

18. Apart from the aforementioned, several 'informal' sources count among the sources of law in Slovenia. Contrary to Anglo-Saxon legal systems, the *case law* does not bind the judges (save the case law of the Court of Justice of the European Union), but nevertheless has a significant influence on their decisions, especially in the case of the aforementioned 'legal opinions' of the plenary sessions of the

17. Article 3/2 of Courts Act. The use of analogy is forbidden in criminal cases, as being contrary to the principle of legality.

Supreme Court.[18] In spite of this lack of a formal binding power of case law, the courts are obliged to be aware of the case law in similar cases. They should either take the same position or provide 'reasonable legal argumentation'[19] if they decide to depart from it.[20] The significance of case law is especially relevant in light of the constitutional principle of equality before the law (Article 14 of the Constitution) and the right to the equal protection of rights (Article 22 of the Constitution).[21] *Customs* (Sl. *običaji*) can be used to interpret and complete the written law under the condition that the latter expressly foresees such application and that the applied customs are not contrary to other legal rules in force.[22] *Business customs* (Sl. *poslovni običaji*) as well as *written customs* (Sl. *uzance*) and *business practice* have an important role in contracts concluded between commercial entities.[23]

III. Judicial System

19. The term 'judiciary' can be defined strictly as covering only the judges and the courts or, more broadly, as also including other subjects participating in the application of the law, such as attorneys, state prosecutors, state attorneys, notaries, and bailiffs.

20. The courts are divided into *courts of general jurisdiction* and *courts of specialized jurisdiction*. In the first group, the courts of first instance are local courts (Sl. *okrajna sodišča*) with jurisdiction in less important civil and criminal matters, as well as in proceedings concerning family matters, inheritance, capacity matters, maintaining the land register, the enforcement of judgments, the disturbance of possession, and some other matters, and district courts (Sl. *okrožna sodišča*), with jurisdiction in more important civil and criminal matters, as well as in all commercial matters, the recognition of foreign judgments, maintaining the register of commercial companies, and some other matters.[24] The *courts of specialized jurisdiction* comprise the courts for labour and social matters and the administrative courts.

---

18. The 'legal opinions' and the 'principled legal opinions' are binding on all the panels of judges of the Supreme Court, but not on the lower instances.
19. Constitutional Court Decisions No. Up 337/00 of 26 Feb. 2002 and No. Up 19/01 of 26 Mar. 2002.
20. For further details, see: Štajnpihler, *Precedenčni učinek sodnih odločb pri pravnem utemeljevanju* [The effect of precedent of the case law in legal argumentation], 90 ff. (GV Založba 2012).
21. For more on the issue of departing from the previous case law, see Galič, *Ustavno civilno procesno pravo* [Constitutional Civil Procedure Law], 315–338 (GV Založba 2004). See also Constitutional Court Decisions No. Up 121/96 of 23 Mar. 2000, No. Up 297/96 of 15 Jun. 1999 and others.
22. Toplak, *Civilno pravo, Splošni del civilnega prava* [Civil Law, General Part of the Civil Law], 61 (Univerza v Mariboru, Pravna fakulteta 2002).
23. See Art. 6 of CO.
24. The organization of the courts is regulated by the Courts Act (Zakon o sodiščih (ZS), Official Gazette RS, No. 19/94, with further amendments). The division of the jurisdiction of local and district courts in civil matters is regulated in Arts 30 and 32 of the Civil Procedure Act (Zakon o pravdnem postopku (ZPP), Official Gazette RS, No. 26/99, with further amendments), as well as some other legislation. For details on courts having jurisdiction in civil matters which typically cover the property law related cases, see Pogorelčnik Vogrinc, *Der Zivilprozess in Slowenien* [Civil Procedure in Slovenia]. In Jahrbuch für Ostrecht, bd. 59, hb. 1, 2018 pp. 25 ff.

21. According to the Constitution and the European Convention on Human Rights, judges in Slovenia have to exercise their office *impartially* and *independently*, as well as accomplish the judicial proceedings *within reasonable time limits* and in respect of the guarantees of a fair trial. Once elected by the National Assembly (on the proposal of the Judicial Council[25]), their *office is permanent* and ceases only by retirement or the judge's own will, as well as on the grounds provided by Article 132 of the Constitution:

(1) If in the performance of the judicial office a judge violates the Constitution or seriously violates the law, the National Assembly may dismiss such judge on the proposal of the Judicial Council.
(2) If a judge is found by a final judgement to have deliberately committed a criminal offence through the abuse of the judicial office, the National Assembly dismisses such judge.

22. Judicial office is *not compatible* with office in other state authorities, in local self-government authorities, and in bodies of political parties, or with other offices and activities as provided by law.[26] Article 134 of the Constitution guarantees judges immunity. It provides:

(1) No one who participates in making judicial decisions may be held accountable for an opinion expressed during decision making in court.
(2) If a judge is suspected of a criminal offence in the performance of judicial office, he or she may not be detained nor may criminal proceedings be initiated against him or her without the consent of the National Assembly.

23. At the courts of first instance, one judge decides the civil litigation. In many criminal cases, however, the law provides for a panel of three or five judges, of which two or three are lay judges (the latter are nominated for five years and can be renominated). The high courts (i.e., the appellate courts, Sl. *višja sodišča*) normally exercise their function in panels of three, and the Supreme Court in panels of five professional judges. In view of the acceleration of the court proceedings in civil matters, the civil procedure legislation provides for a (restricted) possibility that only one judge of the high court decides on the appeal against a judgment of first instance, and a panel of three judges of the Supreme Court decides on the admissibility of the extraordinary legal remedy at parties' disposal – the revision (whereas

25. Article 131 of the Constitution (Judicial Council) provides: 'The Judicial Council is composed of eleven members. The National Assembly elects five members on the proposal of the President of the Republic from among university professors of law, attorneys, and other lawyers, whereas judges holding permanent judicial office elect six members from among their own number. The members of the council select a president from among their own number.'
26. Article 133 of the Constitution. Other texts generally regulating the (in)compatibility of judges' activities are Zakon o sodniški službi (ZSS) [Judicial Service Act], Official Gazette RS, No. 19/94, with further amendments, and Kodeks sodniške etike [Judges Code of Ethics], the latter being adopted by the Slovenian Association of Judges.

the final decision on the substance of the revision is adopted by a panel of five judges). The Constitution provides for a judiciary of a minimum of two instances in all matters.[27]

24. Court proceedings are *public*, with the exception of particularly 'sensitive' matters (matrimonial and children disputes, criminal proceedings concerning minors, etc.). The restrictions of the publicity of the hearings can be based on the law or on the decision of the judge in each particular case.

25. With regard to the other subjects of the judiciary in the broader sense of the word, *state prosecutors* (Sl. *državni tožilci*) have the most important role in criminal proceedings, where they file and present criminal charges, and hold a minor role in civil matters. There, their only responsibility is to file the 'petition for protection of legality' (Sl. *zahteva za varstvo zakonitosti*), an extraordinary legal remedy, the scope of which was considerably reduced by the Civil Procedure Act (CPA)[28] amendment of 2008, and which is envisaged to prevent serious infringements of law, mainly in the cases where revision is not possible.[29] *State attorneys* (Sl. *državni odvetniki*) represent the state in the proceedings before the courts and administrative bodies, as well as in proceedings before international courts, such as the European Court of Human Rights and the Court of Justice of the European Union.[30] The *attorneyship* (the Bar) is an independent service within the system of justice.[31] The *notary service* is a public service with a limited number of notary offices in the country.[32] The judiciary is assisted by certain regulated professions, such as *bailiffs*, entrusted with the task of enforcing civil judgments,[33] *experts* who give expert opinions in different non-legal fields, and *court interpreters*, who officially translate the oral statements in courts and the legal acts and documents.

---

27. The Slovenian Constitution thus broadens the guarantee of two instance proceedings from criminal matters (where such guarantee is already provided by Art. 2 of the Protocol No. 7 to the European Convention on Human Rights) to civil and commercial matters. Two instance judicial control (first instance being the Administrative Court and second instance the Supreme Court) of final administrative decisions is in principle also provided (by Zakon o upravnem sporu (ZUS-1) [Administrative Dispute Act], Official Gazette RS, No. 105/06, with further amendments); however, the Slovenian Constitutional Court has held a single instance control by the Supreme Court sufficient if such control comprises the possibility of verification of the factual findings of the administrative authority and is not limited solely to the questions of law (Decision No. U-I-40/12 of 11 Apr. 2013).
28. Zakon o pravdnem postopku (ZPP) [Civil Procedure Act], Official Gazette RS, No. 26/99, with further amendments.
29. Article 385 of CPA.
30. The regulation of the state attorneys' duties is found in Zakon o državnem odvetništvu (ZDOdv) [State Attorneys Office Act], Official Gazette RS, No. 23/17.
31. The attorneyship, or Bar, is regulated by Zakon o odvetništvu (ZOdv) [Attorneys Act], Official Gazette RS, No. 18/93, with further amendments.
32. The notary service is regulated by Zakon o notariatu (ZN) [Notary Act], Official Gazette RS, No. 13/94, with further amendments.
33. The regulation of the bailiffs' service can be found in the Zakon o izvršbi in zavarovanju (ZIZ) [Claim Enforcement and Security Act (CESA)], Official Gazette RS, No. 51/98, with further amendments.

§3. Introduction to Property Law

26. Property law is a part of civil law, which regulates the ownership and control of things in relations between individuals.[34] The rights regulated by the property law (also called the 'static' law) exist in relation to every other person (Lat. *erga omnes*), whereas the rights regulated by the law of obligations (called also the 'dynamic' law) typically refer to certain conduct and exist only towards another, specifically defined person or persons (Lat. *inter partes*).[35] Property law rights are guaranteed by property law mechanisms as are, in case of the ownership, claims for return (Lat. *rei vindicatio*) and protection from disturbance (Lat. *actio negatoria*); the law of obligations complements the protection under the property law by way of claims for damages and claims for reparation, if the interference in the property rights results in damages or unjust enrichment.[36] The institution of trust does not exist in Slovenian law, at least not in the same sense as in Anglo-Saxon legal systems.

I. Historical Origins and Evolution

A. *Property Law Before 1991*

27. As Slovenia was a part of the Austrian Empire, the ABGB of 1811 was applicable until the First World War. Among other things, this legacy is important because Austria was one of the first countries to introduce the land register and the cadastre[37] (the so-called *Franziszeischer Kataster*, 1817–1861). When Slovenian territory was first included in the State of Slovenians, Croats, and Serbs, and later in the Kingdom of Serbs, Croats, and Slovenians, which eventually became the Kingdom of Yugoslavia, the new legislature did not pass new civil law legislation, and thus the ABGB remained in force.

28. After the Second World War, the revolutionary powers passed a law that annulled all legal acts adopted before 6 April 1941,[38] one of which was the ABGB. This legislation could, nevertheless, still be applied under strict conditions – the most important being that it must not be contrary to the new social order. The provisions of the ABGB concerning property law mostly fulfilled these conditions and could thus be applied until 1980, when the Yugoslav legislature adopted the *Basic Property Law Relations Act* (BPLRA).[39] The latter was, however, restricted in its application to the limited cases of private property existing under the new regime.

34. Several authors, cited by Juhart in *Property Law*, 39.
35. *Ibid.*, 42.
36. *Ibid.*
37. Juhart in *Property Law*, 45.
38. Zakon o razveljavljanju pravnih predpisov, izdanih pred 6. aprilom 1941 in med sovražnikovo okupacijo (ZRPP) [Act on the Annulment of Legal Acts Adopted Before 6 Apr. 1941 and During the Enemy's Occupation], Official Gazette of the Federal People's Republic of Yugoslavia, No. 86/46.
39. Zakon o temeljnih lastninskopravnih razmerjih (ZTLR), Official Gazette of the Socialist Federal Republic of Yugoslavia, No. 6/80.

29. The new political order brought many crucial changes to property relations in Yugoslavia and Slovenia as a constituent part thereof. In the first years after the Second World War, several acts were adopted in order to ensure the *expropriation* of individuals and the creation of the system of state (and later 'social') property.[40] Gavella cites the following important changes in the Yugoslav property law after the Second World War: (1) the dominant collectivistic regulation of ownership, (2) the dualism of the general regulation of property (social property on one side and private property on the other), (3) the priority of the social property to the detriment of the private one, (4) the fragmentation of the law regulating ownership, (5) the inequality of legal subjects and their rights, (6) the breaking of the unity of ownership on the immovables, (7) many special provisions regulating economically important objects, and (8) the stunting of the general institutions of property law.[41]

30. In this era, several assets were *excluded from private ownership* and could only be in state or social property. Such were the so-called means of production and some immovables.[42] All building land was social property, whereas private individuals and legal entities could acquire ownership of the buildings and consequently the right to use the land under the buildings, which was then transferred together with the ownership of the building.[43] The principle of the connection of land and building (Lat. *superficies solo cedit*), later (re-)established by the new Slovenian legislation, was thus disregarded. Regarding the land not envisaged to be the location of buildings, the so-called land maximums were established in order to limit the amount of land one could own; these 'maximums' were also established for the ownership of residential and business buildings.[44] The period of 1945–1991 was marked by a decline in the regulation of immovable property law; consequently, today there still exist some problems in establishing the land register and in the legal transactions related to immovables.[45]

31. Social property was regulated by special law. However, because the *private property* of individuals was not abolished (although in many ways limited), there was further need for classical property law legislation, which explains the use of the ABGB and the later adoption of the BPLRA. The *BPLRA* was built on the basis of the ABGB and upgraded by modern concepts developed on the basis of the newer German property law legislation, especially the objective conception of possession.[46] It was thus comparable to the property law acts in countries with a firm tradition of private property. The difficulty lay in the fact that this federal act only regulated the 'basic' property law relations and envisaged further regulation by the

40. Juhart in *Property Law*, 45.
41. Gavella in Gavella et al., *Stvarno pravo* [Property Law], 13 (Narodne Novine 2007).
42. Juhart in *Property Law*, 46.
43. *Ibid.*
44. *Ibid.*
45. *Ibid.*, 46–47.
46. *Ibid.*, 47. For the objective conception of possession, see s. V of this chapter.

legislatures of the republics.[47] The Slovenian legislature did not adopt such complementary acts; hence, the provisions of the ABGB, as well as the pre-war legal theory and case law, further served to fill these legal gaps.[48] Some of these gaps were also filled by the adoption of the Non-Contentious Civil Procedure Act in 1986.[49] The return to the principle of private property (guaranteed by the Slovenian Constitution of 1991) expanded the application of the BPLRA from the previously limited number of cases to all assets in general, and the Act continued to apply (with the omission of the ideological references) in the new circumstances, until the adoption of the new Slovenian legislation in 2002.

B. Property Law from 1991 until Today

32. The first years of Slovenian independence were marked by the process of *denationalization* of confiscated assets, as well as by ownership transformation[50] and privatization.[51] The Denationalization Act of 1991[52] is the basic act in this field and sets forth the general principle of returning nationalized assets 'in nature', with the payment of pecuniary damages as an exception. Further important legislation includes the Privatization of Real Estate in Social Ownership Act,[53] the Act on Establishing Divided Co-ownership and on Determining the Land Belonging to a Building (AEDC),[54] and other legislation on specific cases of ownership transformation.

---

47. The main reason for such limited regulation on the federal level was the difference in legal traditions among the Yugoslav republics: the ABGB served as the legal basis in Slovenia and Croatia, whereas Serbia and Montenegro built their case law and legal theory on the basis of their national pre-war civil codes. Berden in *CPL with Commentary 2004*, 55.
48. Berden in *CPL with Commentary 2004*, 54.
49. Zakon o nepravdnem postopku (ZNP) [Non-Contentious Civil Procedure Act], Official Gazette of the Socialist RS, No. 30/86, with further amendments. Such legal gap was, for example, the regulation of the so-called way of necessity. Cf. Juhart in *Property Law*, p. 47.
50. See Damjan, *Zapleti pri lastninjenju nekdanjih nepremičnin v družbeni lastnini in urejanju sedanjega (neurejenega) stanja na zemljiščih* [Complications in the Privatization of the Former Socially Owned Real Property and Solving of the Current (Disorderly) Situation],in Pravosodni bilten, 2011, Y. 32, No. 1, pp. 119 ff.
51. Juhart in *Property Law*, 49. For the definitions of the terms 'denationalization', 'ownership transformation', and 'privatization', see Juhart in *Property Law*, 49–50.
52. Zakon o denacionalizaciji (ZDen) [Denationalization Act], Official Gazette RS, No. 27/91, with many further amendments, often ordered by the Constitutional Court.
53. Zakon o lastninjenju nepremičnin v družbeni lastnini (ZLNDL), Official Gazette RS, No. 44/97, with further amendments.
54. Zakon o vzpostavitvi etažne lastnine na predlog pridobitelja posameznega dela stavbe in o določanju pripadajočega zemljišča k stavbi (ZVEtL), Official Gazette RS, No. 45/08, with further amendments, replaced in 2017 by Zakon o vzpostavitvi etažne lastnine na predlog pridobitelja posameznega dela stavbe in o določanju pripadajočega zemljišča k stavbi (ZVEtL-1), Official Gazette RS, No. 34/17.

33. The first Slovenian legislative act to lay the foundations for the (new) law of property was the *Constitution* of 1991. In Article 33, it guarantees the right to private[55] property and inheritance as a basic human right.[56] According to the case law of the Constitutional Court, this provision protects not only the right to ownership of an asset as defined by property law, but of a wider concept of each patrimonial asset a person may manage.[57] Article 67 further provides that the manner in which property is acquired and enjoyed shall be established by law so as to ensure its economic, social, and environmental functions. This provision serves as the basis for all possible limitations of the right of ownership. Article 68 of the Constitution regulates the ownership rights of foreigners to immovable property in Slovenia in the following way: '[a]liens may acquire ownership rights to real estate under conditions provided by law or a treaty ratified by the National Assembly'.[58,59] The Reciprocity Act of 1999[60] laid down the regulation of the condition of reciprocity between the country of origin of the foreigner acquiring the property, and Slovenia where such reciprocity is required.[61] Article 69 of the Constitution regulates expropriation as the most radical interference in ownership rights, which is nevertheless unavoidable also in modern democratic legal systems.[62] It reads: '[o]wnership rights to real estate may be revoked or limited in the public interest with the provision of compensation in kind or monetary compensation under conditions established by

55. The word 'private' is nowadays redundant, because there is only one form of property regardless of the private or public status of the owner. It was introduced into the wording of the Constitution for historical reasons. Juhart in *Property Law*, 53; Tratnik & Vrenčur, *Omejitve lastninske pravice in posebni pravni režimi na nepremčninah* [Limitations of Ownership and Special Legal Regimes on the Immovables], 26–27 (GV Založba 2009).
56. An important means of interpretation of this constitutional provision is the case law of the European Court of Human Rights concerning Art. 1 of the First Protocol to the European Convention on Human Rights.
57. Juhart in *Property Law*, 54.
58. This article was quite problematic and therefore amended twice. Originally it read: 'Aliens may acquire ownership rights to real estate under conditions provided by law. Aliens may not acquire title to land except by inheritance, under the condition of reciprocity.' Following the amendment of 1997, the text of Art. 68 read as follows: 'Aliens may acquire ownership rights to real estate under conditions provided by law or if so provided by a treaty ratified by the National Assembly, under the condition of reciprocity. Such law and treaty from the preceding paragraph shall be adopted by the National Assembly by a two-thirds majority votes of all deputies.' The last amendment resulting in the current text was adopted in 2003 in order to harmonize the Slovenian system with the European acquis.
59. Regarding acquiring ownership of immovables by persons originating in EU candidate countries, the Zakon o pogojih za pridobitev lastninske pravice fizičnih in pravnih oseb držav kandidatk za članstvo v Evropski uniji na nepremičninah (ZPPLPKEU) [Act Governing the Conditions for the Acquisition of Title to Property by Natural Persons and Legal Entities of European Union Candidate Countries], Official Gazette RS, No. 61/06, was adopted in 2006.
60. Zakon o ugotavljanju vzajemnosti (ZUVza) [Reciprocity Act], Official Gazette RS, No. 9/99, replaced in 2017 by a new Reciprocity Act, Official Gazette RS, No. 27/17.
61. For further details on acquisition of ownership on immovables in Slovenia by foreigners, see Vlahek, *Pridobivanje lastninske pravice na nepremičninah v Sloveniji s strani tujcev* [Acquisition of Ownership on Immovables in Slovenia by Foreign Citizens], in Pravnik (Ljubljana: 2008), y. 63, No. 1/3.
62. For more on expropriation, see Part III, Ch. 10. See also Tratnik & Vrenčur, *Omejitve lastninske pravice in posebni pravni režimi na nepremičninah* [Limitations of Ownership and Special Legal Regimes on the Immovables], 44–64 (GV Založba 2009).

law'. Expropriation is possible only in relation to immovable property. Article 70 refers to 'national assets' (i.e., property in public domain) and natural resources; it states that special rights to use national assets may be acquired, subject to conditions established by law,[63] and that the conditions under which natural resources may be exploited shall be established by law. The law may provide that natural resources may also be exploited by foreign persons and in such cases establishes conditions for such exploitation.[64] According to Article 71, the law shall establish special conditions for land utilization in order to ensure its proper use. Special protection of agricultural land shall be provided by law and the state shall promote the economic, cultural, and social advancement of the population living in mountain and hill areas.

34. In 1995, the National Assembly adopted the Land Registry Act.[65] As it contained several disputable legal solutions and considering the fact that the new property law legislation was adopted in 2002, this act was abrogated in 2003 by the new Land Registry Act (LRA).[66] The latter was importantly modified in 2008 and in 2011. Perhaps the biggest achievement of these acts was the establishment of the electronic land register, finalized in 2004.[67]

35. The preparative work for the new Slovenian property law legislation began short after the independence and resulted in a proposal of an act on ownership and other property law rights; this proposal, however, was withdrawn from the legislative procedure in 2001, thus opening the possibility for a thorough reform.[68] The Slovenian *CPL,* as the basic and most important source of Slovenian property law, was adopted in 2002 and entered into force on 1 January 2003. It was formulated on the basis of the BPLRA and modernized and supplemented with provisions on the basic principles, easements in personam, encumbrance, land debt (which was, however, abolished in 2013), the right of superficies, and the 'law of neighbourhood'.[69] According to Article 1 of the CPL, 'this act lays down the basic principles of property law, possession, and property rights and the method of their acquisition, transfer, protection, and expiration'. The CPL is divided into eleven parts (the former Part VII regulated the land debt): Part I – Basic Principles (such as the principle of speciality, the connection between the land and building, the presumption of good faith, trust in the land register, the prohibition of abuse, etc.), Part II – Basic Terms (such as 'the thing' [the asset, the object], the element, the appurtenance, the

---

63. See also Art. 19 of CPL.
64. For more on the legal regime applicable to the property in the public domain, see Tratnik & Vrenčur, *Omejitve lastninske pravice in posebni pravni režimi na nepremičninah* [Limitations of Ownership and Special Legal Regimes on the Immovables], 98–106 (GV Založba 2009).
65. Zakon o zemljiški knjigi (ZZK) [Land Registry Act], Official Gazette RS, No. 33/95, with further amendments.
66. Zakon o zemljiški knjigi (ZZK-1) [Land Registry Act], Official Gazette RS, No. 58/03, with further amendments.
67. Juhart in *Property Law*, 50.
68. Berden in *CPL with Commentary 2004*, 55.
69. Juhart in *Property Law*, 51.

immovable, etc.), Part III – Possession (Sl. *posest*), Part IV – Ownership (Sl. *lastninska pravica*), Part V – Divided Co-ownership (Sl. *etažna lastnina*), Part VI – Lien (Sl. *zastavna pravica*), Part VIII – Transfer as Security (Sl. *prenos lastninske pravice v zavarovanje*), Part IX – Easements (Sl. *služnosti*), Part X – Encumbrance (Sl. *stvarno breme*), Part XI – The Right of Superficies (Sl. *stavbna pravica*), and Part XII – Transitional and Final Provisions. During the seventeen-year application of the CPL, several inconsistencies regarding its substance arose and the courts adopted numerous decisions interpreting this code. In March 2020, an amendment of the CPL was adopted (it partly entered into force in end March 2020 while some of its provisions will enter into force in July 2020 and some in July 2021), mitigating several deficiencies of the code, e.g., defining animals as sensible beings, inserting of a new chapter 'Connected immovables', amending of several rules regarding the non-possessory pledge, and introducing the possibility of a right of superficies unlimited in time.[70] A larger amendment possibly leading to more fundamental changes in property law concepts is still in the preparation process.

36. Slovenian law regulates the following property rights (rights in rem) existing with regard to assets (things): *ownership* (as the basic property right) and the so-called *limited property rights* or property rights to another's property. Limited property rights can exist concurrent to ownership and represent the partial transfer of the owner's rights to another person. All property rights have *erga omnes* (universal, absolute) effect, which means that they can be enforced against all other persons and everybody must refrain from interfering with someone else's property rights.[71] Property rights are also subject to the *numerus clausus* principle: no other property right can be created by the parties outside of the scope provided by the law. The protection of property rights is not subject to the statute of limitations (prescription) and can therefore be legally enforced without any time limits.

37. In addition to the CPL as the basic act in this field, property law is partially regulated by some other acts and regulations: the LRA and the Real-Estate Recording Act,[72] the AEDC, the Maritime Code[73] (regulating the property rights regarding ships), the Obligations and Real Rights in Air Navigation Act[74] (regulating property rights regarding aeroplanes), the Housing Act (HA),[75] the Protection of Buyers of Apartments and Single Occupancy Buildings Act,[76] the Book Entry Securities

70. SPZ-B, Official Gazette RS, No. 23/20.
71. Article 5 of CPL provides that: 'Holders of a property right may enforce their right against any person.'
72. Zakon o evidentiranju nepremičnin (ZEN) [Real-Estate Recording Act], Official Gazette RS, No. 47/06, with further amendments. This act regulates the land cadastre as the factual basis of the land register.
73. Pomorski zakonik (PZ) [Maritime Code], Official Gazette RS, No. 26/01, with further amendments.
74. Zakon o obligacijskih in stvarnopravnih razmerjih v letalstvu (ZOSRL) [Obligations and Real Rights in Air Navigation Act], Official Gazette RS, No.12/00, with further amendments.
75. Stanovanjski zakon (SZ-1) [Housing Act], Official Gazette RS, No. 69/03, with further amendments. This act further regulates divided co-ownership regarding apartment buildings.
76. Zakon o varstvu kupcev stanovanj in enostanovanjskih stavb (ZVKSES) [Protection of Buyers of Apartments and Single Occupancy Buildings Act], Official Gazette RS, No. 18/04.

Act,[77] the Decree on the Register of Non-possessory Liens and Seized Movable Property,[78] the Rules on Land Letter (applicable to land letters established before the abolition of the land debt from the CPL in 2013),[79] etc. The property law is also influenced by the CO, the Family Code[80] (that replaced the Marriage and Family Relations Act (MFRA)),[81] and the Inheritance Act (IA).[82] One must not disregard procedural law: the CPA, the Claim Enforcement and Security Act (CESA),[83] the Non-Contentious Civil Procedure Act (NCCPA),[84] as well as the Financial Operations, Insolvency Proceedings, and Compulsory Dissolution Act (FOIPCDA).[85]

II. Objects of Property Rights

38. According to Article 3 of the CPL, the subject of a property right is '*a thing*' (*an asset, an object*, Sl. *stvar*).[86] The 'thing' is defined as 'an independent corporeal object that can be controlled by man', as well as 'various forms of energy and waves that can be controlled by man'.[87] The basic characteristics of a thing are thus its physical, corporeal nature and the possibility of control by man – the latter being also true for energy and waves as the only (possible) non-corporeal things. The other non-corporeal objects and rights cannot be subjects of property rights, with

77. Zakon o nematerializiranih vrednostnih papirjih (ZNVP-1) [Book Entry Securities Act], Official Gazette RS, No. 75/15, with further amendments.
78. Uredba o registru neposestnih zastavnih pravic in zarubljenih premičnin [Decree on the Register of Non-possessory Liens and Seized Movable Property], Official Gazette RS, No. 23/04, with further amendments.
79. Pravilnik o zemljiškem pismu [Rules on Land Letter], Official Gazette RS, No. 15/03, with further amendments.
80. Družinski zakonik (DZ), Official Gazette RS, No. 15/17, with further amendments.
81. Zakon o zakonski zvezi in družinskih razmerjih (ZZZDR) [Marriage and Family Relations Act], Official Gazette SRS, No. 15/76, with further amendments.
82. Zakon o dedovanju (ZD) [Inheritance Act], Official Gazette SRS, No. 15/76, with further amendments.
83. Zakon o izvršbi in zavarovanju (ZIZ) [Enforcement and Securing of Civil Claims Act (CESA)], Official Gazette RS, No. 51/98, with further amendments.
84. In March 2019, a new Non-Contentious Civil Procedure Act (NCCPA) was enacted (Official Gazette RS, No. 16 /19) replacing the NCCPA of 1986 (Official Gazette SRS, No. 30/86, with further amendments). It started to apply on 15 April 2019.
85. Zakon o finančnem poslovanju, postopkih zaradi insolventnosti in prisilnem prenehanju (ZFPPIPP) [Financial Operations, Insolvency Proceedings, and Compulsory Dissolution Act], Official Gazette RS, No. 126/07, with further amendments.
86. For the definitions of a thing, an element and an appurtenance in comparative law, see Tratnik, *Stvarno pravo: Pojem stvari, njenih sestavnih delov in pritiklin* [Property Law: The Notion of Things, Their Elements and Appurtenances], in Pravna Praksa, No. 45/1999, pp. 4 ff.
87. Article 15 of CPL. An electronic communication signal is an example of such waves, see, e.g., Decision of the High Court in Ljubljana, No. I Cp 2750/2010 of 18 Aug. 2010.

the exception of patrimonial rights, on which lien and usufruct can also be established.[88] In the latter case, the provisions applying to a thing apply *mutatis mutandis* to such right.[89] Parts of the human body are not things as long as they are not separated from the body. If and when they are separated, their definition must depend on ethical standards, and they cannot be automatically treated as things.[90] As for the animals, they are legally deemed to be things, although general rules must be set aside in case of special regulation.[91] Things can be movable or immovable, consumable or inconsumable, uniform or composed, etc. The law can exclude specific things from being subjects of property rights.[92] A thing can cease to exist by way of destruction, consumption, transformation into a new thing, or becoming a part of another thing. At the moment of the ceasing of the existence of the thing, all property rights on such thing extinguish as well.[93]

39. A thing can be composed of different *elements* or components (Sl. *sestavine*). The elements are 'everything which in accordance with general perception is considered to be part of another thing'.[94] According to the principle of speciality and the principle of connection between land and building,[95] '[a]n element is not deemed to be an independent object of property rights until it is separated from the principal thing'.[96] Thus, the property rights on a thing extend also to all its elements.[97] The standard of the 'general conviction' has been adopted because it is impossible to lay down exact criteria when a thing must be considered an element of another thing. The legal theory considers that a thing can be defined as an element if the principal thing and the element have such firm (physical) connection that they cannot be separated without harming one or both things, or if the principal thing is considered incomplete or unfinished without the element.[98] According to the principle *superficies solo cedit*, the building is considered to be an element of the

88. E.g., dematerialized ('book entry') securities (Sl. *nematerializirani vrednostni papirji*) are property rights and can be encumbered by a lien, but, since they are not things, they cannot be the object of a *rei vindicatio*; see Judgment of the Supreme Court RS, No. II Ips 381/2010 of 28 Nov. 2013. Industrial property rights must be duly registered to be considered as property rights; see Judgment of the Supreme Court RS, No. III Ips 33/2009 of 17 Apr. 2012. Computer program is not a thing nor a property right but a creation in the sense of copyright law; see Judgment of High Court in Ljubljana, No. I Cpg 1017/2013 of 12 Dec. 2013.
89. Article 3/2 of CPL.
90. Juhart in *Property Law*, 63. For a comparative analysis, see Tratnik, *Stvarno pravo: Pojem stvari, njenih sestavnih delov in pritiklin* [Property Law: The Notion of Things, their Elements and Appurtenances], in Pravna Praksa, No. 45/1999, pp. 4 ff., No. 1, and Tratnik in *CPL with Commentary 2004*, 116–117.
91. Juhart in *Property Law*, 63; Tratnik in *CPL with Commentary 2004*, 118.
92. Article 4 of CPL.
93. Gavella in Gavella et al., *Stvarno pravo* [Property Law], 73 (Narodne Novine 2007).
94. Article 16/1 of CPL.
95. Tratnik in *CPL with Commentary 2004*, 118.
96. Article 16/2 of CPL.
97. Gavella in Gavella et al., *Stvarno pravo* [Property Law], 73 (Narodne Novine 2007).
98. Tratnik in *CPL with Commentary 2004*, 120. See, e.g., Decision of the High Court in Kranj, No. Cpg 455/2014 of 26 Mar. 2015, where the court deemed that a part of a machine, which can be physically separated from the machine without harming the part or the machine, is not an element of the machine and can be an autonomous thing in legal commerce, although the machine cannot function without such part and the part has no functionality on its own.

land without regard to the respective value or other criteria.[99] If an independent thing becomes an element of another principal thing, its ownership is defined in Articles 54–58 of the CPL (see Part III of this monograph).

40. An element must further be distinguished from an *appurtenance* (Sl. *pritiklina*), which is 'a movable which in accordance with general conviction is intended for commercial use or to embellish a principal thing'.[100] Furthermore, the owner of the appurtenance must have decided that his or her object will relatively permanently serve the purpose of the principal thing.[101] The connection between the appurtenance and the principal thing is weaker, as in the case of an element. The principal thing can be used also without the appurtenance and the appurtenance can be separated from the principal thing without any harm to both of them.[102] An appurtenance can serve the purpose of more than one principal thing.[103] The appurtenance can only be a movable. The appurtenance and the principal thing can be owned by different persons, and the appurtenance can be an independent object of other property rights.[104] However, 'in case of a doubt, an appurtenance shares the fate of the principal thing'[105] – *accessorium sequitur principale.* Furthermore, Article 140/2 of the CPL expressly provides that 'a mortgage also encompasses the appurtenances owned by the mortgagor'.

41. The CPL also defines the so-called *collective thing* (Sl. *zbirna stvar*), where several things are considered as one, without one of them being principal and others 'subordinate'. A collective thing is defined as 'several things which by general comprehension are deemed to be one thing'.[106] Juhart argues that parts of a collective thing are actually its elements, without the existence of a physical connection between them.[107] Such things are, for example, a pair of shoes or a set of cards.[108] The theory emphasizes the difference between a collective thing and a *collectivity*

99. Juhart in *Property Law*, 64–65. For example, a biogas plant is an element of the land it is built on, and the biogas engine is an element of the biogas plant: see Judgment of the High Court in Celje, No. Cpg 27/2015 of 15 Apr. 2015. If a building is built on pieces of land with different owners, and if the immovable property of one of the owners is sold in insolvency proceedings, this means that the part of the building which stands on the other owner's land is not the object of this sale: only the land with the buildings on it is being sold: see Decision of the High Court in Ljubjana, No. Cst 146/2015 of 11 Mar. 2015.

100. Article 17 of CPL. 'The general conviction' is a so-called legal standard which must be defined by courts in each particular situation; the connection is 'functional' and often also 'spatial', thus the technical documentation concerning the immovable cannot be considered as appurtenance: see Judgment of the Supreme Court RS, No. II Ips 299/2014 of 26 Feb. 2015.

101. Gavella in Gavella et al., *Stvarno pravo* [Property Law], 77 (Narodne Novine 2007).

102. Juhart in *Property Law*, 66. For example, a water-heater and a ceiling light are appurtenances and not elements (components) of an apartment: Judgment of the Appellate Court in Ljubljana, No. I Cp 2021/2015 of 23 Sep. 2015.

103. Tratnik in *CPL with Commentary 2004*, 122.

104. Juhart in *Property Law*, 66. See, e.g., Judgment of the High Court in Ljubljana, No. I Cp 2471/2008 of 8 Apr. 2009.

105. Article 17/2 of CPL.

106. Article 21 of CPL.

107. Juhart in *Property Law*, 70.

108. Cf. Vrenčur in *CPL with Commentary 2004*, 133.

of things (Sl. *skupnost stvari*), in which each part of the collectivity still has its autonomy and commercial value, e.g., a herd of sheep, a collection of stamps, a book collection, etc.[109]

42. The CPL provides for the following legal definition of *fruits* (Sl. *plodovi*): '[f]ruits are the direct product of a thing which until separation are an element of the thing but which upon separation become an independent thing'.[110] There exist natural fruits and civil fruits[111] – the former being the fruits given by the principal thing periodically and without damage to its substance (e.g., milk, honey, etc.), whereas the latter are those periodical incomes that are expressed in money or other generic (fungible) things and are based on a legal relationship entered into by the person entitled to the fruits (e.g., interests, rents, etc.).[112] The CPL only regulates the status of the natural fruits. The civil/indirect fruits are regulated by the law of obligations.[113] The owner of the fruit, after its separation from the principal thing, is in principle the owner of the principal thing.[114] 'Under conditions determined by law anyone may acquire ownership of forest fruits, mushrooms, and other freely growing plants.'[115]

43. Even though the conception of ownership in Slovenian law is unitary and there is only one form of ownership, some things are of special public interest and have to be, under certain conditions, accessible to everyone.[116] According to Article 19 of the CPL, *property in public domain* (national assets, Sl. *javno dobro*) is a thing that, in accordance with its purpose, can be used under equal conditions by everyone (general use). Such property cannot be used in a way to exclude or make difficult its use by other persons.[117] The scope of property in public domain and the conditions for general use are determined by law.[118]

44. According to CPL, *patrimonial rights* (Sl. *premoženjske pravice*) can also be objects of specific property rights, that is, the lien and the usufruct. The legal theory speaks of 'a right on a right'.[119] For the purposes of the CPL, a patrimonial right is

109. Juhart in *Property Law*, 69, Vrenčur in *CPL with Commentary* 2004, 133.
110. Article 20 of CPL.
111. Article 20/2 of CPL.
112. Juhart in *Property Law*, 71, 72.
113. Tratnik in *CPL with Commentary 2004*, 130.
114. Article 59/1 of CPL. See also Part III. The fruits of a thing, which is a part of the special property of one of the spouses, are a part of the joint property of the spouses if they came into existence with the work of one or both spouses: see, e.g., Judgment and Decision of the Supreme Court RS, No. II Ips 291/2008 of 14 Oct. 2009.
115. Article 59/3 of CPL. See also Part III.
116. Juhart in *Property Law*, 72.
117. Berden in *CPL with Commentary 2004*, 126.
118. For more details, see *ibid.*, 126–129, and Tratnik, Berden, *Javno dobro* [Property in Public Domain], in Pravna praksa, No. 38/2010, pp. II-VIII. For the regulation of the sea and maritime property as things in public domain, see Kerševan, *Morsko javno dobro: slabo* [Sea as Property in Public Domain: Insufficient], in Podjetje in delo, 6–7/2007, pp. 1430–1438.
119. Sajovic, *Osnove civilnega prava, Splošni del* [Bases of Civil Law, General Part], 75 (ČZ Uradni list RS 1994), cited by Juhart in *Property Law*, 76.

a right that is transferable and whose value can be expressed in money.[120] These rights are thus not tied to a specific person; they can also be inherited.[121] Patrimonial rights are, for example, claims, negotiable instruments (securities), corporate rights, patrimonial intellectual property rights, etc.[122]

A. *Immovable Property*

45. In Slovenian law, immovable property[123] (Sl. *nepremičnina*) is *defined* in Article 18 of the CPL as 'spatially measured parts of the earth's surface together with all their components'. This definition corresponds to Article 8 of the CPL, which enacts the principle of connection between land and building (Lat. *superficies solo cedit*). All other things are considered to be movables. The basic form of an immovable is thus a piece of land, which is registered in the cadastre and in the land register.[124] The regime proper to immovable property applies also to the parts of buildings in case of the establishment of the divided co-ownership, and to the buildings built on the basis of the right of superficies, for the time period of this right.[125] By analogy to the movables, an immovable can be defined as a thing that cannot be moved from one place to another without harming its substance.[126]

46. The regulation of property rights on immovable property shows several particularities in comparison to the regulation of the movables. The first is the publicity of the *ownership* of the immovables.[127] The state of the property rights on the immovables is registered in the land register maintained by the local courts. It must however be noted that as a consequence of the discontinuity of the property rights on immovables after the Second World War (some denationalization procedures are still not concluded), the actual state of the immovables and the state in the land register sometimes still do not correspond (which, to guarantee fair decisions, has been taken into account by the courts when deciding on the ownership of such immovables). Since 2004, the electronic land register has been established which is accessible via the Internet.[128]

---

120. Article 22 of CPL.
121. Berden in *CPL with Commentary 2004*, 72.
122. Juhart in *Property Law*, 77; Tratnik, *Zastavna pravica* [Lien], 281 (GV Založba 2006). According to High Court of Ljubljana, Decision No. I Ip 1202/2015 of 29 May 2015, personal easements, such as habitation, are not patrimonial rights, as they are not transferable.
123. See also Part I.
124. Juhart in *Property Law*, 67.
125. This wider definition originates in the law of the land register, see Art. 11/2/2 of LRA. Tratnik in *CPL with Commentary 2004*, 124–125; Juhart in *Property Law*, 68; Tratnik & Vrenčur, *Omejitve lastninske pravice in posebni pravni režimi na nepremičninah* [Limitations of Ownership and Special Legal Regimes on the Immovables], 29 (GV Založba 2009).
126. Gavella in Gavella et al., *Stvarno pravo* [Property Law], 79 (Narodne Novine 2007).
127. Article 11 of CPL.
128. http://www.sodisce.si/javne_knjige/zemljiska_knjiga/ (accessed on 31 Jul. 2019).

47. The ownership on the immovable property is (in cases of contractual acquisition) acquired only upon its entry in the *land register* (and not by the sole conclusion of the contract of sale, or by any other action as for example, handing over the keys to the house).[129] The principle of trust applies to the land register, which means that nobody can suffer negative consequences if he or she relied in good faith upon information in the land register that was later found out to be erroneous.[130] In cases of acquisitive prescription of an immovable which takes ten years, the ownership is acquired at the moment of the expiry of the ten-year period, while registration of such acquisition in the land register is of pure declaratory nature, whereby the effects of the principle of trust in the land register are of utmost importance for such acquirer as he or she may end up losing his or her non-registered ownership if a third person in good faith relied on the data of the land register and was registered as owner – in that case, ownership acquired on the basis of acquisitive prescription which was not registered ceases to exist.[131] The legal theory deems that the situation where the acquirer is in possession of a permission for inscription of ownership in the land register is analogous to that where the conditions for the acquisitive prescription are fulfilled: the 'new owner' is protected against the registered owner and against third parties which are aware of the factual situation (i.e., are in bad faith), whereas third parties in good faith are protected in legal transactions.[132] Article 243 of the LRA expressly provides that also persons which deem that their obligational (*inter partes*) rights were violated with the inscription in the land register (e.g., the first buyer in cases of multiple sales of the same immovable, if the second buyer registered first)[133] can demand the cancellation of such inscription, however only against persons in bad faith.[134]

48. The attention must be drawn to the case law of the Constitutional Court and the Supreme Court which established limits to the principle of trust in the land register in the enforcement proceedings, i.e., the acquirer who is not yet registered in the land register (but is already in possession of a permission for inscription issued by the registered owner or has acquired ownership by non-derivative acquisition (acquisitive prescription or common ownership of the spouses) can demand that the

129. For further details on acquisition of ownership, see Part III.
130. Article 8 of LRA.
131. For further details, see Part III, Ch. 1, §7. If the acquirer is aware of the prescription, he or she cannot rely on the principle of publicity and will not acquire ownership from the registered owner: Judgment of the Supreme Court RS, No. II Ips 370/2011 of 13 Mar. 2014.
132. Hudej, Ščernjavič, *Ponovni premislek o nekaterih temeljnih izhodiščih stvarnega prava pri prenosu lastninske pravice na nepremičninah* [New Reflections on Some of the Basic Principles of Property Law Regarding the Transfer of Ownership on Immovable Property], in Pravna praksa No. 3/2012, p. 23.
133. *Ibid.*
134. For more on this legal remedy, see Plavšak, *Izbrisna tožba* [Action for Cancellation], in *Zbornik, 2. Dnevi stvarnega in zemljiškoknjižnega prava*, 41–49 (GV Založba 2010), and Vrenčur, *Prenovljena ureditev izbrisne tožbe* [The Amended Regulation of the Action for Cancellation], in Podjetje in delo, 6–7/2010, pp. 1387 ff.

immovable be exempt from enforcement conducted over the property of the registered owner.[135] The ownership is thus considered to already have passed from the registered owner to the person who fulfils all conditions for inscription, as regards the relationship between these parties. Third persons can rely on the registered data when entering into legal transactions with the registered owner, but not in enforcement proceedings.[136] The same is true in insolvency proceedings: the acquirer in possession of a valid permission for inscription can proceed to the registration in the land register even if insolvency proceedings regarding the registered owner have already been initiated at the time of the request for registration.[137]

49. The principle of trust in the land register has thus strongly been mitigated, and the legal theory warns of the possibility of abuse of the fact that the real state of the property of certain persons is not apparent from the public records.[138] For example, a person can obtain a credit because the creditor believes the debtor is the owner of a valuable immovable registered on his or her name, whereas this immovable has already been sold to a third person who has not yet registered the transfer. On the other hand, the new owner can benefit of certain rights because he or she officially does not own any immovable, even though the contract of sale was concluded and he or she is already in possession of the permission to register. In 2016, the Supreme Court decided a case where the lower courts rejected the action for inadmissibility of enforcement of such non-registered owner, since they deemed that the latter abused of his or her right to file such action, whereby he or she omitted to register in the land register as the owner. The Supreme Court judged that: '[the] plaintiff did not abuse of his right to judicial protection by not registering his right of (co)ownership in the land register and filing the action for the inadmissibility of enforcement under Art. 65 of the CESA […], since the registering […] was not his duty and the situation would have been the same if he had registered. The expected ownership prevails over the right of repayment of the claim in the enforcement procedure. Only a creditor who obtained a contractual lien on the immovable can avail him or herself of the information in the land register and the good faith, and not a creditor who obtained the lien only in the enforcement procedure or the procedure for securing of claims (the so-called compulsory lien)'.[139]

---

135. See the Decision of the Constitutional Court RS, No. Up-591/10 of 2 Dec. 2010, and, e.g., the Judgments of the Supreme Court of RS Nos II Ips 475/2008, II Ips 132/2009, and II Ips 220/2006. For the joint ownership of the spouses, see Decision of the Constitutional Court RS, No. Up-128/03 of 27 Jan. 2005.
136. See, e.g., Judgment and Decision of the Supreme Court RS, No. II Ips 60/2014 of 11 Dec. 2014: '[o]nly the acquisition of rights by legal transactions is protected [by the principle of trust in the land register], whereas a lien acquired in the enforcement proceedings is not such right'.
137. Article 94/3/3 of the LRA. See, e.g., Decision of the High Court in Ljubljana, No. I Cpg 1733/2014 of 25 Nov. 2014.
138. Tratnik, *Lastninska pravica na nepremičnini v pričakovanju* [The Expectation of Ownership of an Immovable], in Pravna praksa, No. 2/2013, p. VIII.
139. Decision No. II Ips 284/2015 of 18 Feb. 2016. In this respect, the Supreme Court also cites the Decision of the Constitutional Court No. Up-128/03 and the Decision of the Supreme Court No. II Ips 135/2012.

50. All *limited property rights* can be established on the immovable property. Only the immovables can be the object of the easements in rem, the encumbrance, and the right of superficies (the land debt was abolished from the CPL in 2013).[140] Limited property rights on the immovables are registered in the land register. The lien on the immovable property (the mortgage) does not include the transfer of possession of the object of the lien, which typically remains in the possession of the owner. The publicity of the mortgage and the security of the creditor are guaranteed by the inscription in the land register.

51. Because of the limited number of immovables, *public interest* in their use is much more intense than in movables; therefore, the right of ownership on the immovables is more often the subject of limitations pursuing the economical, ecological, and social functions of the property, as determined in the Constitution.[141] According to Article 69 of the Constitution, expropriation is possible, under strict conditions, only in relation to immovable property.[142]

B. Movable Property

52. The CPL does not provide any *definition* of the movable property.[143,144] The legal theory defines the movables as specifically determined objects that can be moved from one place to another without any harm for their economical substance.[145] In contrast to the immovable property, the number of movables is practically unlimited. There is no register of property rights on the movables, with exception of the register of certain categories of movables that have been seized in enforcement proceedings or on which a non-possessory pledge has been established.[146] However, certain forms of movables – for example, ships – are subject to special regulation.[147] The legal regime applicable to such movables is similar to the

140. Official Gazette RS, No. 91/13.
141. Juhart in *Property Law*, 67.
142. For more on expropriation, see Part III.
143. See also Part II.
144. For more on the definition of movables and immovables, see Tratnik, *Stvarno pravo: O problemih definicije nepremičnine in premičnine* [Property Law: About the Problems of the Definition of an Immovable and a Movable], in Pravna Praksa, No. 46/1999, pp. 8 ff.
145. This definition is based on Art. 293 of the ABGB. Juhart in *Property Law*, 67; Gavella in Gavella et al., *Stvarno pravo* [Property Law], 78 (Narodne Novine 2007).
146. Register of non-possessory liens and attached movables, established by Uredba o registru neposestnih zastavnih pravic in zarubljenih premicnin [Decree on the Register of Non-possessory Liens and Seized Movable Property], Official Gazette RS, No. 23/04, with further amendments.
147. Juhart in *Property Law*, 68. The Maritime Code thus provides that ships and ships in the process of being built are considered to be movables (Art. 219). The same provision regarding airplanes and airplanes in the process of being built is contained in Art. 164 of the Obligations and Real Rights in Air Navigation Act (Zakon o obligacijskih in stvarnopravnih razmerjih v letalstvu (ZOSRL)), Official Gazette RS, No. 27/11.

one that applies to the immovables.[148] Compared to the immovable property, the exercise of the ownership on movable property is very rarely limited in the public interest.

53. The *ownership* of the movables is typically acquired by a non-formal act of delivery (Lat. *traditio*), preceded by a legal transaction, without the interference of the state. Regarding the *limited property rights*, only lien and personal easements can be established on movable property. The lien on movables (pledge, Lat. *pignus*) is typically characterized by the transfer of possession on the object of the lien to the creditor or a third person.[149] According to Article 64 of the CPL, it is possible, under strict conditions (especially the good faith of the acquirer), to acquire ownership on the movables from a non-owner. The *acquisitive prescription* for movables takes effect after three years of possession. Articles 201–206 of the CPL on the transfer of title as security (Lat. *fiducia cum creditore contracta*) and Articles 520 and 521 of the CO[150] on the reservation of title (the conditional sale) also apply to movables only.[151]

III. General (Basic) Principles of the Slovenian Property Law

54. 'The general principles of the Slovenian property law define the latter as an individualist legal branch which stems from the ownership liberty of an individual as the main defining element of the individual's patrimonial situation.'[152] The general principles serve as an *instrument of the interpretation* of property law concepts and the filling of legal gaps.[153] According to the CPL, these principles are the priority principle, the principle of speciality, the connection between land and building, the presumption of good faith, the trust in the land register, the principle of presumption of ownership (the publicity principle), and the prohibition of abuse. The legal theory adds the principle of the limited number (Lat. *numerus clausus*) of property rights (deduced from Article 2 of the CPL), the principle of the universal effect (Lat. *erga omnes*) of the property rights (Article 5 of the CPL), as well as the principle that no one can transfer more rights than he or she has (Lat. *nemo plus iuris tranferre potest quam ipse habet*).[154] Berden also cites the principle of the property rights as a constitutionally guaranteed category, the principle of the property law nature, the principle of the capacity of things, the principle of causality of

148. Tratnik, *Stvarno pravo: O problemih definicije nepremičnine in premičnine* [Property Law: About the Problems of the Definition of an Immovable and a Movable], in Pravna Praksa, No. 46/1999, pp. 8 ff. See also Part III.
149. Although a non-possessory lien in the form of a directly enforceable notarial protocol is also possible under the provisions of Part VI, Ch. 4 of the CPL.
150. Article 520/1 of the CO provides: 'The seller of a specific item of movable property may via a special contractual provision reserve title to the thing once delivered to the buyer until the buyer pays the purchase money.'
151. Examples gathered by Rudolf et al., *National Report on the Transfer of Movables in Slovenia*, in *National Reports on the Transfer of Movables in Europe*, 545 (Eds Faber & Lurger, Sellier 2008).
152. Juhart in *Property Law*, 77.
153. Berden in *CPL with Commentary 2004*, 56.
154. Juhart in *Property Law*, 77–94.

the transfer agreement, the principle of protection of the acquirer in good faith, the principle of deduction (i.e., the analogous application of the rules concerning the founding and transfer of ownership to the founding and transfer of other property law rights), the principle of the perfection of form, and the principle of possession.[155] It must be emphasized that the general principles of private law, such as the equality of parties, the free initiative of the parties, the transferability of rights, the pecuniary sanctions, the dispositive nature of legal provisions, etc., also apply.[156]

A. *Priority Principle*

55. Article 6 of the CPL provides that: '[i]f more than one property right exists over the same thing, the property right of the same type acquired earlier shall have priority over a property right acquired later'. This is the articulation of the Roman law principle *prior tempore potior iure*. Different property rights can exist on the same thing, but the priority principle is only of importance if these rights do not only coexist but also 'compete' with one another – for example, in the case of several liens on the same thing.[157] According to the priority principle, the first creditor to have his or her claim protected by a lien will have his or her claim fully (or to the limited extent if the lien item's value is minor to the creditor's claim) repaid by the proceeds from the sale of the lien item; the second lienor would receive the remaining amount of the purchase money, etc.[158] The priority principle is thus an important sign of distinction between, on one hand, property law, and, on the other hand, the law of obligations, with its principle of equality of the creditors notwithstanding the moment of the establishment of their rights.[159]

56. The legal theory draws attention to the fact that the expression 'the property right of the same type' should not be interpreted in a too restrictive manner, as also the contents of different types of property rights can enter into 'competition'.[160] Such situations will most commonly occur during the realization of the mortgage (or a land debt established before its legislative abolition in 2013) on the same immovable, as well as in cases of the collision between mortgage (or land debt established before 2013) with easements, encumbrances, and rights of superficies.[161] The priority principle is usually also applied to solve such situations,[162] with the exception of the co-existence of a mortgage (or a land debt established before

155. Berden in *CPL with Commentary 2004*, 57–67; Berden, *Reforma stvarnega prava: Načela stvarnega prava* [Reform of Property Law: The Principles of Property Law], in Podjetje in delo, No. 6/2000, pp. 1447 ff.; Berden, *Načela stvarnega prava* [Principles of Property Law], in Pravna Praksa, No. 6/2003, p. 9, No. 8/2003, p. 9, No. 9/2003, p. 13, No. 10/2003, p. 7, No. 12/2003, p. 11, No. 13/2003, p. 9.
156. Berden in *CPL with Commentary 2004*, 57.
157. Juhart in *Property Law*, 81.
158. See also Art. 198 of CESA, Art. 147 of CPL and, for example, Decision of the High Court in Maribor, No. I Ip 215/2009 of 2 Apr. 2009.
159. Tratnik in *CPL with Commentary 2004*, 79.
160. Juhart in *Property Law*, 81–82.
161. Tratnik in *CPL with Commentary 2004*, 79.
162. Juhart in *Property Law*, 81.

2013) and an easement in rem (the easements in rem namely remain despite the sale of the immovable for the realization of a mortgage).[163] This principle is also one of the principles of the law on land register.[164]

B. Principle of Speciality

57. According to Article 7 of the CPL, '[o]nly an individually defined independent thing can be the object of property rights, except where this Act provides otherwise'. A part of a thing can thus be a separate object of a property right only if the law so provides.[165] Such legal provisions are those related to the acquisitive prescription of a part of an immovable, the co-divided ownership, and the right of superficies, as well as those regulating the non-possessory pledge and fiduciary transfer of stored material.[166] The principle of speciality is a distinguishing attribute of property rights because it neither applies to the rights under the law of obligations nor to possession that can exist on a part of a thing.[167] Property rights thus exist on the principal thing, together with its elements (building being an element of the land it is built on) and, in principle, its appurtenances (if the necessary conditions are complied with, i.e., that such movables, in accordance with general perception, are intended for commercial use or to embellish the principal thing). The ideal parts (percentage) of co-owned things can, however, be autonomous objects of the property law rights.[168] The whole patrimony of a person cannot be an independent object of property law rights so that each item belonging to this patrimony must be transferred or encumbered individually, with the exception of the universal transfer in case of the owner's death.[169]

58. It must be stressed that the principle of speciality is only applicable to the property law legal relations and not to the obligational relations such as sale or lease.[170] Thus, a room in an apartment cannot, for example, be the object of a contract of sale (whereas it can be rented) as ownership of a mere part of a thing cannot be transferred.[171]

---

163. Tratnik in *CPL with Commentary 2004*, 79–80. See also Art. 174 of CESA.
164. Article 10 of LRA.
165. Juhart in *Property Law*, 82. See also the legal status of the elements described earlier (Ch. II: Objects of Property Rights).
166. Tratnik in *CPL with Commentary 2004*, 82.
167. Juhart in *Property Law*, 82.
168. Tratnik in *CPL with Commentary 2004*, 80.
169. *Ibid.*, 81.
170. For more details see Tratnik in *CPL with Commentary 2004*, 80.
171. If the heirs who inherited each an ideal part (a percentage) of a land with a house built on it enter an agreement regarding the future use of the house (under which they designate which part will be exclusively used by which heir), they did not thus create new immovables (as this would be the case in the creation of a co-divided ownership, i.e., the creation of separate legal entities in one building); the immovable remains in co-ownership of the heirs: Judgment of the Supreme Court RS, No. II Ips 10/2013 of 5 Feb. 2015. 'A part of a land has no autonomy in property law and cannot be the object of the right of ownership or of the transfer of that right (however, a part of a land

C. Connection Between Land and Building

59. 'Everything which by intention is permanently affixed to or is permanently on an immovable, above it or below it, is an element of the immovable, except where the law provides otherwise.'[172] This principle is generally known by its Latin parallel, *superficies solo cedit.* It not only applies to buildings made by man, but also to all natural things connected to the land, typically the plants.[173] The permanence of the connection must not be appreciated in the absolute way, but according to the will of the parties and the nature of the object, as well as according to the general conviction.[174] The connection must be organic or functional, which means that the object cannot be separated from the land without harming the object or its economical substance.[175] The principle of connection between land and building is crucial for the effective registration of the immovables.

60. The principle of connection between land and building was not respected in the times of the state/social ownership, where all land destined to the building of objects was owned by the state/society and the individual could only acquire ownership on the building and the right to use the land underneath this building.[176] Today, this principle has regained its basic character and importance, but not entirely without exceptions. Such exceptions are the co-divided ownership on apartment buildings (Sl. *etažna lastnina*), where the land is co-owned by the owners of the apartments, and the right of superficies (Sl. *stavbna pravica*), where the land and the building are legally separated and owned by different persons.[177]

D. Presumption of Good Faith

61. 'Good faith is presumed unless indicated otherwise.'[178] Good faith is the most important in acquiring the property rights and not as much in their execution, which is limited only by the prohibition of the abuse of rights set down in Article

---

can be the object of a legal transaction under the law of obligations [if it is sufficiently determined] since the principle of speciality does not apply to such transactions)': Judgment of the Supreme Court RS, No. II Ips 571/2009 of 6 June 2013.

172. Article 8 of CPL. See, e.g., Judgment of the Supreme Court RS, No. II Ips 163/2008 of 26 May 2011, where the court held that it is not possible to succeed with the demand that the ownership of the building be established, without also demanding the establishment of the ownership of the land under this building.
173. Tratnik in *CPL with Commentary 2004*, 83.
174. *Ibid.*, 84.
175. *Ibid.* See also Juhart in *Property Law*, 84. The Supreme Court RS has held that a bee house (Judgment No. II Ips 295/2008 of 15 Dec. 2011) or a publicity board (Judgment No. I Ips 281/2007 of 13 Sep. 2007) were not permanently affixed to the land and were thus not objects of the principle *superficies solo cedit.* On the contrary, a road barrier was considered an element of the immovable (Decision of the High Court in Ljubljana, No. II Cp 2194/2015 of 16 Sep. 2015).
176. Juhart in *Property Law*, 84.
177. See, e.g., Decision of the High Court in Maribor, No. I Ip 759/2015 of 26 Oct. 2015.
178. Article 9 of CPL.

12 of the CPL.[179] The acquirer must be in good faith to be able to acquire ownership by acquisitive prescription (Article 43 of the CPL) or from a non-owner (Article 64 of the CPL as to movables, and Article 8 of the CPL as to immovables),[180] sometimes also to acquire ownership of the fruits (Article 59 of the CPL) and in some other cases.[181]

62. Article 9 of the CPL has, above all, the role of a general rule of evidence.[182] When the existence of good faith is legally important, good faith is presumed and does not have to be proven. This presumption can, however, be rebutted by evidence of the lack of good faith.[183] The Supreme Court held that:

> [e]veryone must be diligent when acquiring possession, whereas it cannot be expected that the possessor, after acquiring possession in good faith, constantly controls their legal situation; such possessor later becomes of bad faith if they actually find out that they have no right to possess, but still continue possessing; on the other hand, the possessor is not in bad faith if a possibility existed for them to find out about lacking the right to possess, but they nevertheless did not find that out; certain diligence must be expected also from the owner who is aware of the difference between the registered and the actual situation and who must prevent the fulfilment of the conditions for acquiring ownership by acquisitive prescription.[184]

E. Trust in the Land Register

63. 'Anyone who acts honestly in legal transactions and relies on information about rights entered in the land register shall not suffer detrimental consequences as a result.'[185] This principle has the central role in the legal relations concerning the immovables.[186] The legal theory points out two faces of this principle: from the negative point of view, it means that a right on an immovable does not exist if it is not registered in the land register; the positive approach leads to the conclusion that only those rights that are registered in the land register exist on the immovable.[187]

64. The principle of trust in the land register is organically linked to the principle of good faith because it can only be successfully availed of by a person in good faith – that is, a person who does not know and does not have to know that the state

179. Juhart in *Property Law*, 84–85.
180. The Supreme Court of RS held that 'a proprietary possessor is in good faith when his or her error about his or her ownership is excusable, i.e. a person who does not know and who cannot know that he or she is not the owner of the thing': Judgment No. II Ips 115/2012 of 30 Oct. 2014.
181. See also Arts 47, 95, 98, 99, 156 and 217 of CPL.
182. Tratnik in *CPL with Commentary 2004*, 85.
183. See, e.g., Judgment of the Supreme Court RS, No. II Ips 115/2012 of 30 Oct. 2014.
184. Judgment No. II Ips 622/2008 of 19 Jan. 2012.
185. Article 10 of CPL. Very similar provision is to be found in Art. 8/1 of the LRA.
186. Juhart in *Property Law*, 85; Juhart in *CPL with Commentary 2004*, 85.
187. Juhart in *Property Law*, 85–86.

of the registered rights is incorrect.[188] It is also an expression of the land register law principle of publicity, which lays down the presumption of awareness of the existence of the registered rights.[189] This principle is fundamental for the achievement of efficacy of the land register, because it provides legal protection to the one who was aware of the registered rights and trusted in good faith their correctness. It also indirectly forces the person who fulfils the conditions for the registration of his or her right to proceed to such registration, because they will have to bear the consequences that could follow their not doing so.[190]

65. However, as explained above, the case law has mitigated the absolute nature of this principle. The Constitutional Court of RS and the Supreme Court of RS have held that only third persons entering into legal transactions with the registered owner can, provided their good faith, rely on the registered data, whereas a creditor in the enforcement proceedings conducted against the registered owner, cannot, if the new owner acquired his/her ownership in a non-derivative manner (via acquisitive prescription or the establishment of joint ownership of the spouses) or if the new owner is already in possession of the permission to be registered in the land register.[191] Another exception has been introduced by the Supreme Court of RS stating that immovables having the status of a 'plot belonging to a building' cannot be validly transferred as individual immovables regardless of any good faith of the acquirer.[192]

66. The principle of trust is limited to the sole registered rights. It does not apply to the factual information about the immovable that is originally registered in the cadastre (there is no such principle as the principle of trust in the cadastre).[193]

67. This principle is also linked to another land register law principle: the principle of the constitutive effect of the entry in the land register:[194] the property rights generally come into being, are modified, or become extinct at the moment of the validity of this entry.[195] There exist certain possibilities of acquiring the property rights on immovables outside of this general rule – for example, the acquisition by prescription – but such acquisition is only effective in the relationship between the former and the new owner and does not yet apply to the third party in good faith

188. *Ibid.*, 86–88.
189. *Ibid.*, 86.
190. Article 8/2 of LRA. For more on this topic, see Tratnik, *Stvarnopravni zakonik in obligacijsko pravo* [Code of Property Law and the Law of Obligations], in Podjetje in delo, No. 6/2002, pp. 1392 ff.; Vrenčur, *Vpisovanje obligacijskih pravic v zemljiško knjigo* [Entry of the Obligational Rights in the Land Register], in Pravna Praksa, No. 26/2006, pp. 16 ff.
191. For a thorough presentation and evaluation of this case law, see Tratnik, *Lastninska pravica na nepremičnini v pričakovanju* [The Expectation of Ownership of an Immovable], in Pravna praksa, No. 2/2013, pp. II-VIII.
192. See the following Decisions taken by the Supreme Court of RS: II Ips 420/2011 of 19 Sep. 2013 and II Ips 369/29 of 27 May 2013. For further details on the concept of 'plot belonging to a building', see paras. 112, 115, 142, 423 of this monograph.
193. Juhart in *Property Law*, 86.
194. Article 7 of LRA.
195. Juhart in *Property Law*, 87.

who could acquire the ownership and enter his or her right in the land register before the person who became an out-of-register owner by prescription.[196] The above-mentioned case law of the highest courts, granting, in specific circumstances, the non-registered acquirers to invoke their ownership of the immovable, mitigates this principle, too.

F. Principle of Publicity (Presumption of Ownership)

68. 'It shall be presumed that the owner of an immovable is the person entered in the land register. It shall be presumed that the proprietary possessor of a movable is its owner.'[197] As the property rights have *erga omnes* effect, there must be an objective sign of their existence, or, in other words, their publicity must be assured. This is true above all for the most important of the property rights – the ownership. The publicity of the ownership is based on facts that reflect the highest real-life probability of justifying the aforementioned presumption, although it can be rebutted by opposite evidence.[198]

69. As a rule, the ownership on the immovables is acquired upon entry in the land register. The presumption of ownership of immovables is thus linked to the principle of trust in the land register (see Part III, Chapter 1, Section 7 on the Principle of Trust in the Land Register for the exceptions). It is established on the day after the court has notified in the land register the receipt of the demand for entry.[199] There is logically no register for the movables, so that the sign of the ownership is different, namely, the 'proprietary possession'.[200] The entitlement to possess is, namely, the core of the right of ownership.[201] The term 'proprietary possession' is defined in Article 27 of the CPL as follows: '[a]nyone who has a thing in his or her possession as his or her own is the proprietary possessor'. The element that distinguishes the proprietary from the non-proprietary possession is the intention of possessing as the owner and without the recognition of 'the higher legal control of an indirect possessor'.[202] The Supreme Court RS held that the conditions for proprietary possession in good faith are fulfilled when the possessor justifiably deems all prerequisites for the transfer of ownership fulfilled, i.e., legal title, act of delivery, capacity of the transferor; however, the validity of the legal title is not required.[203] The possession is clearly a much less reliable reference for the presumption of ownership than the land register in case of immovables, because the possessor can have possession on other grounds than ownership. Despite the clear definition, the proprietary character of the possession will thus probably be difficult to recognize for

196. Article 44 of CPL; Juhart in *Property Law*, 87–88.
197. Article 11 of CPL.
198. For such rebuttal see, e.g., Judgment of the Supreme Court, No. II Ips 370/2011 of 13 Mar. 2014.
199. Art. 6/1 LRA, Juhart in *CPL with Commentary 2004*, 91.
200. Cf. *ibid.*
201. *Ibid.*
202. Article 27/2 of CPL.
203. Judgment No. II Ips 359/2010 of 19 Dec. 2013.

the third parties. The trust in the publicity principle in movables is protected, for example, by Article 64 of the CPL, which regulates the acquiring of ownership on movables from a non-owner.[204]

G. Prohibition of Abuse

70. Article 12 of the CPL provides: '[t]he owner of a thing or the holder of another property right is limited by the same rights of others. Ownership and other property rights must be exercised in accordance with the fundamental principles of this Act, with their purpose and with the nature of the thing. If the holder of a right acts with the sole or clear intention of harming another person, it shall be considered a sham exercise of that right'. The holder of a property right is thus limited in its exercise by the same rights of others (the typical case being the collision between two ownerships), by the purpose of the right and the nature of the thing, and by the prohibition of intentionally harming another person. In all of these cases, the third parties can claim the cessation of such exercise because it is presumed to be abusive.[205] The prohibition of abuse is especially important in the law of neighbourhood, in the cases of co-ownership, and in other property law relationships involving several persons.[206]

71. The prohibition of exercising a property right with the intention of harming others is considered to be the basic example of abuse.[207] However, it is especially difficult to establish because it is based both on the objective criterion of causing harm and on the subjective criterion of the intention of harming others.[208] Some authors name slightly different criteria of abuse: the intentional criterion (the holder of a right exercises this right with intention of harming another person) and the functional criterion (the holder of a right exercises this right with no justified purpose).[209] The Supreme Court emphasized the role of time: judicial protection is only necessary when the disturbance of ownership is continuous or when it is probable that without the intervention of the court the disturbance will be repeated.[210]

72. The notion of abuse of a right itself has been much discussed.[211] The legal theory problematizes above all the obligation of exercising the property right according to its purpose and the nature of the thing. The right to ownership is,

204. Juhart in *CPL with Commentary 2004*, 92.
205. Cf. Berden in *CPL with Commentary 2004*, 93, and Juhart in *Property Law*, 92.
206. Tratnik & Vrenčur, *Omejitve lastninske pravice in posebni pravni režimi na nepremičninah* [Limitations of Ownership and Special Legal Regimes on the Immovables], 184 (GV Založba 2009).
207. Juhart in *Property Law*, 92.
208. *Ibid.*, 93. The Supreme Court RS held that putting up a fence at the beginning of the road on which another person has an easement in rem is an exercise of the right of ownership and it suffices that the owner give the holder of the easement the keys for opening the fence, as the easement must be exercised in such a way that the ownership is least encumbered: Decision No. II Ips 749/2005 of 22 Feb. 2007.
209. Berden in *CPL with Commentary 2004*, 93.
210. Judgment No. II Ips 343/2010 of 9 Jun. 2011.
211. For abuse of a property right, see Berden in *CPL with Commentary 2004*, 93–107.

namely, a right that includes also the right of destruction of the thing. The rights should be limited in this regard only by a concrete interest of another person or a concrete public interest, and not merely on the basis of an abstract judgment of the holders' actions as being non-economical, not useful, or lacking sense.[212]

73. An interesting case of abuse of rights is the multiple sale of the same immovable. The courts have developed case law regarding such sales, under which the second sale was contrary to the moral and therefore null and void; in consequence, if the second buyer succeeded to register their ownership and was in bad faith, the first buyer could demand that he/she issues him/her the permission to register.[213] Currently, such situations are better addressed via the action for cancellation regulated in the LRA (and mentioned above).

H. Principle of the Limited Number (Numerus Clausus) of Property Rights

74. Because property rights have universal effect and must be respected by everybody and not just the parties to the contract, it is necessary that their forms are defined by law. Contrary to the law of obligations, the parties cannot establish other legal relationships outside those included in the CPL that would have effects in the field of property law.[214] The principle of *numerus clausus* is not expressly included in the CPL, but can be deduced from Article 2 of the CPL enumerating the property rights. These are: the ownership as the basic property right and the limited property rights or the rights on a foreign thing: lien, easements, encumbrance, and right of superficies. The criterion for establishing whether a right is a property right is thus the legislature's definition.[215]

75. The principle of the limited number of property rights does not demand an *ex ante* definition of content of the property rights; they can and, in some instances, must be determined according to each specific case. The legal theory cites the encumbrance and the easement in rem as typical examples of the 'abstractly defined' property rights requiring concretization.[216]

*I. Principle of the Universal Effect (*Erga Omnes*) of the Property Rights*

76. Property rights must be respected by everyone and can be enforced against everyone who would interfere with the exercise of these rights by the owner or the

212. Juhart in *Property Law*, 92.
213. See, e.g., Judgment of the Supreme Court RS, No. II Ips 567/2009 of 30 Jun. 2011.
214. Juhart in *Property Law*, 78.
215. Berden in Berden et al., *Novo stvarno pravo* [New Property Law], 18 (Codex Iuris 2002).
216. Juhart in *Property Law*, 78.

person entitled to a limited property right.[217] The person entitled to a limited property right can protect his or her right also against the owner. A typical form of judicial protection of property rights are the claims for omission of interference – for example, the *rei vindicatio*, in the case of alienation of a thing from its owner, and the *actio negatoria*, in the case of interference with the exercise of the right to ownership other than alienation.

77. The universal effect of property rights is of crucial importance in insolvency and enforcement proceedings.[218] The owner of the thing in possession of the insolvent debtor can demand that his or her thing be returned to him or her and thus separated from the estate of the insolvent debtor, which will later be divided among the creditors.[219] The creditor whose claim is protected by a lien can demand that his or her claim be paid prior to other claims and in whole. Consequently, he or she will return the lien thing into the estate of the insolvent debtor.[220] In the enforcement proceedings against the holder of the thing, the person who proves the probability of the existence of his or her right on the thing which prevents the enforcement (typically the ownership) can file a so-called third-party objection, demanding that the court forbid the enforcement regarding this thing.[221]

78. The rights on immovables provided by the law of obligations get the *erga omnes* effect only by inscription in the land register (whereas not all of these rights can be registered in all circumstances);[222] otherwise, they can only produce effects *inter partes* – that is, between the parties to the contract. Such rights are the prohibition to alienate or encumber the thing,[223] the lease,[224] the right of preemption,[225] the right of repurchase,[226] and the special right to use the property in public domain and other rights if the law so provides.[227]

217. Article 5 of CPL provides: 'Holders of a property right may enforce their right against any person.'
218. Cf. Juhart in *Property Law*, 81.
219. Article 22 of FOIPCDA.
220. Article 19 of FOIPCDA.
221. Articles 64 ff. of CESA.
222. See, e.g., Art. 38 of CPL.
223. Articles 38/2, 38/3 and 38/4 of CPL.
224. Articles 587 ff. of CO.
225. Articles 507–512 of CO.
226. Article 38/2 of CPL.
227. Article 13/2 of LRA, cited earlier. For more on this question, see Vrenčur, *Vpisovanje obligacijskih pravic v zemljiško knjigo* [The Registration of Obligational Rights in the Land Register], in Pravna praksa, No. 26/2006, pp. 16 ff., and Šuler, *Pomen vpisa obligacijskih pravic v zemljiško knjigo* [The Importance of the Registration of Obligational Rights in the Land Register], in Pravna praksa, No. 18/2013, pp. 14 ff.

J. *Principle of the Impossible Transfer of Rights One Is Not Entitled to (*Nemo Plus Iuris Transferre Potest Quam Ipse Habet*)*

79. According to this principle, no one can effectively transfer a right he or she is not entitled to. This principle is expressly put forward in several provisions of the CPL; it is also expressed in the law of the land register as the principle of the legal predecessor.[228]

80. In spite of its fundamental importance in the property law, this principle is not absolute. Article 64 of the CPL provides: '[o]wnership of a movable is acquired even if the transferor did not have the authority to alienate the thing if the acquirer was in good faith at the moment of delivery and acquired the thing on the basis of an onerous legal transaction … '. Only three situations permit the transfer of ownership in this manner: if the movable was sold at a public auction, if the transferor put such movables into circulation as part of his or her activity, or if the transferor acquired possession of the movable by will of its owner. Good faith of the acquirer is an inevitable condition for such transfer. The previous owner is, however, not entirely denied his or her statute: Article 64/5 of the CPL provides that within one year of the expiration of ownership, the previous owner may require the acquirer to sell the movable to him or her at the market price if it has a special importance for him or her.[229]

81. The acquisition of ownership on an immovable from a non-owner is exceptionally also possible on grounds of trust in the land register[230] (i.e., under the condition that the acquirer is in good faith) if, for example, the actual owner acquired his or her ownership on grounds of the acquisitive prescription and has not yet demanded the entry in the land register.[231]

IV. Concept of Ownership

82. The right to ownership (Sl. *lastninska pravica*) is a basic *human right*, defined as such in Article 33 of the Slovenian Constitution,[232] as well as in Article 1 of the Protocol No. 1 to the European Convention on Human Rights, which was ratified by the Slovenian parliament[233] and is thus directly applicable in the Slovenian legal system. The right to ownership is also guaranteed by Article 17 of the

228. Juhart in *Property Law*, 93.
229. For further details, see Part III.
230. Juhart in *Property Law*, 94.
231. For further details, see Part III.
232. The Internet site Ius Info which records Slovenian case law concerning the legislation in force, reports that only the Constitutional Court, competent for the interpretation of the Slovenian Constitution, rendered 858 decisions (including the ones rejecting such judicial protection) with regard to Art. 33 of the Constitution from 1991 until January 2016 (http://www.iusinfo.si).
233. Zakon o ratifikaciji Konvencije o varstvu človekovih pravic in temeljnih svoboščin, spremenjene s protokoli št. 3, 5 in 8 ter dopolnjene s protokolom št. 2, ter njenih protokolov št. 1, 4, 6, 7, 9, 10 in 11 [Act ratifying the Convention on Human Rights and Fundamental Freedoms as amended by

United Nations' Universal Declaration of Human Rights of 1948 and by Article 17 of the Charter of Fundamental Rights of the European Union.

83. The *ownership* as the basic property right is composed of several entitlements (Sl. *upravičenja*) of the owner, as well as of some obligations according to the social, economic, and ecological functions of the property. According to Article 37/1 of the CPL, the right of ownership is defined as a right to possess a thing, to use and enjoy it in the fullest manner, and to dispose of it (i.e., to alienate or encumber the thing). The legal theory defines ownership as the will of the owner to use and dispose of a thing in the fullest manner (positive aspect of ownership) and to exclude all other people of doing the same (negative aspect).[234] The Supreme Court RS held: 'If the owner transfers one or more of his/her entitlements to other persons […] he/she still holds the substantial entitlement arising from the ownership to defend themselves against any intervention of third parties and to request the return of the thing from anybody who alienated the thing.'[235] The right of ownership also includes the right of the owner to destroy the thing.[236]

84. The object of ownership is a *thing* as defined in Article 15 of the CPL. The ownership is not possible regarding the patrimonial rights, because those are not legally considered to be things.

85. The restrictions on use, enjoyment, and disposal can only be determined by law. Article 37/2 of the CPL provides that ownership cannot be limited in time or be conditional unless otherwise determined by law. Such exceptions are, for example, the fiduciary transfer of ownership and the reservation of title. Some of the entitlements can be separately transferred to other persons in the form of *limited property rights*. According to Article 2 of the CPL, these are the lien (the pledge, the mortgage, Sl. *zastavna pravica*), the right of encumbrance (Sl. *stvarno breme*), the right of superficies or the building lease (Sl. *stavbna pravica*), and the easements or the servitudes (Sl. *služnosti*) in rem and in personam.

86. Article 38 of the CPL regulates *the restrictions of ownership at the will of the owner*, which can be established unless expressly prohibited. A *prohibition of disposal* (Sl. *prepoved odtujitve in obremenitve*)[237] of a thing or a property right by means of a legal transaction or last will is, however, binding only on the first owner

---

Protocols Nos 3, 5 and 8 and amended by Protocol No. 2 and its Protocols Nos 1, 4, 6, 7, 9, 10 and 11], Official Gazette RS – International Treaties, No. 7/94.

234. Berden in *CPL with Commentary 2004*, 213; Tratnik & Vrenčur, *Omejitve lastninske pravice in posebni pravni režimi na nepremičninah* [Limitations of Ownership and Special Legal Regimes on the Immovables], 27 (GV Založba, 2009).

235. Decision No. II Ips 528/2004 of 20 Sep. 2006.

236. Tratnik & Vrenčur, *Omejitve lastninske pravice in posebni pravni režimi na nepremičninah* [Limitations of Ownership and Special Legal Regimes on the Immovables], 27 (GV Založba 2009).

237. In Slovenia, this restriction literally means the prohibition to alienate and encumber; however, under the case law, this is a unitary legal concept and cannot be divided in the way that the parties would only agree on the prohibition to alienate, without the prohibition to encumber: Decision of the High Court in Koper, No. CDn 27/2014 of 11 Feb. 2014.

and not on his or her legal successors.[238] It can be entered in the land register if it is agreed between spouses or cohabiting partners, parents and their children, as well as adopted children and adoptive parents. In this case, the prohibition also has effects against third persons.[239] An owner can conclude a contract establishing the *right of repurchase* (Sl. *odkupna pravica*), stating that he or she will sell a certain thing to the other contracting party on request under agreed conditions. This right cannot be transferred and expires upon death or dissolution of the other contracting party. It has effects against third persons if it is entered in the land register.[240]

87. The basic right of the owner is to demand from the possessor of the thing to return the thing (Lat. *rei vindicatio,* Sl. *reivindikacijska tožba, lastninska tožba*).[241] In this claim, the owner must specify the thing and prove that he or she is the owner and that the defendant is the possessor of this thing.[242] If the latter possesses the thing on the grounds of a valid legal title – for example, a lease – the burden of proof regarding the existence of such title lies on him or her. The action for return of the thing is not subject to the statute of limitations.[243] The owner can also demand the cessation of disturbance of his or her exercise of ownership by third persons (Lat. *actio negatoria*, Sl. *negatorna tožba*).[244] The Supreme Court drew attention to the fact that it is sometimes difficult to determine whether *rei vindicatio* or *actio negatoria* should be filed, especially in the case of disturbance of the exercise of ownership on a part of an immovable.[245]

88. There is only one form of ownership, even though the constitutional provision on the right to 'private' property could suggest that different forms of ownership exist in Slovenian law. This provision is, namely, the expression of the legal situation in times of writing of the Constitution when social property as a distinct form of property still existed. The contents (the entitlements of the holder) of the right to ownership are not conditioned by the owner, but by the nature of the asset.[246]

---

238. See, e.g., Decision of the High Court in Koper, No. CDn 150/2014 of 29 May 2014.
239. The registration does not, however, expand the effects of the prohibition to the subsequent owners. Courts will delete such entry on their own motion when the right of ownership is being registered in favour of a new owner. See Decision of the High Court in Koper, No. CDn 150/2014 of 29 May 2014, and Art. 47/4 of LRA.
240. For the right of repurchase, see, e.g., Decision of the High Court in Celje, No. Cp 318/2014 of 4 Sep. 2014. For details on the prohibition to alienate and encumber and on the right of repurchase, see Vrenčur in *CPL with Commentary 2004*, 223–237. For the restrictions of disposal in immovables, see Vrenčur, *Omejitev razpolaganja po volji lastnika na področju nepremičnin* [Restriction of Disposal at the Will of the Owner Regarding Immovables], in Pravna Praksa, No. 26/2003, pp. 5 ff.
241. Article 92 of CPL.
242. Article 92/2 of CPL. See, e.g., Judgment of the High Court in Ljubljana, No. II Cp 2341/2015 of 18 Nov. 2015.
243. Article 92/3 of CPL.
244. Article 99 of CPL.
245. The courts should thus regard the goal of these actions (they are both intended to protect the ownership) and the goal of the owner (the question whether the owner will attain his or her goal with the action he or she filed): Judgment No. II Ips 93/2013 of 3 Apr. 2014.
246. Juhart in *Property Law*, 53.

89. According to Article 13 of the CPL, the provisions of this act on acquisition, transfer, protection, and expiration of ownership rights apply *mutatis mutandis* to the creation and transfer of other property rights.

V. Concept of Possession

90. Since the BPLRA, the Slovenian law has opted for the *objective conception* of possession (Sl. *posest*), according to which the sole actual control over a thing suffices and the intention to own the thing (*animus domini*) is no longer required.[247] The subjective element is, however, still important regarding the distinction between the proprietary and non-proprietary possession. Possession is thus an actual control over a thing,[248] in contrast to the right, which is a legal control over a thing.[249] As explained later, one must nevertheless be cautious regarding this definition because it is not absolute: the so-called detentor also exercises actual control over a thing, but is not a possessor, whereas the indirect possessor does not have this control but still has possession. It is possible to demand judicial protection against disturbance of the exercise of an easement,[250] but not in the case of the so-called negative easements, as e.g., the easement of sight or of light – under the case law, there is namely no actual control over such elements.[251]

91. Possession can be exercised by more than one person, either by them possessing the thing together or by each of them exclusively possessing a specific part of the thing (*joint possession*, Sl. *skupna posest*).[252]

92. Especially in movables, possession is an important sign of the ownership of the thing.[253] The possession is also important in the acquiring of property rights, for the acquisitive prescription, for the acquiring of fruits, etc.

93. Article 24 of the CPL distinguishes between *direct* and *indirect possession*. Direct possession is a direct, actual control over a thing,[254] whereas indirect possession is a possession held by a person who exercises actual control over a thing through another person who has direct possession based on any form of legal

247. Vrenčur in *CPL with Commentary 2004*, 143–145.
248. According to the objective concept of possession, possession of a right is not possible. Vrenčur in *CPL with Commentary 2004*, 149.
249. Vrenčur in *CPL with Commentary 2004*, 144.
250. See, e.g., Decision of the High Court in Ljubljana, No. II Cp 3197/2008 of 17 Sep. 2008.
251. Decisions of the High Court in Ljubljana, Nos II Cp 3197/2008 of 17 Sep. 2008, I Cp 2214/2013 of 29 Jan. 2014, and I Cp 642/2015 of 13 May 2015.
252. Article 25 of CPL. An example of joint possession is the possession of a road by the owner of the land and the holder of the easement in rem consisting of the use of such road: Decision of the Supreme Court RS, No. II Ips 669/2007 of 1 Oct. 2009.
253. See, for example, the presumption of ownership in Art. 11/2 of CPL.
254. The actual control over the thing need nevertheless not be exercised incessantly; the possession is not lost because of the lack of its exercise. Vrenčur in *CPL with Commentary 2004*, 148.

title.[255] The indirect possessor does not have actual control over the thing – his or her statute of indirect possessor is based on a legal relationship between him or her and the direct possessor.[256] Before the CPL, the BPLRA enumerated several examples of such legal relationship: a usufruct, a lease, or a deposit.[257] If the direct possessor loses his or her possession, also the indirect possessor loses his or her possession, with the exception of the previous direct possessor becoming the indirect possessor.[258] More than one indirect possessor can exist if the direct possessor transfers the possession further to another person who thereby becomes the (new) direct possessor.[259]

94. The CPL further distinguishes between *proprietary* and *non-proprietary possession*. According to Article 27, the proprietary possessor is an individual who has a thing in his or her possession as his or her own, whereas the non-proprietary possessor has it in possession without wishing to have it as his or her own and who recognizes the higher legal control of the indirect possessor. The element of distinction is, thus, the will of the possessor.[260] This distinction can be important for the acquisition of ownership – for example, by prescription.[261]

95. The most important right of a possessor is the *right to 'self-help'*, which is, however, subject to strict conditions. According to Article 31 of the CPL, the possessor has the right to self-help against a person who, without justification, disturbs his or her possession or deprives him or her of it, under the condition that the danger is direct, that the self-help is immediate and urgent, and that the method of self-help is appropriate to the circumstances in which the danger exists.[262]

96. The possessor can also claim *judicial protection* in case of disturbance or deprivation of possession (a 'possessory dispute' or the 'dispute over disturbance of possession', Sl. *spor o motenju posesti*).[263] The Supreme Court defined disturbance as:

---

255. This control must, however, not necessarily be physical: the person holding the key to a building thus exercises actual control of the building and the transfer of direct possession can also be operated with the delivery of the key: Judgment of the High Court in Ljubljana, No. II Cp 1902/2012 of 12 Dec. 2012.
256. Vrenčur, *Posest: Posredna in neposredna posest stvari* [Possession: Indirect and Direct Possession of a Thing], in Podjetje in delo, No. 6/1999, pp. 1040 ff.
257. Article 70/2 of BPLRA.
258. Article 30/2 of CPL.
259. Vrenčur in *CPL with Commentary 2004*, 150.
260. Vrenčur, *Reforma stvarnega prava: Lastniška posest* [Reform of the Property Law: Proprietary Possession], in Podjetje in delo, No. 6/2000, pp. 1454 ff. The author cites the example of a leaseholder who has non-proprietary possession of an asset on the basis of the contract of lease, but becomes a proprietary possessor if he or she refuses to return the asset and keeps it as his or her own.
261. Vrenčur, *Reforma stvarnega prava: Lastniška posest* [Reform of the Property Law: Proprietary Possession], in Podjetje in delo, No. 6/2000, pp. 1454 ff.
262. In the case where the possessor changed the locks approximately one month after finding out about the disturbance, self-help is not immediate and thus not permitted: Decision of the High Court in Ljubljana, No. II Cp 332/2015 of 18 Mar. 2015.
263. The possessory dispute is regulated among the so-called special proceedings in the CPA (Arts 424–430).

> an action regarding a thing possessed by another person, by which a new, different state of possession is established; the disturbance has two complementary effects regarding the possessed thing: the actual possession of the previous possessor ceases or becomes limited, whereas, on the other hand, new actual control of the thing by the disturber is established or his or her previous actual control of the thing is expanded or liberated from previous restrictions.[264]

The disturbance must reach a certain threshold of severity in order to be judicially protected.[265] The case law emphasizes that judicial protection against disturbance is justified if the disturbance is continuous or it is probable that the disturbing actions will be repeated; a one-time disturbance does not suffice.[266] The protection against the disturbance of possession can be requested against the person who directly commits the disturbing action, against the person who ordered such action, as well as the person who later approves such action which was committed to his or her benefit.[267] A disturbance can also occur between two or more possessors of the same thing.[268] Provisional measures in proceedings in disputes for disturbance of possession are also available.[269]

97. Because the possession is not a right but an actual situation, and concerning the legal basis for the decision of the court, this judicial protection is limited. First, it can be claimed only within thirty days of the day on which the possessor learned of the disturbance and of the perpetrator and no later than one year after the disturbance occurred. Second, 'the court shall give judicial protection with respect to the last state of the possession and any disturbance that has occurred; in this regard the right to possession and the good faith of the possessor are not taken into account'.[270] Nevertheless, the possessor shall not have legal protection if the disturbance or dispossession was based on a legal provision.[271] A possessor who obtained possession by force, secretly, or by abuse of trust also has the right to protection, except against the person from whom he or she gained possession in this manner, if that person exercised permitted self-help.[272] The procedure regarding a

---

264. Decision No. II Ips 568/2008 of 27 Jan. 2011.
265. See, e.g., Decision of the High Court in Ljubljana, No. II Cp 2479/2015 of 28 Oct. 2015, where the defendant objected that such threshold was not reached, but the court disagreed.
266. See, e.g., Supreme Court RS, Judgment No. II Ips 343/2010 of 9 Jun. 2011, and Decision of the High Court in Maribor, No. I Cp 548/2015 of 22 Sep. 2015.
267. Decision of the High Court in Ljubljana, No. I Cp 2482/2015 of 23 Sep. 2015.
268. See, e.g., Decision of the High Court in Ljubljana, No. I Cp 2170/2015 of 5 Aug. 2015.
269. For further details, see Pogorelčnik Vogrinc, *Začasne odredbe v postopkih v pravdah zaradi motenja posesti* [Provisional Measures in Proceedings in Disputes for Disturbance of Possession]. In Pravnik, No. 5–6, pp. 303 ff.
270. Article 33/1 of CPL. See, e.g., Decisions of the High Court in Ljubljana, Nos Cp 2291/2015 of 21 Oct. 2015 (regarding the right of possession) and II Cp 332/2015 of 18 Mar. 2015 (regarding the bad faith of the possessor).
271. Article 33/3 of CPL. See, e.g., Decision of the High Court in Celje, No. Cp 181/2015 of 9 Apr. 2015.
272. Article 33/2 of CPL.

possessory dispute can be led at the same time and without prejudice to the 'petitory dispute' – that is, the dispute over the right to possession (most often the ownership). The issue of the possessory dispute does not become final (*res iudicata* effect) regarding the determination of the right to possession. The procedure regarding a possessory dispute is led according to the special provisions of the CPA, whereas the procedure regarding a petitory dispute is led as a normal civil contentious procedure, according to the generally applicable procedural provisions.

98. Another situation of an actual control over a thing – the *detention* (holding) (Sl. *imetništvo*) – must be distinguished from the (direct) possession. Article 26 of the CPL defines the concept of detention as the exercise of actual control over a thing for another person under obligation to act in accordance with that person's instructions (typically as the possessor's employee). This lack of independence in exercising the control over the thing is the element that distinguishes detention from direct possession.[273] The holder does thus not have possession, but has some of the rights the possessor has in relation to third persons. For example, the holder can exercise self-help (for the possessor) but cannot institute a possessory dispute. It is not possible to acquire ownership from a detentor on the basis of Article 64 of the CPL.[274]

99. According to Slovenian case law, the detentor can exercise actual control on the basis of a legal transaction, but such relationship is characterized by submission and superiority, i.e., social dependence.[275] A typical detentor is, e.g., a sales person in the supermarket concerning the things that are being sold in such supermarket, or a policeman concerning his uniform.[276] Also, according to case law, detentor is a person who holds the thing for the purpose of repairing it on the basis of a guarantee,[277] as well as the representative of a legal entity which possesses the premises.[278] However, a person who rents a thing is a (direct non-proprietary) possessor, because such person is considered to be autonomous in their use of the thing.[279]

100. The High Court in Koper defined the differences between a direct possessor, an indirect possessor, and a detentor as follows:

> The difference between a non-proprietary direct possessor and the detentor is that the detentor exercises actual control over the thing for another person and

---

273. Vrenčur, *Posest: Posredna in neposredna posest stvari* [Possession: Indirect and Direct Possession of a Thing], in Podjetje in delo, No. 6/1999, pp. 1040 ff. In a case where the defendant used the premises of another person for occasionally training the horses of that other person, such defendant is not a possessor; his position is comparable of that of a detentor: Judgment of the Supreme Court RS, No. II Ips 100/2013 of 24 Apr. 2014.
274. Vrenčur in *CPL with Commentary 2004*, 170.
275. Judgment of the High Court in Koper, No. Cp 999/2007 of 23 Oct. 2007.
276. Vrenčur in *Property Law*, 117, 118.
277. Judgment of the High Court in Ljubljana, No. I Cp 3574/2009 of 16 Dec. 2009.
278. Decision of the High Court in Ljubljana, No. I Cp 2799/2014 of 29 Oct. 2014.
279. Vrenčur in *CPL with Commentary 2004*, 168.

under their orders, whereas the non-proprietary direct possessor exercises actual control over the thing for himself, but recognizes a higher form of possession to the indirect possessor. A legal relationship must exist between the indirect and the direct possessor, for example a lease, a deposit, a contract of work, a mandate, a commission agency, or a similar contract. A detentor, too, can exercise actual control over the thing on the basis of a legal relationship, but such relationship is characterized by submission and superiority, i.e., a social dependence.[280]

VI. Concept of Patrimony

101. The English word 'patrimony' is usually defined as either the inherited property (inheritance, Sl. *dediščina*) or the sum of all personal and real entitlements, including movable and immovable property, belonging to a person (assets, property, Sl. *premoženje*).

102. The notion of patrimony in the sense of assets or property is not expressly defined in Slovenian law, but it is used relatively often in acts and statutes, as well as in legal writing. It is generally defined as the sum of all the property rights belonging to a certain person,[281] although in specific legal fields – for example, the law of inheritance and the company law, the term 'patrimony' comprises not only the rights, but also the obligations (the debts).

103. In principle, *one person can only have one patrimony*. An exception to this rule is the whole of the *company law*,[282] where physical or legal persons create other legal persons and transfer a part of their patrimony to them. The most evident example of such division of patrimony is the formation of a limited liability company by only one person, which results in dividing the patrimony of this person into his or her personal patrimony and the company's patrimony.

104. The notion of patrimony is also important in *insolvency* law, where the whole patrimony of a legal person forms 'the bankrupt's estate' (the estate from which the debts will be (partly) repaid).[283]

---

280. Judgment No. Cp 999/2007 of 23 Oct. 2007, see also Decision of the High Court of Ljubljana, No. I Cpg 146/2011 of 12 Apr. 2011.
281. Klarič & Vedriš, *Građansko pravo*, 95 (Narodne Novine 2009). Some also opt for the general definition based on the Roman law according to which the patrimony is composed of rights and obligations of an individual: *Pravni leksikon* [Legal Glossary], cited by Skubic, *Premoženje* [Patrimony], in Pravna Praksa, 12/2007, p. 34.
282. Company law is regulated in Zakon o gospodarskih družbah (ZGD-1) [Companies Act], Official Gazette RS, No. 42/06, with further amendments.
283. The insolvency law is regulated in the FOIPCDA of 2007. FOIPCDA regulates insolvency proceedings concerning legal persons, individuals, and inheritance. The insolvency of individuals and inheritance represented, at the time of the adoption of the act, a novelty in Slovenian law. For further details, see Part III, Ch. 11.

105. Another exception from the rule of one sole patrimony per person occurs in legal relations between *spouses*. The Slovenian law speaks of joint patrimony or joint ownership or undivided ownership (Sl. *skupno premoženje*) of the spouses.[284] Family law[285] provides that the patrimony of each spouse is divided into special and joint patrimony. Special patrimony is composed of the assets the spouse had owned before entering the marriage, as well as the assets he or she obtains during the marriage but not on behalf of his or her work (e.g., heritage, prizes, gifts, pecuniary damages for injury, etc.). Joint patrimony is composed of the assets both spouses obtained during the marriage on behalf of their work, typically all the salaries they have earned. The acquisition of a non-defined part of the joint patrimony is of a non-derivative nature and does not depend on the registration in the land register.[286] The joint patrimony is divided after the death of one spouse, after divorce, or after the annulment of marriage. During the marriage, joint patrimony can be divided at the joint request of the spouses, at the request of one spouse or on the request of a spouse's creditor.[287] Such division is decided upon in the non-contentious procedure.[288] Since the entry into force of the Family Code in 2019, (future) spouses can depart from the property regime described above by a contract on the regulation of patrimonial relations (Sl. *pogodba o ureditvi premoženjskopravnih razmerij*).[289] Before that time, future spouses could conclude a prenuptial contract regarding the status of their patrimony, but it could not contradict the legal regime,[290] which means that the future spouses had very little room for manoeuvre. They could not, e.g., decide that the patrimony acquired on behalf of their work during the marriage would not become joint property; they could, however, decide that their special property would become joint property.[291]

106. The two meanings of the English word 'patrimony' come together in case of its transfer. The entire patrimony can be transferred by universal succession. In the case of an individual (natural person), this means by *inheritance* (*mortis causa*).[292] The patrimony (including the debts) of a person passes into the joint patrimony of the heirs at the moment of the predecessor's (testator's) death,[293] even if the heirs are not yet known nominally. This kind of patrimony is normally of temporary nature: upon request of one of the heirs, it will be divided among them according to the law or the last will and will cease to exist.[294] The heirs are liable for the debts of the *de cujus* up to the amount of their inherited share.[295] The only way of avoiding the liability for such debts is to disclaim the inheritance (and thus

284. Also: common property or community property. For further details, see Part I, Ch. 5, §3.
285. Article 67 of FC.
286. See, e.g., Judgment of the Supreme Court RS, No. II Ips 428/2011 of 20 Feb. 2014.
287. Article 71 of FC.
288. Articles 162–164 of the new NCCPA.
289. Articles 85 ff. of FC.
290. Zupančič, *Družinsko pravo* [Family Law], 77 (ČZ Uradni list RS 1999).
291. Novak, *Družinsko pravo* [Family Law], 96, 97 (Uradni list 2014).
292. The contracts of inheritance – that is, the contracts by which one party is entitled to get the entire patrimony of another upon the latter's death – are prohibited and null in Slovenian law.
293. Article 132 of IA.
294. For further details on acquisition of ownership in case of death, see Part III.
295. Article 142/1 of IA.

also the benefits therefrom).[296] In case of a patrimony of a legal entity, the universal successor can be another entity that overtakes the patrimony of a liquidated company or the (former) partners.[297]

VII. Trust and Fiduciary Mechanisms

107. Slovenian law does not provide for the institution of trust as it exists in Anglo-Saxon legal systems.[298] The transfer of property to another person in view of this person's managing the property for a third person is, in principle, possible on a contractual basis, but it will be regarded as a normal transfer of property, and in case of breach of contract by the other party, the only possibility will be the claim for damages. Slovenia has not ratified The Hague Convention of 1 July 1985 on the Law Applicable to Trusts and on Their Recognition.[299]

108. The fiduciary mechanisms of the Roman law have partly evolved into new forms of contracts, where similar effect is obtained without a transfer of property. Thus, *fiducia cum amico contracta* has evolved into, on the one hand, the loan for use contract (*commodatum*) regulated in Articles 579 ff. of the CO, and, on the other hand, into the contract of deposit (*depositum*) regulated in Articles 729 ff. of the CO.[300] *Fiducia cum creditore contracta* has generally developed into the lien regulated in Part VI of the CPL.[301] Nevertheless, there still exist situations where transfer of property best serves the intention of the parties. The Slovenian law regulates the fiduciary transfer of title and the fiduciary transfer of claims (fiduciary assignment), both based on the Roman *fiducia cum creditore*.[302] Before the entry into force of the CPL, the *fiduciary transfer of title* was not legally regulated. On grounds of the possibility of *fiduciary assignment* regulated in the CO,[303] the legal theory nevertheless concluded that the fiduciary transfer of title should also be allowed.[304] The legislature decided to include this institution into the new CPL.[305] Articles 201–206 of the CPL now regulate the fiduciary transfer of ownership on movables, and Articles 207–209 the fiduciary assignment. The characteristics of the *fiducia cum*

296. Article 142/2 of IA.
297. For more on the universal succession in legal entities see Žgavec, *Univerzalno pravno nasledstvo pri statusnih preoblikovanjih gospodarskih družb* [Universal Legal Succession in the Change of Status of Commercial Companies], in Pravna praksa, Nos 24–25/2010, pp. 8 ff.
298. See also Part IV and Part V.
299. https://www.hcch.net/en/instruments/conventions/full-text/?cid=59, accessed on 31 Jul. 2019.
300. Kranjc, *Rimsko pravo* [Roman Law], 385 (GV Založba 2010).
301. *Ibid.*
302. Cf. *Ibid.*
303. Article 426 of CO.
304. Vrenčur in *Property Law*, 525–526. Juhart, *Prenos lastninske pravice v zavarovanje* [Fiduciary Transfer of Property], in Pravnik, Nos 1–3/1995, p. 55. Tratnik in Tratnik et al., *Stvarnopravna zavarovanja* [Securities under Property Law], 149 (IARS 2001).
305. For details, see Tratnik in *CPL with Commentary 2004*, 833–870; Vrenčur, *Ureditev fiduciarnega prenosa lastninske pravice v zavarovanje v novem slovenskem pravu* [Regulation of the Fiduciary Transfer of Ownership in the New Slovenian Law], in Pravna Praksa, No. 42/2003, pp. 37 ff.

amico can also be found in several mechanisms of today's law.[306] For more on fiduciary mechanisms in Slovenian law, see Part IV.

306. Žnidaršič Skubic cites the following examples: the commission agency contract (Sl. *komisijska pogodba*), the notary's fiduciary account (Sl. *skrbniški račun notarja*), the fiduciary account of the brokerage company (Sl. *fiduciarni račun pri borznoposredniški družbi*) and the fiduciary money account of the insolvency administrator (Sl. *fiduciarni denarni račun stečajnega upravitelja*). Žnidaršič Skubic, *Zasebna ustanova,* trust, *fiduciarni pravni posli in njihov vpliv na dedovanje* [Private Foundation, Trust, Fiduciary Transactions and their Impact on Inheritance], 81, 82 (Uradni list 2015).

Part I. Immovable Property

Chapter 1. General Classification

109. Immovable property is *defined* in Article 18/1 of the CPL as 'spatially measured parts of the earth's surface together with all their components'. According to Article 18/2 of the CPL, all other things are considered to be movables. By analogy to one of the non-legislative definitions of movables, an immovable can also be defined as a thing that cannot be moved from one place to another without harming its substance.[307] The definition of immovable as set out in Article 18/1 of the CPL corresponds to Article 8 of the CPL, which enacts the principle of *superficies solo cedit*, i.e., the principle of connection between land and building stating that, except where the law provides otherwise, everything which by intention is permanently affixed to or is permanently on an immovable, above it or below it, is an element of the immovable.[308] The building or other thing integrated in the plot of land is thus considered to be an element of the land without regard to the respective value of the component in comparison to the land or to any other criteria.[309] The basic form of an immovable is thus a piece of land, which is (as a rule) registered in the cadastre and in the land register.[310] In deviation from this definition, the immovable property regime applies also to the parts of buildings in case of the establishment of the divided co-ownership,[311] and to the buildings built on the basis of the right of superficies,[312] for the time period of this right.[313]

110. The CPL amendments of 2020 inserted into the CPL a novel concept of 'connected immovables' (Sl. *povezane nepremičnine*) consisted of a 'main immovable' (Sl. *glavna nepremičnina*) and an 'auxiliary immovable' (Sl. *pomožna napremičnina*). If the use of the auxiliary immovable is permanently required for

307. Gavella in Gavella et al., *Stvarno pravo* [Property Law], 79 (Narodne Novine 2007).
308. For further details as to the *superficies solo cedit* principle, see General Introduction, §3, III, C.
309. Juhart in *Property Law*, 64–65.
310. *Ibid.*, 67. Some immovables are still not registered and represent an obstacle to legal certainty in legal transactions with such immovable. Application of specific provisions, such as those of the otherwise invalidated chapter of CESA on contractual lien, is required. See Tratnik in *Property Law*, 455.
311. For further details, see Part I, Ch. 5, §3.
312. For further details, see Part I, Ch. 4, §4.
313. This wider definition originates in the law of the land register, see Art. 11/2/2 of LRA. Tratnik in *CPL with Commentary 2004*, 124–125; Juhart in *Property Law*, 68; Tratnik & Vrenčur, *Omejitve lastninske pravice in posebni pravni režimi na nepremičninah* [Limitations of Ownership and Special Legal Regimes on the Immovables], 29 (GV Založba 2009).

the use of one or more other immovables and/or apartments, the owner of the auxiliary immovable may connect his or her ownership on such immovable with his or her ownership of the main immovable so that the connected immovables may be disposed of as a whole.[314]

111. The regulation of property rights on immovable property shows several *particularities in comparison to the regulation of the movables*. The first is the publicity of the ownership. According to Article 11 of the CPL, the person registered as owner in the land register is deemed to be the owner of the immovable, while the proprietary possessor of a movable is deemed to be an owner of the movable. As a consequence of the discontinuity of the property rights on immovables after the Second World War (e.g., some denationalization procedures are still not concluded), as well as due to the fact that the land register had for a long time in fact not played an important role in the process of acquiring immovables, there is, unfortunately, a discrepancy in the actual state of the immovables and their corresponding status in the land register. This represents a great anomaly in the property law system of Slovenia.

112. The second difference in the regulation of immovables to that of movables is the transfer of ownership. In cases of contractual acquisition, the ownership on the immovable property is *acquired* only upon its entry in the land register (and not by the sole conclusion of the contract of sale, or by delivery as in case of movables).[315] In cases of acquisitive prescription of immovables, the ownership is acquired at the moment of the expiry of the ten-years period of continuous possession of an immovable in good faith (three years in case of movables),[316] while registration of such acquisition in the land register is of pure declarative nature, whereby the effects of the principle of trust in the land register are of great importance for such acquirer.[317] According to the principle of trust in the land register, nobody (at least if acquiring the immovable on the basis of a legal transaction and – according to the case law of the Supreme Court of RS – under the proviso that the immovable in question does not have the status of a 'plot belonging to a building', as such immovables cannot be validly transferred as individual immovables regardless of the fact that they have their own parcel numbers and regardless of any good faith of their acquirer[318])[319] can suffer negative consequences if he or she relied in good faith upon information in the land register that was later found out to be erroneous. The person who acquired ownership on an immovable via the rules on acquisitive prescription, may end up losing his or her non-registered ownership if a

314. See Arts 127.a–127.č of the CPL.
315. For further details on contractual acquisition of ownership, see Part III, Ch. 1.
316. For further details on acquisitive prescription, see Part III, Ch. 3.
317. For further details on the principle of trust in the land register, see Part III, Ch. 1, §7.
318. See the following Decisions taken by the Supreme Court of RS: Nos II Ips 420/2011 of 19 Sep. 2013 and II Ips 369/29 of 27 May 2013. For further details on the concept of »plot belonging to a building«, see also paras. 65, 115, 142, 423 of this monograph.
319. For further details on how principle of trust in the land register has been loosened by the courts, see General Introduction, §3, II, A and General Introduction, §3, III, E.

third person relied in good faith on the data of the land register and was consequently registered as owner – in that case, non-registered ownership acquired on the basis of acquisitive prescription ceases to exist. In cases of acquisition on the basis of a decision issued by a public authority (courts or administrative authorities), ownership on immovable is acquired the moment such decision becomes final (the same system applies to movable property).[320] In inheritance cases, ownership on the decedent's immovable (as well as movables) is acquired at the moment of the decedent's death.[321]

113. In contrast to movables on which only pledge and personal easements may be established, all *limited property rights* can be established on the immovable property. Namely, only immovables can be the object of the easements in rem, the encumbrance, the right of superficies (also of the land debt if the land debt was established between 1 January 2003 and 5 November 2013). Limited property rights on the immovables are registered in the land register.

114. Further, because of the limited number of immovables, *public interest* in their use is much more intense than in movables. Therefore, the right of ownership on the immovables is more often the subject of limitations pursuing the economical, ecological, and social functions of the property, as determined in the Constitution.[322] According to Article 69 of the Constitution, expropriation is possible, under strict conditions, only in relation to immovable property.[323] In addition, some restraints exist as to acquisition of ownership on immovables by foreigners, i.e., by persons lacking Slovenian citizenship and undertakings not having their seat in Slovenia, while acquisition of ownership on movables is in general not restricted to foreigners.[324]

115. Immovables in particular may be determined as *property in public domain* (Sl. *javno dobro*) being of special public interest and accessible to everyone. According to Article 19 of the CPL, property in public domain is a thing that, in accordance with its purpose, can be used under equal conditions by everyone (so-called general use, Sl. *splošna raba*). Such property cannot be used in a way to exclude or make difficult its use by other persons. The scope of property in public domain and the conditions for their general use are determined by law. It is, however, to be emphasized that regulation of public domain in Slovenia is dispersed in various legal acts and is extremely unclear. It is, for example, not clear whether public domain may exist on private land, whether in such cases citizens are to be paid damages (as in cases of expropriation and easements in the public interest), etc. It must also be stressed that recently, Slovenian municipalities have started proclaiming hundreds or better say thousands of plots in Slovenia still registered in the land register as social property or as general people's property (and have not yet been

320. For further details on acquisition, see introduction to Part III, and Part III, Chs 10 and 11.
321. For further details on transfer of property by death, see Part II, Ch. 2.
322. Juhart in *Property Law*, 67.
323. For more on expropriation, see Part III, Ch. 10.
324. For further details on acquisition of immovables by foreign persons, see Part I, Ch. 3.

registered as private ownership of their real legal owner) as property of the municipality and proclaiming them as property in public domain. Such practice has no valid legal basis and was performed by referring abusively to somewhat ambiguously formulated Article 212 of the Construction Act.[325] Instead of determining first who the real owner is of such immovables, and finally assisting the real owner in registering his or her private ownership in the land register (or at least waiting for the courts to decide on who the rightful owner is[326]), municipalities are now taking advantage of improper, i.e., obsolete registrations claiming that they are the owners of these immovables. Mass nationalization of immovables in private ownership to the detriment of their rightful owners (and then possibly sale of such immovables to third persons (or even to rightful owners themselves) for the benefit of the municipal budgets) started taking place in Slovenia. Slovenian courts have detected this problem and have stressed that such unilateral municipal decisions do not preclude civil courts from determining the legal status of immovables, and that no prior annulment of such decisions is required before civil courts are allowed to assess the ownership status of the immovables.[327] In order to prevent abusive and illegal practices of the municipalities, a rule enabling the annulment of such municipal decisions has eventually been clearly set out in the amended AEDC.

---

325. Zakon o graditvi objektov (ZGO-1) [Construction Act], Official Gazette RS, No. 110/02, with further amendments, replaced in 2017 by the new Building Act (Sl. *Gradbeni zakon (GZ)*), Official Gazette RS, No. 61/17. See the following Judgments of the High Court in Ljubljana: Nos I Cp 3289/2014 of 5 May 2015, II Cp 2676/2009 of 11 Nov. 2009.
326. Private parties will be claiming that they had become owners of such immovables *ex lege* when the legislation transposing their 'right to use land in social ownership' into private ownership of the land entered into force in 1997. Acquisition of ownership by prescription could be their alternative claim. As of 2008, most of such cases are assessed in non-contentious proceedings according to the rules set out in the AEDC. This act enables the courts to assess if and to what extent a certain plot of land (Sl. *funkcionalno zemljišče*, now called *pripadajoče zemljišče*) 'belongs' to a certain building to which it serves (i.e., it is necessary for its regular use), i.e., if and to what extent it is in ownership of the owner of the plot with the building. For further details on this procedure, see Fajs, *ZVEtL in ovire za njegovo izvajanje v praksi* [ZVEtL and the Obstacles for its Application in Practice], in Pravna praksa, Y. 30, No.28/29, pp. 9–11; Vlahek, *Problematika skupnih površin in skupnosti lastnikov v vzorčnih soseskah* [Problems of Common Immovables and the Community of Owners in Sample Housing Estates], in Zbornik, 14–15 (GV Založba 2016) ; Damjan, Ude, Vlahek, *Strokovno mnenje o predlogu Zakona o vzpostavitvi etažne lastnine na določenih stavbah in o ugotavljanju pripadajočega zemljišča* [Professional Opinion on the draft ZVEtL], Inštitut za primerjalno pravo pri Pravni fakulteti v Ljubljani, 2016.
327. See the following Decisions of the High Court in Ljubljana: Nos VSL I Cp 3289/2014 of 5 May 2015 and VSL I Cp 251/2015 of 5 May 2015.

Chapter 2. Registration of Immovable Property

116. Registration of immovable property in the RS is based on the old Austrian systems of land cadastre and land register, which are based on the system of real estate folios with an individual plot of land as its central element.[328]

117. Different cadastres – for example, land cadastre (Sl. *zemljiški kataster*), building cadastre (Sl. *kataster stavb*), cadastre of public infrastructure facilities (Sl. *kataster gospodarske javne infrastrukture*),[329] the data of which are put together in the register of immovables (Sl. *register nepremičnin*) – reveal the factual status of immovable property. The register and the cadastres are regulated in the Real-Estate Recording Act[330] and maintained by the Surveying and Mapping Authority of the RS (Sl. *Geodetska uprava Republike Slovenije*).[331] The land register (Sl. *zemljiška knjiga*), on the other hand, is a register of legal status on immovable property. The land register data on factual status of an immovable (such as size, use, etc.) is synchronized with that of the relevant cadastre. The following is registered as an 'immovable' in the land register: plot of land; building within the superficies regime; the right of superficies itself; building in divided co-ownership; and individual parts of the building in divided co-ownership.[332] Each immovable has its own 'ID' (Sl. '*ID*') (identification number of each data registered) as well as 'ID sign' (Sl. '*ID znak*') (composed of the number of the cadastral municipality in which the immovable is located, and the parcel number of the immovable as ensues from the cadastre). It can be searched in the electronic land register by both criteria.

118. The land register is currently governed by the LRA of 2003[333] (as amended in 2008, 2009, 2011, 2015, 2017, 2018, and 2019) and several secondary legislations.[334] If the LRA does not provide for an answer on a procedural matter, the NCCPA applies.[335]

---

328. Juhart in *Property Law*, 135, 150–151.
329. All the cadastres and other relevant information on the factual status of immovables are published on the Internet site of The Surveying and Mapping Authority of the RS. It is in Slovene language only, http://e-prostor.gov.si/, accessed on 31 Jul. 2019.
330. Zakon o evidentiranju nepremičnin (ZEN) [Real-Estate Recording Act], Official Gazette RS, No. 47/06, with further amendments.
331. See www.gu.gov.si/en/ and its new website www.gov.si/en/public-authorities/bodies-within -ministries/surveying-and-mapping-authority/, accessed on 31 Jul. 2019.
332. Article 11 of LRA.
333. Zakon o zemljiški knjigi (ZZK-1) [Land Registry Act], Official Gazette RS, No. 58/03, with further amendments.
334. Pravilnik o elektronski izmenjavi podatkov med zemljiško knjigo in katastri [Rules on electronic exchange of data between land register and cadastres], Official Gazette RS, No. 30/11; Pravilnik o zemljiški knjigi [Rules of land register], Official Gazette RS, No. 30/11, with further amendments; Pravilnik o zemljiškem pismu [Rules on land letter], Official Gazette RS, No. 15/03, with further amendments.
335. Article 120/2 of the LRA. For further details on the (previous version of the) NCCPA, see Šinkovec & Tratar, *Zakon o nepravdnem postopku s komentarjem, vzorci in sodno prakso* [Non-Contentious Civil Procedure Act with Commentary, Forms and Case-law] (Primath 2003).

119. Slovenian land registry system is based on the old Austrian land register. Up until the collapse of the Habsburg Monarchy in 1918, the territory of Slovenia formed part of the Austrian Empire and later Austria-Hungary. *Allgemeines Grundbuchsgesetz - AGBG* of 1871 and other relevant legislation applied also to Slovenian territory. In 1930, Land Registry Act (almost entirely a copy of the AGBG of 1871) was enacted in the Kingdom of Yugoslavia.[336] After the Second World War, land registry regulation in Slovenia was for a long time somewhat schizophrenic: old Austrian land registers were used, legal rules of the Land Registry Act enacted in 1930 in the Kingdom of Yugoslavia were applied next to some novel legislation regulating specific land registry issues, such as registration of divided co-ownership, registration of ownership on buildings on land in social property, etc.

120. New land registry legislation of independent Slovenia was first enacted in 1995[337] modernizing the land registry and enabling its computerization. After the new Slovenian Code of Property Law was enacted in 2002 (entering into force on 1 January 2003), the Land Registry Act of 1995 (Sl. *Zakon o zemljiški knjigi – ZZK*) was replaced in 2003 by a new Land Registry Act (Sl. *Zakon o zemljiški knjigi – ZZK-1*) in order to correspond to the novelties enforced by the new property law regime. In 2004, the electronic land register was established, and the judiciary was working on the modernization and easier accessibility of this register via the Internet, the accessibility of the land register being of crucial importance for anyone wishing to acquire property rights on immovables. Both the LRA of 1995 and the LRA of 2003 are, however, still predominantly based on the same principles as ensuing from the older land registry regulation.[338]

121. The LRA of 2003 was amended twice in 2008 and once in 2009,2011, 2015, 2017, 2018, and 2019. In 2008, the new Court Fees Act[339] first deleted the provision of the LRA requesting the court to check in its preliminary assessment of the party's land registry application whether proof of payment of a court fee is attached to the application. The second amendment of the LRA in 2008 which entered into force in May 2008, was important for mainly three reasons: first, it enabled that as of 1 May 2011, land registry applications are submitted with any of the local courts in Slovenia regardless of where the respective immovable is located (whereas before, the application had to be submitted with the court in whose territory the respective immovable was located); second, it enabled electronic submission of applications via the notaries while all other applications (i.e., those not filed by the notaries) still had to be filed in writing (such new regime was to be applied as of 1 May 2011); and third, if the parties visit a notary for the purposes of concluding an agreement in the form of a notarial deed or for the purposes of attesting a signature on the land registry permission, the notary is (as of 1 May 2009) to file

336. Juhart in *Property Law*, 150.
337. Official Gazette RS, No. 33/95, with further amendments.
338. Juhart in *Property Law*, 150.
339. Zakon o sodnih taksah (ZST-1) [Court Fees Act], Official Gazette RS, No. 37/08, with further amendments.

their application with the court unless directed otherwise by the parties.[340] The 2009 amendment merely abolished some of the inconsistencies of the second 2008 amendment regarding the provisions setting out when the novelties of the 2008 amendment start applying.[341]

122. In 2011, the LRA was amended extensively.[342] A new information system of electronic land register and a new portal of electronic land register were launched with the Information Centre of the Supreme Court of RS. One of the main features of the amendment was the abolishment of the land registry sheets in which under certain circumstances more than one immovable could be registered (i.e., if all immovable were located in the same cadastral municipality, and if the ownership status was the same on these immovables). In the new regime, each immovable is registered separately in an electronic document titled 'land registry statement' (Sl. *izpisek iz zemljiške knjige*). Division of the sheets into parts A, B, and C that enabled an immediate and clear identification of an immovable's status, were unfortunately also abolished. New terminology, such as 'basic legal status of an immovable', 'ID sign', 'source of ID sign', 'ID', 'ID of the basic legal status of an immovable', etc., was introduced causing quite some dissatisfaction with the new regime with the users. Further, registration of immovables in divided co-ownership was altered, new types of notations were introduced. One of the most important amendments concerned the rules on filing land registry applications: in principle, the application (as well as all documents) has to be filed electronically by a notary, attorney, real estate agent, state or municipal attorney, or by the party him- or herself using a safe electronic signature, while applications in writing may no longer be filed by the parties themselves. They may, however, exceptionally file an application by going to one of the local courts' land registry divisions and requesting the official person of the court to file an electronic application on the basis of their oral request. All decisions and other documents issued by the court are also issued in an electronic form and are forwarded to the notaries, attorneys, and other persons who have filed applications via their secure electronic inbox. Decisions are only exceptionally issued and sent in writing. All contracts and other documents, which were the basis for registration, are kept in an electronic form. Land registry cases are disseminated electronically to judicial assistants of the land registry divisions of local courts in Slovenia, taking account of their availability according to the data on the amount of their (un)solved cases. The High Court in Koper was *a novo* vested with exclusive jurisdiction in second instance land registry cases. Access to the land register is free of charge and publicly available on the Internet.

123. Further amendments of the LRA that took place in 2015, 2017, 2018, and 2019, were minor amendments of specific LRA provisions corresponding mostly to the novelties introduced by other legislation, such as the Act Regulating Measures

---

340. Zakon o spremembah in dopolnitvah Zakona o zemljiški knjigi (ZZK-1A) [Act Amending the Land Register Act], Official Gazette RS, No. 45/08.
341. Zakon o spremembah in dopolnitvah Zakona o zemljiški knjigi (ZZK-1B) [Act Amending the Land Register Act], Official Gazette RS, No. 28/09.
342. Zakon o spremembah in dopolnitvah Zakona o zemljiški knjigi (ZZK-1C) [Act Amending the Land Register Act], Official Gazette RS, No. 25/11.

Aimed at Fiscal Balance of Municipalities,[343] the SECA, and the NCCPA. The 2017 amendments that were introduced by the Act Amending the Land Registered Act amended the provisions of the LRA of the procedure for registering non-registered immovables (so-called procedure for supplementing the land register (Sl. *postopek dopolnitve zemljiške knjige*)). A new amendment to the LRA is currently being drafted on the basis of the CPL amendments introducing a novel concept of 'connected immovables'.[344]

124. Land registry regulation is based on the following *land registry principles*: principle of publicity of the land register; principle of filing effects; principle of publicity effects of registration; principle of trust in the land register; priority principle; principle of legal ancestor; and principle of constitutive effects of registration. According to the principle of publicity of the land register, all registrations in the land register are publicly available (whereas public access to the collection of documents is conditioned upon showing legitimate interest).[345] The principle of filing effects states that registrations of rights and legal facts into the land register have effects as of the moment the land registry received application for registration, or the document on the basis of which it performed registration ex officio.[346] According to the principle of publicity effects of registration, everyone is deemed knowing of the registrations of rights or legal facts from the day following the day when the land registry registered receipt of land registry application which was eventually approved by the land registry, or from the day following the day when the land registry registered receipt of documents on the basis of which the land registry had to perform an ex officio registration; no one can claim that he or she was not aware of the registrations, while on the other hand, it is deemed that the third person was not aware of such right or legal fact if it is not registered.[347] The principle of trust in the land register[348] states that no one can suffer negative consequences if he or she relied in good faith on the registered information on the legal status of an immovable although such information was erroneous or it did not reveal all relevant information about the current or anticipated legal status of the immovable.[349] The principle of constitutive effects of registration states that, in principle, entries in the land register have constitutive effect, while declaratory effect of entries is an exception (as, for example, in the case of acquisitive prescription of immovables where ownership is acquired at the moment of the expiry of the ten-years period, while registration of such acquisition in the land register is of pure declaratory nature).[350]

343. Zakon o ukrepih za uravnoteženje javnih financ občin (ZUUJFO) [Act Regulating Measures Aimed at Fiscal Balance of Municipalities], Official Gazette RS, No. 14/15.
344. See paras. 35, 110 of this monograph.
345. Article 4 of LRA.
346. Article 5 of LRA.
347. Article 6 of LRA.
348. Article 8 of LRA.
349. For further details, see General Introduction, §3, II, A and General Introduction, §3, III, E. Exceptions to this rule are explained in Part III, Ch. 1, §7 and para. 112 of this monograph.
350. Article 7 of LRA.

The principle of legal ancestor requires that entries are made against the person registered as the holder of the right who is also the person against which the document serving as basis for the entry is oriented, while entries are made in favour of the person in whose favour such document is oriented.[351] The land registry system is governed also by the priority principle which means that as decisive for the order of registration is the exact time when an application is submitted for registration to the land registry – applications must be assessed according to the sequence of their submission, an earlier application thus has to be assessed before the one received afterwards.[352]

125. Specific principles apply also to the land registry proceedings. The principle of expediency of the proceedings requires the land registry to act expedient.[353] The principle of priority of assessment of land registry applications is also one of the principles underpinning land registry proceedings requiring that applications are assessed according to the sequence of their submission. The principle of orality is restricted in land registry proceedings as the first instance land registry cases are (save in exceptional cases) determined without enabling the participants in the proceedings to express their opinion on the filed application or other submitted documents aiming at amending the entries in the land register.[354] The principle of formality of the proceedings requires the land registry to decide on the entries only on the basis of the documents which may be submitted to the land registry in order to succeed with the application, and on the basis of the legal status as ensues from the land register.[355] The principle of party autonomy states that the land registry, as a rule, assess cases only on the basis of applications and is bound by the claim as determined in the application.[356] One of the novel principles of Slovenian land registry proceedings is the principle of obligatory electronic submission of applications and other documents, electronic handling of cases and electronic communication between the land registry and the participants in the proceedings – in exceptional cases, however, written submissions and communication are still required.[357]

126. All property rights on immovables (i.e., ownership, easement, right of superficies, right of encumbrance, mortgage, land debt) are registered in the land register. If an immovable is owned by two or more persons, co-ownership (with the exact shares belonging to each of the co-owners) or joint ownership is registered. If a limited property right is established for a specific time or for a specific time of year, this is also evidenced in the land register.[358] Further, *some of the obligatory rights* – that is, those important for transactions with immovables – are also registered in the land register. According to the CPL and LRA, the following obligatory

351. Article 9 of LRA.
352. Article 10 of LRA.
353. Article 121 of LRA.
354. Article 123 of LRA.
355. Article 124 of LRA.
356. Article 125 of LRA.
357. Articles 125a–125dof LRA.
358. Article 21 of the LRA states that date of expiry of a right must be registered in the land register in all those cases where rights are limited in time.

rights may be registered: rights of tenancy and lease, pre-emption rights based on a legal transaction,[359] repurchase rights, certain types of rights of prohibition of alienating and encumbering the immovable,[360] and special rights of use of property in public domain.

127. Rights (property and obligatory) are registered by the so-called *incorporation* into the land register (Sl. *vknjižba, intabulacija*, Ger. *Einverleibung*).[361] Incorporation of property rights can be of a constitutive or of a declaratory nature. If it is constitutive, property rights are acquired, amended, or abolished by the incorporation of acquisition, amendment, or abolishment of the right, while in cases of declaratory incorporations the rights are acquired, amended, or abolished regardless of the incorporation. The latter may, however, be of significance due to the principle of trust in the land register according to which no one can suffer negative consequences if he or she relied in good faith on the registered information about the legal status of an immovable although such information was erroneous.[362]

128. Further, property rights may be registered conditionally by the so-called *prenotation* or priority notice (Sl. *predznamba*, *prenotacija*, Lat. *prenotatio,* Ger. *Vormerkung*). It is a conditional entry aimed at becoming fully incorporated once the applicant demonstrates that the registration prerequisite that was not met at the time of prenotation is finally met. For example, a buyer can pre-notate his or her ownership on an immovable he or she had bought, but for which he or she has not yet obtained the seller's land registry permission or has obtained the permission which has not yet been properly signed by the seller, i.e., it does not contain the sellers signature attested by a notary (usually due to the fact that the buyer has not yet paid the purchase price); once he or she pays the price and therefore obtains the permission (or files an action against the seller who is unwilling to issue the permission), he or she will be able to justify the prenotation (in a set time limit of one month after the pre-notated right was registered in the land register[363]) and thereby register his or her ownership. Rights obtained by a court decision which has not yet become final may also be pre-notated – once they become final, the prenotation may be justified in a period of two months.[364] The purpose of prenotation is to secure the priority of the entry – if the prenotation is justified in the provided time limit,[365] then it is deemed that the registration of ownership was applied at the time the application for prenotation was filed, and not only at the time it was justified. Hence, all

359. Statutory pre-emption rights are not registered.

360. Only those acquired on the basis of contract of a lifelong maintenance (Arts 557–563 of CO) and those acquired on the basis of a legal transaction between spouses or civil partners, or between parents and children or adopters and adoptees (Art. 38 of CPL).

361. For further details as to incorporation, see Arts 39–47 of the LRA.

362. Article 10 of CPL; Art. 8 of LRA. For further details as to the principle of trust in the land register, see General Introduction, §3, II, A, General Introduction, §3, III, E and Part III, Ch. 1, §7.

363. Interpretation of the time of registration of the pre-notated right varies in practice. Some courts and notaries deem that the one-month period starst running only as of the finality of the registration request, not already upon its filing.

364. Article 53 of the LRA sets out detailed rules on when this period starts to run.

365. One month in cases the pre-notated right is being established on a basis of a legal transaction, and two months in other cases.

other applications filed after the prenotation do not jeopardize the pre-notated right. The same prenotation may generally be filed only once.[366]

129. Some of the legal facts and other circumstances important for the transactions with a particular immovable are registered in the land register by the so-called *notation* (Sl. *zaznamba, adnotacija*, Lat. *adnotatio*, Ger. *Anmerkung*).[367] A few examples include the information that an immovable is a property in public domain, that the immovable has a status of an immovable monument or of protected farm or that it is located on a protected area or is otherwise under a certain public regime, that the owner lacks authority to dispose of his or her immovable, that the owner is insolvent, that an immovable is subject of enforcement or litigation, that *actio hypothecaria* was filed, that an immovable is being expropriated or used without a building permit, that it is under the super mortgage regime, etc. One of the most important notations for the legal transactions in practice is the so-called notation of sequence (Sl. *zaznamba vrstnega reda*) enabling the owner of an immovable to secure a sequence of acquiring ownership or superficies, or of acquiring, transferring, or terminating a mortgage on his or her immovable.[368] Such notation is valid for one year after it was registered in the land register on the basis of a notary's request on behalf of the owner. It typically serves the same purpose as the prenotation, i.e. secures the acquirer his or her order until he or she submits the required documents for finalizing the transaction. On the basis of these, the owner informs his or her tutelary notary that he or she is transferring to the acquirer the right to dispose of the notated sequence by depositing with the notary a statement informing of the transfer. Notation of sequence is more expensive but secures the acquirers' interests for a longer period of time than prenotation.

130. Apart from incorporations, priority notices and notations that are forms of a main entry, two assistant entries – *links* (Sl. *poočitev*) and *seals* (Sl. *plomba*) – serve as registration of further relevant data regarding a particular immovable. Links are intended to synchronize the land register data with that of the cadastres or of the Central population register (e.g., amendment of the immovable's ID sign, amendment of the owner's ID, etc.).[369] Seals are registered in the section titled 'Seals' located at the beginning of the land registry statement right after the section containing the basic identification information on the immovable, and before the section on the basic legal status of the immovable. Seals are of extreme importance for the transactions with immovables. Seals are entries that reveal that certain land registry applications regarding an immovable have been made. At the moment the land registry receives an application, it denotes (seals) it ex officio in the land registry. In case of multiple applications regarding the same immovable, the land registry must solve the applications one after another in accordance with the principle of priority – the application handed in first has priority over the one handed in afterwards,

366. For further details as to prenotation, see Arts 48–62 of the LRA.

367. For further details as to notations, see Arts 63–113 and 245 of the LRA. Some provisions on notations (regarding personal status of the owners as well as the procedure for the division of co-ownership) are laid down also in the NCCPA.

368. See Arts 68–76 of the LRA.

369. For further details as to links, see Arts 114–119 of the LRA.

whereby the receipt of the application by the land registry is decisive for determining priority. If there are no seals registered, it is stated in the 'Seals' section that 'No non-final land registry case is pending with regard to this immovable.'[370]

131. Land register (Sl. *zemljiška knjiga*, Ger. *Grundbuch*) is composed of the so-called *main register* – a ledger (Sl. *glavna knjiga*), and the so-called *collection of documents* (Sl. *zbirka listin*). Both are maintained in an electronic form only, hence e-land register, e-main register, and e-collection of documents.

132. Each of the land registry departments of the forty-four local courts in Slovenia register data in their main register, while the substance of all main registers forms the central main register database of the land register of RS. An electronic main land register, replacing the manual main land register, was established in 2004 on the basis of the LRA of 2003. It is accessible via the Internet site of the Supreme Court of the RS[371] and is linked to the cadastres and other immovables' databases as well as to the Central population register and other databases containing data relevant for the land register. The user can have an insight into and can download (free of charge as of 2011) different land registry statements (i.e., the so-called regular land registry statements as well as the so-called historical land registry statements) for every immovable in Slovenia. It is to be underscored that the electronic land register only supports searches by immovables, while the personal search criterion is not enabled. Thus, a search regarding all immovables owned by one individual is not executable. Anyone can also order (against payment) that any local court, notary or one of the state bodies, further specified in the LRA, issues him or her a verified printed extract of the land registry statement irrespective of where the immovable is located. Until 2011 when the LRA of 2003 was extensively amended, the main register was composed of the *land registry sheets* (folios, Ger. *Grunbuchblatt*) in which immovables and rights on them were registered. In principle, each immovable was registered in a separate land registry sheet. However, more immovables could be registered in the same land registry sheet (if the land registry found it fit), provided they were located in the same cadastral municipality and had the same ownership status. According to the Decree on Loading and Keeping of Land Register by Application of Computer Technology and on Harmonization of Data with the Land Cadastre Data, land registry sheet consisted of parts A, B, and C. Part A contained specifications of the immovable registered in the land registry sheet.[372] Ownership on immovables was evident from part B of the land registry sheet of a particular immovable, whereas any limited property rights were registered in part C of the same land registry sheet.[373] In 2011, land registry sheets were abolished as a term

370. For further details as to seals, see Arts 134–138 of the LRA.

371. It is in Slovene only, https://evlozisce.sodisce.si/esodstvo/index.html, accessed on 31 Jul. 2019.

372. Part A consisted of the heading, where the number of the land registry sheet, the cadastral municipality, and the court maintaining the main register were registered; subpart A1, where data on the immovable copied from the land cadastre were registered; and subpart A2, where changes regarding the data on the immovable contained in A1, as well as other relevant data or rights existent in favour of this immovable (e.g., a real easement in favour of this immovable), were registered.

373. Part C was divided in subparts C1, C2, and C3. In subpart C1, the following rights were registered: personal easements, rights of encumbrance, rights of tenancy, pre-emption and repurchase rights,

as well as the document in which more than one immovable could be registered. In the new regime, each immovable is registered separately in an electronic document titled 'land registry statement' (Sl. *izpisek iz zemljiške knjige*). Division of the sheets into parts A, B, and C that enabled an immediate and clear identification of an immovable's status, were unfortunately also abolished. New terminology, such as 'basic legal status of an immovable' (Sl. *osnovni pravni položaj nepremičnine*), 'ID sign' (Sl. *ID znak*), 'source of ID sign' (Sl. *vir ID znaka*), 'ID' (Sl. *ID*), 'ID of the basic legal status of an immovable', etc., was introduced causing quite some dissatisfaction with the new regime with the users.

133. The *collection of documents* is composed of folders containing documents regarding a particular immovable – that is, land registry decisions and all documents that were the basis of the entries made with regard to a particular immovable. In land registry cases initiated after 1 May 2011, the documents are maintained in an electronic form and form the e-collection of documents. In contrast to the main register, which is open to the public,[374] only persons demonstrating a legitimate interest may request the court to issue him or her a copy of such document on which the court attests that the original of the document is contained in the collection of documents.[375] Such request must be in writing and must provide reasons. A land registry judge decides on it – in cases of documents contained in the physical collections of documents maintained by the local courts deciding on the case, the judge of that court decides on the request, while in cases of documents contained in the e-collection of documents, any judge has the power to do so.[376]

134. The land registry cases in the RS are handled by the *local courts*. According to one of the 2008 amendments of the LRA (as was additionally amended in 2009), all of the forty-four local courts have, as of 1 May 2011, general jurisdiction to perform registrations regardless of where in the RS the immovable is located, whereas before, the application had to be submitted with the court in whose territory the respective immovable was located. The same amendment introduced a new regulation of filing land registry applications – before 1 May 2009, the parties could file written applications with the local courts only; after that date, notaries were to file applications in the name of the party when attesting signatures on land registry permissions or forming notarial protocols, unless the party expressly opposes to it, while after 1 May 2011, the notaries must do so with electronic applications. One of the most important novelties of the 2011 LRA amendment additionally changed the rules on filing land registry applications which set out the following: in principle, the application (as well as all documents) has to be filed electronically by a notary, attorney, real estate agent, state or municipal attorney or by the party him or herself using a safe electronic signature, while applications in writing may no longer

---

rights of prohibition of alienating and encumbering the immovable. In subpart C3, mortgages were registered, while in subpart C2, other rights (e.g., real easements and rights of superficies encumbering the immovable) were registered.

374. Article 195 of LRA.

375. This prerequisite does, however, not apply to documents of the still pending cases.

376. Article 196 of LRA.

be filed by the parties themselves. They may, however, exceptionally file an application by going to one of the local courts' land registry divisions and requesting the official person of the court to file an electronic application on the basis of their oral request. Some other writings to the court must, however, still be in writing.[377]

135. The applications are processed by land registry judicial assistants (Sl. *zemljiškoknjižni sodniški pomočnik*) and/or individual land registry judges (Sl. *zemljiškoknjižni sodnik*).[378] Judges handle more complicated applications (e.g., in cases of land registry completion, i.e., in cases of registering non-registered immovables;[379] in objections to some applications, for example to applications for restoration of documents relevant for registration,[380] etc.), while all others are handled by land registry judicial assistants. In the latter case, however, an objection against the judicial assistant's decision (Sl. *ugovor*) can be filed in eight days after receiving the assistant's decision,[381] and is handled by a land registry judge. In some exceptional cases (i.e., with regard to setting up main land registers in the areas where to date they have not yet been set up) a panel composed of one judge and two judicial assistants decides the cases.[382] Land registry cases are disseminated electronically to judicial assistants of the land registry divisions of local courts in Slovenia irrespective of where the respective immovable is located,[383] taking account of their availability according to the data on the number of their (un)solved cases.

136. It should be stressed that when handling applications, the judicial assistant/judge merely checks whether all formal prerequisites for the requested registration are met – all legal remedies – that is, objections and/or appeals – can therefore refer to such issues only. If, however, the performed registrations are substantively invalid (e.g., a contract that was the basis for registration, is void, and therefore – according to the principle of causality – the registration is void, too), a so-called deletion claim or 'claim for removal from the land register' (Sl. *zahtevek za izbris izpodbijane vknjižbe*) can be filed via the so-called deletion action or 'action for removal from the land register' (Sl. *izbrisna tožba*) in order to restore the previous legal state. The fact that a deletion action has been initiated is notated in the land register.[384]

---

377. Article 125c of LRA.
378. See Arts 126 and 127 of the LRA.
379. For further details on the procedure of registering non-registered immovables into the land register (the so-called procedure for the supplementation of the land register), see Arts 229–233 of the LRA.
380. For further details on land registry restoration of documents, see Arts 234–242 of the LRA.
381. Articles 157 and 158 of LRA.
382. For further details on the procedure of setting up main land registers, see Arts 213–228 of the LRA.
383. Some land registry issues are, however, handled by the court of the territory of the respective immovable. See Art. 126 of the LRA.
384. Articles 243–245 of LRA. For further details on the deletion claim, see Hudej, Ščernjavič. *Aktualna vprašanja izbrisne tožbe* [Current Issues of Action for Deletion], in Zbornik, 15–26 (GV Založba2016); Hudej, *Izbrisna tožba – analiza aktualne sodne prakse s komentarjem* [Deletion Claim – analysis and commentary of case law], in Podjetje in delo, 2014, Y. 40, No. 8,

137. All decisions and other documents issued by the court are also issued in an electronic form and are forwarded to the notaries, attorneys, and other persons who have filed applications via their secure electronic inbox.[385] Writings of the court are only exceptionally issued and sent in writing.[386] All contracts and other documents which were the basis for registration are also kept in an electronic form.

138. Before the 2011 LRA amendment, appeals were handled by all four High Courts in the RS, while the 2011 amendment vested High Court in Koper with exclusive jurisdiction in land registry appeal cases. Accordingly, as of 1 May 2011, High Court in Koper is the only second instance court in the RS in land registry cases.[387] Appeals must be submitted in fifteen days after receiving the land registry judge's decision and must not submit any new facts or evidence.[388] Extraordinary remedies of revision and of opening of the proceedings, as well as reversion to the previous state of affairs are not allowed in land registry cases.[389]

---

pp. 1445 ff.; Pavčnik, *Izbrisna tožba: (analiza prakse višjih sodišč)* [Deletion Claim: (Analysis of high courts' case law)], in Pravosodni bilten, 2012, Y. 33, No. 1, pp. 165 ff.

385. Article 125b of LRA.
386. Article 125č of LRA.
387. Article 126/4 of LRA.
388. Articles 159 and 160 of LRA.
389. Article 120/3 of LRA.

Chapter 3. Ownership on Immovables

139. The right to ownership (Sl. *lastninska pravica*) is a basic *human right*, defined as such in Article 33 of the Slovenian Constitution, as well as in Article 1 of the Protocol No. 1 to the European Convention on Human Rights, which was ratified by the Slovenian parliament and is thus directly applicable in the Slovenian legal system. The right to ownership is also guaranteed by Article 17 of the United Nations' Universal Declaration of Human Rights of 1948 and by Article 17 of the Charter of Fundamental Rights of the European Union.

140. The right to ownership as the basic property right is composed of several entitlements (Sl. *upravičenja*) of the owner, as well as of some obligations according to the social, economic, and ecological functions of the property as set out in Article 67 of the Slovenian Constitution and further detailed in various Slovenian legal acts. According to Article 37/1 of the CPL, the right of ownership is defined as a right to possess a thing, to use and enjoy it in the fullest manner, and to dispose of it (i.e., to alienate or encumber the thing in ownership). The legal theory defines ownership (Sl. *lastnina*) as the will of the owner to use and dispose of a thing in the fullest manner (positive aspect of ownership) and to exclude all other people from doing the same (negative aspect of ownership).[390] The right of ownership also includes the right of the owner to destroy the thing (except in cases where such disposition is forbidden).[391]

141. Article 37/2 of the CPL provides that ownership cannot be limited in time or be conditional unless otherwise determined by law. Such exceptions are, for example, the fiduciary transfer of ownership and the reservation of title. Some of the entitlements can be separately transferred to other persons in the form of *limited property rights*. According to Article 2 of the CPL, these are the lien (the pledge, the mortgage, Sl. *zastavna pravica*), the right of encumbrance (Sl. *stvarno breme*), the right of superficies (Sl. *stavbna pravica*), the easements (Sl. *služnosti*) in rem and in personam, and the land debt (Sl. *zemljiški dolg*) which can no longer be established as the CPL amendment of 2013 deleted the whole chapter on land debt with the effect as of 6 November 2013, while all land debts established during 1 January 2003 (when land debt was introduced into Slovenian property law) and 5 November 2013 continue to exist.

142. Only one form of ownership exists in Slovenia, even though the constitutional provision on the right to 'private' property (Article 33) could suggest that different forms of ownership exist in Slovenian law. This provision is, namely, the expression of the legal situation in times of writing of the Constitution when social property as a distinct form of property still existed. The contents (the entitlements

---

390. Berden in *CPL with Commentary 2004*, 213; Tratnik & Vrenčur, *Omejitve lastninske pravice in posebni pravni režimi na nepremičninah* [Limitations of Ownership and Special Legal Regimes on the Immovables], 27 (GV Založba 2009).
391. Tratnik & Vrenčur, *Omejitve lastninske pravice in posebni pravni režimi na nepremičninah* [Limitations of Ownership and Special Legal Regimes on the Immovables], 27 (GV Založba 2009).

of the holder) of the right to ownership are not conditioned by the owner, but by the nature of the asset.[392] Unfortunately, loads of immovables in Slovenia are still registered in the land register as 'social ownership' (Sl. *družbena lastnina*) or as 'general peoples' property' (Sl. *splošno ljudsko premoženje*).[393] Such registered status does of course not accord to the real proprietary status of these immovables that is yet to be determined and registered accordingly. Recently, Slovenian municipalities have started proclaiming such immovables as property of the municipality and subsequently as property in public domain. Such practice has no valid legal basis and was performed by referring abusively to somewhat ambiguously formulated Article 212 of the Construction Act.[394] Instead of determining first who the real owner is of such immovables and finally assisting the real owner in registering his or her private ownership in the land register (or at least waiting for the courts to decide on who the rightful owner is[395]), municipalities have been taking advantage of improper, i.e., obsolete registrations claiming that they are the owners of these immovables. Mass nationalization of immovables in private ownership was to take place until the legislator and the courts have detected such practices and started addressing them accordingly.

143. The object of ownership is a *thing* as defined in Article 15 of the CPL. Ownership is not possible on patrimonial rights, because those are not legally considered to be things.

392. Juhart in *Property Law*, 53.
393. Today, this is in particular the case with common parts of multi-unit buildings and with common parts in bedroom communities (common playgrounds, parks, waste collection points, parking spaces, etc.) where the owners of apartments or individual houses in bedroom communities obtained (when buying the apartment or the house) but never registered their right to use these plots in social ownership. The legal status of these plots remained unaddressed for decades. Only in recent years, people have started to realize that it is of utmost importance for them to register their ownership on these plots as otherwise the municipalities or the state that have been for decades totally inactive as regards these plots, will (clearly in bad faith) sell them or encumber them to the detriment of real owners of these plots.
394. Zakon o graditvi objektov (ZGO-1) [Construction Act], Official Gazette RS, No. 110/02, with further amendments, replaced in 2017 by the new Building Act (Sl. *Gradbeni zakon (GZ)*), Official Gazette RS, No. 61/17.
395. Private parties will be claiming that they had become owners *ex lege* when the legislation transposing their right to use land in public ownership into private ownership of the land entered into force in 1997. Acquisition of ownership by prescription could be their alternative claim. As of 2008, most of such cases are assessed in non-contentious proceedings according to the rules set out in the Zakon o vzpostavitvi etažne lastnine na predlog pridobitelja posameznega dela stavbe in o določanju pripadajočega zemljišča k stavbi (ZVEtL) [Act on Establishing Divided Co-ownership and on Determining the Land Belonging to a Building], Official Gazette RS, Nos 45/08 and 59/11. This act enables the courts to assess if and to what extent a certain plot of land (Sl. *funkcionalno zemljišče, pripadajoče zemljišče*) 'belongs' to a certain building to which it serves, i.e., if and to what extent it is in ownership of the owner of the plot with the building.

144. A thing may be owned by one, as well as by two or more persons. In the latter case, the thing is in joint ownership or in co-ownership.[396] A specific type of ownership is divided co-ownership existent in cases of apartment and/or offices buildings.[397]

145. Article 67 of the Slovenian Constitution requires that ownership is exercised according to its social, economic, and ecological functions. The Constitution itself regulates some of the restrictions of property in the public interest, such as expropriation, acquisition of ownership on immovables by foreign citizens, while these and other restrictions on use, enjoyment, and disposal of ownership are further determined by law. Various laws regulate them: the CPL (e.g., rules on neighbourhood law, on statutory pre-emption right in cases of co-ownership of immovables and in some cases of divided co-ownership, etc.), laws on spatial planning, laws on construction of buildings, laws on forests, laws on agricultural land, etc.

146. Restraints as to acquisition of ownership on immovables exist in terms of citizenship of the acquirer. Namely, not all foreigners, i.e., persons lacking Slovenian citizenship and undertakings not having their seat in Slovenia, may unconditionally acquire ownership on Slovenian immovables. Article 68 of the Slovenian Constitution regulates the ownership rights of foreigners to immovable property in Slovenia. It currently reads as follows: '[a]liens may acquire ownership rights to real estate under conditions provided by law or a treaty ratified by the National Assembly'. Article 68 of the Slovenian Constitution was quite problematic and therefore amended twice. Originally it read: 'Aliens may acquire ownership rights to real estate under conditions provided by law. Aliens may not acquire title to land except by inheritance, under the condition of reciprocity.' Following the amendment of 1997, the text of Article 68 read as follows: 'Aliens may acquire ownership rights to real estate under conditions provided by law or if so provided by a treaty ratified by the National Assembly, under the condition of reciprocity. Such law and treaty from the preceding paragraph shall be adopted by the National Assembly by a two-thirds majority vote of all deputies.' The Reciprocity Act of 1999,[398] which was replaced in 2017 by the new Reciprocity Act,[399] laid down the regulation of the condition of reciprocity between the country of origin of the foreigner acquiring the property, and Slovenia where such reciprocity is required. The last amendment of Article 68 of the Slovenian Constitution resulting in the current text was adopted in 2003 in order to harmonize the Slovenian system with the European acquis. Accordingly, all EU and EFTA citizens can acquire ownership on Slovenian immovables unconditionally after 1 May 2004.[400] According to EU legislation, a special regime

396. For further details as to joint ownership and co-ownership, see Part I, Ch. 5, §1 and §2.
397. For further details on divided co-ownership, see Part I, Ch. 5, §3.
398. Zakon o ugotavljanju vzajemnosti (ZUVza) [Reciprocity Act], Official Gazette RS, No. 9/99.
399. Zakon o ugotavljanju vzajemnosti (ZUVza-1) [Reciprocity Act], Official Gazette RS, No. 27/17.
400. EU citizens could acquire Slovenian immovables even before Slovenia acceded to the EU. As of 1999 when the so-called Spanish compromise was signed, EU citizens could acquire immovables also on a contractual basis (by buying immovables, not only by inheriting them as was the general rule on acquiring immovables by foreigners) under the condition of reciprocity. Between 1999 and

is provided for Swiss citizens who may, under certain conditions, buy Slovenian immovables (not merely inherit them under the general scheme of acquiring immovables by foreigners) as of 1 April 2006. Citizens of the US are most plausibly governed by the same regime as EU citizens on the basis of a Most Favoured Nation (MFN) clause set out in an old trade agreement signed between the US and the Princedom of Serbia in 1881[401] which is supposed to be binding on Slovenia on the basis of succession. After Slovenia acceded to the EU, quite a number of EU citizens bought immovables in the coastal area as well as in Prekmurje where prices of immovables are lower and where immovables are largely available. A special legislation was adopted in 2006 setting out specific rules on acquisition of ownership on Slovenian immovables by persons originating in EU candidate countries.[402] A specific regulation of acquiring immovables in Slovenia is set out also in the Act on Relations between the Republic of Slovenia and Slovenians abroad according to which all persons of Slovenian nationality not having Slovenian citizenship may also unconditionally acquire immovables in Slovenia.[403] All other foreigners can acquire ownership only by inheritance under the condition of reciprocity (Article 6 of the IA) as set out in the Reciprocity Act of 1999. Reciprocity is assessed by the Ministry of Justice (in case of foreign states and international governmental organizations acquiring immovables in Slovenia by the Ministry for foreign affairs).[404]

147. Apart from restrictions in the public interest, ownership may be restricted also by the will of the owner. Article 38 of the CPL regulates *the restrictions of ownership at the will of the owner*, which can be established unless expressly prohibited. Article 38 of the CPL sets out detailed provisions on *the right on prohibition of encumbrance and disposal* (Sl. *prepoved obremenitve in odtujitve*)[405] as well as

2003, however, that was possible only if they had their residence in Slovenia for at least three years, whereas between 1 Feb. 2003 and 1 May 2004, the prerequisite of residence was no longer required. The EU Accession Treaty of 16 Apr. 2004 (Official Treaty RS, International Contracts, No. 3/I/2004) set out a safeguard clause enabling Slovenia to restrict acquisition of immovables to EU citizens up to 1 May 2011.

401. Serbian Official Gazette, No. 268/1882.

402. Zakon o pogojih za pridobitev lastninske pravice fizičnih in pravnih oseb držav kandidatk za članstvo v Evropski uniji na nepremičninah (ZPPLPKEU) [Act Governing the Conditions for the Acquisition of Title to Property by Natural Persons and Legal Entities of European Union Candidate Countries], Official Gazette RS, No. 61/06.

403. Zakon o odnosih Republike Slovenije s Slovenci zunaj njenih meja (ZORSSZNM) [Act on Relations between the Republic of Slovenia and Slovenians abroad], Official Gazette RS, No. 43/06, with further amendments.

404. For further details on acquisition of ownership on immovables in Slovenia by foreigners, see Vlahek, *Pridobivanje lastninske pravice na nepremičninah v Sloveniji s strani tujcev* [Acquisition of Ownership on Immovables in Slovenia by Foreign Citizens], in Pravnik (Ljubljana: 2008), y. 63, No. 1/3, pp. 7 ff.

405. A prohibition of encumbrance and disposal of a thing or a property right by means of a legal transaction or last will is, however, binding only on the first owner and not on his or her legal successors. It can be entered in the land register if it is agreed between spouses or cohabiting partners, parents, and their children, as well as adopted children and adoptive parents. In this case, the prohibition also has effects against third persons. For details on the prohibition to alienate and encumber and on the right of repurchase, see Vrenčur in *CPL with Commentary 2004*, 223–237.

on the *right of repurchase* (Sl. *odkupna pravica*),[406] while all other restrictions of ownership at the will of the owner are regulated in other chapters of the CPL (e.g., in chapters on limited property rights) as well as in other legal acts (the CO, for example, regulates the contractual right of *pre-emption* (Sl. *predkupna pravica*), the lease contract (Sl. *najemna pogodba*), etc.). As of the CPL 2020 amendment, Article 38 explicitly states that in case the encumbered thing is divided, the restrictions apply to all of its parts.

148. The basic right of protection of the owner is to demand from the possessor of the thing to return the thing (*rei vindicatio*, Sl. *lastninska tožba*, *vrnitvena tožba*, *reivindikacijska tožba*).[407] In this claim, the owner must specify the thing and prove that he or she is the owner, and that the defendant is the possessor of this thing. If the latter possesses the thing on the grounds of a valid legal title – for example, a lease – the burden of proof lies on him or her. In cases where the thing was not taken from the owner who is merely disturbed in his or her exercise of ownership, the owner can demand the cessation of disturbance (*actio negatoria*, Sl. *negatorna tožba*, *tožba zaradi vznemirjanja*).[408] *Rei vindicatio* and *actio negatoria* are not subject to any statute of limitations.

149. Ownership on immovables can be acquired by inheritance, by a final decision of a public authority, i.e., court or administrative body (sale in non-contentious proceedings, sale in enforcement proceedings, sale in insolvency, expropriation, commassation, rounding off, denationalization, building over a boundary), by a law, i.e., by a statutory provision (acquisitive prescription, acquisition *a non domino*) or by registration on the basis of a legal transaction.[409]

150. According to Article 13 of the CPL, the provisions of the CPL on acquisition, transfer, protection, and loss of ownership rights apply *mutatis mutandis* to the creation, transfer, and loss of other property rights.

---

406. An owner can conclude a contract establishing the right of repurchase, stating that he or she will sell a certain thing to the other contracting party on request under agreed conditions. This right cannot be transferred and expires upon death or dissolution of the other contracting party. It has effects against third persons if it is entered in the land register. For the restrictions of disposal in immovables, see Vrenčur, *Omejitev razpolaganja po volji lastnika na področju nepremičnin* [Restriction of Disposal at the Will of the Owner Regarding Immovables], in Pravna Praksa, No. 26/2003, pp. 5 ff.
407. Article 92 of CPL.
408. Article 99 of CPL.
409. Article 39 of CPL.

Chapter 4. Limited Property Rights on Immovables

151. Under Slovenian law as it stands now, four types of limited property rights may be established as encumbrances of ownership: easement, mortgage, superficies, and the right of encumbrance (land charge). According to the principle of *numerus clausus*,[410] only these property rights may exist on things next to the right of ownership, whereby certain of these rights are plausible as encumbrances of immovables only.

152. The CPL of 2003 introduced two new property rights into the Slovenian property law: superficies and land debt. The institute of land debt, however, ceased to exist in Slovenian legislation in 2013 when the whole chapter of CPL on land debt was repealed after it was claimed to be abused by the businessmen facing criminal charges in order to safeguard their property from confiscation. Under heavy media and political criticism, the instrument of land debt was erased from the Code of Property Law with effect as of 6 November 2013. Land debts which were successfully applied for incorporation before that (i.e., between 1 January 2003 and 5 November 2013) are, however, still valid. In view of property law, professors and practising lawyers, existent or, if needed, novel measures against the abuse of land debt could have been applied instead of simply erasing it from Slovenian property law even before a single proceeding aiming at claiming and proving the abuse was initiated.

§1. Easements

I. Concept

153. Easement (Sl. *služnost*, Lat. *servitus*, Ger. *Dienstbarkeit*) is a right to use another's property or to exploit another's right (i.e., the so-called *positive easement*) or to demand from the owner of a property that he or she refrain from actions that he or she would otherwise have the right to carry out on his or her property (i.e., the so-called *negative easement*).[411] The property encumbered with an easement is called the 'servient property'.

154. In contrast to the right of encumbrance, an easement cannot bind the owner of the servient property to a particular action.[412] As ensues from the definition of an easement, it may only bind the owner to refrain from a particular action, or to tolerate a particular action of the holder of the right of easement on the servient property.

410. See General Introduction, §3, III H.

411. Article 210 of CPL. Only real easements may be negative easements, while personal easements are always positive easements. Vrenčur in *CPL with Commentary 2004*, 617.

412. Article 213/2 of CPL.

155. Following the Roman law model, easements may be real (those established in the interest of a particular immovable) or personal (those established in the interest of a particular person). The former are regulated in Articles 213–226 of the CPL and the latter in Articles 227–248 of the CPL, while Articles 211 and 212 of the CPL provide for general rules on easements. The CPL regulates also the so-called non-genuine real easements which are real easements in their substance, but are (in contrast to genuine real easements) not established in the interest of a particular immovable, but in the interest of a particular individual or public interest. Easements in the public interest are regulated in the Spatial Planning Act (SPA),[413] as well as in special legislation on telecommunications, energy, etc.

II. Real Easements

156. Real easement (Sl. *stvarna služnost*) is a right of an owner of an immovable (the so-called *dominant immovable*, Lat. *praedium dominians*) to carry out for the needs of that immovable certain actions on another's immovable (the *servient immovable*, Lat. *praedium serviens*) or to demand that the owner of such immovable refrain from certain actions that he or she would otherwise have the right to carry out on his or her immovable.[414] Apart from establishing the real easement for an indefinite time, which is usually the case, it may also be established for a specific time or for a specific time of year.[415]

157. The basic characteristic of real easements is that they are *established in the interest of a particular immovable*, and not in the interest of a particular person. Whoever owns the dominant immovable thus profits from the easement. Likewise, whoever owns the servient immovable must tolerate performance of the easement his or her immovable is encumbered with. Transfer of ownership on the dominant or servient immovable does, therefore, in principle not affect the existence of real easements.

158. The provisions relating to the owners of the dominant and of the servient immovables apply *mutatis mutandis* to a usufructuary and a holder of the right of superficies. They, too, can thus establish easements (be it an encumbrance of the immovable they hold a right on, be it an easement on another's immovable, and in favour of the immovable they hold a right on). If they encumber the immovable, they must, however, not encumber it for longer than the duration of their right.[416]

413. Zakon o urejanju prostora (ZUreP-2) [Spatial Planning Act], Official Gazette RS, No. 61/17..
414. Article 213/1 of CPL.
415. Article 213/3 of CPL.
416. Article 213/4 of CPL.

A. Creation of Real Easements

159. A real easement is created by *law* (e.g., by acquisitive prescription), on the basis of an *agreement*, or by *decision of a state body.*[417]

160. If it is created on the basis of an agreement (the so-called contract on the establishment of the easement, Sl. *pogodba o ustanovitvi služnosti*), the land registry permission and an entry in the land register are required in addition to a valid agreement from which the obligation to establish an easement derives.[418] The contract on the establishment of the easement must contain the name of the owners of the dominant and servient immovables, the land register designation of both immovables, a precise description of the easement, and any compensation that must be paid by the owner of the dominant immovable to the owner of the servient immovable. The compensation can be fixed as a one-off payment or as periodically maturing instalments.

161. If an easement is created by a decision of a state body, it is created on the day when the court decision or the decision of an administrative body becomes final.[419] Although such easement is established without registration, registering it in the land register is of utmost importance to the holder of the right due to the possible detrimental effects of the principle of trust in the land register. One of such easements is the so-called way of necessity which is regulated in Articles 88–91 of the CPL.[420] Another such easement is the easement in the public interest which is regulated in Articles 211–215 of the SPA as well as in special legislation on telecommunications, energy, etc., and is created by a final decision of an administrative unit.

162. Further, a (positive) real easement is created by prescription, if the owner of the dominant immovable has actually been exercising the easement in good faith for ten years (the so-called regular prescription, Sl. *pravo priposestvovanje*).[421] A real easement is also created by prescription if the owner of the dominant immovable has actually been exercising the easement for twenty years (despite the lack of good faith, *sic!*), and the owner of the servient property has not opposed it (the so-called irregular prescription, Sl. *nepravo priposestvovanje*).[422] However, real

417. Articles 211 and 214 of CPL.
418. Article 215 of CPL. A real easement is registered as a limited property right existent on the servient immovable, while with the dominant immovable it is registered as a right existent in its favour. Before the land registry was reformed in –, easements were registered in part C2 of the land registry sheet of the servient immovable, while with the dominant immovable they were registered in part A2 of the land registry sheet as a right existing in the immovable's favour.
419. Article 216 of CPL.
420. For further details as to the way of necessity, see Part I, Ch. 6, §10.
421. Article 217 of CPL. For further details as to the assessment of the acquirer's good faith, see Part III, Ch. 3, §3.
422. Such regime was introduced by the Yugoslav federal Law on Property Relations of 1980 (Sl. *Zakon o temeljnih lastninskopravnih razmerjih*) that regulated only the irregular acquisitive prescription of easements. In contrast to, for example, Croatian legislator, the Slovenian legislator has obviously not decided to alter it and has regulated it next to the regular ABGB like prescription.

easements cannot be acquired by prescription if the owner of the dominant immovable abused the trust of the owner or the direct possessor of the servient property, if the easement was exercised by force or by deception, or if the easement was permitted only until revoked. Negative easements can, though, never be acquired by prescription. For example, if the owner of an immovable has not been exercising his or her right on the immovable by planting flowers on it for twenty years, the owners of another immovable may not claim that they acquired an easement prohibiting the first owner to plant flowers on his or her land.

163. A person entitled to an easement may request that the existence of the easement is established against the owner of the servient immovable.[423]

B. *Exercise of Real Easements*

164. A real easement must be exercised in the manner that least encumbers the object of the easement.[424]

165. If the exercise of a real easement requires the use of a device or if a particular action is required, the costs of maintenance or the costs of the action are covered by the owner of the dominant property. However, if the device is also used by the owner of the servient property or if the action is also in his or her interest, the costs of maintenance of the device and the costs of the action are to be covered by the owner of the dominant property and the owner of the servient property in proportion to the benefit they derive from using the encumbered part of the servient property.[425]

C. *Expiration of Real Easements*

166. A real easement expires on the basis of an *agreement*, on the basis of a state body *decision,* or on the basis of a *law*.[426]

167. First, an easement expires with its deletion from the land register on the basis of a legal agreement concluded between the owner of the dominant and the owner of the servient immovable.[427]

168. Second, the owner of the servient property may request the expiration of the easement if it ceases to be beneficial for use of the dominant property or if there

---

423. Article 218 of CPL.
424. Article 219/1 of CPL.
425. Article 219/2,3 of CPL.
426. Article 220 of CPL.
427. Article 221 of CPL.

has been a substantial change in the circumstance under which it was established.[428] In such cases, the real easement expires when the court decision or the decision of an administrative body becomes final.

169. Further, a real easement expires by law if the owner of the servient property opposes its exercise and the owner of the dominant property has not exercised his or her right for three consecutive years (*usucapio libertatis*, Sl. *osvoboditev služnosti*). It also expires if it is not exercised during the time necessary for its acquisition by prescription (Sl. *zastaranje služnosti*)[429] as well as if the dominant or the servient property is destroyed.[430]

170. An easement which is not registered in the land register (i.e., which was created outside the register, e.g., in cases of acquisitive prescription) expires also in cases where the principle of trust in the land register is applied, i.e., where a third person relied in good faith on the data set out in the land register where the easement was not registered, and acquired ownership on the immovable without the easement. Such cases are very common in Slovenia as easements – irrespective of their substance and purpose – had in the past been rarely registered in the land register. In recent years, the courts are faced in particular with disputes regarding various networks that were built on immovables which were acquired by new owners who are claiming that they have not known of the easements and that they have relied in good faith on the land register where the easements are not registered. According to Article 9 of the CPL, good faith is presumed unless proven otherwise. The burden of proving that the acquirer was operating in bad faith is, therefore, on the holder of the easement. According to theory and case law analysing the issue in question in the first years after the enactment of the CPL and the LRA, the acquirer did not need to check the factual status of an immovable in order to be in good faith and could merely rely on the data registered in the land register (provided he or she is not proven knowing of the fact that someone has acquired an easement on the immovable[431]).[432] More recent theory and case law have, however, departed from such position requiring in practice the acquirer to check the actual status of an immovable in order to be able to rely on the principle of trust in the land register.[433] The factual state of possession of an immovable and/or statements made about it to

428. Article 222 of CPL. For further details, see Vlahek, *Prestavitev služnostne poti* [Alteration of Easements], in Pravna Praksa, No. 8/2008, 21–22, pp. 21 ff.

429. Juhart states that the period is that of the irregular prescription, i.e., twenty years. Juhart in *CPL with Commentary 2004*, 611.

430. Article 223 of CPL.

431. See the following Judgment of the High Court in Ljubljana: No. VSL I Cp 1198/2011 of 4 Apr. 2012.

432. See Vlahek, *Odprta vprašanja načela zaupanja v zemljiško knjigo* [Issues Relating to the Principle of Trust in the Land Register], in *Izbrane teme civilnega prava II*, 111–129 (Ed. Ude, Institute of Comparative Law at the Faculty of Law in Ljubljana 2007).

433. See, for example, Tratnik, *Pridobitev lastnine in drugih stvarnih pravic na nepremičnini na podlagi zaupanja v zemljiško knjigo* [Acquisition of Ownership and other Property Rights on Immovables on the Basis of Trust in the Land Register], 139 (Ed. Ude, Institute of Comparative Law at the Faculty of Law in Ljubljana 2007); Juhart, *Dobrovernost kot pogoj za učinkovanje načela zaupanja v zemljiško knjigo*, [Good Faith Prerequisite of the Principle of Trust in the Land Register],

the acquirer may, taking into account all the relevant circumstances of each particular case, be relevant for assessing his or her good faith. Gross negligence of the acquirer in not knowing about the actual state of the immovable has become the relevant standard. In cases of visible easements (e.g., in cases of paths used by third persons, electricity poles), the holder of the easement will thus quite easily prove that the acquirer of the immovable knew or could have easily known of the existent easement, while in cases where the easement is carried out invisibly (e.g., in cases of cables or other networks installed under the surface), it will be harder to prove that the acquirer was not in good faith as he or she might not have the possibility to detect the easement. As in Slovenia, the Consolidated Cadastre of Public Infrastructure (Sl. *zbirni kataster gospodarske javne infrastrukture*) has been set up as of 2006, the question has arisen recently in the theory whether network easements which are not registered in the land register, but are registered in the cadastre and shown also on the maps available on the official site of the Surveying and Mapping Authority of RS,[434] should have effect on third persons acquiring land, in particular how the entry of infrastructure in the cadastre affects the good faith of the purchaser of the burdened plot of land.[435] So far, attempts of addressing this issue in legal theory and case law have been scarce,[436] but it is presumed that the courts will eventually be burdened with solving loads of disputes regarding this issue.

171. According to legal theory and case law as they stand now, only *derivative inter vivos transactions* (concluded by the registered person and a third person in good faith) can lead to acquisition of ownership on an immovable free of any easements. This is inferred from the wording of the CPL and the LRA, which use the term *legal commerce* (Sl. *pravni promet*) to denote the sphere of relationships in which acquisition free of limited property rights encumbering immovables can occur.[437] *Mortis causa* transactions, for example, do not qualify as transactions to which the principle of trust in the land register would apply. In these cases, preference is given to out-of-register holders of easements (e.g., acquirers of easements by acquisitive prescription) instead of heirs irrespective of the heirs' good faith in

156–157 (Ed. Ude, Institute of Comparative Law at the Faculty of Law in Ljubljana 2007). See also the following Judgment of the Supreme Court of RS: No. II Ips 397/2006 of 15 Jan. 2009.

434. See http://www.e-prostor.gov.si/ (available in Slovene only), accessed on 31 Jul. 2019.

435. See Damjan & Vlahek, *Priposestvovanje služnosti v javno korist* [Acquisitive Prescription of an Easement in Public Interest]., in Pravnik, Nos 3–4/2014, pp. 149 ff.; see also Damjan, *Pravne podlage za ureditev položaja infrastrukturnih omrežij na tujih zemljiščih* [Legal basis for regulating the position of infrastructure networks on others' property], in Pravni letopis 2013, pp. 85 ff.

436. See Damjan & Vlahek, *Priposestvovanje služnosti v javno korist* [Acquisitive Prescription of an Easement in Public Interest]., in Pravnik, Nos 3–4/2014, pp. 149 ff. See also Damjan & Bergant Rakočević, *Dobra vera pri priposestvovanju služnosti: vidik pridobitelja služeče nepremičnine* [Good Faith in Acquisitve Prescription of Easements on Immovables: Position of the Acquirer of Encumbered Immovable], in Pravnik, No. 5/6 (2015), pp. 307 ff. See also the Judgment of the High Court of Ljubljana No. I Cp 1662/2012 of 12 Sep. 2012.

437. See Vlahek, *Odprta vprašanja načela zaupanja v zemljiško knjigo* [Issues Relating to the Principle of Trust in the Land Register], in *Izbrane teme civilnega prava II*, 111–129 (Ed. Ude, Institute of Comparative Law at the Faculty of Law in Ljubljana, 2007).

the decedent's registered ownership free of encumbrances.[438] Whether applicability of principle of trust in the land register is limited on transactions made for consideration is not expressly settled in legislation, and it is the legal theory and courts that are to interpret the term *legal commerce* accordingly.[439] Acquisition of ownership of immovables in enforcement proceedings does, under certain prerequisites, also not enable acquisition of the debtor's land free of real easements. Personal easements, superficies, and rights of encumbrance cease to exist unless they were registered in the land register prior to the registration of the rights of the creditors, or unless the new owner agrees to their existence.[440] Easements in the public interest remain in existence. With regard to real easements, such regulation seems unfair as it treats differently buyers obtaining ownership on the basis of an agreement with the owner, from those obtaining ownership in enforcement proceedings.

172. Moreover, a real easement expires if the same person becomes the owner of the dominant and the servient immovable.[441] If the immovables once again come under the ownership of different owners, the real easement is restored, provided it has not been deleted from the land register in the interim period. A written declaration of the will of the owner containing the land registry permission is sufficient for the deletion of the real easement in the interim period.

D. Division of Immovables

173. If the dominant immovable is divided, a real easement remains on all of its parts.[442] If the servient immovable is divided, the easement remains only on those parts on which it was exercised.[443]

E. Non-genuine Real Easements

174. A non-genuine real easement is an easement that, by its content, is a genuine real easement but is established for the benefit of a particular person, and not for

438. Vlahek, *Odprta vprašanja načela zaupanja v zemljiško knjigo* [Issues Relating to the Principle of Trust in the Land Register], in *Izbrane teme civilnega prava II*, 120 (Ed. Ude, Institute of Comparative Law at the Faculty of Law in Ljubljana 2007); Tratnik. *Pridobitev lastnine in drugih stvarnih pravic na nepremičnini na podlagi zaupanja v zemljiško knjigo* [Acquisition of Ownership and other Property Rights on Immovables on the Basis of Trust in the Land Register], 133 (Ed. Ude, Institute of Comparative Law at the Faculty of Law in Ljubljana 2007). See also the following Judgments of the Supreme Court of RS, Nos VS RS II Ips 622/2008 of 19 Jan. 2012, II Ips 1030/2008 of 16 Feb. 2012, and VSL II Cp 2602/2010 of 10 Nov. 2010.

439. See Vlahek, *Odprta vprašanja načela zaupanja v zemljiško knjigo* [Issues Relating to the Principle of Trust in the Land Register], in *Izbrane teme civilnega prava II*, 122 (Ed. Ude, Institute of Comparative Law at the Faculty of Law in Ljubljana 2007).

440. Article 174 of CESA.

441. Article 224 of CPL.

442. Article 225/1 of CPL.

443. Article 225/2 of CPL.

the benefit of a particular immovable as in the case of genuine real easements. Parties may want to establish such easements when they want to establish them only in favour of a particular natural or legal person owning a particular immovable, not in favour of every owner of this immovable. Article 226 of the CPL states that in these cases, the provisions of the CPL applying to personal easements apply with respect to the creation and expiration of the easement, while otherwise, provisions on genuine real easements apply.

175. Because a non-genuine easement has all the characteristics of genuine real easements, except that it is not established in the interest of another immovable, it corresponds well also to some circumstances where no link between two immovables can be established. *Easements in the public interest* regulated in the SPA which are usually established for setting up of public infrastructure networks (such as telecommunications infrastructure, sewerage system, water distribution system, heating system, etc.), are the most common examples of that.[444] No dominant immovable exists in these cases, the easement usually exists in favour of the (operator of a) particular infrastructure network (usually serving the public interest) installed in private land. If rules on non-genuine easements are strictly applied to such easements, then they are to be established in favour of a particular legal person and may last only thirty years (as rules on personal easements apply to non-genuine easements with regard to their establishment and expiration). The possibility to establish easements for an unlimited period and in the public interest in favour of the network itself, or in favour of the public interest itself, or at least in favour of every network operator (and not only in favour of a particular operator) would, however, better suit this type of easements. Some of the special sectoral laws regulating such easements (e.g., the Energy Act[445]) have thus already set out that such easements are established in favour of every operator in charge of the network. In cases of networks where such specific regulation does not exist, the parties tried to register such easements as genuine real easements by stating that the immovable from which the network originated represents the dominant immovable, but the courts did not accept such legal construction. They were also not particularly benevolent to attempts of registering such easements in favour of 'every operator of the network', the parties thus had to register such easements in favour of the particular legal person in charge of the network at the time of the registration that caused problems in cases where the operator was to be altered. The CPL amendment of 2020, has eventually set out explicitly that such network easements in the public interest may be established for longer than thirty years or even for an indefinite time unless another law stipulates otherwise. It also set out that in case the operator of the network is altered, the easement is transferred to the new operator.[446] The possibility of acquiring such network easements by acquisitive prescription is also highly debated as personal easements (regulation of which applies also to non-genuine easements as to their establishment and expiration) may according

444. See also Part III, Ch. 10.
445. Energetski zakon (EZ-1), Official Gazette RS, No. 17/14, with further amendments.
446. Article 226/2,3 CPL.

to some Slovenian legal authors not be acquired by acquisitive prescription.[447] Due to these difficulties in establishing proper relationship between traditional easements and easements in the public interest, legal theory started to denote such easements as *sui generis* easements eliminating thereby the obstacles of applying on them provisions on traditional easements. The possibility of acquiring network easements by acquisitive prescription is of utmost importance in cases where the network cables or pipes were installed in private land decades ago, usually on the basis of an oral agreement with the owner of the land, or on the basis of the owner's written consent, whereby the right of the operator to instal the cables or pipes was never processed in the land register in order to establish an easement.[448] Agreements suitable for registration were usually not concluded, and easements were for this reason not registered in the land register and did thus not even legally exist. In the last couple of years, the owners of land in which the cables or pipes are installed (in particular the successors of those who agreed to the instalment), have started claiming that the infrastructure is installed in their land without any contractual basis and are requesting the operators to pay them for the use of their land. The operators are on the other hand claiming that they have acquired easements by acquisitive prescription. This has been one of the highly debated issues of Slovenian property law. Acquisitive prescription of easements in the public interest under the previously and currently valid regimes in Slovenia is being analysed focusing also on the question on the admissibility of such acquisition by prescription in the light of constitutional provisions coupled with the issue of obligation to pay compensation – one of such cases has been under review by the Constitutional Court of RS.[449] In October 2015, however, the Supreme Court of RS has opted for confirming (non-compensatory) acquisitive prescription as valid legal basis for acquiring network easements in the

447. Vrenčur is opposing the possibility to acquire such easements by acquisitive prescription, while Pavčnik, Damjan and Vlahek are in favour of it. In October 2015, the Supreme Court of RS has ruled in favour of acquisitive prescription of network easements in the public interest (II Ips 210/2014). For further details, see Vrenčur, *Pravni temelji pridobitve služnosti v javno korist s komentarjem najnovejše sodne prakse* [Legal basis of acquisition of easements in the public interest with commentary of the novel case law], in *Sodobno stvarno pravo*, 253 ff. (Eds Juhart, Plavšak, Vrenčur, Pravna fakulteta v Ljubljani, Planet GV, TaxFinLex 2016); Pavčnik, *Usklajenost sodne prakse glede priposestvovanja služnosti v javno korist* [Harmony of Judicial Decisions on Acquisition of Easements in the Public Interest], in *Sodobno stvarno pravo*, 271 ff. (Eds Juhart, Plavšak, Vrenčur, Pravna fakulteta v Ljubljani, Planet GV, TaxFinLex 2016); Damjan & Vlahek, *Priposestvovanje služnosti v javno korist* [Acquisitive Prescription of Easements in the Public Interest]., in Pravnik, Nos 3–4/2014, pp. 149 ff.; Damjan, *Služnost v javno korist* [Easement in the Public Interest], in Pravosodni bilten,Y. 37, No. 1, 2016, pp. 69 ff.; Damjan, *Služnost v javno korist* [Easement in the Public Interest], in Zbornik, 2016, pp. 89–113.

448. See Damjan & Vlahek, *Priposestvovanje služnosti v javno korist* [Acquisitive Prescription of an Easement in Public Interest], in Pravnik, Nos 3–4/2014, pp. 149 ff.; see also Damjan, *Pravne podlage za ureditev položaja infrastrukturnih omrežij na tujih zemljiščih* [Legal basis for regulating the position of infrastructure networks on others' property], in Pravni letopis 2013, pp. 85 ff. See also the recent Judgment of the Supreme Court od RS No. II Ips 186/2011 of 22 May 2014.

449. See Damjan & Vlahek, *Priposestvovanje služnosti v javno korist* [Acquisitive Prescription of an Easement in Public Interest], in Pravnik, Nos 3–4/2014, pp. 149 ff.

public interest putting forward pragmatic and reasonable arguments for such decision.[450] Another interesting question regarding network easements is whether non-registered network easements have effect on a third person acquiring the land, in particular how the entry of infrastructure in the Consolidated Cadastre of Public Infrastructure (Sl. *kataster gospodarske javne infrastrukture*) affects the good faith of the purchaser of the burdened plot of land.[451]

III. Personal Easements

A. General

176. In contrast to real easements, where the easement is established for the benefit of a particular immovable, personal easements are established for the benefit of a particular person, be it a *legal entity* or an *individual.* A personal easement (Sl. *osebna služnost*) is defined as the right of the holder to use another's property (be it *immovable* or *movable*) or to exploit another's *right.* If a personal easement is established for the benefit of an individual, it lasts until his or her death (unless established for a certain period), while its duration may not be more than thirty years if the holder of an easement is a legal entity.[452] Personal easements are not inheritable. They are also not transferable; however, a holder of a personal easement may in some cases (i.e., in cases of usufruct) transfer its exercise.[453]

177. Slovenian property law provides for the following *three types* of personal easements: usufruct, use, and habitation.[454] With the exception of usufruct, which may be established by a court decision, personal easements may be established on the basis of a legal transaction only.[455] While habitation can encumber immovables only, the rights of usufruct and use can be established on immovables as well as movables (usufruct also on property rights).

B. Usufruct

178. Usufruct (Sl. *užitek*, Lat. *ususfructus*) is a personal easement that confers the right to use and enjoy another's property or right such that its substance is preserved.[456] It is an extensive property right that usually leaves the owner of the

450. No. II Ips 210/2014.
451. See Damjan & Vlahek, *Priposestvovanje služnosti v javno korist* [Acquisitive Prescription of an Easement in Public Interest], in Pravnik, Nos 3–4/2014, pp. 149 ff.; see also Damjan, *Pravne podlage za ureditev položaja infrastrukturnih omrežij na tujih zemljiščih* [Legal basis for regulating the position of infrastructure networks on others' property]., n Pravni letopis 2013, pp. 85 ff.
452. Article 227 of CPL. If parties wish so, they may of course establish a new personal easement with the same substance.
453. Article 229 of CPL.
454. Article 228 of CPL.
455. Vrenčur in *CPL with Commentary 2004*, 618.
456. Article 230 of CPL.

encumbered thing with a bare right (Lat. *nuda proprietas*, Sl. *gola lastninska pravica*). In contrast to the other two personal easements, usufruct confers on the holder of the easement not only the right to use another's property, but also to enjoy it. The object of a usufruct can be a *non-consumable thing* or *a right from which interest or other benefits derive*.[457] A co-ownership share can also be the object of a usufruct.[458] A usufruct can also be established on part of an immovable so that the immovable is jointly used and enjoyed by the owner and the usufructuary.[459]

179. As was already emphasized, the usufructuary may not transfer his or her right[460] but may transfer its exercise. This is another distinctive factor between usufruct on the one hand and the easements of use and habitation on the other. The owner of the thing encumbered with usufruct may transfer his or her ownership, but the transfer does not affect the existence of usufruct.

180. A usufruct is created on the basis of an agreement or a *court decision*.[461] In addition to a valid legal agreement from which the obligation to establish a usufruct derives, the creation of a usufruct on the basis of an agreement requires the land registry permission and an entry in the land register in case of immovables, delivery in case of movables, and the transaction necessary for the transfer of the right in case of rights.[462] If the usufruct is created on the basis of court decision, it is created on the day when the court decision becomes final.[463]

181. The usufructuary must inform the owner about all important circumstances concerning the encumbered thing and allow him or her to examine it once a year.[464]

---

457. For example, usufruct on a book entry security may be established in the form of the right to payment of dividends or other profits deriving from such security according to the Zakon o nematerializiranih vrednostnih papirjih (ZNVP-1) [Book Entry Securities Act], Official Gazette RS, No. 75/15, with further amendments.
458. In this case, the usufructuary has the right to exercise the usufruct in the extent of the co-ownership share (Art. 231 of CPL).
459. Article 232 of CPL. In their mutual relationship, the usufruct is deemed to encumber the co-ownership share corresponding to the extent of the use of the thing to the benefit of the usufructuary. In relations with third persons, however, the immovable is deemed to be encumbered as a whole. A new Art. 239a was inserted into the CPL by its 2020 amendments stating that in case the thing encumbered with an usufruct is divided, each of the new parts is fully encumbered with the usufruct.
460. The CO, however, regulates an exception to this rule in cases of contracts on delivery and distribution of property concluded among owners of such property and their descendants. Art. 551 of the CO provides that during delivery and distribution, the deliverer may reserve for him- or herself, his or her spouse, or any other person the right to usufruct on all or part of the delivered property or claim a lifelong annuity in kind or in cash, lifelong maintenance, or any other compensation. If usufruct or a lifelong annuity is agreed for the deliverer and his or her spouse together, in the event of the death of one of them, the usufruct or lifelong annuity pertains to the other in its entirety until the death of the other, unless agreed otherwise or unless it follows otherwise from the circumstances of the case.
461. Article 233 of CPL.
462. Article 234 of CPL.
463. Article 235 of CPL.
464. Article 236 of CPL.

182. For the duration of the usufruct, the usufructuary must maintain the thing with the diligence of a good manager in accordance with its economic purpose. The usufructuary must bear all the costs of use as well as encumbrances and public contributions regardless of the benefit he or she derives from the usufruct.[465] If the usufructuary fails to fulfil any of these obligations and the substance of the thing is jeopardized, the owner may demand appropriate security from him or her. If the usufructuary fails to provide the owner with such security, the owner may demand the premature expiration of the usufruct. In this case, the usufructuary has the right to compensation for the premature expiration, which is determined by the court, taking into account the condition of the thing and the expected duration of the usufruct.[466]

183. If the thing in usufruct requires *repair exceeding the bounds of ordinary maintenance due to* force majeure *or because it is worn out*, the usufructuary must inform the owner of this without delay.[467] The owner must carry out the repair at his or her own expense (the usufructuary bears the costs of ordinary maintenance only).[468] If the owner does not wish to carry out the repair within a reasonable period, the usufructuary may carry it out at his or her own expense. The reimbursement of these costs may be demanded upon the expiration of the usufruct in accordance with the rules applying to a possessor in good faith.[469]

184. For the duration of the usufruct, the usufructuary must *permit the owner* of the thing to carry out improvements to the thing at his or her own expense. For the period when the usufructuary's right is restricted as a result of the performance of this work, the owner must provide the usufructuary with monetary compensation.[470]

185. Upon the expiration of the usufruct, the usufructuary must *return the thing* to its owner.[471] If it is not possible to return the thing in the condition it maintained at the moment the usufruct was established, the owner may demand compensation for loss as a result of the deterioration. The usufructuary is not liable for deterioration resulting from the normal use of the thing or the force majeure.

465. Article 237/1 of CPL.
466. Article 237/2 of CPL.
467. Article 238 of CPL.
468. According to the CPL, the usufructuary owes interest to the owner on the value of the work carried out in order to return the condition of the thing to what it was when the usufruct was established. The interest falls due for payment at the end of each calendar year and for the last year upon the expiration of the usufruct.
469. Article 95 of CPL.
470. Article 239 of CPL.
471. Article 240 of CPL.

186. If the usufruct was established for a particular period, it *expires* when the time for which the right was established lapses. It always expires upon death or dissolution of the usufructuary.[472] Further, the usufruct expires on the basis of an agreement between the owner and the usufructuary. It also expires when the usufructuary gives notice – that is, a unilateral declaration that he or she is waiving his or her right of usufruct.[473] A usufruct expires also if the thing is destroyed.[474] The owner may also request the expiration of the usufruct if the usufructuary breaches his or her obligations, etc.

187. Consumable things and rights that do not give interest or benefits may also be subject to usufruct (the so-called *non-genuine usufruct, irregular usufruct,* Sl. *nepravi užitek*).[475] In this case, it is considered that the monetary value of a thing or right which upon expiration of the usufruct is returned to the owner was given in usufruct. Where specifically agreed, the usufructuary must return the revalued principal.

188. All claims for compensation arising from the relationship between the owner and the usufructuary are subject to a one-year statute of limitation.[476]

C. Use

189. Use (Sl. *raba*, Lat. *usus*) is a personal easement that gives the right to use the thing of another person in accordance with its economic purpose for the benefit of the holder of the easement in such manner that its substance is preserved.[477] Only non-consumable things may be subject to use.[478] The holder of the right of use may use the thing to the extent set out in the legal title on the basis of which the right of use was established.[479] In contrast to the usufruct, the holder may not transfer the exercise of the use to a third person.

190. Apart from the aforementioned specific provisions on use, the provisions of the CPL on usufruct apply *mutatis mutandis* to the personal easement of use.[480]

---

472. Article 241 of CPL.
473. If the object of the usufruct is an immovable, the usufruct expires with its deletion from the land register.
474. If a new thing or right takes the place of the destroyed thing, then the usufruct is transferred to that thing or right.
475. Article 242 of CPL. Provisions relating to a usufruct apply *mutatis mutandis* to a non-genuine usufruct.
476. Article 243 of CPL.
477. Article 244/1 of CPL.
478. Article 244/2 of CPL.
479. Article 245 of CPL.
480. Article 246 of CPL. For further details, see Keresteš in *CPL with Commentary 2004*, 972–978.

D. Habitation

191. Habitation (Sl. *stanovanje*, Lat. *habitatio*) is a personal easement that gives the right to use the residence or a part thereof of another person for the benefit of the holder of the easement and his or her family in such manner that its substance is preserved.[481] The holder of the right of habitation also has the right to use the common parts of a residential house. In contrast to the usufruct, the exercise of habitation cannot be transferred to a third person. The personal easement of habitation must also not be equated to the obligatory right of lease.[482]

192. As in case of use, in case of habitation, the provisions of the CPL on usufruct apply *mutatis mutandis* regarding those matters that are not specifically regulated in the CPL's chapter on habitation.[483]

IV. Protection of Easements

193. If anyone (be it a third person or the owner of the encumbered property) unjustifiably disturbs the person entitled to a (real or personal) easement in his or her exercise of that easement, the latter may file a suit to request that the obstruction or disturbance cease.[484] Such claim for the protection of the right of easement is called *actio confessoria* (Sl. *konfesorna tožba*) and is equivalent to the *actio negatoria* used for protection of ownership. It is, therefore, not subject to the statute of limitations and can thus be legally enforced without any time limits.[485]

194. A holder of an easement may want to opt for *possessory protection* instead of petitory protection of the easement. As is often the case with owners who rather opt for possessory claim instead of the *rei vindicatio* or *actio negatoria,* which are often characterized as *probatio diabolica*, holders of easements, too, tend to make use of procedurally more attractive alternative – that is, a general possessory claim – and not the *actio confessoria*. However, petitory protection is not always plausible. For example, in cases of negative easements, only petitory protection is available because possession of another's property is not a characteristic of negative easements. Further, it is subject to the statute of limitations – it must be filed for within thirty days of the day on which the possessor learned of the disturbance and

481. Article 247 of CPL. For further details, see Keresteš in *CPL with Commentary 2004*, 979–981; Vrenčur in *CPL with Commentary 2004*, 645–647.
482. For further details, see Vrenčur in *CPL with Commentary 2004*, 646–647.
483. Article 248 of CPL.
484. Article 212 of CPL.
485. Article 99/3 of the CPL *mutatis mutandis*.

of the violator, and no later than one year after the disturbance originated.[486] If prerequisites for *self-help* are met, a holder of an easement may also protect his or her right by making an immediate stand against an unlawful intervention in his or her legal and factual position.[487]

195. A holder of an easement may always request *damages* in case the obstruction or disturbance had induced them.

§2. MORTGAGE

196. A mortgage (Sl. *hipoteka*) is a lien on an immovable.[488] A lien established on immovable property is characterized by many specifics, which upgrade the general regime of the lien.[489]

I. Concept

197. A mortgage is a non-possessory lien on an immovable.[490] It encompasses the immovable as a whole as well as all of its elements and fruits until such time as they are severed from the principal thing. A mortgage also encompasses the appurtenances owned by the mortgagor, while appurtenances of immovable under mortgage which are in ownership of other persons, are not encompassed in the mortgage.[491] According to the principle of speciality, a mortgage cannot be established on a part of an immovable.

198. Mortgage may exist on registered immovables only. On those rare but, to date, existent immovables that are not yet registered in the land register, a non-possessory lien, similar to that on movables, may be established according to the rules of the CESA.[492] CESA provides that the legal transaction on the establishment of a lien on a non-registered immovable must be concluded in the form of a directly enforceable notarial protocol. The lien is established at the moment of the completion of the notarial protocol.[493]

199. Each co-owner may establish a mortgage on his or her ideal share without the consent of the other co-owners, while the contractual establishment of a mortgage on the entire immovable that is the object of the co-ownership requires the

486. Article 32 of CPL.
487. Articles 31 of the CPL and 139 of the CO apply. For further details, see Juhart in *CPL with Commentary 2004*, 876; Vrenčur in *CPL with Commentary 2004*, 188–190. See General Introduction, §3, V.
488. Article 138 of CPL.
489. For details on the lien, see Part V.
490. Article 138 of CPL.
491. Article 140 of CPL.
492. Articles 249–254 of CESA.
493. For further details, see Vrenčur in *CPL with Commentary 2004*, 455.

agreement of all co-owners. If an immovable is jointly owned, a mortgage can only be established on the immovable as a whole.[494]

200. More than one mortgage may be established on the same immovable.[495] An agreement whereby the mortgagor undertakes not to establish any further mortgages on the immovable is null and void.[496] According to the priority principle, the first creditor to have his or her claim protected by a mortgage will have his or her claim fully repaid by the proceeds from the sale of the immovable; the second mortgagor would receive the remaining amount of the purchase money, etc.[497]

201. A mortgage is intended to secure a claim until its final repayment. If a claim is partly repaid, the mortgage is not reduced. On the division of an immovable encumbered with a mortgage, each of the parts of the immovable is encumbered with the mortgage in full. If a mortgage is established on a whole thing in co-ownership, each co-owner may pay the whole debt. Upon payment, the co-owner acquires the secured claim together with the mortgage.[498]

II. Creation of a Mortgage

A. *Contractual Mortgage*

202. The acquisition of a mortgage on the basis of a legal transaction (Sl. *pogodbena hipoteka*) requires an entry in the land register. In addition to the general provisions on lien,[499] the CPL sets down special provisions on the contractual establishment of a mortgage.[500]

203. Registration is performed on the basis of a valid obligatory mortgage contract (Sl. *zastavna pogodba*) and on the basis of a valid document containing the land registry permission.[501] Such document must consist of a designation of the mortgagee and the debtor of the secured claim (as well as the mortgagor, if the mortgagor is not at the same time the debtor of the secured claim), the legal basis, the land registry designation of the immovable on which the mortgage is established, and the amount and due date of the secured claim.

204. If a mortgage serves as security for consumer credit, the rules of the Consumer Credit Act apply.[502] The consumer mortgage credit contract must be concluded in the form of a notarial protocol. If the owner of the immovable is a

494. Article 139 of CPL.
495. Article 147/1 of CPL.
496. Article 147/2 of CPL.
497. Article 147/3,4 of CPL.
498. Article 150 of CPL.
499. Articles 131–133 of CPL. For further details, see Part V.
500. Articles 141–142 of CPL.
501. Article 141 of CPL.
502. Zakon o potrošniških kreditih (ZPotK-2) [Consumer Credit Act], Official Gazette RS, No. 77/16.

consumer, he or she must be present during the conclusion of such contract and must be informed by the notary of the legal consequences of such contract and its security as well as of the legal consequences of non-payment. The owner has to attest that he or she was informed of that by signing the notarial protocol.[503]

B. Notarial Mortgage

205. A proprietary legal transaction on the establishment of a mortgage – that is basically, the land registry permission of the owner of a mortgaged immovable – may be concluded in the form of a directly enforceable notarial protocol in which the mortgagor agrees to secure the claim with the registration of a mortgage on the mortgagor's immovable and agrees that after the claim has fallen due the claim can be repaid from the proceeds from the sale of the immovable, and that the immovable shall be vacated and handed over within one month of the sale.[504] A notarial mortgage (Sl. *notarska hipoteka*) is thus a type of a contractual mortgage, with some specific characteristics deviating from the general rules on contractual mortgages (whereby the mortgagee is deemed to consent to such declaration).

206. The direct enforceability of the notarial protocol is noted in the land register and takes effect against any subsequent acquirer of ownership of the mortgaged immovable. The registration of the mortgage (which is of a constitutive nature) and the noting of the enforceability must be requested by the notary immediately after the transaction is concluded.[505]

C. Coercive Mortgage

207. A coercive mortgage (Sl. *prisilna hipoteka*), such as a mortgage in enforcement proceedings, a mortgage in security proceedings, and a mortgage on the basis of a preliminary measure (pre-notated, preliminary mortgage),[506] is created on the basis of a court decision, upon its entry in the land register.[507] It is, therefore, not established at the moment of finality of the court decision (as is the case with all other property rights established on the basis of a court decision, including liens on movables[508]); registration is of a constitutive effect.

503. Article 51 of the Consumer Credit Act.
504. Article 142/1 of CPL.
505. Article 142/2,3 of CPL.
506. These mortgages are regulated in the CESA. For further details, see Keresteš in *CPL with Commentary 2004*, 643–646.
507. Article 143 of CPL.
508. Article 135 of CPL.

D. Statutory Mortgage

208. A statutory mortgage (Sl. *zakonita hipoteka*) is created the moment the conditions prescribed by law are fulfilled.[509] Its entry into the land register is, therefore, not of a constitutive nature, but can be of importance in case any third person in good faith acquires the immovable or any other right colliding with the statutory mortgage (i.e., according to the principle of trust in the land register).

209. There are few cases of statutory mortgage in Slovenian law. For example, the CPL provides that in cases of division of co-ownership where one of the co-owners obtains full ownership on the thing, the other co-owners have a statutory lien on the thing until the shares of the other co-owners are fully paid off.[510] Another example is a statutory lien of heirs in those cases where one of the heirs requests that some of the descendant's things, which would otherwise fall to another heir's share, be ascribed to him or her due to a special interest he or she has in them – the other heirs have a statutory lien on such things until the payment of their value by the heir to whom the things are ascribed.[511] Further, a statutory mortgage is provided in the interest of the RS according to the construction legislation: the state has a mortgage on all those immovables on which illegal edifices were built as security for the costs incurred and penalties imposed during inspection proceedings. Such statutory mortgage is registered into the land register ex officio.[512]

III. Special Types of Mortgages

A. Joint Mortgage

210. A mortgage can be established on more than one immovable (owned by one or more persons) as security for the same claim. A so-called principal immovable (Sl. *glavna nepremičnina*) is determined for the purposes of registration of joint mortgage (Sl. *skupna hipoteka*) in the land register.[513] A joint mortgage is registered as an encumbrance of the principal immovable as well as of all the other immovables, where also the ID of the principal immovable is stated. Due to registration simplification, entries regarding the joint mortgage are performed in the basic legal status of the principal immovable only, but they apply to all other immovables.

211. The mortgagee may demand repayment of his or her claim from the proceeds of the sale of any of the immovables and may do so in any order regardless

509. Article 144 of CPL.
510. Article 71 of CPL. For further details, see Part I, Ch. 6.
511. Article 147 of IA.
512. Article 79 of the Building Act (Sl. *Gradbeni zakon (GZ)*), Official Gazette RS, No. 61/17.
513. Article 17 of LRA.

of whether an immovable is designated as principal immovable or not, and regardless of whether an immovable is owned by the debtor him- or herself or by another person.[514]

B. Maximum Mortgage

212. A mortgage can also be established by determining a maximum amount up to which an immovable guarantees a secured claim.[515] Such maximum mortgage (Sl. *maksimalna hipoteka*) may secure an individual claim or claims originating in a specific debtor-creditor legal relationship, whose amount is not determined at the moment the mortgage is established. Therefore, data on the debtor-creditor relationship, and not data on the secured claims, are registered in the land register. The mortgagee's right to repayment does not necessarily reach the maximum amount because it depends on the value of the secured claims, which are, at the time of the establishment of the maximum mortgage, not yet determinable. Such value may, at a particular moment, be lower or higher than the maximum amount, or may even not exist.[516] With a maximum mortgage, all the interest and costs of the secured claim are also secured up to the maximum amount.

213. In the case of an assignment of a claim secured with a maximum mortgage, the transfer of the mortgage is excluded. This rule is an exception to the general principle that a mortgage is transferred with the transfer of a secured claim. However, if the whole debtor-creditor relationship is transferred, the maximum mortgage is transferred, too.[517]

214. A maximum mortgage exists as long as the debtor-creditor relationship exists and, in contrast to an ordinary mortgage, does not end with the expiration of a particular claim. A maximum mortgage is accessory to the debtor-creditor relationship from which claims might arise, and not to particular secured claims.[518]

C. Super mortgage

215. A so-called super mortgage (Sl. *nadhipoteka*) is a lien on a claim secured with a mortgage.[519] Because it is a lien on a claim and not a lien on an immovable, it is actually not a mortgage. It is also not a mortgage on a mortgage as would ensue from its denomination. The provisions regulating a lien on a claim, therefore, apply to a super mortgage.[520]

---

514. Article 145 of CPL. For further details, see Keresteš in *CPL with Commentary 2004*, 656–657.
515. Article 146 of CPL.
516. Vrenčur in *CPL with Commentary 2004*, 454.
517. *Ibid*, 453.
518. For further details, see Keresteš in *CPL with Commentary 2004*, 657–664 and 703.
519. Article 149/1 of CPL.
520. Article 149/3 of CPL. Lien on a claim is regulated in Arts 178–186 of the CPL. For further details, see Part V.

216. The mortgagee may establish a super mortgage for the benefit of a third person without the consent of the pledgor.[521] According to Article 179 of the CPL regulating establishment of a lien on a right, a super mortgage is created the moment the debtor of the pledged claim receives notification from the pledgor (i.e., the mortgagee) that the claim (secured by a mortgage) is pledged. A super mortgage is merely notated in the land register.[522] Notation is not a prerequisite for the establishment of a super mortgage.

IV. Relationship between the Mortgagor and Mortgagee before the Secured Claim Falls Due

A. *Transfer of a Mortgage*

217. Unless agreed otherwise, a mortgage is transferred together with the transfer of a secured claim.[523] The transfer of a mortgage takes effect only upon its entry into the land register on the basis of the mortgagee's (i.e., the assignor's) land registry permission.[524]

B. *Devastation Claim*

218. In certain cases, an immovable secured with a mortgage may be sold even before the maturity of the claim. Namely, if, by his or her actions, the mortgagor reduces the value of a mortgaged immovable or in some other way worsens its state, the mortgagee may ask the court (by filing the so-called devastation claim, Sl. *devastacijska tožba*) to instruct the mortgagor to cease such actions. If the mortgagor fails to do so, the mortgagee may request compulsory enforcement of the claim secured with the mortgage even before the claim falls due.[525]

C. *Prohibition of Antichresis*

219. An agreement on antichresis (Lat. *pactum antichreticum*) – that is, an agreement by which a mortgagee reserves him- or herself the right to collect the fruits of the mortgaged immovable or to exploit the immovable in some other way – is null and void.[526] Legal theory explains that such possibility would contradict the very purpose and nature of a mortgage. The latter is a non-possessory security,

521. Article 149/2 of CPL.
522. Article 63/2 of LRA.
523. Article 148 of CPL. See special regulation of effects of transferring claims in cases of maximum mortgage.
524. For further details, see Vrenčur in *CPL with Commentary 2004*, 442–443.
525. Article 151 of CPL. To obtain an enforcement title, the mortgagee must file the so-called *actio hypothecaria*.
526. Article 152 of CPL.

enabling the mortgagor to possess and enjoy his or her immovable during the relationship with his or her creditor. As is often the case with non-possessory liens on movables, the fact that the pledged thing remains in possession of the pledgor is usually of his or her great interest.

D. Disposal with the Mortgaged Immovable

220. The mortgagor and the mortgagee may agree that the mortgagor is prohibited from disposing of his or her immovable. Generally, however, such prohibition produces relative effects only. Disposition with the immovable in breach of an agreement is thus generally valid. The prohibition can induce absolute effect only by its registration in the land register. According to the CPL, however, only prohibitions agreed among parties to a contract of a lifelong maintenance,[527] and those agreed among spouses or civil partners, as well as among parents/adopters and children/adoptees,[528] may be registered. In other cases – for example, agreements prohibiting disposal concluded between a bank as a creditor and the owner of the mortgaged immovable – prohibitions are not registered and thus provide relative effects only.[529]

E. Establishing Further Mortgages

221. An agreement under which the mortgagor is precluded from establishing any further mortgages on the immovable is null and void.[530]

V. Repayment from a Mortgage

222. If the debtor fails to pay a debt within the deadline, the creditor may *request in court that the mortgaged immovable be sold* (the so-called *actio hypothecaria*, Sl. *hipotekarna tožba*).[531] The creditor thereby requests the mortgagor to acknowledge that the creditor is authorized to demand payment of his or her claim from the mortgaged immovable and to allow repayment from the mortgaged immovable in enforcement proceedings.[532] On the basis of a final judgment issued upon *actio hypothecaria*, the creditor may start enforcement proceedings.[533]

527. Articles 557–563 of CO.
528. Article 38 of CPL.
529. An exception to this rule is set down in the Zakon o varstvu kupcev stanovanj in enostanovanjskih stavb (ZVKSES) [Protection of Buyers of Apartments and Single Occupancy Buildings Act], Official Gazette RS, No. 18/04, which provides that a prohibition of disposal burdening the seller of apartments is registered in the land register in the interest of the tutelary notary.
530. Article 147/2 of CPL.
531. Article 153/1 of CPL.
532. In case an immovable was mortgaged by the debtor him- or herself, the creditor may request that the court order payment of the secured claim. In this case, the creditor obtains a general title, which provides that he or she is repaid from any of the debtor's property (as a non-privileged creditor

223. If, however, the mortgage was created on the basis of a directly enforceable notarial protocol (the so-called notarial mortgage),[534] the creditor *need not file the actio hypothecaria*. He or she may demand that the notary establish that the claim has matured, sell the pledged immovable, and repay the creditors or start enforcement proceedings.[535]

224. The immovable is usually sold at a public auction. The parties may also agree on a direct sale. These proceedings are regulated in the CESA.[536] After the public auction is finished, or after the direct sales contract is concluded, the court issues a decision on the attachment of the immovable. After such decision is final and the purchase price is paid, the court issues a decision on the delivery of the immovable to the buyer, and on his or her registration as the owner of the immovable in the land register. The buyer acquires ownership the moment such decision is final; registration of his or her right is thus of a mere declaratory nature.[537]

225. Although acquisition of ownership is, in such cases, original and not derivative, the buyer does not acquire ownership on the immovable free of all encumbrances (the so-called deletion principle versus takeover principle in enforcement proceedings). Real easements remain as encumbrances of the immovable regardless of the time they were established, while personal easements, rights of encumbrance, and rights of superficies that were registered after the mortgagee's rights generally cease to exist, leaving their holders with a right to compensation.[538] Further, the buyer of an immovable may – giving a notice period of one month, and regardless of the statutory or contractual cancellation deadlines – cancel in writing a contract on the use of the immovable (in particular a tenancy or lease contract) concluded after the establishment of the mortgage.[539] The fate of rights of preemption and repurchase is regulated in the CO and the CESA.[540]

VI. Expiration of a Mortgage

226. A mortgage expires *by deletion from the land register*.[541] The deletion of a mortgage may be demanded:

---

though), and not only from the mortgaged immovable. Such cannot be claimed if the mortgagor and debtor are not the same person. For further details, see Vrenčur in *CPL with Commentary 2004*, 444–445; Tratnik in *CPL with Commentary 2016*, 836–838.

533. Article 153/2 of CPL. For further details, see Vrenčur in *CPL with Commentary 2004*, 444–448; Tratnik in *CPL with Commentary 2016*, 835–836, 838–845.
534. See Part I, Ch. 4, §2, II, B.
535. For further details, see Tratnik in *CPL with Commentary 2016*, 838–839.
536. Articles 166–211 of CESA.
537. For further details, see Tratnik in *CPL with Commentary 2016*, 838–841.
538. See Arts 173–175 of the CESA. For further details, see Tratnik in *CPL with Commentary 2016*, 841–845.
539. Article 153/3 of CPL.
540. See Art. 510 of the CO and Art. 182 of the CESA.
541. Article 154 of CPL, Art. 175 of CESA.

- if the debtor pays off the claim which is secured with the mortgage;
- if the claim secured with the mortgage ceases to exist;
- if the mortgagee renounces the mortgage;
- if the same person becomes the owner of the immovable and the holder of the mortgage on this immovable;
- if the mortgage ceases to exist by lapse of time, that is, ten years from the day on which the secured claim fell due; and
- if the pledged property is sold for repayment of the secured claim.

227. If, under any title whatsoever, an owner of an immovable encumbered with a mortgage receives some other immovable in compensation (as in cases of rounding off, commassation, and expropriation), the mortgage transfers (*ex lege*) to such immovable.

§3. Land Debt

I. Concept

228. The right of a land debt (Sl. *zemljiški dolg*, Ger. *Grundschuld*) is *a new property right*, which was unknown to Slovenian law prior to the CPL. In addition to the right of superficies, it represents one of the most important novelties of the new Slovenian property law system. The legislature decided to regulate it after it proved successful in Germany as an alternative to mortgage. Provisions on land debt were set out in Articles 192–200 (Chapter VII) of the CPL, following mostly the German and Swiss model of land-debt regulation. Because a land debt is an instrument, similar to a mortgage, the CPL stated that unless provided otherwise by the CPL, provisions on mortgages apply *mutatis mutandis*.[542]

229. The institute of land debt, however, ceased to exist in Slovenian legislation in 2013 when the whole chapter of the CPL on land debt was repealed after it was claimed to be abused by the businessmen facing criminal charges and damages claims in order to safeguard their property from enforcement and/or confiscation. In the last couple of years before land debt was repealed from Slovenian property law, an extensive amount of land debts were established, in particular by such businessmen who had supposedly established them solely for the purpose of safeguarding their property from their creditors. By establishing land debts, they were convinced that the creditors could not take hold of their property as the property was in the first place encumbered with the land debt (in favour of the owner him- or herself, or in favour of someone else in possession of the land letter) meaning that any later security of the creditors on the immovable would take a second place in the priority

542. Article 193 of CPL. These are, for example, provisions on the establishment of a mortgage on immovables in joint ownership or in co-ownership, and on its ideal share (Art. 139 of the CPL); provision on the prohibition of lex commissoria (Art. 132 of CPL); provisions on the indivisibility of mortgage (Art. 150 of CPL); etc. For further details, see Keresteš in *CPL with Commentary 2004*, 803–805.

order and would thus be of no value (land debts were usually established for a very high amount exceeding the value of the encumbered immovable). In some of these cases, the claims secured by the land debt did not even exist or were fictitiously agreed upon. Under heavy media and political criticism, the instrument of land debt was erased from the CPL with effect as of 6 November 2013. Land debts which were registered or at least successfully applied for incorporation before that (i.e., between 1 January 2003 and 5 November 2013) are, however, still valid, whereby Articles 108/2, 110/2, 111 of the CPL (regulating some aspects of mortgage) and Articles 192–200 of the pre-amended CPL (i.e., the repealed chapter on land debt) continue to apply to them. In view of property law professors and practising lawyers, existent or, if needed, novel measures against the abuse of land debt could have been applied (e.g., the *actio Pauliana*) instead of simply erasing it from Slovenian property law even before one single proceedings aiming at claiming and proving the abuse were initiated. The removal of the right of land debt from Slovenian property law also defamed all those land debts which were established legally without any intentions of circumventing the creditors, and prevented further use of land debt in the cases where its particularities were advantageous to those of the mortgage. Even the fact that the creditor of the claim secured by land debt was not evidenced in the land register, was sometimes of enough importance for the parties to choose land debt over mortgage. The already established land debts, which were the reason for the CPL amendment, however, still exist. In order to safeguard the interest of the creditors of the owners who had established land debts on their immovable, the Slovenian legislator decided in 2014 to regulate enforcement of such creditors' claims by inserting new articles in the CESA.[543] According to the new Article 172a of the ECSSA, the court in enforcement proceedings must (at the latest by issuing an order on the establishment of the value of the immovable) publish on the notice board of the court and on the website of the court an announcement with summons to the holder of the land letter to inform the court of his or her ID and to submit to the court the original land letter in three months after the announcement has been published. The announcement is ex officio notated in the land register. If the holder does not do that, it is presumed that the owner of the immovable who established the land letter and was the first holder of the land letter, is the current holder of the land letter, unless proved otherwise at the latest at the hearing for distribution. If the owner of the immovable is held the holder of the land letter, the land letter will not have priority over security of the creditors and will not be able to safeguard the property of the owner who established the land debt and did not transfer it to his or her creditor.

230. A land debt is a right to demand repayment of a specified money sum from the value of an immovable prior to other creditors with an inferior ranking.[544] In its substance and purpose, a land debt is similar to a mortgage, but it differs significantly: land debt is not dependent on the existence of the secured claim; it was

543. Zakon o spremembah in dopolnitvah Zakona o izvršbi in zavarovanju (ZIZ-J) [Act Amending the Enforcement and Securing of Civil Claims Act], Official Gazette RS, No. 53/14.
544. Article 192 of CPL.

established and it exists regardless of the secured claim and is thus more flexible than a mortgage.[545] Further, a land debt can serve several purposes, and not only to secure claims.[546]

II. Creation of a Land Debt

231. A land debt could be established by the owner of the immovable (the so-called *proprietary land debt*). It could also be established by a mortgagee who, in agreement with the owner of the encumbered immovable, converted his or her already existent mortgage into one or more land debts (the so-called *non-proprietary land debt*). In such cases, the encumbrance of an immovable under land debts could not exceed the encumbrance under the mortgage. The conversion did not require the consent of other holders of the land debt or mortgage having the same or subsequent ranking.

232. A land debt could be created on the basis of a legal transaction only. No statutory or public authority decision-based land debts could be established. It could only be created upon entry in the land register and upon issuing of a land letter on the basis of a valid unilateral legal transaction.[547]

233. A unilateral legal transaction on the establishment of a land debt (issued by the owner of the immovable or by the mortgagee transforming his or her mortgage into a land debt[548]) had to be in the form of a notarial protocol, which had to contain the name of the founder, the land register designation of the encumbered immovable, and the amount and conditions attaching to the maturity of the land-debt sum.[549] Such unilateral legal transaction represented a real agreement, while a fiduciary (most often security) contract between the owner of the immovable and his or her creditor, in whose interest the land debt is actually established, was most often the underlying obligatory agreement.

---

545. The CPL, therefore, states that the payment of a land debt must not be bound by a condition (such that the payment would be accessory to the secured claim). For further details, see Kercsteš in *CPL with Commentary 2004*, 802–803.
546. Theory differentiates the so-called security land debt from the so-called isolated land debt. Vrenčur in *Property Law*, 511.
547. Article 194 of CPL.
548. In case of a non-proprietorial land debt, the consent of the owner of the immovable to the conversion of a mortgage into a land debt must be in a written declaration added to the unilateral real transaction (in case of a super mortgage, consent of the holder of the super mortgage is required, too). The owner's signature on the declaration must be attested by the notary. Vrenčur in *Property Law*, 514–515.
549. Article 195 of CPL. The amount of a land debt is fixed nominally and in any currency. It is written in the land register and in the land letter and is unalterable. Land debt does not bear interest and must, therefore, be fixed in the amount that covers the interests of the secured claim besides the principal. Vrenčur in *Property Law*, 516.

234. Registration of a land debt is regulated in the LRA[550] as well as in the Rules on Land Letter.[551] Provisions on registration of a maximum mortgage apply unless special provisions on the registration of a land debt exist. A land debt was registered on request of an owner of an immovable who wished to encumber his or her immovable with a land debt, or on request of a mortgagee who wished to alter his or her mortgage into a land debt, and it is registered in the interest of a holder of a land letter. A land debt is registered as a limited property right existing on the encumbered immovable. In contrast to other limited property rights that – if they are established on the basis of a legal transaction – are created at the moment they are registered in the land register, creation of a land debt required a further prerequisite – that is, the issuing of the so-called land letter.

235. A land letter (Sl. *zemljiško pismo*) was issued to the founder of the land debt by the court that keeps the land register for the encumbered immovable after the land debt had been entered in the register.[552] A land letter is a negotiable instrument payable to order.[553] The CPL provides that it must contain the name of the court that issued it, all the details the unilateral act on the establishment of a land debt must contain, the time of issuing the land letter, and the stamp of the court issuing it. The founder is deemed to be the first holder of the land letter. A land debt can be deleted only upon submission of the land letter to the land registry. Further details on the types, substance, form, and invalidation of a land letter, as well as the procedure of registration of a land debt and the procedure of issuing a land letter and keeping records of it, are regulated in the LRA and in the aforementioned Rules on Land Letter.

III. Disposal of a Land Debt

236. A land debt is transferred out-of-register together with the land letter.[554] In contrast to a mortgage, the entry in the land register is not required. The Slovenian legislature has thus opted for the so-called letter land debt and not for the so-called registry land debt.[555] The land letter is transferred by endorsement, which represents a real agreement, and by delivery of the paper.[556]

550. Articles 20 and 44 of LRA.
551. Pravilnik o zemljiškem pismu [Rules on Land Letter], Official Gazette RS, No. 15/03, with further amendments.
552. Article 196 of CPL. To be precise, a land letter was issued only after the decision on the entry of a land debt into the land register was final. Vrenčur in *Property Law*, 516–517.
553. In this respect, provisions of the CO on negotiable instruments apply.
554. Article 197 of CPL.
555. Vrenčur in *Property Law*, 515.
556. For further details, see Keresteš in *CPL with Commentary 2004*, 820–824; Vrenčur, *Moderne oblike zavarovanja plačil* [Modern Methods of Securing Payments], 297–302 (GV Založba 2005).

237. A land debt is *independently pledgeable.*[557] Rules on placing negotiable instruments payable to order under a pledge apply. A land letter, and thereby a land debt, is pledged by the pledge endorsement.[558]

IV. Payment of a Land Debt

238. The owner of an encumbered immovable must pay the land debt on maturity to the *entitled holder of the land letter.*[559] The entitled holder of the land letter is the one having the letter in his or her possession and demonstrating a continuous chain of endorsements.[560]

239. A land letter is *an enforceable title.*[561] If the owner of the encumbered immovable does not pay the land debt, the creditor may request for enforcement according to the CESA.[562]

V. Expiration of a Land Debt

240. A land debt expires *upon its deletion from the land register,* which can be performed *upon submission of the land letter.*[563] Apart from allowing the deletion of the land debt, the land registry also decides on the invalidation of the land letter. Once the decision on the deletion and invalidation is final, the registry marks the letter as 'invalidated' and files it in the land registry collection of documents.[564]

241. Because land debt is not an accessory to the claim secured by it, payment of the claim itself does not affect the land debt directly. However, the owner of the encumbered immovable usually has the right, deriving from the underlying obligatory contract, to request retransfer of the land debt. However, once the owner of the immovable takes hold of the land letter, he or she may request the deletion of the land debt from the land register. The owner may also keep the land letter in order to employ it for any future securitization of loans.[565]

---

557. Article 198 of CPL.
558. For further details, see Keresteš in *CPL with Commentary 2004*, 824–825.
559. Article 199 of CPL. To avoid causing damage to the creditors, the CPL prevents the owner of an encumbered immovable from demanding payment of the land debt. For further details, see Keresteš in *CPL with Commentary 2004*, 826–827; Vrenčur, *Moderne oblike zavarovanja plačil* [Modern Methods of Securing Payments], 306 (GV Založba 2005).
560. Vrenčur in *Property Law*, 519.
561. Article 199/2 of CPL.
562. For further details, see Vrenčur in *Property Law*, 519.
563. Article 200 of CPL.
564. Keresteš in *CPL with Commentary 2004*, 832.
565. Vrenčur in *Property Law*, 520.

242. If an immovable is sold in enforcement proceedings, the land debt ceases to exist, unless agreed otherwise, the moment the decision on the delivery of the immovable to its buyer becomes final.[566]

§4. SUPERFICIES

I. Concept

243. Before the CPL entered into force in 2003, Slovenian law did not regulate the right of superficies (Sl. *stavbna pravica*). However, once the principle of *superficies solo cedit* was reintroduced in Slovenian legal system, the right of superficies could be introduced as an exception to this rule. In Yugoslavia in the period of the social property, a similar, but conceptually entirely different 'right to use the social property' (Sl. *pravica uporabe stvari v družbeni lastnini*) was the means to own edifices on someone else's immovable. It enabled citizens and private entities to own edifices on the land in social property on which they had the so-called right to use the social property that was inseparably linked and transferred with the ownership on the edifice. Although social property was abolished after Slovenia's independence in 1991, the principle of *superficies solo cedit* was not formally introduced until 2003.[567]

244. The CPL does not limit the possibility to establish the right of superficies to any particular person or group of persons. Every person who owns an immovable may encumber it with the right of superficies. And every person may become the holder of the right of superficies. As the latter is also the owner of the fictitious immovable and the building, rules restricting foreigners to acquire ownership on Slovenian land[568] are applicable as ensues from Article 5 of the Reciprocity Act[569] stating that 'reciprocity is to be established also in cases of acquiring the right of superficies on an immovable' . The Slovenian legislator obviously equates the right of superficies with ownership of the land although in the case of superficies, ownership of the real immovable is not transferred to a foreigner who is merely an owner of the fictitious immovable and the building being its part; as the real immovable, i.e., the plot of land, remains in the ownership of a person who obviously may own land in Slovenia, and as superficies is by its definition limited in time (nota bene: as of 2020, superficies may be established also for an unlimited period), interpretation in favour of the possibility to obtain superficies without restrictions might as well be plausible. Taking into account that in cases of superficies the owner is usually left with the bare ownership while the holder of the right of superficies acts as if he or she was the owner, the existent legislative solution is, however, not that unreasonable. If this was the ratio behind such solution, it should be noted that the usufructuary, for example, is in a similar position but may nevertheless acquire the

566. Vrenčur in *Property Law*, 520.
567. For further details, see Vlahek in *CPL with Commentary 2004*, 1011–1014.
568. See Part I, Ch. 3.
569. Zakon o ugotavljanju vzajemnosti (ZUVza-1) [Reciprocity Act], Official Gazette RS, No. 27/17.

easement. It is true, however, that the usufructuary is not the owner of the building which is obviously in the focus of the legislator irrespective of the legal status of the encumbered immovable.

245. In Slovenia, the right of superficies is employed mostly by the municipalities and the state on the immovables which are of importance to them and are therefore not willing to sell them, but are willing to put them in use in favour of the public interest as well as to gain additional financial sources.[570] It is beneficial also for the cases where complex buildings of several individual interests aimed at establishing separate ownership on each of the buildings (or their parts) planned to be built on one immovable (e.g., shopping malls with parking garages beneath them). Apart from the CPL, the right of superficies is regulated also in the Public-Private Partnership Act that sets out some specific rules on superficies derogating those of the CPL.[571] The CPL defines the right of superficies as the right to own a building on, above, or beneath an immovable of another person.[572] Because the land is owned by one person and a building on it by another person, *the right of superficies deviates from the principle of superficies solo cedit*, according to which a building is considered to be an element of the land and thereby in ownership of the person owning the land. The right of superficies *also deviates from the principle of speciality*, according to which only an individually defined independent thing can be the object of property rights: because a building is an element of the land on which it is built, it is not an independent thing. In cases of right of superficies, however, a building is an independent object of ownership. To minimize such deviation from the principles of *superficies solo cedit* and speciality, the Slovenian theory (following German and Austrian legislation and theory) deems the building to be an element of the right of superficies, which is equated to a fictitious immovable (Ger. *juristisches Grundstück* as opposed to the real, physically existent immovable – Ger. *natürliches Grundstück*).[573] Both the building and the right of superficies are treated as separate immovables for the purposes of registration in the land register.[574]

246. A right of superficies can mathematically be described as the ownership of a building plus the more or less extensive right to use and enjoy the land on which

570. An analysis of some of these cases is provided in Vlahek, *Stavbna pravica – sedem let po njeni uveljavitvi* [The Right of Superficies – Seven Years of its Regulation], in Pravni letopis 2010, Ljubljana, pp. 165 ff., 173–176, 180–185. See also Zidar Sambolec, *Stavbna pravica in posebnosti njene ureditve ter uporabe v javnem sektorju* [The Right of Superficies - Special Features of Regulation and Use in the Public Sector], Master Thesis, University of Ljubljana, 2016.

571. Zakon o javno-zasebnem partnerstvu (ZJZP) [Public-Private Partnership Act], Official Gazette RS, No. 127/06.

572. Article 256/1 of CPL. According to High Court in Koper, the right of superficies may, according to Slovenian law, not be established in favour of the owner of the encumbered land (Decision No. CDn 376/2012 of 9 Oct. 2012). Referring to definition of the right of superficies set out in the CPL, the court states that the owner of the land and the holder of the right of superficies must be different persons. Legal theory and business practice favour the opposite interpretation.

573. For further details, see Vlahek in *CPL with Commentary 2004*, 1014–1015; Vlahek, *Stavbna pravica – sedem let po njeni uveljavitvi* [The Right of Superficies – Seven Years of its Regulation], in Pravni letopis 2010, Ljubljana, pp. 165 ff., 166–167.

574. Article 11 of LRA.

such building is located for the duration of the right of superficies. A right of superficies is, in substance, somewhat similar to easements because holders of both rights are entitled to use and enjoy someone else's immovable. However, in case of the right of superficies, the holder of the right becomes an owner of the building, while in case of easements, ownership remains with the owner of the immovable. The right of superficies should also not be misidentified for lease which is a relationship based on an obligatory lease contract producing mere obligations for the parties, not property rights. As in case of easements, in case of lease, too, ownership of the building is not transferred.

247. The CPL does not define the term 'edifice' being of the basic elements of the right of superficies and the purpose of its establishment. Referral to Slovenian legislation on construction defining edifices, buildings, etc., or to comparative law may thus be helpful.[575] An edifice built on an immovable encumbered with a right of superficies may be split up into divided co-ownership, provided the conditions for forming the divided co-ownership are fulfilled. In this case, the owners of individual parts who are also co-owners of the common parts of the building have a right to use the land in accordance with their ideal shares.[576]

248. Because a right of superficies is an exception to the rule of *superficies solo cedit*, the initial regulation set out in the CPL limited its existence to the maximum of *ninety-nine years*.[577] Within this limit, the duration of the right of superficies was left to the parties to determine. However, the parties could always establish anew a right of superficies with the same substance and thereby de facto prolong the duration of the superficies.[578] The CPL 2020 amendment, however, enables the parties to establish a superficies for an indefinite period.

249. A right of superficies is transferable. The provisions applying to the transfer of title to immovables apply *mutatis mutandis* to the transfer of a right of superficies.[579] Parties to the contract on establishment of the right of superficies sometimes agree on the owner's right on prohibition of encumbrance and disposal of the right of superficies by its holder. Unless registered in the land register (only in exceptional cases listed in Article 38 of the CPL) such right has mere *inter partes* effects.[580]

575. For further details on the definition of edifice within the superficies regime, see Vlahek, *Stavbna pravica – sedem let po njeni uveljavitvi* [The Right of Superficies – Seven Years of its Regulation], in Pravni letopis 2010, Ljubljana, pp. 165 ff., 167–170.
576. Article 258 of CPL.
577. Article 256/2 of CPL.
578. Vlahek in *CPL with Commentary 2004*, 1022–1024; Vlahek, *Stavbna pravica – sedem let po njeni uveljavitvi* [The Right of Superficies – Seven Years of its Regulation], in Pravni letopis 2010, Ljubljana, pp. 165 ff., 171–172.
579. Article 256/3 of CPL.
580. See Vlahek, *Stavbna pravica – sedem let po njeni uveljavitvi* [The Right of Superficies – Seven Years of its Regulation], in Pravni letopis 2010, Ljubljana, pp. 165 ff., 176.

II. Establishment of the Right of Superficies

250. The right of superficies can be established *on the basis of a legal transaction.* In addition to a valid legal transaction from which the obligation to establish a right of superficies derives, the creation of a right of superficies also requires the land registry permission and an entry in the land register.[581]

251. A contract on the establishment of a right of superficies (Sl. *pogodba o ustanovitvi stavbne pravice*) must contain the name of the owner of the immovable, the land register designation of the immovable, a precise description of the right of superficies,[582] the duration of the right of superficies, and the compensation the holder of the right of superficies must pay to the owner of the immovable if so agreed.[583] The contract must not contain any resolutory conditions,[584] except in cases of public-private partnership where the duration of superficies may be conditioned upon the existence of the partnership.[585]

252. Before the LRA was amended in 2011, the right of superficies was registered in a special land registry sheet (the so-called *sheet for registration of superficies*, Sl. *vložek za vpis stavbne pravice*) where the holder of the right was registered and the immovable encumbered with the superficies (which was registered in a separate sheet) was indicated. If an edifice was built on the immovable encumbered with a superficies, the edifice was also registered in the sheet for the registration of superficies. After the LRA amendment of 2011, the right of superficies is – similarly to the previous system – deemed an immovable for the purposes of registration meaning that the right of superficies is registered separately as an immovable.[586] In the land registry statement of the encumbered immovable, the right of superficies is registered as a limited property right. The ID sign of the right

581. The LRA requires that the date of expiry of every limited property right, which is established for a specified time, is registered in the land register. Despite that, the courts often register only the time for which the right is established, not the exact date of its expiry what might cause difficulties in establishing the exact date of expiry as sometimes the contracts on the basis of which the right of superficies is established, are concluded some time before the registration takes place. According to the rule that the right of superficies is established only at its registration, the contracted period should probably start running from the date of registration. See Vlahek, *Stavbna pravica – sedem let po njeni uveljavitvi* [The Right of Superficies – Seven Years of its Regulation], in Pravni letopis 2010, Ljubljana, pp. 165 ff., 171–173, 181–184.
582. Article 259 of the CPL additionally provides that an agreement on the manner of use and maintenance of the land surface above the building must be part of the contract if the right of superficies relates to a building beneath an immovable. Even if such provision was lacking, the determination of the manner of use and maintenance of the land surface above the building would ensue from the general requirements for the substance of the contract on the establishment of a right of superficies. For further details as to the description of the substance of the right of superficies, see Vlahek, *Stavbna pravica – sedem let po njeni uveljavitvi* [The Right of Superficies – Seven Years of its Regulation], in Pravni letopis 2010, Ljubljana, pp. 165 ff., 184–185.
583. For further details as to compensation, see Vlahek, *Stavbna pravica – sedem let po njeni uveljavitvi* [The Right of Superficies – Seven Years of its Regulation], in Pravni letopis 2010, Ljubljana, pp. 165 ff., 172–173.
584. Article 257 of CPL.
585. Article 73/2 of the Public-Private Partnership Act.
586. Articles 11 and 20.a of LRA.

of superficies, its substance,[587] its duration, and the holder of the right of superficies are stated therein. In the land registry statement of the encumbered immovable, the holder of the limited property right encumbering the immovable, i.e., the holder of the right of superficies, is not stated by name, but abstractly as follows: 'every owner of the immovable: right of superficies No. X cadastre municipality Y', while the exact current holder of the right of superficies, i.e., the owner of the immovable called 'the right of superficies' (who is at the same time the owner of the building if it exists) is evident only from the land registry statement of the right of superficies. If a building is built on the basis of the right of superficies, the holder may request that the building is registered as well, whereby the right of superficies is registered as the building's basic legal status; such registration has the effect of an incorporation of ownership in favour of every holder of the right of superficies.

253. Encumbrances of the right of superficies (most often a mortgage) are also registered in the land registry statement of the right of superficies.[588] General rules on registration of divided co-ownership apply *mutatis mutandis* should the edifice as part of the superficies be in divided co-ownership. There is, however, an exceptional legal situation in which *superficies arises by law*, and not on the basis of a legal transaction. If, in accordance with the regulations on social property the land and the building on the land were subject to two different 'rights of use' which were later transformed into two different ownerships[589] (one on the land, the other on the building built on this land) which existed up until the day the CPL entered into force, the building became an element of the immovable if the owner of the land and of the building were one and the same person. If, in such cases, the owner was not the same, the building became an element of the immovable on the day the CPL entered into force, and the owner of the building acquired a right of superficies on the immovable that lasts as long as the building stands (thereby deviating from the general rule that the right of superficies may not last more than ninety-nine years). The owner of the immovable and the holder of the right of superficies were obliged to regulate their mutual relations with a contract within three years from the entry into force of the CPL – that is, until 1 January 2006. If such an agreement is not reached, each of the owners may request that the content of the agreement be determined by the court in a non-contentious civil procedure. In determining the content, the court must take into account the circumstances in which the building was

587. For further details on registration of the substance in the land register, see Vlahek, *Stavbna pravica – sedem let po njeni uveljavitvi* [The Right of Superficies – Seven Years of its Regulation], in Pravni letopis 2010, Ljubljana, pp. 165 ff., 184–185.

588. The 2020 CPL amendment added that in case the immovable encumbered with a right of superficies is divided into smaller immovables, the right of superficies ceases to exist on those newly established immovables that were not in fact encumbered with the superficies.

589. The transformation was enacted by the Zakon o lastninjenju nepremičnin v družbeni lastnini (ZLNDL) [Privatization of Real Estate in Social Ownership Act], Official Gazette RS, No. 44/97, with further amendments. With regard to some types of immovables, special legislation on transformation of ownership from social to private was enacted.

erected and past relationships between the owners. In setting compensation, the court must take account of the provisions of the law regulating expropriation.[590]

254. Although the CPL does not expressly provide for such establishment, part of Slovenian legal theory is of the opinion that a right of superficies may also be established by way of acquisitive prescription.[591] The theory probably bases it upon the provisions on acquisitive prescription of ownership. In opting for allowing such establishment of the right of superficies, the authors focus on tabular acquisitive prescription – as Slovenian courts have acknowledged contratabular acquisitive prescription of ownership on immovables, contratabular acquisitive prescription of superficies should also be acknowledged. It is not entirely clear what effects the acquisitive prescription would have in terms of the period for which superficies was established. As with many other issues regarding superficies, which are not regulated in the CPL, this, too, will have to be addressed by the courts. So far, the courts have not accepted such interpretation.[592]

255. Another exception to the general rule providing that the right of superficies is established on the basis of a legal transaction is establishment of a *right of superficies as a special right of use of a particular property in public domain.*[593] Provided this does not interfere with the general use of property in the public domain, an administrative decision may be issued on the establishment of a right of superficies as a special right of use of a property in public domain. According to the LRA, every special right of use of an immovable in public domain is registered in the land register.[594]

III. Expiration of the Right of Superficies

256. There are *three manners* in which the right of superficies can expire. It regularly expires at the moment it is deleted from the land register due to the *expiry*

---

590. Article 271 of CPL. For further details, see Vlahek, *Stavbna pravica – sedem let po njeni uveljavitvi* [The Right of Superficies – Seven Years of its Regulation], n Pravni letopis 2010, Ljubljana, pp. 165 ff., 177–179. See, for example, the following decisions finding mostly that prerequisites for applying Art. 271 of the CPL are not met: Supreme Court of RS, No. II Ips 186/2011 of 22 May 2014; High Court in Ljubljana, No. I Cp 1864/2004 of 15 Jun. 2005; High Court in Koper, No. I Cp 683/2006 of 6 Sep. 2006; High Court in Ljubljana, No. I Cp 2383/2008 of 20 Aug. 2008; High Court in Ljubljana, No. I Cpg 1147/2007 of 10 Sep. 2008; Supreme Court of RS, No. II Ips 259/2006 of 9 Oct. 2008; High Court in Ljubljana, No. II Cp 3724/2008 of 25 Feb. 2009; High Court in Ljubljana, No. I Cp 4738/2008 of 4 Mar. 2009; High Court in Ljubljana, No. II Cp 4334/2009 of 5 May 2010; High Court in Ljubljana, No. VSL II Cp 145/2015 of 18 Mar. 2015.
591. Juhart in *Property Law*, 667. Tratnik in Tratnik et al., *Stavbna pravica in služnosti* [The Right of Superficies and Easements], 19 (Inštitut za nepremičninsko pravo Maribor 2007).
592. See, for example, the following Judgments: High Court in Ljubljana, No. I Cp 2970/2009 of 6 Jan. 2010; High Court in Celje, No. Cp 1014/2007 of 14 Feb. 2008; High Court in Ljubljana, No. I Cp 167/2009 of 10 Jun. 2009.
593. Article 265 of CPL. See also Art. 19 of the CPL, and Art. 70 of the Constitution of the RS.
594. Article 13/2 of LRA. The fact that an immovable is in public domain is noted in the land register (Art. 111 of LRA).

of the time for which it was established.[595] The owner of the land (or the holder of the right of superficies) is to require deletion and thereby attain desistance of superficies.

257. Further, a right of superficies might cease to exist prematurely *on the basis of a legal transaction* with which the owner of the immovable and the holder of the right of superficies agree on the expiration. The provisions of the CPL regulating the creation of a right of superficies apply *mutatis mutandis* to the contract on expiration. However, if the right of superficies was mortgaged, a written declaration from the creditor confirming that he or she consents to the expiration is required in order for the contract to be valid.[596] The rationale behind such requirement is to avoid the decrease in the value of the creditor's security. Namely, upon expiration of the superficies, the creditor's security transforms from the right of superficies to the compensation the previous holder of the right of superficies has against the owner of the immovable (which can be of lesser value than the value of the superficies).

258. Finally, a right of superficies might expire prematurely due to a *violation by its holder*. Namely, the owner of an immovable may require that a right of superficies expire if the holder of the right of superficies does not pay the compensation[597] or if he or she exercises the right of superficies in excess of the agreed extent. The holder of the right, on the contrary, may not request premature expiration if the owner is the one in breach. Upon such expiration of the right of superficies, the court must set appropriate compensation, which the owner of the immovable must pay to the holder of the right of superficies.[598] In contrast to other methods of expiration, where the agreed compensation to the holder of the right of superficies upon expiration may, unless provided otherwise by the law, not be less than half of the increase in the market value of the immovable, the court may, in cases of premature expiration due to a violation, set appropriate compensation regardless of the increase in the market value of the immovable.

259. The CPL lists only these three types of expiry of the right of superficies. It does not enable expiry on other grounds, available in comparative law, for example, if superficies would not be exercised for a specific period of time. Some other rules the application of which would result in expiration of superficies, such as rules on expropriation, are also of relevance.

595. Article 260 of CPL. According to Art. 21 of the LRA, date of expiry of a right must be registered in the land register in all those cases where rights are limited in time.
596. Article 261 of CPL.
597. It is not clear how many non-payments suffice for requesting premature expiration.
598. Article 262 of CPL.

IV. Consequences of Expiration

260. The basic consequence of the expiration of the right of superficies is that *the building becomes an element of the immovable.*[599] The principle of *superficies solo cedit* is thereby restored. Because the value of the immovable increases upon accession of the building to the immovable, the owner of the immovable must provide *compensation* to the holder of the right of superficies upon expiration. Although compensation is agreed to by the parties, the CPL initially required that it may not be less than half of the increase in the market value of the immovable.[600] Special legislation on public-private partnership, however, allowed for a deviation from this rule as it sets out that the compensation is to be agreed in the contract on public-private partnership irrespective of the CPL rules on the consequences of expiration of superficies.[601] Municipalities and the state usually condition the establishment of the right of superficies on their immovables by excluding any payments to the holder of the right of superficies upon its expiry.[602] As of 2020, the CPL no longer sets the minimum 50 % amount of compensation but sets a general rule of 100 % compensation unless the parties determine it otherwise or the law sets it otherwise.

261. The compensation paid by the owner to the holder of the right of superficies upon expiration is reasonable in cases where the holder him- or herself built the building after the right of superficies was established – he or she invested funds into the building (which is in his or her ownership during the existence of the right of superficies) and most possibly paid the owner of the land for using the land. Once the right of superficies expires, the ownership on the building is transferred from the person who financed and owned the building, to the owner of the land. The latter is to compensate the previous owner for the value of the building (calculated as the difference between the value of the land encompassing the building, and the value of the land without it), while he or she retains the payments made by the holder for using the owner's land. In cases where the building had already been built at the moment of establishing the right of superficies (it was built by the owner of the land, or was financed by the owner of the land, or was otherwise beforehand in the ownership of the owner of the land), the owner of the land must be extremely cautious when concluding the contract as it might at that moment overlook the important legal consequences of the establishment and expiry of superficies on his or her financial situation. Despite the described circumstances, the owner might possibly (having regard to the wording of the relevant CPL provision) have to compensate the holder who had not invested any resources into the building. The holder had, however, obtained ownership on the building and could even transfer the right of superficies (encompassing ownership of the building). At the expiry of the right of superficies, its value that the holder loses, has to be compensated. One way for

599. Article 263/1 of CPL.
600. Article 263/2 of CPL.
601. Article 73/3 of the Public-Private Partnership Act.
602. See the cases analysed in Vlahek, *Stavbna pravica – sedem let po njeni uveljavitvi* [The Right of Superficies – Seven Years of its Regulation], in Pravni letopis 2010, Ljubljana, pp. 165 ff., 175.

protecting the interests of the owner would be to require payment for the building when establishing superficies or to encompass somehow the value of the building into the payment(s) of the holder for the use of the land.

V. Mortgage on the Right of Superficies

262. A right of superficies may be mortgaged and has, to date, quite often been used (in particular by banks) in Slovenia as a means of security, especially in those cases where the planned building has not yet been built and is credited by the mortgagee accepting the right of superficies as security. However, upon the expiration of the right of superficies, the creditor acquires a lien on the claim of the previous holder of the right of superficies for payment of the compensation.[603] Because the compensation need not necessarily correspond to the value of the superficies, creditors must take into account that their security might be reduced upon expiration of the superficies.[604]

263. Legal theory and business practice have opted also for the possibility to encumber the right of superficies with the right of superficies (so-called sub-superficies (Sl. *podstavbna pravica*)), but the courts have so far not accepted such instrument stating purely formalistically that the CPL does not regulate it.[605]

§5. Encumbrance

I. Concept

264. Although in everyday life encumbrance (land charge, Sl. *stvarno breme,* Ger. *Reallast*) in the form of supplying food and other necessities had, for decades, been part of different personal relationships – in particular, in rural areas and between elderly people and their descendants or other persons taking care of the elderly and their property in exchange for acquiring such property – prior to the CPL, Slovenian law did not expressly regulate it. However, according to the Yugoslav legislation enabling application of the rules in force prior to the end of the Second World War (provided they do not contravene the new social order), ABGB (which does set down rules on encumbrance) was applied as legal rules up to Slovenia's independence in 1991 and remained an important rule until the CPL entered into force in 2003. Accordingly, both the LRA of 1995 and the Courts Act of 1994, as well as the case law, referred to encumbrance as one of the property rights.

603. Article 264 of CPL.

604. It seems that the banks have not always taken this into account and have somewhat negligently accepted superficies as security for their claims. See also Vlahek, *Stavbna pravica – sedem let po njeni uveljavitvi* [The Right of Superficies – Seven Years of its Regulation], in Pravni letopis 2010, Ljubljana, pp. 165 ff., 187–190.

605. See Judgment of High Court in Koper, No. CDn 309/2013 of 3 Sep. 2013.

265. The CPL defines 'encumbrance' as a right on the basis of which the owner of an encumbered immovable is *bound to a future charge or service* for the benefit of a specific person (personal encumbrance) or for the benefit of the owner of a specific immovable (predial encumbrance).[606] It is one of the limited property rights that can exist only with regard to immovables. In contrast to easements, where only inactivity of the owner of the servient immovable is required, an encumbrance consists of the obligation of a debtor to perform a particular action. Further, the owner of an encumbered immovable covers the costs arising out of the encumbrance, as opposed to easements, where the beneficiary generally covers the costs of establishment and maintenance of the easement.[607]

266. An encumbrance is a legal mechanism that creates an obligation of the debtor and, at the same time, establishes *a security for this debt*. The owner of an encumbered immovable is liable to the extent of the value of the immovable for all the obligations arising from the encumbrance.[608] Thus, it is not a mechanism destined to secure a debt arising from other legal relationships.

267. If an encumbered immovable is divided, each owner is liable with his or her immovable as a joint and several debtor. If an immovable in the interest of which the encumbrance is established, is divided, the encumbrance remains, for the benefit of each individual part of the immovable.[609]

268. The provisions of the CPL on easements apply *mutatis mutandis* to encumbrances, while the provisions on mortgages apply *mutatis mutandis* with regard to individual fulfilments.[610]

II. Creation of the Right of Encumbrance

269. An encumbrance can be created on the basis of an *agreement* or by a *law*. In the former case, the creation requires a land registry permission and entry in the land register in addition to a valid legal transaction from which the obligation to establish an encumbrance derives.[611] If it is created by a law, encumbrance is created the moment the conditions determined by the law are fulfilled.[612]

270. The right of encumbrance is, to date, most often a part of a relationship arising out of the so-called contract on delivery of property (Sl. *izročilna pogodba*), according to which the deliverer undertakes to deliver and distribute property to his or her descendants, adopted children, or adopted children's descendants, but may (in

606. Articles 249 and 250 of CPL.
607. Vrenčur in *Property Law*, 652.
608. Article 253 of CPL.
609. Article 254 of CPL.
610. Article 255 of CPL.
611. Articles 250 and 251 of CPL. An encumbrance is registered as a limited property right of the encumbered immovable.
612. Article 252 of CPL.

turn of transferring the ownership) reserve for him- or herself, his or her spouse, or any other person the right to usufruct on all or part of the delivered property or claim a lifelong annuity in kind or in cash, lifelong maintenance, or any other compensation.[613] It is oftentimes also a part of a relationship arising out of the contract of subsistence (Sl. *pogodba o preužitku*) through which the subsistee undertakes to transfer title to specific immovable property to the recipient (irrespective of any family ties), who (also in turn of receiving ownership on the immovable property) undertakes to provide specific benefits and services to the subsistee or any other person until death thereof.[614] Both contract on delivery of property and contract of subsistence must be concluded in the form of a notarial protocol.[615]

271. An example of a statutory encumbrance is the predial encumbrance existent in case of divided co-ownership. If an immovable has more than two divided co-owners and more than eight individual parts, an encumbrance on an individual part in divided co-ownership exists to the benefit of the other divided co-owners for the costs of management and payments into the compulsory reserve fund up to the amount of five times the minimum payment into the reserve fund.[616] Statutory encumbrance is acquired *ex lege* the moment the prerequisites for its formation are met. In case of divided co-ownership with more than two divided co-owners and more than eight individual parts, it arises the moment the divided co-ownership is formed. Because such encumbrance has the highest security ranking, and because it secures insignificant values and therefore leads to enforcement on the individual parts in cases of non-payments of such insignificant values, some authors believe that such encumbrance represents an excessive encroachment upon the ownership of the divided co-owners.[617]

613. Articles 546–556 of CO.
614. Articles 564–568 of CO. If the recipient disposes of the received immovables, the new acquirer is also liable for the performance of the obligations in the contract of subsistence if the subsistence is recorded in the land register.
615. Articles 547 and 567 of CO. If the land registry permission is in a separate document, and not part of the obligatory contract, only the owner's signature must be authenticated by the notary, while the land registry permission itself need not be in the form of a notarial protocol.
616. Article 120 of CPL.
617. See Vrenčur in *Property Law*, 658–659.

Chapter 5. Ownership by Two or More Persons

272. Slovenian law regulates two types of ownership by two or more persons: co-ownership (Sl. *solastnina*) and joint ownership (Sl. *skupna lastnina*). General rules on co-ownership are set down in Articles 65–71 of the CPL and, in principle, apply *mutatis mutandis* to joint ownership. General rules on joint ownership are set down in Article 72 of the CPL, while several types of joint ownership are regulated in specific legislation. Rules on the procedure for the division of co-ownership and rules on the procedure for the regulation of relationships between co-owners are laid down in the NCCPA.[618]

273. A specific form of co-ownership is the co-ownership of common parts of a multi-unit building, provided the building is in the so-called divided co-ownership (storey ownership, floor ownership (Sl. *etažna lastnina*)). Divided co-ownership encompasses individual ownership of an individual apartment or another unit in a multi-unit building and co-ownership on common parts of such building. It is regulated in the CPL (Articles 105–127) as well as in the Housing Act (HA)[619] representing *lex specialis* compared with the CPL,[620] and secondary legislation issued on their basis.[621] To some extent, the provisions of the HA apply even to cases where in multi-unit buildings only a de facto divided co-ownership is established.[622] Some aspects of divided co-ownership of business multi-unit buildings (e.g., on renting such units) are still regulated in the old Yugoslav Law of 1974 on business buildings and business units,[623] while all other aspects regarding such premises are regulated in the CPL being the *lex generalis* compared to the law of 1974. It is unfortunate that the Slovenian legislator has not regulated relationships regarding such premises in a special legislation or has not at least set out that the HA generally applies to them as well. Some further special rules on co-divided ownership are set out also in the Personal Data Protection Act.[624] An important piece of legislation for determining (and registering) existent but not yet (properly) registered divided co-ownership is the AEDC.As of 2020, the CPL sets out also specific rules for cases of co-ownership of the so-called auxiliary immovables that are connected to several main immovables.[625]

---

618. Articles 149–161 of the new NCCPA.
619. Stanovanjski zakon (SZ-1) [Housing Act], Official Gazette RS, No. 69/03, with further amendments.
620. Article 1/2 of HA.
621. See Part I, Ch. 5, §3.
622. Article 9/3 of HA.
623. Zakon o poslovnih stavbah in poslovnih prostorih (ZPSPP) [Act on business buildings and business units], Official Gazette SRS, No. 18/74, with further amendments.
624. Zakon o varstvu osebnih podatkov (ZVOP-1), Official Gazette RS, No. 86/04, with further amendments.
625. See paras. 35, 110 of this monograph.

§1. CO-OWNERSHIP

I. Ideal Shares

274. According to the CPL, two or more persons have co-ownership of an undivided thing if the share of each of them in the thing is determined as a proportion of the whole (the so-called ideal share, Sl. *solastniški delež, idealni delež, alikvotni delež*). When drafting a contract, it is irrelevant how the shares are determined (in fractional numbers, in percentage, descriptively, etc.); in the land register (and, therefore, in the land registry applications), however, co-ownership on immovables is determined *in fractional numbers*. According to the LRA, each co-ownership and its holder and his or her share is registered in the land registry statement of the immovable as a separate basic legal status.[626] If one of the co-owners has acquired his or her shares consecutively, the shares are merged into one share unless the shares are registered with different rights and/or legal facts.[627]

275. If the shares are not determined, *it is presumed that they are equal.*[628] This presumption does not, however, apply to co-ownership on an immovable because the shares must, according to the land registry legislation, be determined in the underlying documents in order for the entry in the land register to be performed. Unless the shares are already determined by the parties, the land registry repudiates the application and may neither determine the shares by itself nor on the basis of the aforementioned presumption.[629]

II. Acquisition of Co-ownership

276. Co-ownership is acquired on the same basis as ownership: by *inheritance*, by a *decision of a public authority* (i.e., court or administrative body), by a *statutory provision* (e.g., by acquisitive prescription where good faith of each co-owner is required and assessed independently),[630] or *on a contractual basis.*[631]

277. Establishment of co-ownership by agreement is, for example, specifically regulated in Article 48 of the CPL with regard to cases of *improvements of an existent building* by someone else with the consent of the owner of the building. If someone erects, adds to, or improves a building with the consent of the owner of an immovable, he or she does not generally acquire ownership of the immovable but may only claim from the owner of the immovable the amount by which the owner was enriched due to the improvement. However, the CPL expressly states that the owner and the builder may agree on establishing co-ownership of the immovable that is acquired when registered in the land register on the basis of a contract with

626. Article 15/2 of LRA.
627. Article 15/3,4 of LRA.
628. Article 65 of CPL.
629. Juhart in *Property Law*, 312.
630. Article 45/3 of CPL.
631. See Part III.

which the owner of the immovable obliges to acknowledge co-ownership to the builder, and on the basis of a corresponding *clausula intabulandi*.[632]

278. A statutory provision providing for the acquisition of co-ownership is for example Article 55 of the CPL regulating *merging* of movables in a non-hierarchical relationship and belonging to different owners. The movables become elements of a merged movable, whereby previous owners of the contributing movables acquire co-ownership of the new movable in proportion to the value their movables had prior to the merger.[633]

III. Entitlements of Co-owners

279. Generally, a co-owner has the *right to possess* the thing in co-ownership and *to use* it together with other co-owners in proportion to his or her ideal share. By doing that, the co-owner must not violate the rights of the other co-owners.

280. Further, *the fruits* of the thing in co-ownership are divided among the co-owners in accordance with their ideal shares. If this is not possible, then the fruits are co-owned by the co-owners of the principal thing. *Costs of use, management, and other burdens* that refer to the entire thing are also covered by the co-owners in proportion to the size of their ideal shares.[634]

281. Co-owners may *dispose of the thing in co-ownership as a whole* only if all of them consent to it, while each co-owner may *dispose of his or her ideal share* in a way of singular or universal succession without the consent of the other co-owners. If the subject of the co-ownership is an immovable, then the other co-owners have a right of pre-emption in case the ideal share is being sold. The purpose of such rule is to avoid any possible tensions that are likely to arise between new co-owners, as well as to gradually attain substitution of co-ownership, which is regarded as *mater rixarium*, with ordinary ownership of only one person. If the right of pre-emption is exercised simultaneously by two or more co-owners, each of them may exercise their right in proportion to their ideal share.[635] An ideal share may also be placed under lien and encumbered with personal easements; a land debt could also be established on an ideal share of an immovable between 1 January 2004 and 5 November 2013.[636]

282. As shown in more detail in the following sections, co-owners also have the right *to manage* the co-owned thing and *to demand its division*.

---

632. For further details, see Part III, Ch. 4.
633. For further details, see Part III, Ch. 5.
634. Article 68 of CPL.
635. Article 66 of CPL. Co-owners usually have priority in exercising the right of pre-emption in those cases where other interests are to be safeguarded when certain property (e.g., agricultural land, forest, farm) is sold. See Art. 23 of the Zakon o kmetijskih zemljiščih (ZKZ) [Agricultural Land Act], Official Gazette RS, No. 59/96, with further amendments.
636. Juhart in *Property Law*, 315.

IV. Management of the Thing in Co-ownership

283. Co-owners have the right to manage a co-owned thing jointly. Transactions concerning *regular management* of the thing (Sl. *posli rednega upravljanja*) – that is, transactions required for the functioning and for the maintenance of the thing in order to achieve its purpose[637] – require the consent of the co-owners whose ideal shares comprise more than half of its value. If the co-owners are unable to reach an agreement on a specific regular management transaction and the transaction is urgent for the regular maintenance of the thing, the court decides on whether the works are to be performed on request of one (or more) of the co-owners in a non-contentious civil procedure.[638] In that case, the costs of the transaction are borne by all the co-owners, not merely by the one requesting it. *Transactions exceeding the bounds of regular management* (Sl. *posli, ki presegajo redno upravljanje*) such as, in particular, disposing of the entire thing, determining the method of use, determining the manager of the thing, and deciding on the division of the thing) require the consent of all the co-owners.[639] If one of the co-owners is not reachable for a longer period, the other co-owners may request that a trustee be appointed for him or her for a specific case.[640] If the co-owners are unable to reach an agreement on a specific transaction exceeding the bounds of regular management, the court decides on request of the co-owners with more than a half of co-ownership shares in a non-contentious civil procedure on whether the works are to be performed.[641]

284. Decisions adopted by the co-owners concerning the management of the thing also have the effect of benefiting and burdening the legal successors of the co-owners.[642]

V. Division of the Thing in Co-ownership

285. A co-owner may always *request the division* of the thing, except at an inappropriate time.[643] A legal transaction with which a co-owner waives the right to

637. Article 67/3 of CPL.
638. Article 67/4 of CPL. The rules on the procedure are laid down in Arts 112–117 of the NCCPA. For further details on the procedure, see Šinkovec & Tratar, *Zakon o nepravdnem postopku s komentarjem, vzorci in sodno prakso* [Non-Contentious Civil Procedure Act with Commentary, Forms and Case-law], 201–213 (Primath 2003).
639. Article 67/5 of CPL.
640. Article 67/7 of CPL.
641. Article 67/6 of CPL. In deciding on such request, the court must pay due regard to the type of the transaction, sharing of the burdens between the co-owners and the consequences for those co-owners who were not in favour of the transaction, as well as the amount of monetary gain in case the transaction is about disposing of the shared property.
642. Article 67/8 of CPL which was a novelty introduced into Slovenian property law by the CPL. Some legal authors – Juhart for example – disagree with general application of such rule to all decisions of the co-owners. For further details, see Juhart in *Property Law*, 320–321.
643. Article 69/1 of CPL. In case of divided co-ownership, however, the co-owners may not request a division of the co-ownership of the common parts (Art. 105 of CPL).

demand division of the thing for a longer period is void.[644] If a co-owner waives the right to demand the division of the thing for a specific period, the waiver binds his legal successors, too.[645] The rules on the procedure for the division are laid down in the NCCPA.[646]

286. The co-owners determine *the method of division* of a thing by agreement.[647] If they are unable to agree on the method of division, the method is decided by the court in a non-contentious civil procedure in such a way that the co-owners acquire in kind that part of the thing for which they demonstrate a justified interest.[648] If the physical *division of a thing in kind* is not possible even with the payment of the difference in value, or if it is possible only with a substantial reduction of the value of the thing, the court may decide that the thing be sold and the proceeds divided up between the former co-owners (*civil division*).[649] At the request of one of the co-owners, the court may decide that, instead of being sold, the thing is vested in full in that co-owner if he or she pays off the other co-owners by paying them a proportionate part of the selling price of the thing as determined by the court.[650]

287. If any of the co-ownership shares is encumbered with a limited property right, the limitation may in case of a division refer only to one or some of the newly established things if the holder of such limited property right agrees to it or if the courts decides so in non-contentious proceedings taking into account the interests of the holder whose position may not be deteriorated by the court's decision.[651]

288. The other co-owners are liable to the co-owner (who obtains the thing or its part by means of a division) for *legal and factual defects* up to the extent of their

644. Article 69/2 of CPL.
645. Article 69/3 of CPL.
646. Articles 156–161 of the new NCCPA. For further details on these provisions as laid down in the previous NCCPA, see Šinkovec & Tratar, *Zakon o nepravdnem postopku s komentarjem, vzorci in sodno prakso* [Non-Contentious Civil Procedure Act with Commentary, Forms and Case-law], 214–236 (Primath 2003).
647. Article 70/1 of CPL. In such cases, the provisions regulating the acquisition of ownership by means of a legal transaction apply *mutatis mutandis* to the acquisition of ownership by division of co-ownership.
648. Article 70/2,3 of CPL. The court may thereby defer the division for a maximum of three years if any of the co-owners demonstrates a stronger interest in not having the thing divided for some time than the interest of the co-owner requesting its division.
649. Article 70/4 of CPL.
650. Article 70/5,6 of CPL. If such a request is made by two or more co-owners, the court shall determine which co-owner has priority, taking into account the size of the ideal shares, the manner in which the thing was used until that time, and the needs of the co-owners. The co-owner obtaining the thing acquires ownership of the thing when the court decision becomes final. He or she must pay off the shares of the other co-owners no later than three months from when the decision becomes final, together with interest at the rate at which money deposited in a bank for a period of three months in the place where the immovable is located earns interest. The other co-owners have a statutory lien on the thing until the full payment.
651. Article 70/1.

ideal shares.[652] If the object of the division is an immovable, the other co-owners have a lien on the immovable until payment and up to the value of their ideal shares as established in the agreement on the division. If the object of the division is movable property, the co-owners retain ownership of it until payment and up to the value of their ideal shares as established in the agreement on the division.[653]

§2. Joint Ownership

I. General on Joint Ownership

289. According to Article 72 of the CPL which sets out the general rules on joint ownership, two or more persons can have joint ownership of an undivided thing when their *shares are not determined in advance* (but are at all times determinable).[654] In case of co-ownership, the thing is undivided, too, but the shares of co-owners are determined.

290. Joint owners jointly use and dispose of the property and are jointly and severally liable for obligations arising out of it.[655] If one of the joint owners independently disposes of a thing in joint ownership, the third person is deemed to be in good faith and the transaction is deemed valid. However, it is deemed that the third person was in bad faith regarding the transferor's right to dispose if they knew that the thing was jointly owned and that it was disposed of without the consent of the other joint owner(s).[656]

291. Each joint owner or his or her creditor may always demand the division of the thing in joint ownership, except at an inappropriate time.

292. Slovenian legal theory is not uniform on the question whether joint ownership can be freely agreed upon as in the case of co-ownership. Some authors stress that only cases of joint ownership determined by the law may exist,[657] while others are of the opinion (with which the author of this chapter concurs) that it can be agreed upon freely.[658] In any case, the law in force recognizes only a small number of cases where joint ownership arises – for example, joint ownership of spouses and

652. The provisions applying to a contract of sale as set out in the CO apply *mutatis mutandis* to the liability for factual and legal defects of the thing.
653. Article 71 of CPL.
654. Article 72/1 of CPL.
655. Article 72/2 of CPL.
656. Article 72/3 of CPL.
657. See, for example, Rijavec in *CPL with Commentary 2004*, 364, who bases her argument on the fact that the property law code in force prior to the CPL (i.e., the Basic Property Law Relations Act – BPLRA) expressly provided that joint ownership may arise only in cases provided for by the law. Additionally, Rijavec believes that granting the parties the right to freely form joint ownership would undermine the protection of third parties who would contract with such owners.
658. See Juhart in *Property Law*, 325–326, who bases his argument on the fact that the CPL does not expressly provide that joint ownership may arise only in cases provided by the law, as was the case of the BPLRA in force prior to the CPL. Juhart is of the opinion that by removing such provision

civil partners set down in the MFRA; a specific type of joint ownership of heirs regulated in the IA; joint ownership on the boundary between two neighbouring immovables, regulated in the CPL; and, according to the HA, joint ownership on those common parts that serve the purposes of several, and not only one, multi-unit buildings in divided co-ownership (and are therefore not in co-ownership as is otherwise the case). Cases that fall under these categories, are, however, very frequent.

293. The provisions on co-ownership apply *mutatis mutandis* to joint ownership unless otherwise determined by law – that is, by the general rules of the CPL on joint ownership (Article 72 of the CPL), as well as by specific rules on specific types of joint ownership.

II. Joint Ownership of Spouses, Cohabiting Partners and Registered Same-Sex Civil Partners

294. Until 15 April 2019, joint ownership of heterosexual spouses and heterosexual cohabiting partners was regulated in Articles 51–61 of the MFRA. The MFRA was enacted by the assembly of the Socialist Republic of Slovenia in 1976 and entered into force on 1 January 1977. It was applicable in the Republic of Slovenia as Slovenian legislation[659] until 15 April 2019 when the new Family Code (FC) of 2017 started to apply.[660] According to the MFRA and the FC, heterosexual cohabiting partners[661] are equated with heterosexual spouses in their mutual rights and obligations as are set out in the MFRA.[662]

295. The institute of cohabitation of heterosexuals was one of the main features of the MFRA which opted (already in 1976) for a legal equality of marriage and out-of-marriage cohabitation as regards mutual rights and obligations of the partners. The main purpose behind such regulation was to safeguard the weaker partner (usually female) from being financially exploited by the other partner (usually male) and left without any financial means after the termination of the partnership

from the code, the legislature intended to change the former rule. Further, he stresses that third parties are sufficiently protected by the rules on good faith and, therefore, need not be protected by prohibiting contractual establishment of joint ownership.

659. For further details as to the development of Slovenian family law, see Podobnik & Vlahek, *Chronology of Development of Private Law in Slovenia*, in *Private Law Reform*, 283 ff., 300–302, 315 (Hurdik ed., Acta Universitatis Brunensis, Iuridica, Editio Scientia, Masaryk University, Brno 2014).

660. Družinski zakonik (DZ), Official Gazette RS, No. 15/17, with further amendments.

661. The MFRA and the Constitution of RS (Art. 53/2) use the term 'out-of-marriage relationship' (Sl. *zunajzakonska zveza*).

662. Article 12 of MFRA, now Art. 4 of FC. The MFRA and the FC state that other legislation (i.e., legislation outside the regulation of the MFRA/FC, such as inheritance law, housing law, tax law, contract law, property law, laws on civil and criminal procedure, laws on pension and disability insurance, etc.) applies to cohabiting partners only if so provided by that legislation. Cohabiting partners were, however, not entirely equated with spouses – the MFRA, for example, enabled joint adoption of non-biological children only to spouses (this rule was amended by the new FC so as to cover also cohabiting partners). For further details, see Novak, *Družinsko pravo* [Family Law], 125 (Uradni list 2014); Novak in *FC with Commentary*, 39–49.

although he or she has contributed to the increase of property of the other partner by taking care of their children, their household, etc.[663] According to the MFRA (and now the FC), out-of-marriage cohabitation is created informally, without any registration, at the moment the criteria of the definition of cohabitation are met (irrespective of the will of the parties as to the application of the legal consequences of the existence of cohabitation – if the prerequisites are met, the relationship is the relationship of cohabitation as regulated in the MFRA/FC): a longer lasting cohabitation of a man and a woman who are not married, provided that no reasons exist why a marriage between them would be invalid.[664] Cohabitation is proven *ex post facto* in each individual case whenever establishing the existence of cohabitation is relevant.[665] It is to be underscored that the rules of the MFRA/FC regulating property relationships between the spouses apply also to cohabiting partners. The following paragraphs analysing property relationships between the spouses thus apply also to cohabiting partners.

296. The basic rule is that the *property obtained by the spouses during their marriage on the basis of their work or for consideration*, as well the property obtained on the basis of such property, becomes their joint property, while all other property (i.e., property obtained before marriage, as well as property obtained during marriage but not on the basis of their work) remains or becomes separate property of each of the spouses, and they may dispose of it individually without any consent or other participation of the other spouse.[666] A novelty of the FC is that the spouses (same goes for cohabiting partners) may conclude a contract on their patrimonial relations (Sl. *pogodba o ureditvi premoženjskih razmerij*).[667] In such cases, the legal regime of the FC on the joint/individual property of the spouses does not apply.

297. The spouses manage and dispose of their joint property jointly and unanimously.[668] They may, however, agree that only one spouse manages and disposes of their joint property, taking account of the interests of the other spouse. Each of the

663. For further details, see Zupančič, *Zakonska zveza in družinska razmerja* [Marriage and Family Relations], 10–13 (Časopisni zavod Uradni list SR Slovenije 1989); Novak, *Družinsko pravo* [Family Law], 117–120 (Uradni list 2014).

664. Art. 4 of FC. See Novak, *Družinsko pravo* [Family Law], 118 (Uradni list 2014); Novak in *FC with Commentary*, 39–49.

665. For further details, see Novak, *Družinsko pravo* [Family Law], 120–122, 126 (Uradni list 2014); Novak in *FC with Commentary*, 39–49.

666. Article 51 of MFRA, now Arts 63–84 of the FC. The part of the provision “or for consideration” was not included in Art. 51 of the MFRA. According to the FC, special provisions apply in cases of the spouses’ joint entrepreneurship. Detailed provisions are also set out in the FC for cases of investments made by one of the spouses into the other spouses’ individual property. For further details see Žnidaršič Skubic in *FC with Commentary*, 186–193, 218–220; Vrtačnik in *FC with Commentary*, 220–226; Dugar in *FC with Commentary*, 227–246.

667. Articles 65–67 and 85–94 of FC. For further details, see Žnidaršič Skubic, Erjavec, Novak and Podgoršek in *FC with Commentary*, 260–299.

668. Article 52 of MFRA, now Art. 69 of the FC. The FC states that in case one of the spouses disposes of a movable of a lesser value or performs legal transactions of regular management of the joint property, he or she is deemed to have consesus of the other spouse. For further details, see Žnidaršič Skubic in *FC with Commentary*, 193–194.

spouses may terminate such agreement under the proviso that the termination does not take place at an inappropriate time.[669]

298. A spouse may not dispose of his or her undivided share of joint property by *inter vivos* transactions; more specifically, he or she may not transfer or encumber it.[670]

299. As regards immovables, joint ownership of the spouses is entered into the land register as their joint ownership with undivided shares. The LRA sets out that in case of joint ownership all joint owners are registered as holders of the right of ownership.[671] It should, however, be stressed that joint ownership of spouses is acquired the moment the prerequisites for the joint ownership to arise are met (i.e., as stated in the FC, when a spouse obtains property during marriage with his or her work or for consideration) and not at the moment of registration of joint ownership in the land register. If the relationship of joint ownership does not ensue from the land register (e.g., only one of the spouses is registered as the owner of an immovable), acquirers of the immovable who rely in good faith on the data entered in the land register are protected as against the joint owner who was not registered as such. It is not unusual that only one of the spouses is registered as the sole owner while, legally, the immovable is in joint ownership of the spouses: if the registered spouse disposes of the immovable or encumbers it (e.g., with a mortgage), his or her contracting party, if they are in good faith, acquires ownership or other property interest regardless of the fact that the other spouse did not consent to the transaction.[672] In case the immovable which is registered only in favour of one of the spouses while it is in fact in joint property of both spouses, is mortgaged, the creditors may rely on the principle of trust in the land register only in case of contractual mortgage, and not in case of a mortgage acquired in enforcement proceedings.[673]

300. Spouses are liable with their separate property as well as with their share on the joint ownership for their individual obligations they contracted to before or after the marriage. For the obligations that generally burden both spouses, the obligations that arise with regard to their joint property, as well as the obligations that are contracted to by one of the spouses for the regular needs of their living, the

669. Article 53 of MFRA, now Art. 70 of the FC. For further details, see Žnidaršič Skubic in *FC with Commentary*, 195–196.

670. Article 54 of MFRA, now Art. 68 of the FC. For further details, see Žnidaršič Skubic in *FC with Commentary*, 191–193.

671. Article 15/3 of LRA.

672. See also Novak, *Družinsko pravo* [Family Law], 94–96 (Uradni list 2014).

673. Judgment of the Constitutional Court of RS, No. Up-128/03 of 27 Jan. 2005. Although only one of the spouses is registered as the owner of the immovable on which a mortgage is established in enforcement proceedings, interests of the creditor of the registered spouse do not take precedence over the interests of the other spouse, regardless of the creditor's good faith. See Juhart in *Property Law*, 330; Vlahek, *Odprta vprašanja načela zaupanja v zemljiško knjigo* [Issues Relating to the Principle of Trust in the Land Register], in *Izbrane teme civilnega prava II*, (Ed. Ude, Institute of Comparative Law at the Faculty of Law in Ljubljana 2007).

spouses are liable jointly and severally with their separate as well as their joint property. The spouse who paid off a joint debt may request his or her partner the return of the amount exceeding his or her part of the debt.[674]

301. On the basis of a final court judgment, a creditor of one of the spouses may request that the court determine the spouse's share on the joint property and may afterwards file for enforcement regarding such share. If a share of one of the spouses is sold in enforcement proceedings, the other spouse has a right of pre-emption.[675]

302. Joint property of the spouses is divided if a marriage is terminated or invalidated. During the marriage, the spouses may agree that their joint ownership be divided. Each of the spouses may also request the partition.[676] It is deemed that the shares of the spouses are equal. Each of them may, however, prove that they have contributed to their joint property in different proportion.[677] In case of a dispute regarding their shares, the court must take into account all circumstances of their relationship (e.g., help offered to a spouse, upbringing and taking care of their children, housekeeping, etc.) and not only their income. The spouses may agree on their shares, or request that the court determine them. After determining the shares, the property is divided according to the rules regulating the division of co-ownership. Each of the spouses may thereby request to acquire the assets needed for performing his or her trade or other activities that enable him or her to earn an income, as well as the things needed for his or her personal use.

303. Very similar rules on joint property to those of MFRA as regards heterosexual spouses and heterosexual cohabiting partners were set out in the Registration of a Same-Sex Civil Partnership Act of 2005[678] as regards registered same-sex civil partners (while the rights and obligations of non-registered same-sex partners were – in contrast to heterosexual cohabiting partners – not specifically regulated – but were nevertheless covered by various provisions of various legislation as well as by the Constitution[679]).[680] The Registration of a Same-Sex Civil Partnership Act enabled homosexual partners to register their partnership in Slovenia as of July 2006. It regulated the prerequisites and the procedure for registering the partnership

674. Article 56 of MFRA, now Art. 82 of the FC.

675. Article 57 of MFRA, now Art. 83 of the FC where additional rules for cases of personal bankruptcy of one of the spouses and the determination of the other spouse's share in joint property are laid down. For further details, see Dugar in *FC with Commentary*, 248–260.

676. Articles 58–61 of MFRA, now Arts 71–76 of the FC. For further details, see Žnidaršič Skubic and Vrtačnik in *FC with Commentary*, 196–218.

677. Debts and claims of the spouses with regard to their joint ownership must be determined (Art. 61/1 of MFRA, now Art. 72 of FC).

678. Zakon o registraciji istospolne partnerske skupnosti (ZRIPS) [The Registration of a Same-Sex Civil Partnership Act]Official Gazette RS, No. 65/05, with further amendments.

679. The Constitutional Court of RS recognized in March 2013 that non-registered same-sex partners who are in a longer lasting cohabitation (provided that no reasons exist why a registered partnership between them would be invalid) have the right to inherit under the same rules as are set out for registered same-sex partners (ECLI:SI:USRS:2013:U.I.212.10).

680. For further details on regulation of same-sex non-registered partnerships, see Novak, *Družinsko pravo* [Family Law], 149–150 (Uradni list, 2014).

(not denoted as marriage by the legislator; the registration procedure is also different to that of the marriage of heterosexual partners); legal consequences of such registration (also to some extent different to those of the marriage of heterosexual spouses); ways of termination of the partnership and rights and obligations of the partners afterwards (while the most disputed questions, such as adoption of children, were left outside the act leaving the general provisions of the MFRA on adoptions apply setting out that only (heterosexual) spouses may jointly adopt children).[681] According to Article 9 of the Registration of a Same-Sex Civil Partnership Act, *property obtained by the registered same-sex partners on the basis of their work during their partnership* became their joint property, while all other property (i.e., property obtained before registration, as well as property obtained during their partnership but not on the basis of their work) remained or became separate property of each of the registered partners, etc.

304. In March 2015, an act amending the MFRA was passed in the Slovenian National Assembly (but did not enter into force after failure on the referendum in December 2015) equating fully heterosexual and homosexual couples with regard to all their rights and obligations (including those regulating adoption).[682] Were it successful, the Registration of a Same-Sex Civil Partnership Act would have been repealed. The terms 'marriage' and 'out-of-marriage community' were to be redefined so as to encompass all communities of two persons. The act provided that the amendments are to apply after six months after the act is enforced. The National Council of the RS decided not to veto the act.[683] However, a much debated referendum (allowed by the Constitutional Court of RS) was eventually held in December 2015 rejecting the amendments by 63.51%.

In 2016, a Civil Union Act[684] *was adopted repealing the Registration of a Same-Sex Civil Partnership Act.*[685] It regulates both "concluded" and "non-concluded" same-sex partnerships. The FC applies *mutatis mutandis* unless the Civil Union Act states otherwise. The "concluded" partnership (called "partnership") has the same legal consequences as marriage of heterosexual persons unless the Civil Union Act states otherwise. The "non-concluded partnership" is defined in the same way as the out-of-marriage cohabitation of heterosexual persons and has (as regards the relationship between the partners themselves) the same legal consequences as the concluded same-sex partnership as well as (unless the Civil Union Act states otherwise) as the out-of-marriage cohabitation of heterosexual persons. The Civil Union Act

---

681. For further details on regulation of same-sex registered partnerships, see Novak, *Družinsko pravo* [Family Law], 126–149 (Uradni list 2014).
682. Some differences would still exist between the category of (hetero or homosexual) spouses and the category of (hetero or homosexual) cohabiting partners.
683. The National Council of RS may, according to the Slovenian Constitution, within seven days of the passing of a law and prior to its promulgation require the National Assembly to decide again on such law.
684. Zakon o partnerski zvezi (ZPZ), Official Gazette of RS, No. 33/16, date of application 24 Feb. 2017.
685. This act, however, still applied six months after the new Civil Union Act started to apply on 24 Feb 2017, whereby new partnerships could no longer be established under the old act.

states explicitly that same-sex partners may not jointly adopt children and are not granted procedures of fertilization with biomedical assistance.

III. Joint Ownership of Heirs

305. A specific type of joint ownership, which does not correspond fully to the general scheme of joint ownership as regulated in the CPL, is joint ownership of heirs.

306. From the moment of the decedent's death to the moment of division of the heritage, the decedent's heirs[686] form a so-called *community* or *partnership of co-heirs* and jointly manage and dispose of the inherited assets.[687] The heirs have aliquot inheritance shares on the estate as a whole, while each of the individual things forming the estate is in joint ownership of the heirs without any shares existing on it.[688] This is so all up until the estate is divided between the heirs in accordance with their inheritance shares in the estate as have been determined by the court in its decision. The decision of the court does therefore not have any effect on the community of heirs and their property status.[689]

307. Each of the co-heirs may, at any time,[690] request the division of the inherited estate.[691] Once the division is performed, individual (co-)ownership of each of the heirs on each individual thing of the inherited estate is established.[692]

IV. Joint Ownership of the Boundary Between Two Neighbouring Immovables

308. According to Article 80 of the CPL, it is presumed that *boundary fences, walls, trees, ditches, and other things intended to demarcate the boundary* are in joint ownership of the owners of the neighbouring immovables. Boundary markers must be maintained in the customary local manner, where the costs of maintenance are to be covered equally by the owners of the neighbouring immovables. The owners of the neighbouring immovables are also jointly and severally liable for damage caused to third persons as a result of non-maintenance of their boundary.

---

686. Legatees to whom the testator may destine only specific things or rights, and not aliquot parts of his or her estate, do not take part in the community of co-heirs.
687. Article 145/1 of IA. Each co-heir may only dispose of his or her inheritance share in favour of other co-heirs (Art. 146 of IA).
688. Zupančič & Žnidaršic Skubic, *Dedno pravo* [Inheritance Law], 219–220 (GV Založba 2009).
689. Zupančič & Žnidaršic Skubic, *Dedno pravo* [Inheritance Law], 220 (GV Založba 2009).
690. Though not at an inappropriate time (Art. 144/1 of IA).
691. Because the IA does not entail rules on the division, rules of the CPL on division of a thing in joint ownership apply (Arts 69–71 of CPL). For further details as to the division, see Zupančič & Žnidaršic Skubic, *Dedno pravo* [Inheritance Law], 224–229 (GV Založba 2009).
692. Zupančič & Žnidaršic Skubic, *Dedno pravo* [Inheritance Law], 220, 224–229 (GV Založba 2009).

V. Joint Ownership on Common Parts That Serve the Purposes of Several Immovables

309. According to Article 23 of the HA, those common parts that serve the purposes of several buildings in divided co-ownership or other immovables (e.g., boiler house, shelter house),[693] and not only the purposes of one building in divided co-ownership, are in *joint ownership of the owners of all units* in all multi-unit buildings or owners of all immovables sharing the common part in question. If such parts were to serve the purposes of one multi-unit building alone, they would be in co-ownership as provided by the general rules on divided co-ownership. Such common parts are managed by the managers of those buildings in divided co-ownership, the purposes of which the common parts serve. Since March 2020, a similar situation is regulated also in Art. 105/6 of the CPL. It is stated that in case a unit in a multi-unit building or an immovable serves the purposes of two or more multi-unit buildings or serves the purposes of one or more multi-unit buildings and one or more individual immovables, such unit or immovable is deemed a common part in co-ownership of owners of units in multi-unit buildings (and owners of individual immovables respectively). The new rules of the CPL on "auxiliary immovables" apply as regards the acquisition, management, and termination of such common part. It is not entirely clear how these two provisions laid down in different acts (i.e. in Article 23 of the HA and Article 105/6 of the CPL) are to be applied in cases where they intersect. The principle *lex posterior derogate legi priori* would probably prevail.

310. The common parts may, however, serve also the purposes of several immovables that are not in divided co-ownership, e.g., the purposes of several individual houses within a housing estate that includes also common parts (e.g., shelter house, parking spaces, parks, recreational plots, etc.) that are used by all owners of such individual houses. It is, however, to be noted that such situations have until recently not been satisfactorily regulated in Slovenian property law. The owners of land and houses being physically part of such housing estates have thus been faced with problems as regards the managing of their immovables and in particular the managing of the common parts. Although being part of a housing estate community is almost identical to being part of a community of divided co-owners living in multi-unit buildings, the CPL and the HA had set out the specific rules of divided co-ownership for multi-unit buildings only. It was important for proper functioning of such estates that the courts applied the rules of divided co-ownership to such cases *mutatis mutandis*, and that the legislator eventually regulated in more detail the relationships in such communities. The novel rules of the CPL on "connected immovables" now enable that common parts in housing communities are connected to the main immovables of such communities. However, the most problematic issue in regard to such housing estates is that they were built in times of the regime of social property, and that the common parts have not yet been registered as joint (shared) private ownership of all of the owners of individual plots with houses. As has already been explained, some municipalities tend to take advantage of this

693. Such parts may be part of another immovable or may form an independent immovable.

anomaly and insert such common parts in their property (and register as their owners without any proper legal basis). By doing this, they have been expropriating without any legal ground and without any compensation the real owners of the common parts, and eventually declare such common parts as property in public domain, or even sell them to third persons and thus foster the degradation of the environment and lower the quality of living in such estates.[694] The AEDC has eventually addressed this problem and now explicitly states that the common "functional" parts of multiple immovables as determined according to the AEDC are in *joint ownership* of all the owners of individual immovables to which these common parts serve. The joint owners of such common parts are thus all those persons that are at the relevant moment individual owners of the individual immovables. Joint ownership thus follows the ownership on individual immovables. Further, the CPL 2020 amendment laid down the rules on the novel concept of "connected immovables" stating that" auxiliary immovables" that are connected to several "main immovables" are in *co-ownership* of owners of the main immovables whereby the rules on divided co-ownership are to be applied *mutatis mutandis*.[695]

§3. Divided Co-ownership

I. Concept of Divided Co-ownership

311. Divided co-ownership (Sl. *etažna lastnina*) is full ownership of an individual part (unit, Sl. *posamezni del*) in a multi-unit building, and co-ownership of the common parts (Sl. *skupni deli*) of such building. An individual part of a building must represent an independent functional unit suitable for independent use, such as an apartment, an office, or some other independent premises, while common parts of a building are other parts intended for common use by the divided co-owners (such as stairways, elevators, roof, facade, etc., including the land on which the multi-unit building is built).[696] The HA sets out three categories of common parts: (i) common areas, (ii) common construction elements, (iii) common devices, fixtures and fittings, and lists the most typical common parts of each of these categories.[697] The categorization is, for example, relevant for determining the method of taking decisions of management of these parts, for determining whether certain common parts may be determined as so-called special common parts (Sl. *posebni skupni deli*), etc. Only common areas and devices may be determined by all of the divided co-owners as special common parts meaning that only a part of divided co-owners use them as their common parts, manage them and cover their costs (thus 'special common parts' as opposed to 'common parts' which are used and managed

694. See paras. 115, 142, 453 of this monograph.
695. See paras. 110, 123, 273, 310, 313 of this monograph.
696. Article 105/1,2,3 of CPL. Similarly also Arts 3–8 of HA.
697. Article 5 of HA.

by all the divided co-owners).[698] Special common parts are in co-ownership of these divided co-owners only, not in co-ownership of all the divided co-owners of the multi-unit building.

312. The Slovenian system of divided co-ownership follows the dualistic system of divided co-ownership (ownership on an individual part plus co-ownership on common parts), not the unitary system where divided co-ownership is merely a type of co-ownership.[699] The dualistic system was introduced in 1976 by one of the acts enacted by the SRS[700] which provided for joint ownership (not co-ownership as set out in the current legislation) on common parts.[701] In 1991, however, the first Housing Act[702] set out the unitary system which was replaced by the dualistic system in 2003 with the enactment of the currently valid Housing Act. It should therefore be emphasized that the term 'divided co-ownership' does not accord fully to the substance of the divided co-ownership as set out in Slovenian legislation. Owners of individual parts are not co-owners of these parts as would ensue from the words 'divided *co-ownership*'. They are sole owners of the individual parts. Only the common parts are in their co-ownership. Therefore, more general terms as 'floor ownership' 'storey ownership', or more precise 'flat ownership' or 'unit ownership' would better correspond to the type of ownership in multi-unit buildings as regulated in Slovenian law (and its denomination in Slovene language).

313. Divided co-ownership is regulated in the CPL (Articles 105–127) as well as in the Housing Act (HA)[703] representing *lex specialis* compared with the CPL,[704] and secondary legislation issued on their basis.[705] Some aspects of divided

---

698. Article 3/4 of HA.
699. Juhart in *Property Law*, 332.
700. Zakon o pravicah na delih stavb (ZPDS) [Act on Rights on Parts of Buildings], Official Gazette SRS, No. 19/76, with further amendments.
701. Vlahek, *Solastnina skupnih delov v etažni lastnini* [Co-ownership of common parts in relationship of divided co-ownership], in Zbornik stvarnega in zemljiškoknjižnega prava, 26–28 (GV založba 2010).
702. Stanovanjski zakon (SZ) [Housing Act], Official Gazette RS, No. 18/91, with further amendments.
703. Stanovanjski zakon (SZ-1) [Housing Act], Official Gazette RS, No. 69/03, with further amendments.
704. Article 1/2 of HA.
705. Pravilnik o merilih za določitev prispevka etažnega lastnika v rezervni sklad in najnižji vrednosti prispevka [Rules on criteria for determining contributions of apartment owners into the reserve fund and the lowest rate of contribution], Official Gazette RS, No. 11/04; Pravilnik o standardih vzdrževanja stanovanjskih stavb in stanovanj [Rules on standards for the maintenance of apartment buildings and apartments], Official Gazette RS, No. 20/04, with further amendments; Pravilnik o upravljanju večstanovanjskih stavb [Rules on management of multiple dwellings], Official Gazette RS, No. 60/09, with further amendments; Pravilnik o minimalnih tehničnih zahtevah za graditev stanovanjskih stavb in stanovanj [Rules on minimum technical requirements for the construction of apartment buildings and apartments], Official Gazette RS, No. 1/11, with further amendments; Akt o ustanovitvi Stanovanjskega sklada Republike Slovenije kot javnega sklada [Act on the establishment of the Housing Fund of the Republic of Slovenia as a public fund], Official Gazette RS, No. 6/11, with further amendments; [Rules of procedure of work of the Housing Council], Official Gazette RS, No. 54/12; Pravilnik o določitvi vrednosti točke za ugotovitev vrednosti stanovanja [Rules establishing the point value for assessing the apartment value], Official Gazette RS, No. 138/06; Uredba o označevanju stanovanj in poslovnih prostorov [Decree on the marking of apartments

co-ownership of business multi-unit buildings (e.g., on renting such units) are still regulated in the old Yugoslav Law of 1974 on business buildings and business units,[706] while all other aspects regarding such premises are regulated in the CPL being the *lex generalis* compared to the law of 1974. It is unfortunate that the Slovenian legislator has not regulated relationships regarding such premises in a special legislation or has not at least set out that the HA generally applies to them as well. Some further special rules on co-divided ownership are set out also in the Personal Data Protection Act.[707] Legislation on divided co-ownership is far from being user-friendly in particular because the same issues are sometimes regulated in the CPL as well as in the HA (sometimes identically and sometimes differently). It is also not entirely clear to which situations the HA applies (combined apartment-business multi-unit buildings, business multi-unit buildings) whereby terraced houses forming a housing estate with several common parts (such as parks, playgrounds, parking spaces, etc.) had long been left out of any specific regulation, and it is not always clear who the owner is of these common parts, what type of ownership exists on them,[708] and how they are to be managed by the owners of the

---

and business premises], Official Gazette RS, No. 63/06; Pravilnik o programu izobraževanja in navodilu o usposabljanju za točkovanje stanovanj [Rules on the programme and instructions for the training in the point-rating of apartments], Official Gazette RS, No. 97/05; Pravilnik o minimalnih tehničnih zahtevah, ki jih morajo izpolnjevati bivalne enote, namenjene začasnemu reševanju stanovanjskih potreb socialno ogroženih oseb [Rules on minimum technical requirements to be met by residential units intended as temporary solutions to housing needs of economically deprived persons], Official Gazette RS, No. 123/04, with further amendments; Pravilnik o minimalnih tehničnih zahtevah za graditev oskrbovanih stanovanj za starejše ter o načinu zagotavljanja pogojev za njihovo obratovanje [Rules on minimum technical requirements for the construction of residential care homes for elderly and on ensuring conditions for their operation], Official Gazette RS, No. 110/04, with further amendments; Navodilo o izdelavi poročila o upravnikovem delu [Instructions on the drawing-up of a report on manager's work], Official Gazette RS, No. 108/04; Pravilnik o dodeljevanju neprofitnih stanovanj v najem [Rules on the rental of non-profit apartments], Official Gazette RS, No. 14/04, with further amendments; Uredba o metodologiji za oblikovanje najemnin v neprofitnih stanovanjih ter merilih in postopku za uveljavljanje subvencioniranih najemnin [Decree on the methodology of determination of rents for non-profit housing and the criteria and procedure for the implementation of subsidised rents], Official Gazette RS, No. 131/03, with further amendments; Pravilnik o posebnih pogojih delovanja neprofitnih stanovanjskih organizacij [Rules on non-profit apartment organizations], Official Gazette RS, No. 64/93, with further amendments.

706. Zakon o poslovnih stavbah in poslovnih prostorih (ZPSPP) [Act on business buildings and business units], Official Gazette SRS, No. 18/74, with further amendments.

707. Zakon o varstvu osebnih podatkov (ZVOP-1), Official Gazette RS, No. 86/04, with further amendments.

708. In Slovenia, such common parts are often registered as ownership of the municipalities who provided land for erection of the housing estates decades ago in the times of social property, or even as ownership of the undertakings who erected the houses in agreement with the municipalities and then sold them to final customers (whereby most of these undertakings are bankrupt). This is an expression of how the Slovenian legislator has not dealt properly with the transformation from public to private ownership coupled with the transformation from out-of-register handling of property relations to giving the land register a central position in the system of property law. At the time of crisis, the municipalities who are registered as owners of such common parts are selling them to third persons or even to owners of the terraced houses although the latter were supposed to be and in fact are real owners of the common parts. Instead of taking care of or at least fostering the registration of the buyers of terraced houses (and common parts of the housing estates) at the conclusion of the sales contracts with the municipality or with the construction undertaking, some

houses. The AEDC of 2008 (renewed in 2017) has to some extent addressed these issues followed by the novel rules on the concept of "connected immovables" inserted in the CPL in 2020.[709]

314. An important piece of legislation for determining (and registering) existent but not yet (properly) registered divided co-ownership is the AEDC of 2008 (renewed in 2017). This act enables efficient determination and registration of divided co-ownership in all those (older) cases of divided co-ownership where divided co-ownership was in fact existent but had never been registered as such in accordance with the modern rules of land registration what led to difficulties with disposing and using such property as well as with taking decisions regarding the common parts, e.g., regarding their maintenance, distribution of the costs, etc. The act provides for non-contentious proceedings in which the courts assess such cases.

315. Co-ownership of the common parts is inseparably linked to the ownership of an individual part and is therefore also transferred together with it. Co-ownership of common parts cannot be waived, and (in contrast to 'regular' co-owners) none of the co-owners may request a division of the co-ownership of the common parts;[710] they may also not dispose of their co-ownership shares on common parts separately from the ownership of the individual part.[711] The co-ownership share of each divided co-owner of the common parts is determined by taking into account the actual value of each individual part in divided co-ownership as a proportion of the total actual value of the immovable, unless otherwise provided by law or agreement.[712] The rights and obligations of divided co-owners with respect to common parts are proportionate to their co-ownership shares, unless otherwise provided by law or agreement.[713] The shares are to be determined already at the creation of divided co-ownership, i.e., by the agreement or by the court decision on the creation of divided co-ownership. As at the time of enactment of the CPL (entering into force on 1 January 2003), a lot of cases of divided co-ownership existed without the shares being determined, the CPL set out in its final provisions that until 1 January 2004 the shares are to be determined or otherwise every co-owner or manager of the multi-unit building may request the court to determine the shares.[714] Further detailed provisions on determination of shares in the absence of the co-owners'

---

municipalities are now even trying to take advantage from the fact that they are still registered as owners in the land register. In the recent years, Slovenian courts have been tackling with this and similar issues of disorderly status of immovables. Eventually, the AEDC was adopted addressing these problems.

709. See para. 110 of this monograph.
710. Article 105/4,5 of CPL.
711. Save those cases where a part of common parts is transformed into an individual part by the will of the divided co-owners according to Art. 113 of the CPL.
712. Article 106 of CPL.
713. Article 115 of CPL. The Pravilnik o upravljanju večstanovanjskih stavb [Rules on management of multiple dwellings], Official Gazette RS, No. 60/09, with further amendments, sets out detailed rules as to how the costs of functioning of the building are divided between the divided co-owners. The divided co-owners may derogate from these rules by agreeing on a different division of the costs between them.
714. Article 270 of CPL.

agreement, are set out also in the HA.[715] Ten and more years afterwards, a lot of multi-unit buildings without the determined shares still exist in Slovenia.

II. Creation of Divided Co-ownership

316. Divided co-ownership is created *on the basis of an agreement or by court decision, followed by the entry in the land register.*[716] An agreement for the acquisition of divided co-ownership can be an agreement on the division of co-ownership into the divided co-ownership (i.e., where the multi-unit building has thus far been in co-ownership) or a unilateral legal transaction (i.e., where the multi-unit building has thus far been owned by one person, which is most often upon its erection).

317. An agreement on the creation of divided co-ownership must contain the names of the divided co-owners, the land register designation of the immovable, a precise description of the individual part of the building in relation to the other parts, a description of the common parts, a determination of the co-ownership shares of the common parts, and a contractual regulation of the mutual relations among the divided co-owners. If any of the co-ownership shares of the immovable is encumbered with a mortgage or a land debt, a division agreement is possible only with the consent of the creditor, while a mortgage and a land debt that encumber the entire immovable are transferred to all the individual parts in divided co-ownership.[717] A division agreement must determine the individual part of the building in divided co-ownership to which the encumbrance transfers.[718]

318. The owner of an immovable may divide his or her ownership of the immovable into divided co-ownership with a unilateral legal transaction. This transaction must have the same elements as an agreement of the co-owners presented in the preceding paragraph.[719]

319. Each co-owner of an immovable may request that the court, in a non-contentious civil procedure, alter the co-ownership of the immovable into divided co-ownership if such division is possible.[720] If any of the co-ownership shares of the immovable are encumbered with a mortgage or a land debt, the court issues a ruling determining to which individual part in divided co-ownership the encumbrance transfers in order that the division does not worsen the position of the creditor. The court ruling must also contain all the elements of an agreement of the co-owners presented earlier.

715. Article 182 of HA.
716. Article 107 of CPL.
717. Article 111 of CPL.
718. Article 108 of CPL.
719. Article 109 of CPL.
720. Article 110 of CPL.

320. Naturally, the owners of individual parts may dispose of their ownership, whereby the provisions of the CPL regulating the disposal of immovables apply.[721] Together with the ownership on an individual part, corresponding co-ownership of the common parts is transferred.

321. Divided co-ownership is registered in the land register. According to Article 15a that was inserted into the LRA as part of the reform of the land register in 2011, the following is registered in the land register: (i) the building (although according to the principle of *superficies solo cedit*, the building itself is not an immovable but merely a part of the land on which it is erected, Slovenian new land register registers it as an immovable in its own land registry entry),[722] (b) its individual parts,[723] (c) plot of land being common part of divided co-owners (i.e., in co-ownership of the owners of all apartments whoever they are in a certain moment), (d) plot of land being common part of only a part of divided co-owners. Prior to the reform of the land register, registration of divided co-ownership was far more clear and user-friendly.

III. Changing Common Parts into Individual Parts

322. Divided co-owners may conclude a written agreement that certain common parts become part of a particular individual part in divided co-ownership, if this is possible. Divided co-owners may also agree that a new individual part in divided co-ownership be created from the common parts.[724] Such agreement must be concluded unanimously.[725]

IV. Division and Merger of Individual Parts

323. A divided co-owner may, by a legal transaction, divide his or her individual part into two or more new individual parts, if this is possible. The co-ownership share of the common parts belonging to the divided individual part is thereby divided into new co-ownership shares for each of the new individual parts. The legal transaction must contain the land register designation of the individual part of the building, a description, and a demarcation of the newly created individual parts, as well as a determination of the co-ownership shares of the common

721. Article 112 of CPL.
722. In this land register entry, the building's common plots of land and individual apartments or other individual parts in the building are listed (here, ideal co-ownership shares on common parts are registered). Land register IDs of these common parts and individual parts are also stated there.
723. The owner of a particular individual part is listed. His or her ideal co-ownership share on common parts is registered. Any encumbrances of this individual part are also registered.
724. Article 113 of CPL.
725. Article 29/2 of HA.

parts for each new individual part in divided co-ownership. All costs incurred by the division are covered by the divided co-owner of the individual part being divided.[726]

324. Similarly, two or more individual parts in divided co-ownership may be merged on the basis of a legal transaction into a new individual part in divided co-ownership. The provisions regulating the division of an individual part in divided co-ownership apply *mutatis mutandis* to this legal transaction.

325. However, the contract on mutual relations concluded among the divided co-owners upon the establishment of the divided co-ownership may determine that a division or a merger may not be carried out or that they are dependent on the agreement of the other divided co-owners. The rationale behind setting out such rule is the possibility of the divided co-owners to prevent the enlargement of the community of divided co-owners against their will.

V. Contract on Mutual Relations

326. Divided co-owners must conclude a so-called contract on mutual relations (Sl. *pogodba o medsebojnih razmerjih*)[727] to regulate, in particular:

- the costs and obligations encumbering the divided co-owners if they deviate from the rules of the CPL;
- the method of forming a reserve fund if it exceeds the minimum amount set down in the CPL and other legislation;
- any special restrictions on the use of individual parts in divided co-ownership;
- the manner in which common parts are used;
- the purpose of use of individual parts in divided co-ownership;
- the conduct of divided co-owners in legal transactions;
- the manner in which common parts are managed;
- the use of individual parts in divided co-ownership for particular purposes;
- the insurance of the building as a whole; and
- the powers of the manager if they deviate from those set down in the CPL.

327. A contract on mutual relations must be concluded *in writing* and *has effect against any new divided co-owner*. According to the HA, more than three-quarters of the co-ownership shares of the common parts are required for the valid conclusion of the contract as regards the issues set out in the HA (except for those issues where consensus is required according to the HA – these are to be regulated in a specific written agreement concluded by all the divided co-owners).[728]

726. Article 114 of CPL.
727. Article 116 of CPL.
728. Article 32 of HA.

VI. Management of the Common Parts

328. The CPL states that the provisions of the CPL regulating the management of a thing in co-ownership apply *mutatis mutandis* to the management of common parts, unless otherwise provided in the contract on mutual relations.[729] The CPL itself, however, sets out some specific rules applicable to cases of divided co-ownership.[730] Additionally, the HA being the *lex specialis* compared to the CPL sets out some specific provisions on the managements which supplement and/or differ extensively to those of the CPL.

329. According to the CPL, transactions concerning *regular management* of the thing in co-ownership – that is, transactions required for the functioning and for the maintenance of the thing in order to achieve its purpose[731] – require the consent of the co-owners whose ideal shares comprise more than half of its value. If the co-owners are unable to reach an agreement and the transaction is urgent for the regular maintenance of the thing, the court decides on whether the works are to be performed on request of one (or more) of the co-owners in a non-contentious civil procedure.[732] Similar, but not identical rules are set out also in the HA.[733] Consent of more than one-half of the divided co-owners' ideal shares are required to pass a vote on a regular management transaction – if a proposal is not voted, the next vote requires only the consent of more than one-half of ideal shares of the divided co-owners' present at voting.[734] The manager of the multi-unit building (if nominated) must require the court to decide on an urgent transaction if the divided co-owners are unable to pass a vote on it;[735] the divided co-owners voting against the urgent transaction are to cover the costs of court proceedings if the court decides that the transaction is to be performed.[736] The HA lists the most typical regular transactions in more detail than the CPL: transactions for the functioning and maintenance of the building; election and discharge of the manager and of the supervisory board of the building; passing the house rules; leasing common parts to third persons; taking decisions with regard to the reserve fund; installation of additional counters and similar devices; and all other transactions required for a normal living in the multi-unit building. The HA also states that smaller maintenance works may be performed by the manager alone without any divided co-owners' decision required.[737] It is to be underscored that according to the HA, the divided co-owners must agree (by a vote of more than 50% of shares) on a building maintenance plan drafted by the manager for the period from one to five years.[738] If they fail to do so,

729. Article 117/1 of CPL.
730. For example, in Art. 117/2 of the CPL.
731. Article 67/3 of CPL.
732. Article 67/4 of CPL.
733. Article 25 of HA.
734. Article 37 of HA.
735. Article 28/2 of HA.
736. Article 28/4 of HA.
737. Article 51 of HA.
738. Article 26 of HA. Every divided co-owner may request the court to appoint in non-contentious proceedings an expert to assess the maintenance plan if the divided co-owner is of the opinion that the

the housing inspectorate may issue on request of one of the divided co-owners the maintenance plan with the effect until the decision of the court is issued in non-contentious proceedings initiated by one of the divided co-owners.

330. With regard to *transactions exceeding the bounds of regular management*, the CPL requires the consent of all the (regular as well as divided) co-owners.[739] The HA, however, differentiates two types of transactions exceeding the bounds of regular management requiring two different consents of the divided co-owners: (i) those requiring full consent of the divided co-owners: amendment of the agreement on the determination of the ideal shares of the divided co-owners; amendment of the ratio of individual parts/common parts; special restraints of use of the individual and/or common parts; agreement on the special common parts and ideal shares on such parts; all construction works requiring construction permit; using an apartment for other purposes than living there or performing a business activity; deciding on a manager in buildings where having a manager is not obligatory, and (ii) all other transactions exceeding the bounds of regular management (such as works not requiring a construction permit; insurance of the building; conclusion of the contract on mutual relations; using an apartment for business activities) – these require only the consent of more than three-quarters of the divided co-owners' ideal shares.[740]

331. The CPL states that if the divided co-owners do not reach agreement on a transaction exceeding regular management, then divided co-owners having more than half of the co-ownership shares of the common parts may request that the court make a decision on the transaction in a non-contentious civil procedure, whereby in reaching its decision, the court must pay particular attention to the type of transaction, the division of the encumbrances, and the consequences for the divided co-owners who opposed the transaction.[741] The same rule is set out in the HA as regards transactions exceeding the bounds of regular management that require full consent,[742] while the HA is silent on if and how the court is to decide in cases of those transactions exceeding the bounds of regular management that require a consent of more than three-quarters of the ideal shares.[743] The HA states only that if a divided co-owner opposes the works which do not require the construction permit, he or she may request the court to decide on the works.[744] Special rules on taking decisions with regard to common parts, are set out in the Personal Data Protection Act that requires a consent of more than 70% of the divided co-owners' ideal shares

---

plan does not guarantee proper maintenance of the building. If the divided co-owner succeeds, the costs of the expert are covered from all the divided co-owners.

739. Article 67/5 of CPL.

740. Article 29 of HA.

741. Article 117 of CPL. This rule applies also to the amendments to a contract on mutual relations in the part concerning regular management of common parts.

742. Article 28/4 of HA.

743. The general rules of Art. 117/2 of the CPL should apply.

744. Article 28/3,5 of HA.

to decide on setting up video control of the entrance of the building and of the common parts of the building (but not of the entrances of individual parts) for the purposes of safeguarding property or life.[745]

332. The divided co-owners take their decisions on the management of the common parts in two types of proceedings regulated in the HA: at the assembly of the divided co-owners[746] or by signing a document containing a reasoned proposal of a decision made by one of the divided co-owners or the supervisory board and made available for no longer than three months for signature to the other divided co-owners.[747] The assembly may be called for by the manager, by the divided co-owners having at least 20% of the ideal shares, or by the supervisory board, whereby the manager is obliged to call for an assembly at least once per year. The voting may start if so many co-owners' shares are present as are required for the decision to be taken depending on the substance of the proposal (i.e., more than 50% or more than 70% or more than 75% or 100%). If they are not present, then the assembly must be called for anew within fourteen days. The decisions regarding regular management of the common parts may then be taken by a majority of the shares voting.

VII. Manager of the Multi-unit Building and Supervisory Board

333. If an immovable has more than two divided co-owners and more than eight individual parts, the divided co-owners must appoint a manager (Sl. *upravnik*).[748] In other cases of divided co-ownership, i.e., when an immovable has less than nine individual parts or has less than three divided co-owners, the manager is not obligatory – if the divided co-owners do not decide to appoint the manager, they are to manage the common parts by themselves.[749]

334. The appointment of a manager is considered a regular management transaction.[750] If a manager is not appointed, each of the divided co-owners may request that the court appoint a manager in a non-contentious civil procedure.[751]

335. The manager is a natural or a legal person registered in the register of managers. One of the divided co-owners may also be appointed the manager.[752] The divided co-owners enter into a contract with the manager which has effects towards

745. Article 76 of the Personal Data Protection Act.
746. Articles 34 and 36 of HA.
747. Articles 34 and 35–38 of HA.
748. Article 118/1 of CPL. For further details, see Arts 48–67 of HA.
749. Article 48/3 of HA.
750. Article 118/2 of CPL, Art. 49/1 of HA.
751. Article 118/3 of CPL, Art. 49/3 of HA. Art. 40/3 of HA states that in cases where the manager is not appointed, one of the divided co-owners may call for a meeting of divided co-owners on which they must first appoint the manager. If not, every divided co-owner may request the court to appoint the manager.
752. Article 49/2 of HA.

all the divided co-owners (including those who voted against it, and those, who had not voted at all, be it the current or future divided co-owners at the time of voting).[753]

336. The manager has the following powers: to carry out the decisions of the divided co-owners; to ensure regular maintenance and functioning of common parts; to ensure division and enforcement of obligations; to manage the reserve fund and joint money; to represent the divided co-owners in management transactions and to file in the name of divided co-owners an enforcement suit and a suit for payment of costs and liabilities encumbering a divided co-owner, etc.[754] In carrying out his or her activities, the manager must always act in accordance with the interests of the divided co-owners.[755] The divided co-owners may appoint a supervisory board whose tasks are to supervise the work of the manager, to make proposals of decisions and make them available for signature by the divided co-owners, and to make proposals to the manager.[756] Unless agreed otherwise by the divided co-owners, the supervisory board has three members, of which one is their president. The divided co-owners may also decide on the assembly that the manager is to be supervised by one of the divided co-owners only.

337. Irrespective of the number of individual parts and the number of divided co-owners, the manager is not appointed in cases where the divided co-owners have registered a legal person called 'community of divided co-owners' (Sl. *skupnost lastnikov*) whose registered activity is management of the multi-unit building.[757] In these cases, the building is managed by the divided co-owners themselves (forming the so-called assembly of divided co-owners, Sl. *zbor etažnih lastnikov*) who are represented by their president (Sl. *predsednik*). The legal person is set up by consensus of all divided co-owners who must draft a statute of the community and register it in the court register. The funds of the legal person are consisted of the divided co-owners' monthly payments for the purposes of management of the common parts and of the payments into the reserve fund. In contrast to the regular divided co-ownership where joint and several liability of the divided co-owners towards third persons with regard to the costs of common parts is explicitly prohibited, the divided co-owners that have established the community are jointly and severally liable for the obligations of the community towards third persons.

753. The conclusion of the contract, its substance, its effects, and its termination are regulated in detail in Arts 53–62 of HA.
754. Article 118 of CPL. Further details as to the manager's powers are set out in Arts 50–52 of HA. The contract on mutual relations may set out further manager's powers and rights and obligations (Arts 50/2 and 53/1 of HA).
755. Article 118/5 of CPL.
756. Article 39 of HA.
757. Articles 72–82 of HA.

VIII. Reserve Fund

338. If an immovable has more than two divided co-owners and more than eight individual parts, the divided co-owners must set up a reserve fund (Sl. *rezervni sklad*) to cover future costs of regular management.[758] In other cases of divided co-ownership, i.e., when an immovable has less than nine individual parts or has less than three divided co-owners, the reserve fund is not obligatory.

339. The funds in the reserve fund are in joint property of the divided co-owners and are managed by the manager of the building separately in a special bank account.[759] The funds in the reserve fund may be used only to meet the costs of maintenance and necessary improvements and to pay off loans taken on for these purposes. Enforcement on the funds in the reserve fund, too, is permitted only for these purposes.[760] The manager's creditors may not take hold of the funds of the reserve fund, the fund may also not form the manager's insolvency estate.[761]

340. The criteria for determining the contribution of each divided co-owner to the reserve fund, and the amount of the minimum contribution, are laid down in the executive regulations.[762]

341. A divided co-owner neither has the right to demand reimbursement of payments made into the reserve fund nor to demand its division.[763] If he or she transfers the ownership on the apartment to another person, his or her contribution in the fund transfers as well.

342. If a divided co-owner fails to pay his or her contribution into the reserve fund, the manager must call on him or her to do so. Such call by the manager must be in writing and is considered to be the authentic document within the meaning of the CESA.[764]

IX. Statutory Encumbrance

343. *If an immovable has more than two divided co-owners and more than eight individual parts*, a statutory encumbrance on an individual part in divided co-ownership is set up by the CPL to the benefit of the other divided co-owners for

758. Article 119 of CPL, Arts 41–47 of HA.
759. Article 119/1,2 of CPL. Further details on the management of the funds by the manager are set out in Arts 42 and 43 of the HA.
760. Article 119/4 of CPL, Art. 46 of HA.
761. Article 45 of HA.
762. According to Art. 119/3 of the CPL, the Minister of Justice issued the Pravilnik o merilih za določitev prispevka etažnega lastnika v rezervni sklad in najnižji vrednosti prispevka [Rules on Criteria for Determining Contributions of Apartment Owners into the Reserve Fund and the Lowest Rate of Contribution], Official Gazette RS, No. 11/04.
763. Article 119/5 of CPL.
764. Article 119/6 of CPL, Art. 44/3 of HA.

the costs of management and the payments into the compulsory reserve fund up to the amount of five times the minimum payment into the reserve fund. In case of multiple encumbrances, such encumbrance has the highest ranking.[765]

X. Obligations of a Divided Co-owner

344. A divided co-owner must, at an appropriate time, ensure repairs to his or her individual part if this is necessary to avert damage being caused to other parts of the building.[766]

345. A divided co-owner must also allow access to his or her individual part for the purpose of carrying out the repairs and improvements to common parts that could otherwise not be carried out or that could otherwise only be carried out at a disproportionate cost. If a divided co-owner does not allow access, a court decides the matter in a non-contentious civil procedure upon a request from the manager of the building or from the other divided co-owners. Repairs or improvements must, however, be carried out in the shortest possible time and with the least possible disturbance to the divided co-owner. A divided co-owner must be given suitable notice of the work planned.[767]

346. Divided co-owners must also provide the manager and the other divided co-owners with the information and the documents necessary for managing the common parts.[768]

XI. Alterations to Individual Parts in Divided Co-ownership

347. A divided co-owner may (without the consent of the other divided co-owners) carry out alterations to his or her individual part, provided they do not cause the deterioration of any other part of the immovable. Whenever alterations to an individual part in divided co-ownership also represent a major intervention in the common parts, the divided co-owner may not commence the work without the consent of the divided co-owners having more than half of the co-ownership shares of the common parts.[769]

348. The HA also sets down the conditions for carrying out economic activity in an individual part by its owner or tenant.[770]

765. Article 120 of CPL.
766. Article 121/1 of CPL.
767. Article 121/2,3,4,5 of CPL.
768. Article 121/6 of CPL.
769. Article 122 of CPL.
770. Article 14 of HA. Vlahek & Damjan, *Slovenian regulation of short-term apartment rentals via digital platforms*, in *Sharing economy in Europe: opportunities and challenges*, 119 ff. (Hojnik, Zavod 14, Ljubljana, European Liberal Forum, Brussels, 2018).

XII. Action for Exclusion of a Divided Co-owner

349. If a divided co-owner or other user of an individual part in divided co-ownership seriously violates the basic rules of neighbourly cohabitation or his or her obligations under the contract on mutual relations in such a way that the community with him or her is unbearable, divided co-owners having more than half of the co-ownership shares of the common parts may *agree to warn the violator*. If, in spite of the warning, the violator continues with his or her behaviour, divided co-owners having more than half of the co-ownership shares of the common parts may *decide to file a suit for his or her exclusion and for the sale of his or her individual part*. A judgment on exclusion is enforced with the sale of the individual part in divided co-ownership in accordance with the rules regulating enforcement on immovables.[771] The HA additionally sets out that the divided co-owners may also list serious violations in their housing order (that may be passed by more than half of the co-ownership shares)[772] in case of which the proceedings for exclusion of a divided co-owner may also be initiated.[773]

XIII. Pre-emption Right

350. If an immovable has two or more divided co-owners and no more than five individual parts, the other divided co-owners have a right of pre-emption in the event one of the individual parts in divided co-ownership is being sold.[774] This a specific rule applying only to cases of divided co-ownership, where setting out the pre-emption right is reasonable only in smaller multi-unit buildings where the other divided co-owners have an interest in deciding who is to enter their close relationship. In cases of regular co-ownership of immovables, the co-owners have a general pre-emption right in the event of one of the co-ownership shares being sold irrespective of the number of the co-owners.

XIV. Expiration of Divided Co-ownership

351. Divided co-ownership can be converted into co-ownership or ownership of the immovable on the basis of a legal transaction. The provisions regulating the creation of divided co-ownership apply *mutatis mutandis*.[775] The parties usually wish to convert ownership or co-ownership into divided co-ownership, and not *vice versa*.

352. Further, divided co-ownership expires upon the destruction of the entire building. In this case, the divided co-owners become co-owners of the immovable

771. Article 123 of CPL.
772. Article 27 of HA.
773. Article 52 of HA.
774. Article 124 of CPL. General rules of the CO on the right of pre-emption apply.
775. Article 125 of CPL.

(the land) and of the remains of the building in accordance with their ideal share of the common parts.[776] Similarly, if an individual part in divided co-ownership is destroyed and cannot be renovated, the divided co-ownership of this part expires.[777]

776. Article 126 of CPL.
777. Article 127 of CPL.

Chapter 6. Neighbourhood Law

353. Neighbourhood relations are regulated in Articles 73–91 of the CPL as well as in several administrative acts (e.g., on construction, noise, spatial planning, protection of environment, etc.). Additionally, nuisance is further regulated in the CO. In this monograph, mainly civil law, and not administrative law aspects, are presented. The Yugoslav federal BPLRA of 1980 did not regulate neighbourhood law, and the rules of the ABGB therefore further applied all up to the enforcement of the CPL in 2003.

§1. Prohibition of Mutual Disturbance

354. Article 73 of the CPL sets down a general prohibition of mutual disturbance which is concretized in other provisions of the CPL. Owners of neighbouring or spatially connected immovables (the so-called neighbouring immovables, Sl. *sosednje nepremičnine*) must exercise their right of ownership in such a way that they do not disturb or cause damage to each other.[778] Rights that restrict the right of ownership of the owner of a neighbouring immovable must be exercised in good faith in accordance with local customs and in a way that least burdens the owner of the immovable.

§2. Prohibition of Nuisance

355. According to Article 75 of the CPL, the owner must refrain from actions and must remedy causes arising from his or her immovable that hinder the use of the other immovable beyond a level that, in view of the nature and purpose of the immovable and in view of the local customs, is normal or that cause substantial damage (the so-called prohibited indirect nuisance). Any disturbance by means of special devices (the so-called direct nuisance) without specific legal title is also prohibited. Direct nuisance is thus always prohibited unless specific legal title exists, while indirect nuisance is prohibited only if it causes substantial damage or if it hinders the use of the other immovable beyond a level that, in view of the nature and purpose of an immovable and in view of the local customs, is normal. According to the prevailing theory and case law, these criteria – and thus property law protection against prohibited nuisance – are applied regardless of any administrative legislation setting levels of admissible noise, pollution, etc.[779]

356. In addition to the CPL, nuisance in the form of a source of danger threatening to cause greater damage to a certain person or an indeterminate number of persons is regulated in Article 133 of the CO, granting a broader protection to claimants than the CPL. According to the CO, anyone may request that another person

778. According to Art. 74 of the CPL, the provisions of the CPL on neighbourhood law applying to an owner shall also apply *mutatis mutandis* to a direct possessor (e.g., tenant).
779. For further details, see Vrenčur in *Property Law*, 362–375.

removes a source of danger threatening to cause greater damage to a certain person or an indeterminate number of persons, and refrains from performing activities causing disturbance or danger for damage, if the occurrence of disturbance or damage cannot be prevented by appropriate measures.[780] Such *actio popularis* (Sl. *popularna tožba*) is granted to a broader number of claimants (because every potentially wronged party may file a request) and in a broader number of cases (because threat of damage suffices)[781] than the *actio negatoria* encompassed in the CPL. At the request of an interested person, the court will order appropriate measures to prevent the occurrence of damage or disturbance or to remove the source of danger. Such measures are to be taken at the expense of the possessor should the latter fail to act. If damage arises during the performance of activities of general interest for which permission has been given by the relevant authority, however, it is only possible to demand the reimbursement of damage that exceeds the customary boundaries. Nevertheless, appropriate measures to prevent the occurrence of damage or to reduce it may also be demanded in such a case.

§3. Temporary Use of the Neighbouring Immovable

I. Maintenance Work

357. According to Article 76 of the CPL, the owner of an immovable urgently requiring works that are necessary for the use and exploitation of the immovable may temporarily use the neighbouring immovable in order to carry out the works, if this works cannot be carried out in some other way or if they can only be carried out otherwise at disproportionate cost. Such use is a form of a legal easement. Before the works are commenced, the owner and possessor of the other immovable must be informed of the works at an appropriate time and in an appropriate manner. After the use, the neighbouring immovable must be restored to its previous condition, and appropriate compensation must be paid on request of the owner of the neighbouring immovable.

II. Pursuit of Animals

358. According to Article 84 of the CPL, domestic and domesticated animals may be pursued by their owner onto another's immovable (a form of a legal easement is thereby established). The owner or the possessor of the immovable may, however, prohibit access to the immovable by the owner of the animals if he or she him- or herself delivers the animals to the owner without delay.

780. For further details, see Damjan, *Idealne imisije industrijskih in infrastrukturnih objektov* [The Ideal Immissions of Industrial and Infrastructural Facilities], in Pravnik, 2010, Y. 65, No. 9/10, pp. 573 ff.

781. See Vrenčur in *Property Law*, 373–375. The threat must, however, be concrete, direct, and not uncertain.

§4. REGULATION OF BOUNDARIES

I. Determination of Boundaries

359. Boundaries are primarily determined in the geodetic (cadastral) administrative proceedings according to Articles 26–44 of the Real-Estate Recording Act,[782] while in some cases, parties start civil proceedings where boundaries are determined according to Articles 77 and 78 of the CPL.

A. Determination of Boundaries in Cadastral Proceedings

360. The cadastral procedure for determining boundaries consists of three phases. The first phase is a procedure for determining a boundary consisting of activities of a geodesist making a detailed report on the boundary on the basis of a boundary hearing. The second phase is an administrative procedure of recording a determined boundary (Sl. *določena meja*) by a surveying and mapping authority (Sl. *geodetska uprava*) on the basis of the geodesist's report. Finally, the recorded boundary is marked in nature.

361. A geodesist performs a boundary hearing,[783] where he or she shows the owners of the neighbouring immovables where the boundary is drawn in the cadastre and to where on its left and right the field of deviation in which the boundary may be set in cadastral proceedings extends (the so-called boundary according to the cadastral data, Sl. *meja po podatkih zemljiškega katastra*), and asks them to show where, in their view, the boundary is (the so-called shown boundary, Sl. *pokazana meja*).

362. If the shown boundary falls outside the limits of the boundary according to the cadastral data, the geodesist warns the parties that such boundary cannot be recorded as a determined boundary in the cadastre. If the neighbours agree on the boundary and show it in the limits of the boundary according to the cadastral data, the geodesist denotes it as a so-called suggested boundary (Sl. *predlagana meja*), which afterwards becomes the determined boundary. If the neighbours, however, show two different boundaries within the limits of the boundary according to the

782. Zakon o evidentiranju nepremičnin (ZEN) [Real-Estate Recording Act], Official Gazette RS, No. 47/06, with further amendments.

783. Usually on request of one of the owners of the immovables, sometimes performing an official duty. It is to be underscored that a large number of immovables in Slovenia is still registered as 'social property' or as 'general people's property' and that in these cases, the real owner of the immovable should be determined in order to perform proper boundary hearing and boundary administrative proceedings. What happens in practice is that municipalities wishing to take illegally hold of such immovables (or at least encumber them or proclaim them as immovable in public domain) although they are in reality in ownership of private parties, hire geodesists in order to determine the boundary between immovables that are not in ownership of municipalities. For further details on the status of such immovables, see Part I, Ch. 2 and Ch. 3.

cadastral data, the geodesist must try to reach an agreement between the parties. If he or she does not succeed, he or she him- or herself denotes the suggested boundary as he or she thinks fit.

363. A party initiating the administrative geodetic procedure must enclose the boundary report drafted by a geodesist. The surveying and mapping authority first invites all owners of immovables who had not participated in the boundary hearing to make statements in writing on whether they agree with the suggested boundary. When the boundary report provides for one or more shown boundaries that do not correspond to the suggested boundary, an oral hearing must be held. If it seems that the neighbours could agree on the boundary within the cadastre limits, but not as suggested in the boundary report, a new report is to be made, and the boundary is held to be determined as agreed upon. If, however, there is no agreement on the boundary, the surveying and mapping authority invites the parties to start court proceedings in thirty days and provide evidence thereof. If court proceedings are not initiated within thirty days, it is presumed that the parties agree to the suggested boundary. Once court proceedings are activated, the surveying and mapping authority must suspend administration proceedings, and after the court regulates the boundary, administration proceedings must be discontinued.

B. Determination of Boundaries in Court Proceedings

364. As explained in the preceding paragraph, if a boundary is disputed among neighbours (or if it is not disputed, but is not within the limits of the boundary according to the cadastral data), it cannot generally be determined in cadastral proceedings; the neighbours are requested to initiate court proceedings, and only if they fail to do so, is the boundary determined in cadastral proceedings whereby it is presumed that the parties have agreed to the suggested boundary. A boundary may also be determined in court proceedings if the boundary has not yet been determined at all; initiation of cadastral proceedings is, therefore, not a prerequisite for activating court proceedings. Further, once a boundary is determined in cadastral proceedings, it may always be determined anew in court proceedings. On the contrary, once the boundary is determined in court proceedings, it cannot be determined anew in cadastral or court proceedings.[784]

365. Boundaries are generally determined in a non-contentious procedure regulated in the NCCPA (Articles 167–174 of the new NCCPA).[785] As presented later, the boundary can also be determined in a contentious procedure. Substantive provisions for regulating boundaries are set down in Articles 77 and 78 of the CPL.

784. For further details, see Rijavec in Rijavec et al., *Pravna ureditev nepremičnin* [Legal Regulation of Immovables], 162–174 (GV Založba 2006).

785. Šinkovec & Tratar, *Zakon o nepravdnem postopku s komentarjem, vzorci in sodno prakso* [Non-Contentious Civil Procedure Act with Commentary, Forms and Case-law], 236–256 (Primath 2003).

According to the CPL, the court regulates the boundary on the basis of the following three criteria: (i) the stronger right, (ii) the last peaceful enjoyment of possession, and (iii) the fair assessment.

366. First, the court must regulate a boundary on the basis of the stronger right, which is presumed to attach to the boundary that had already been regulated in the cadastral proceedings. However, if the value of the disputed boundary area[786] exceeds twice the value for determining a small claims procedure (i.e., two times EUR 2,000, according to the CPA), the court may regulate the boundary on the basis of the stronger right (e.g., as determined in cadastral proceedings or when ownership was acquired and the boundary moved by acquisitive prescription) only if the parties agree so. If they do not agree so, or if the stronger right is not proven, the court determines the boundary according to the last peaceful enjoyment of possession (i.e., possession that had been enjoyed peacefully by the parties for a longer period of time before the dispute arose),[787] and, if this is not possible, on the grounds of a fair assessment of the court (provided there are no specific characteristics of the land to be divided, courts usually divide the disputed area by halves).[788] If they do not agree to the application of the stronger right criteria in the non-contentious procedure, each of the parties may, however, claim the stronger right in a civil contentious procedure within three months of the court's final decision on the determination of the boundary (issued in the non-contentious procedure).[789]

II. Use of the Boundary

367. According to Article 79 of the CPL, the owner of an immovable may use the fence, ditch, wall, or other things intended to demarcate the boundary up to half of the width from his or her side of the boundary.

III. Boundary Markers

368. According to Article 80 of the CPL, it is presumed that boundary fences, walls, trees, ditches, and other things intended to demarcate the boundary are *in*

786. Usually, this will be the market value. If the parties agree on the value, the court will, in principle, not investigate the value of the area. Rijavec in Rijavec et al., *Pravna ureditev nepremičnin* [Legal Regulation of Immovables], 170 (GV Založba 2006).

787. Rijavec in Rijavec et al., *Pravna ureditev nepremičnin* [Legal Regulation of Immovables], 170 (GV Založba 2006), citing two Decisions of the Supreme Court of the RS interpreting the notion of the last quiet enjoyment of possession (Nos I Cp 233/97 of 25 Feb. 1997, I Cp 173/98 of 23 Sep. 1998).

788. Rijavec in Rijavec et al., *Pravna ureditev nepremičnin* [Legal Regulation of Immovables], 171 (GV Založba 2006).

789. *Ibid.*, 169.

joint ownership of the owners of the neighbouring immovables.[790] Boundary markers must be maintained in the customary local manner, where the costs of maintenance are covered equally by the owners of the neighbouring immovables. The owners of the neighbouring immovables are also jointly and severally liable for damage caused to third persons as a result of non-maintenance of their boundary.

IV. Trees on a Boundary

369. According to Article 81 of the CPL, the fruits of a tree that grows on a boundary are to be *divided equally* between the owners of the neighbouring immovables. If such tree obstructs the use of any neighbouring immovable, the owner of the immovable *may require the tree to be removed at the owners' joint cost.*

V. Building over a Boundary

370. Article 47 of the CPL regulates constructions extending over the boundary of an immovable onto the neighbouring immovable. It sets down an exception to the rule on accession as it enables the neighbours to request that the court decide the arrangement of their mutual relationship – either by requesting the builder to pull down the structure and restore the neighbouring immovable to its original condition, or by setting appropriate compensation for his or her neighbour and issuing a ruling establishing a new border between the neighbouring immovables and requesting the builder to compensate the neighbour for the part of the immovable that has come into the builder's ownership.[791]

§5. Fruits Falling on a Neighbouring Immovable

371. In contrast to Article 81 of the CPL, which regulates ownership on fruits falling from a tree growing on the boundary, Article 82 of the CPL regulates ownership of fruits that fall onto a neighbouring immovable from a tree that grows on someone else's immovable. Ownership of such fruits *is acquired by the owner of the neighbouring immovable the moment the fruits are severed from the tree and fall onto his or her land*, and thus not by the owner of the tree as would normally be the case according to the rule that the owner of a principal thing becomes owner of its fruits.

§6. Right to Remove Branches and Roots

372. Article 83 of the CPL sets down rules in cases where branches of a neighbour's tree extend into the airspace above someone's immovable or where roots of

790. For further details on joint ownership, see Part I, Ch. 5, §2.
791. For details, see Part III, Ch. 4.

a neighbour's tree grow into someone's immovable. The owner of an immovable has *the right to remove and appropriate such branches and roots if they disturb him or her and if the owner of the neighbouring immovable fails to do so at his or her request*. If the owner of the neighbouring immovable is prohibited by special regulation from performing such actions (e.g., the tree has a status of a natural monument), his or her neighbour has only the right to compensation for such disturbance. Further, fruits from branches extending into the airspace of a neighbouring immovable become the property of the owner of that immovable upon severance. These provisions, however, do not apply to forests, where it is presumed that the branches and roots do not disturb the neighbouring owners, who thus do not have the right to remove and appropriate them.

§7. Prohibition Against Excavation

373. According to Article 85 of the CPL, the owner of an immovable may not excavate his or her immovable or interfere with it in such a way that would cause a neighbouring immovable to lose solidity, stability, or support. The owner of an immovable whose solidity, stability, or support is endangered by the interference *may demand a ban on the continuation of the works until suitable measures are carried out to prevent the loss of solidity, stability, and support*. If such measures cannot be carried out, the owner may demand that the interference be prohibited. If the owner erected special supports and constructions while excavating and interfering with his or her immovable in order to ensure the stability of another's immovable, the owner is obliged to maintain them regularly. He or she is liable for damage arising as a result of these supports and constructions regardless of fault.

§8. Prohibition Against Altering a Watercourse

374. According to Article 86 of the CPL, the owner of an immovable may not (on his or her immovable) alter the flow, strength, quantity, or quality of water flowing over his or her immovable to the detriment of a neighbouring immovable.

§9. Run-Off of Precipitation

375. According to Article 87 of the CPL, the owner of an immovable must do everything necessary to ensure that precipitation coming off his or her building does not run off or fall onto another's immovable.

§10. Way of Necessity

376. The way of necessity is regulated in Articles 88–91 of the CPL and enables acquisition of easement on someone else's immovable by a final court decision. The court establishes a way of necessity *for an immovable that does not have the necessary connection with a public road for regular use (or with other public infrastructure)*[792] *or when such connection would be associated with disproportionate costs*. It permits a way of necessity provided it does not prevent or substantially obstruct the use of the immovable over which it is to run, and it determines it in such a way as to minimize the burden on the other immovable. The entitled person must pay appropriate compensation to the person under obligation for the permitted way of necessity. A way of necessity may be altered or abolished if it is no longer necessary owing to changed circumstances. The rules on the procedure for determining the way of necessity are laid down in the NCCPA.[793]

792. According to Art. 91 of the CPL, the provisions on the way of necessity also apply *mutatis mutandis* to connection to public infrastructure if the owner of the immovable demanding it fulfils the conditions for connecting to such infrastructure.
793. Articles 175–179 of the new NCCPA.

Part II. Movable Property and Personal Property/Chattels

377. Property rights can be established with regard to movable and immovable assets, as well as with regard to patrimonial rights. The regulation of property rights on immovables differs considerably from that of property rights on movables, whereas the latter applies *mutatis mutandis* to property rights that can be established on patrimonial rights.[794] For this reason, property rights on movables and on patrimonial rights are treated together here in Part II. Attention will be drawn to the specific characteristics of movables, while general characteristics common to movables and immovables are presented in the chapter Introduction to Property Law in the General Introduction of this monograph. Funds are a special form of patrimony, which is not regulated by the Slovenian property law. They will be also presented in this part of the monograph.

794. Article 3/2 of CPL.

Chapter 1. General Classification

§1. MOVABLE PROPERTY

378. Article 18 of the CPL determines that an immovable is a spatially defined area of land together with all its elements, whereas all other things are movables.[795] Thus, the CPL does not provide for a positive definition of movable property. The legal theory *defines* movables as specifically determined objects that can be moved from one place to another without their economical substance being harmed in any way.[796] A movable is distinguished from other things as being a separate thing according to the common understanding in legal relationships.[797] Various forms of energy and waves that can be controlled by man, which for the purposes of the CPL are deemed to be things (Article 15/2 of the CPL), must also be considered to be movables.[798] Money is also a movable.[799] Movables can be consumable or non-consumable. This distinction has greater importance in the law of obligations, but is important also in property law, as, for example, personal easements can only be established on non-consumable things.[800]

379. As already explained in the General Introduction to this monograph, movables are sometimes considered as elements of immovables or their appurtenances (e.g., tools for working the land are appurtenances of a farm). In principle, such movables share the legal regime applicable to the immovable they 'belong' to, i.e., they are transferred together with the immovable, the mortgage usually encompasses them, etc.

380. In contrast to immovable property, the number of movables is practically unlimited. Therefore, there is no register of movables that would ensure the *publicity of property rights* with regard to such property.[801] Such publicity can thus only be marked by possession of the object, which is, however, not a very reliable sign. One exception regarding specific categories of movables is the Register of Attached Movables and Non-possessory Pledges,[802] which enables anyone to verify if a certain movable has been attached (seized) in enforcement proceedings or placed under a non-possessory pledge. Further examples are the register of ships and the register of aircrafts.[803]

---

795. For the definition of a thing, see General Introduction, §3, II.
796. This definition is based on Art. 293 of the ABGB. Juhart in *Property Law*, 67; Gavella in Gavella et al., *Stvarno pravo* [Property Law], 78 (Narodne Novine 2007).
797. Gavella in Gavella et al., *Stvarno pravo* [Property Law], 78 (Narodne Novine 2007).
798. An electronic communication signal is an example of such waves, see, e.g., Decision of the High Court in Ljubljana, No. I Cp 2750/2010 of 18 Aug. 2010.
799. Juhart in *Property Law*, 68.
800. *Ibid.*, 68 and 69.
801. Certain categories of movables (e.g., ships) are, however, subject to special regulation and registers.
802. For more on this register, see Part V.
803. For more, see paras. 414 and 415 of this monograph.

381. Compared with immovable property, the exercise of ownership of movable property is very rarely limited in the *public interest*.

§2. Patrimonial Rights

382. According to the CPL, patrimonial rights (Sl. *premoženjske pravice*) can also be the object of specific property rights – that is, the lien and the usufruct – although they are not considered to be 'things'.[804] The doctrine denominates them as 'a right on a right'.[805] The right of ownership can thus not exist on a right; nevertheless, each patrimonial right naturally belongs to someone and constitutes a part of this person's patrimony, which is protected by a fundamental constitutional right to ownership.[806] Having a patrimonial right is thus a parallel to owning a thing.

383. For the purposes of property law, a patrimonial right is a right that is *transferable* and whose *value can be expressed in money*.[807] Thus, according to High Court in Ljubljana, personal easements, such as habitation, are not patrimonial rights, as they are not transferable.[808] The establishment of a lien or usufruct on a patrimonial right usually results in the limitation of the latter, which is possible only if the patrimonial right is transferable.[809] The possibility of expressing the value of a right in money is of special importance in the case of the establishment of a lien, the latter being the right of priority in the payment of a claim by way of selling the lien object or right.[810] Patrimonial rights are, for example, claims, corporate rights, patrimonial intellectual property rights,[811] etc.[812]

384. The provisions of the CPL on the *transfer* of ownership are applicable also to the disposal of all other patrimonial rights and can thus be designated as general rules of civil law.[813] However, it must be noted that outside the requirement regarding the capacity to dispose of the patrimonial right, the requirements regarding the

804. Article 3/3 of CPL.
805. B. Sajovic, *Osnove civilnega prava, Splošni del* [Bases of Civil law, General Part], 75 (ČZ Uradni list RS 1994), cited by Juhart in *Property Law*, 76.
806. Juhart in *Property Law*, 79.
807. Article 22 of CPL.
808. See High Court in Ljubljana, Decision No. I Ip 1202/2015 of 29 May 2015.
809. Juhart in *Property Law*, 76.
810. *Ibid.*, 76–77.
811. Industrial property rights must be duly registered to be considered as property rights; see Judgment of the Supreme Court RS, No. III Ips 33/2009 of 17 Apr. 2012. Computer program is not a thing nor a property right but a creation in the sense of copyright law; see Judgment of High Court in Ljubljana, No. I Cpg 1017/2013 of 12 Dec. 2013.
812. Juhart in *Property Law*, 77.
813. Tratnik in *Property Law*, 249.

content and form of the necessary legal acts can differ considerably.[814] For the transfer of a patrimonial right, an assignment is generally necessary in order for the transfer to gain property law effects.[815] Assignment is thus analogous to delivery regarding the transfer of movables and to entry into the land register regarding immovables.

§3. Funds

385. In Slovenian law, funds are not subject to property law regulation. *Public funds* are regulated by the Public Funds Act[816] and are subject to public law. *Investment funds* are regulated by the Investment Funds and Management Companies Act.[817] In Article 5/1, they are defined as collective investment undertakings whose sole purpose is the collecting of the assets of the investors and investing these assets according to the previously determined investment politics into different kinds of investments to the sole benefit of the holders of the units of such investment fund.

386. In this context, another form of patrimony can be mentioned – the *foundation*. Foundations are regulated by the Foundations Act of 1995.[818] They are defined as a patrimony with a defined purpose. They are legal persons subject to private law; however, under Article 3 of the Foundations Act, the ministry responsible for the field of the purpose of a foundation has legally determined tasks in the founding, the functioning and the cessation of such foundation. The purpose of a foundation must be of general or charitable interest and, as a general rule, durable.[819] Thus, in Slovenian law, a foundation cannot have a private purpose.[820] Even if the circle of beneficiaries of a foundation is limited, they cannot be designated by name or a family connection.[821] A foundation can be established by a natural or a legal person, by way of a notarial protocol, or by a last will.[822] The patrimony of a foundation can be money, movables, immovables, or patrimonial rights.[823]

814. *Ibid.*, 249.
815. Vrenčur in *Property Law*, 577.
816. Zakon o javnih skladih (ZJS-1) [Public Funds Act], Official Gazette RS, No 77/08, with further amendments.
817. Zakon o investicijskih skladih in družbah za upravljanje (ZISDU-3) [Investment Funds and Management Companies Act], Official Gazette RS, No. 31/15, with further amendments.
818. Zakon o ustanovah (ZU) [Foundations Act], Official Gazette RS, No. 60/95, with further amendments.
819. Article 2/1 of Foundations Act.
820. Žnidaršič Skubic, *Zasebna ustanova,* trust, *fiduciarni pravni posli in njihov vpliv na dedovanje* [Private Foundation, Trust, Fiduciary Transactions and their Influence on Inheritance], 12 (Uradni list 2015).
821. Article 2/4 of Foundations Act. See also Žnidaršič Skubic, *Zasebna ustanova,* trust, *fiduciarni pravni posli in njihov vpliv na dedovanje* [Private Foundation, Trust, Fiduciary Transactions and their Influence on Inheritance], 14 (Uradni list, 2015).
822. Articles 4–8 of Foundations Act.
823. Articles 9 of Foundations Act.

Chapter 2. Legal Interests: Limited Property Rights on Movables and Patrimonial Rights

387. Limited property rights, which can be established with regard to movables, are pledge and personal easements. Patrimonial rights can be the object of a lien and of a usufruct. For more on the pledge on movables and the lien on patrimonial rights, see Part V of this monograph.

388. The personal easements regulated in Slovenian law comprise *usufruct*,[824] *use*,[825] and *habitation*.[826] A personal easement is the right of its holder to use a thing or a right that belong to another person; it extinguishes at the time of the holder's death at the latest.[827] If the holder of a personal easement is a legal entity, the duration of the easement is of maximum thirty years.[828] According to Article 229 of the CPL, it is not possible to transfer personal easements to other persons;[829] however, it is possible to transfer the right of exercise of the personal easement if the CPL provides so (i.e., in the case of usufruct, not other personal easements).

389. A usufruct can be established on things and patrimonial rights, whereas use and habitation can only be established on things. According to Article 230 of the CPL, usufruct is a personal easement that confers the right to use and enjoy another's property or right so that its substance is preserved. It can only be established on non-consumable things. A usufruct is established on the basis of a legal transaction or of a judgment.[830] A usufruct on a movable is acquired with the delivery of the movable, whereas a usufruct on a patrimonial right is acquired by a legal transaction necessary for the transfer of such right. On the basis of a judgment, a usufruct is acquired when the judgment becomes final. It can be established on the sole co-owner's part of the thing.[831]

390. Use is defined in Article 244 of the CPL as a personal easement that grants the right to use the thing of another person in accordance with its economic purpose for the needs of the holder of the easement in such a manner that its substance is preserved. Under Article 247 of the CPL, habitation is a personal easement that grants the right to use the residence or part thereof of another person for the needs

824. Articles 230 ff. of CPL.
825. Articles 244 ff. of CPL.
826. Articles 247–248 of CPL.
827. Article 227/1 of CPL.
828. Article 227/2 of CPL.
829. It is also not possible to acquire a personal easement by way of acquisitive prescription (see, e.g., Judgment of the High Court in Ljubljana, No. II Cp 3143/2009 of 3 Feb. 2010), nor in the enforcement proceedings (see, e.g., Decision of the High Court in Koper, No. II Cp 958/2005 of 6 Sep. 2005, and Decision of the High Court in Ljubljana, No. I Ip 1202/2015 of 29 May 2015).
830. Article 233 of CPL.
831. Article 231 of CPL.

of the holder of the easement and his or her family in such a manner that its substance is preserved.[832] Habitation can thus only be established on immovable property. The effects and protection under property law are acquired when habitation is entered in the land register.[833]

391. Personal easements can be established on both movables (except habitation) and immovables; usufruct can also be established on patrimonial rights. The legal regulation of such easements does not differ regarding the nature of their object; see Part I for further details.

832. The parties' will to establish this personal easement must be clearly expressed, for example by the use of the word 'easement' and/or by the issuing of the permission to register the easement in the land register: see, e.g., Judgment of the High Court in Ljubljana, No. I Cp 3046/2013 of 19 Mar. 2014.

833. See, e.g., Judgment of the High Court in Ljubljana, No. I Cp 2605/2013 of 2 Oct. 2013.

Chapter 3. Equitable Interests

392. Slovenian law belongs to the continental legal circle, based on the heritage of Roman law, as was more thoroughly explained in the General Introduction. It does not feature the parallelism of law and equity known to legal systems based on common law. Equitable interests thus do not exist in Slovenia.

Chapter 4. Security Interests

393. In Slovenian law, securities with regard to movable property are the following:[834] the possessory and the non-possessory pledge, the right of retention, the reservation of title, and the fiduciary transfer of property. Lien can also be established on patrimonial rights. The aforementioned securities are presented in detail in Parts IV and V of this monograph.

834. See also Part I, Part IV, and Part V.

Part III. Acquisition of Property Rights

394. According to Article 39 of the CPL, ownership can be acquired by inheritance, by a decision of a public authority (i.e., court or administrative body), by a law (i.e., by a statutory provision), or on the basis of an agreement.[835] According to Article 13 of the CPL, the provisions of the CPL regulating acquisition of ownership apply *mutatis mutandis* to acquisition of other property rights.

395. Bases for acquiring ownership on movables partially differ from those on immovables and are the following:

- delivery on the basis of an agreement (Articles 40 and 60–63 of the CPL);
- inheritance (Article 41 of the CPL and Article 132 of the IA);
- final decision of a public authority (Article 42 of the CPL), for example:
  a. sale in non-contentious proceedings (Articles 140–145 of the new NCCPA[836]);
  b. sale in enforcement proceedings (Articles 92–96 of the CESA);
  c. sale in insolvency (Articles 325–347 of the FOIPCDA);
  d. distribution in insolvency (Article 374 of the FOIPCDA);
  e. denationalization (Article 66 of the Denationalization Act[837]); and
  f. confiscation in criminal proceedings (Articles 69 and 73 of the Penal Code[838]).
- statutory provision, for example:
  a. acquisition *a non domino* (Article 64 of the CPL);
  b. acquisitive prescription (Articles 43–46 of the CPL);
  c. appropriation (Article 50 of the CPL);
  d. finding (Articles 51–53 of the CPL);
  e. accession (Article 54 of the CPL);
  f. merging, confusion, and commixture (Articles 55–58 of the CPL); and
  g. acquisition of fruits (Article 59 of the CPL).

whereas bases of acquiring ownership on immovables are:

835. The rules on acquisition of ownership are analogously applied to all other property rights if stated so by the specific rule regulating a property right.
836. For further details (on the relevant provisions of the previous NCCPA), see Šinkovec & Tratar, *Zakon o nepravdnem postopku s komentarjem, vzorci in sodno prakso* [Non-Contentious Civil Procedure Act with Commentary, Forms and Case-law], 197–200 (Primath 2003).
837. Zakon o denacionalizaciji (ZDen) [Denationalization Act], Official Gazette RS, No. 27/91, with further amendments.
838. Kazenski zakonik (KZ-1) [Penal Code], Official Gazette RS, No. 55/08, with further amendments.

- registration on the basis of an agreement (Articles 40 and 49 of the CPL and provisions of the LRA);
- inheritance (Article 41 of the CPL and Article 132 of the IA);
- final decision of a public authority (Article 42 of the CPL), for example:
  a. building over a boundary (Article 47 of the CPL);
  b. sale in non-contentious proceedings (Articles 140–145 of the new NCCPA[839]);
  c. sale in enforcement proceedings (Articles 181–194 of the CESA);
  d. sale in insolvency (Articles 325–347 of the FOIPCDA);
  e. distribution in insolvency (Article 374 of the FOIPCDA);
  f. expropriation (Article 69 of the Constitution and Articles 92–114 of the SPA);
  g. commassation (Articles 115–132 of the SPA and Articles 55–76 of the Agricultural Land Act[840]);
  h. rounding off (Articles 47–54 of the Agricultural Land Act); and
  i. denationalization (Article 66 of the Denationalization Act).
- statutory provision, for example:
  a. acquisitive prescription (Articles 43–46 of the CPL); and
  b. acquisition *a non domino* (Article 8 of the CPL and Article 10 of the LRA).

396. As ensues from the foregoing, apart from provisions of Articles 39–64 of the CPL, acquisition of ownership is also regulated in specific legislation – for example, on the land register, inheritance, insolvency, spatial planning, denationalization, etc.

---

839. For further details (on the relevant provisions of the previous NCCPA), see Šinkovec & Tratar, *Zakon o nepravdnem postopku s komentarjem, vzorci in sodno prakso* [Non-Contentious Civil Procedure Act with Commentary, Forms and Case-law], 197–200 (Primath 2003).

840. Zakon o kmetijskih zemljiščih (ZKZ) [Agricultural Land Act], Official Gazette RS, No. 59/96, with further amendments.

Chapter 1. Transfer of Property by Contract *Inter Vivos*

§1. Basic Principles of the Slovenian Derivative *Inter Vivos* Transfer System

397. Derivative acquisition of ownership presupposes a valid agreement (instituting the obligation to transfer the ownership, Sl. *zavezovalni pravni posel*), a valid real agreement (conveyance, Sl. *razpolagalni pravni posel*), and the fulfilment of other conditions laid down in law that differ according to the type of object of transaction and serve the publicity of the transfer. In case of movables transfer is made by delivery to the acquirer (Sl. *izročitev*), whereas in case of immovables registration in the land register on the basis of the land registry permission (Lat. *clausula intabulandi*, Sl. *intabulacijska klavzula*, *zemljiškoknjižno dovolilo*) is required.

398. Although all *transfer prerequisites* cannot be deduced directly and clearly from the wording of the CPL,[841] they are traditionally fourfold and must be met cumulatively for the ownership and the rights associated with it to pass with full effects:[842]

1. valid underlying contract between the owner and the acquirer;
2. valid real agreement between the owner and the acquirer;
3. delivery in case of movables/registration in case of immovables, aircraft, ships, and securities; and
4. entitlement to dispose (Sl. *razpolagalno upravičenje*[843]).

---

841. Article 40 of the CPL as a general provision on *inter vivos* acquisition of ownership sets down (only) the 'valid underlying contract from which the obligation to transfer the ownership derives' and 'other conditions' as transfer requirements. Art. 60 of the CPL determines only delivery as the prerequisite of the acquisition of ownership on movables. Similarly, Art. 49 of the CPL emphasizes entry in the land register as a prerequisite for acquiring ownership on immovables. It, however, explains that entry in the land register is made on the basis of a document containing the land registry permission, from which a real agreement can be deduced. Some authors (e.g., Tratnik) state that the term 'legal transaction' contained in the titles of Arts 40 and 60 of the CPL ('Acquisition of the right of ownership by legal transaction') refers to the real agreement, which does not accord to the substance of these provisions, at least not to Art. 40 that clearly uses the term 'legal transaction' to denote the underlying obligation. It can, however, undoubtedly be deduced from Arts 49, 142, 171, 202, and 209 of the CPL. See Tratnik in *Property Law*, 223–224. See also Vlahek, *Pogodbeni prenos lastninske pravice na premičninah v evropskem pravnem prostoru* [Contractual Transfer of Ownership on Movables in European Legal Environment], 258–261 (GV Založba, 2010).
842. Some elements that might be important for the parties are not directly linked to the moment of transfer of ownership. The moment of passing of risk, for example, in principle corresponds to the moment of physical delivery (see Arts 436–437 of the CO) and not to the moment of transfer of ownership, although these two usually coincide.
843. Term 'the capacity to dispose' is usually being used but has started being replaced by 'the right to dispose' or 'the entitlement to dispose' in order to stress that it does not relate to the transferor's capacity but to the right of which he or she disposes of which such entitlement is part. For further details, see, e.g., Plavšak, Vrenčur, *Pomen razpolagalnega upravičenja pri razpolaganju z lastninsko pravico na nepremičnini* [The Importance of the Disposal Right for Transactions with Ownership Right on Real Estate], in Podjetje in delo, 2016, pp. 595 ff.; Juhart in *Property Law*, 240.

399. Slovenian transfer system is one of the so-called systems of causal tradition/registration with a separation of underlying obligation and real agreement. The principles enshrined in it – that is, the principle of causality, the principle of delivery/registration, and the principle of separation – are a reflection of the reception of German and, in particular (as regards the causality), Austrian law into the Slovenian legal system. As shown later, some exceptions exist regarding the last two prerequisites mitigating the principle of delivery/registration and the *nemo plus* principle.[844] It is also to be noted that in the case of immovables, recent Slovenian theory and case law have started veering off from the traditional concepts of acquiring immovables by *inter vivos* transactions by differentiating the moment of acquisition of ownership as between the parties (*inter partes*), and the moment of acquisition of ownership *erga omnes*, i.e. with full effects towards everyone.[845] This differentiation is in fact somewhat similar to the French transfer system[846] and has thus to some extent derogated from the traditional understanding of transfer prerequisites in Slovenian property law. It has plausibly been introduced so as to give the not yet registered acquirer who is already in possession of a valid land registry permission issued on the basis of a valid underlying contract (a so-called expected owner (Sl. *pričakovani lastnik*), a novel term in Slovenian legal terminology) certain legal protection, e.g., towards the transferor him- or herself, and in some cases (e.g., in enforcement and insolvency proceedings) even towards third persons.[847]

844. A presentation of the Slovene system in German language is provided in Juhart, *Die Eigentumsübertragung im Recht der Republik Slowenien*, in *Transfer of Title Concerning Movables, Part 1* (Eds Rainer & Filip-Fröschl, Salzburger Studien zum europäischen Privatrecht, Bd. 18, Peter Lang 2006). A detailed analysis of the system in Slovene language is available in Vlahek, *Pogodbeni prenos lastninske pravice na premičninah v evropskem pravnem prostoru* [Contractual Transfer of Ownership on Movables in European Legal Environment] (GV Založba 2010).

845. See, e.g., Decision of the Constitutional Court of RS, No. Up-591/10–15 of 2 Dec. 2010; Plavšak, Vrenčur, *Pomen razpolagalnega upravičenja pri razpolaganju z lastninsko pravico na nepremičnini* [The Importance of the Disposal Right for Transactions with Ownership Right on Real Estate], in Podjetje in delo, 2016, pp. 595 ff.; Juhart, *Nekaj dodatnih premislekov k stvarnopravnim izhodiščem pri prenosu lastninske pravice na nepremičninah* [Some Additional Thoughts on Property Law Principles of Transfer of Ownership on Immovables], Pravna praksa, 17. jan. 2013, Y. 32, No. 2, pp. 6–9; cf. Hudej Jasna & Ščernjavič Iztok, *Ponovni premislek o nekaterih temeljnih izhodiščih stvarnega prava pri prenosu lastninske pravice na nepremičninah* [New Reflections on Some of the Basic Principles of Property Law Regarding the Transfer of Ownership on Immovable Property], in Pravna praksa No. 3/2012, p. 23.

846. See Vlahek, *Pravnoposlovni prenos lastninske pravice na premičninah v francoskem pravnem sistemu* [Derivative Inter Vivos Transfer of Movables in the French Legal System], in Pravnik, 2010, pp. 171 ff.

847. See, e.g., Decision of the Constitutional Court of RS, No. Up-591/10–15 of 2 Dec. 2010; Decisions of the Supreme Court od RS, Nos II Ips 475/2008 of 5 Apr. 2012 and II Ips 385/2012 of 17 May 2012; Plavšak, Vrenčur, *Pomen razpolagalnega upravičenja pri razpolaganju z lastninsko pravico na nepremičnini* [The Importance of the Disposal Right for Transactions with Ownership Right on Real Estate], in Podjetje in delo, 2016, pp. 595 ff.; Verčko, *Uporaba pravil stvarnega prava pri varstvu vknjižene, resnične in pričakovane lastninske pravice* [Application og the Rules of Property Law in the Protection of Registered, real and expected ownership], in *Sodobno stvarno pravo* [Modern Property Law], 99–103 (Eds Juhart et al., Pravna fakulteta v Ljubljani, Planet GV, Tax-Fin-Lex 2016).

§2. Principle of Separation

400. Being influenced by the Germanic legal tradition, the principle of separation (Sl. *načelo ločitve*, Ger. *Trennungsprinzip*) of an *underlying legal transaction*, from which the obligation to transfer ownership derives (Sl. *zavezovalni pravni posel*, Ger. *Verpflichtungsgeschäft*), and a *real agreement* (Sl. *razpolagalni pravni posel*, Ger. *Verfügungsgeschäft*) plays a central role in the Slovenian transfer system. The substance of the underlying contract is merely an obligation to transfer property. The contract has no proprietary effects as is generally immanent to Romanic legal orders.[848] A further real agreement on the passing of ownership (followed by a real act of delivery in case of movables/registration in case of immovables producing *erga omnes* effects of the transfer) must be concluded between the transferor and transferee in order for the ownership to pass. Although the principle of separation is not expressly and unambiguously set down in the legislation, the modern Slovenian legal theory has been cogently stressing its role in the structure of property law. The terminology used by legal scholars and the courts referring to them, however, is at times ambiguous because they do not differentiate unequivocally the separation principle from the doctrine of *titulus* and *modus* that is also immanent to the Slovenian transfer system. Some authors equate *modus* with delivery as a real act, some with the real agreement as a volitional act, while others understand it as composed of both acts. The latter is usually termed as *modus* in the broader meaning, the sole delivery on the other hand as *modus* in the stricter sense.[849] Further, some authors assume tradition as a perceptible part of disposition,[850] whereas others treat it as separated from the disposition;[851] at times, however, some of the authors take both of these views.[852]

848. For further details on French transfer system, see Vlahek, *Pravnoposlovni prenos lastninske pravice na premičninah v francoskem pravnem sistemu* [Derivative Inter Vivos Transfer of Movables in the French Legal System], in Pravnik, 2010, pp. 171 ff.

849. Tratnik in *Property Law*, 223.

850. For example, Juhart in *CPL with Commentary 2004*, 248–250; Juhart, *Die Eigentumsübertragung im Recht der Republik Slowenien*, in *Transfer of Title Concerning Movables, Part 1* (Eds Rainer & Filip-Fröschl, Salzburger Studien zum europäischen Privatrecht, Bd. 18, Peter Lang 2006); Kersteš in Tratnik et al., *Stvarnopravna zavarovanja* [Securities under the Property Law], 98 (IARS 2001); Vrenčur in *Novo stvarno pravo* [New Property Law], 67 (Berden et al., Studio Linea, Zavod Codex Iuris 2002).

851. For example, Tratnik in *CPL with Commentary 2004*, 310; Tratnik, *Stvarnopravni zakonik z uvodnimi pojasnili* [Property Code with Introductory Remarks], 65 (Uradni list 2002); Vrenčur in *Novo stvarno pravo* [New Property Law], 68 (Berden et al., Studio Linea, Zavod Codex Iuris 2002).

852. For further details, see Vlahek, *Pogodbeni prenos lastninske pravice na premičninah v evropskem pravnem prostoru* [Contractual Transfer of Ownership on Movables in European Legal Environment], 261–272 (GV Založba 2010).

I. Underlying Obligation

401. Contracts of sale, exchange, donation, and every other contract giving rise to obligation to transfer ownership can serve as the underlying contract.[853] According to the principle of causality, no transfer of property can take place unless such legal transaction is *valid.*

402. According to Slovenian law of obligations, contracts can be void *ab initio* (null, Sl. *ničen*) or voidable (Sl. *izpodbojen*) – that is, they can be subsequently annulled with an *ex tunc* effect – meaning that it is presumed that the contract had not been valid in the first place. Basic prerequisites for the validity of a legal transaction (be it a unilateral declaration of will or a contract as a bi- or multilateral declaration of will) are the following:

- a real and free declaration of will;
- capacity of the parties;
- defined, permissible, and possible object of the contract as well as permissible *causa* of the contract; and
- form when prescribed (e.g., a written form in case of immovables,[854] a notarial deed in case of contracts regulating property relations between the spouses or cohabiting partners,[855] contracts of subsistence,[856] contracts on delivery of property,[857] etc.).[858]

403. A legal transaction is *null* when, for example:[859]

- the contract violates the Constitution or mandatory provisions, or is contrary to moral principles, unless the purpose of the violated rule refers to another sanction or the rule itself provides for another sanction;[860]
- a party to the contract lacks capacity (i.e., under the age of 15 unless provided otherwise by the law,[861] or is fully deprived of capacity, or is temporarily unable to understand the implications of concluding a contract);
- a contract lacks legal ground;[862]
- the object of the contract is not defined, permissible, or possible;[863] and

853. Their substance is regulated in the CO. For further details on the regulation of contracts in Slovenian law, see Možina & Vlahek, *Contract Law in Slovenia* (Wolters Kluwer, 2019).
854. Article 52 of CO.
855. Article 47 of Zakon o notariatu (ZN) [Notary Act], Official Gazette RS, No. 13/94, with further amendments.
856. Article 567 of CO.
857. Article 547/2 of CO.
858. Možina & Vlahek, *Contract Law in Slovenia* (Wolters Kluwer, 2019), pp. 70–72.
859. For further details on nullity, see Polajnar Pavčnik in *CO with Commentary*, 1st book, 504–523; Možina & Vlahek, *Contract Law in Slovenia* (Wolters Kluwer, 2019), pp. 76–91.
860. Article 86 of CO.
861. Article 146 of the FC (previously Art. 108 of the MFRA) which sets out that in case of important transactions, the approval of the parents is required.
862. Article 39 of CO.
863. Article 35 of CO.

– a contract is usurious.[864]

404. A legal transaction is *voidable* and can be annulled with an effect *ex tunc* when, for example:[865]

– a declaration of will was not real and free;[866]
– a party has limited capacity (i.e., 15–18 years old) and the transaction is such that it requires approval of the party's legal representative and such approval is not obtained *ex ante* or *ex post*;[867]
– a contract stipulates gross disproportion between performances (*laesio enormis*);[868]
– a right of pre-emption had not been respected;[869] and
– fraudulent conveyance occurs.[870]

405. *Avoidance* of the contract in case of breach of contract generally also has an *ex tunc* effect.[871]

II. Real Agreement

406. As already stressed, a further real agreement (disposition agreement, conveyance, Sl. *razpolagalni pravni posel, stvarnopravni posel*) is required beyond the underlying contract for the ownership to pass. It is an agreement between the transferor and the transferee that the ownership shall pass. Regardless of the validity of the underlying obligation, the real agreement must also be *valid* in order for the ownership to be transferred.[872]

407. In case of immovables, the real agreement ensues from the *clausula intabulandi* – that is, the *land registry permission* (Sl. *intabulacijska klavzula, zemljiškoknjižno dovolilo*). According to Article 23 of the CPL, this clause is an express and unconditional written statement of the owner that he or she accords to the registration of the transferee as the new owner of an immovable.[873] Additionally, the LRA

864. Article 119 of CO.
865. For further details on voidability, see Polajnar Pavčnik in *CO with Commentary*, 1st book, 524–533; Možina & Vlahek, *Contract Law in Slovenia* (Wolters Kluwer, 2019), pp. 76–91.
866. Articles 45–50 and 94 of CO.
867. Article 94 of CO.
868. Article 118 of CO.
869. Article 507 of CO.
870. Article 255 of CO.
871. Article 111 of CO. See Možina & Vlahek, *Contract Law in Slovenia* (Wolters Kluwer, 2019), pp. 87–91.
872. General rules on validity of contracts apply. See the CO. Regarding the form of the agreement, special rules of the CPL on *clausula intabulandi* apply in cases of immovables.
873. The land registry permission being a unilateral declaration of the owner could be described as one of the two declarations needed for conclusion of the real agreement. The second declaration, i.e., a declaration of the acquirer that he or she accepts the property right, is presumed, or can be derived from taking hold of the paper containing *clausula intabulandi*. See Tratnik in *Property Law*, 174.

requires that the permission must contain the transferor's statement having the exact substance as set out in Article 23 of the CPL. It also sets out which data on transferor must be included in the land registry permission.[874] The land registry permission is usually incorporated in the sales contract or other obligatory contract or is (rarely) drafted as a separate document. It should be stressed that the owner's signature on the land registry permission must be attested by the notary[875] or else the permission is invalid. In case of immovables, the form requirement for the real agreement (written statement with prescribed substance, and with the transferor's signature attested by the notary) is therefore stricter than the form requirement for the obligatory agreement (written contract). The purpose of the attestation is to check whether the person issuing the land registry permission in fact is the immovable's owner, not someone else. The notarial attestation of land registry permissions is, however, aimed also at guaranteeing that some rules set out in public interest are observed in the course of making transactions in immovable property. In cases of contractual transfer of ownership on an immovable, the LRA requires the notaries to check the citizenship of the acquirer as under Slovenian law, such acquisition of ownership on immovables is not available to all foreign citizens.[876] For that purpose, the acquirer will have to submit to the notary his or her identification card or other public document. If the person acquiring ownership is a Slovenian citizen or one the foreigners who may acquire ownership free of any restriction, the notary will make a note of the document on the land registry permission. Otherwise, he or she will require a submission of any public decisions granting the transferee acquisition of the immovable.[877] Before attesting the transferor's signature on land registry permission, notaries must also verify whether all taxes have been paid[878] and whether any spatial measures apply to the respective immovable restricting the transaction or making it conditional upon any state or municipal decision.[879] In case of movables, the real agreement can be adduced from the underlying contract, and all the more from the act of delivery. As in case of obligatory agreement, no form is required, an exception being the fiduciary transfer where the real agreement must be in the form of notarial protocol.[880]

§3. Principle of Causality

408. The Slovenian transfer system is causal because it requires a valid legal ground (a valid underlying contract – e.g., a sales contract) for the transfer to occur.[881] Unless the underlying legal transaction is valid, the ownership does not pass.

874. Article 32 of LRA.
875. Article 23 of CPL and Art. 33 of LRA.
876. Article 36 of LRA. For further details, see Part I, Ch. 3.
877. *Ibid.*
878. Article 37 of LRA.
879. Article 38 of LRA.
880. Article 202 of CPL.
881. Article 40 of CPL.

409. It should be stressed, however, that before entry into force of the CPL in 2003, the nature of the relationship between the underlying contract and the real agreement was not undisputed. The law preceding the CPL did not address this question expressly and thereby enabled theory to develop opposing standpoints on this matter. Some authors leaning towards German law pleaded for the principle of abstraction (Sl. *abstraktno načelo*, Ger. *Abstraktionsprinzip*),[882] whereas others, implying in particular the will of the Yugoslav legislature to continue with the Austrian ABGB solutions, spoke in favour of the principle of causality (Sl. *kavzalno načelo*, Ger. *Kausalprinzip*).[883] To avoid further dissention, the legislature decided, when drafting the CPL, to settle the issue by regulating it expressly in the code. It opted for the principle of causality: Article 40 of the CPL (as a general provision on *inter vivos* acquisition of ownership) sets down as a transfer prerequisite a *valid* legal transaction from which the obligation to transfer the ownership derives.[884]

§4. Principle of Tradition

410. The principle of delivery (tradition) has always been a part of the Slovenian transfer system and has never been disputed.[885] Setting delivery as a transfer prerequisite serves to manifest the disposition outwardly and thereby ensure the publicity of property relationships. Accordingly, as laid down in Article 11/2 of the CPL, the proprietary possessor of a movable deems to be its owner.

411. According to Article 60 of the CPL, ownership of a movable is acquired with its *delivery into the possession of the acquirer* (Sl. *dejanska izročitev*, Lat. *traditio vera*) in a sense that the latter may exercise his or her control over the movable.[886] According to Article 62 of the CPL, delivery of a movable to a transferee is deemed to have been accomplished if the movable was delivered to his or her representative. Delivery of a movable is also deemed to be accomplished with the

---

882. Abstraction was strongly argued for by Sajovic and Juhart. See, in particular, Juhart, *Zavezovalni in razpolagalni pravni posli – med kavzalnostjo in abstraktnostjo* [Obligatory and Real Legal Transactions – Between Causality and Abstraction], in Zbornik znanstvenih razprav, y. 55, 1995, pp. 129 ff.

883. Leading authors advocating for the system of causality were Tratnik and Vrenčur. See in particular Tratnik & Vrenčur, *O sistemu abstraktne ter kavzalne tradicije v stvarnem pravu* [On the System of Abstract and Causal Tradition in Property Law], in Pravniky. 54, 1999, No. 6/8, pp. 333 ff.

884. Vlahek, *Pogodbeni prenos lastninske pravice na premičninah v evropskem pravnem prostoru* [Contractual Transfer of Ownership on Movables in European Legal Environment], 273–277 (GV Založba 2010).

885. The only issue on which theory differs is whether delivery forms part of the real agreement (being its form) or is separated from it. For further details, see Vlahek, *Pogodbeni prenos lastninske pravice na premičninah v evropskem pravnem prostoru* [Contractual Transfer of Ownership on Movables in European Legal Environment], 277–284 (GV Založba 2010).

886. Tratnik in *Property Law*, 233–234.

delivery of a document on the basis of which the acquirer may dispose of the movable, as well as with the delivery of part of it, or with the exclusion or any other designation of the asset that implies its delivery (*symbolic delivery*, Sl. *simbolična izročitev*, Lat. *traditio symbolica*).[887]

412. Apart from actual delivery, Article 60 of the CPL provides for a list of ownership transfers on the basis of a real agreement only (agreement is a delivery equivalent though) without actual delivery taking place (*constructive, fictitious delivery*; Sl. *fiktivna izročitev*, Lat. *traditio ficta*).[888] First, delivery of a movable is deemed to be accomplished by concluding a legal transaction on the transfer of ownership without its actual delivery if, prior to the concluding of the legal transaction, the movable was already in the possession of the acquirer (Sl. *tradicija na kratko roko*, Lat. *traditio brevi manu*) or if the parties agree that despite the transfer of ownership the movable is to remain in the possession of the transferor (Sl. *posestni konstitut*, Lat. *constitutum possessorium*). Further, if an asset is in the possession of a third person, delivery is deemed to be accomplished at the moment the third person was notified of the transfer of ownership (Sl. *tradicija na dolgo roko*, Lat. *traditio longa manu*). The transferor thereby transfers his or her indirect possession to the transferee.

§5. Principle of Registration

I. Movables

413. Ownership on some types of movables is transferred by registration and not by delivery. In case of derivative acquisition, ownership of registered aircraft and watercraft is fully transferred at the moment of registration in the corresponding register. As in the case of immovables, delivery plays no role in transferring ownership on these movables. Ownership on vehicles, motorbikes, bikes, etc., is, in contrast to common opinion, transferred by mere delivery and not by any other act, despite the existence of certain registers of those movables (e.g., police register of vehicles).[889]

887. Article 60 of CPL.
888. Tratnik in *Property Law*, 235.
889. All movables having the so-called uniform identification mark as laid down in the Uredba o registru neposestnih zastavnih pravic in zarubljenih premičnin [Decree on the Register of Non-possessory Liens and Seized Movable Property], Official Gazette RS, No. 23/04, with further amendments (i.e., stored material, equipment, motor and track vehicles, motorcycles, trailers, semi-trailers, and certain animals) may, however, be objects of the registered non-possessory lien. The registration in the Register of Non-possessory Liens and Seized Movable Property, however, relates only to non-possessory pledge, and not to ownership on these movables. For further details, see Part V.

414. According to the Maritime Code,[890] ships, boats,[891] and floating devices[892] are registered into the *Slovenian Register of Ships* (Sl. *Slovenski ladijski register*),[893] which is maintained by the Slovenian Maritime Administration (Sl. *Uprava Republike Slovenije za pomorstvo*).[894] The Slovenian Register of Ships consists of several separate registers: register of merchant ships, register of yachts, register of trawlers, register of public ships, register of ships under construction in a Slovenian shipyard, register of military ships, register of boats, and register of floating devices. The register (following the model of the land register as was in force before 2011 when the land register was reformed) consists of a main public register with folios A (data on the ship), B (data on the owner and other relevant persons), and C (data on any limited property rights, other restrictions, etc.), and of a collection of documents that form the basis of the registration. Ownership on Seacraft registered in the Slovenian Register of Ships is, in cases of derivate acquisition, acquired upon entry into the register on the basis of a written legal transaction and transferor's *clausula intabuladi*.[895] The same rule applies to inland watercraft.[896]

415. In addition, ownership on aircraft registered in the *Aircraft Register of the Republic of Slovenia* (Sl. *Register zrakoplovov Republike Slovenije*) can, in cases of derivative acquisition, be transferred upon registration only. Obligations and Real Rights in Air Navigation Act[897] requires that it be, in principle, made on a basis of a written legal transaction.[898] The Aircraft Register is maintained by the Ministry of Transport (Sl. *Ministrstvo za promet*) and follows the model of the land register, too.

890. Pomorski zakonik (PZ) [Maritime Code], Official Gazette RS, No. 26/01, with further amendments. For further details on the regulation, see Vlačič et al., *Pomorsko pravo* [Maritime Law] (Uradni list 2008).
891. Save boats under 3 m of length (unless its engine power exceeds 3.7 kW), boats that belong to another craft, and sports boats (rowing boats, kayaks and the like). A boat is defined as a craft under 24 m of length. Otherwise, it is a ship.
892. Only those longer than 15 m and wider than 3 m.
893. Ships that are more than half owned by Slovenian/EU citizens or legal entities can be registered, Ships that are more than half owned by foreigners, but whose operator is a Slovene/EU citizen or legal entity, can also be registered if the owner of the ship agrees to the registration.
894. See Arts 201–218 of the Maritime Code. Register of military ships and boats is maintained by the Ministry of Defence.
895. Articles 221 and 317 of the Maritime Code. While this rule is expressly settled for ships, it is less clear whether it also applies to other watercraft (boats and floating devices). If it does not, then ownership on these is despite registration acquired by tradition.
896. According to the Zakon o plovbi po celinskih vodah (ZPCV) [Inland Waterways Navigation Act], Official Gazette RS, No. 30/02, with further amendments, Slovenian Maritime Administration registers inland ships, whereas inland boats [except boats that belong to another craft, sports boats, and boats less than 5 m long (unless their engine power exceeds 3.7 kW) – these, too, must be registered if they are used for commercial activities] and floating devices (those longer than 10 m and wider than 3 m) are registered by the local office for administration where the boat or device is located and used, except military boats and ships that are registered by the Ministry of Defence.
897. Zakon o obligacijskih in stvarnopravnih razmerjih v letalstvu (ZOSRL) [Obligations and Real Rights in Air Navigation Act], Official Gazette RS, No. 12/00, with further amendments. Zakon o letalstvu (ZLet) [Aviation Act], Official Gazette RS, No. 18/01, with further amendments, also applies.
898. Articles 169 and 170 of the Obligations and Real Rights in Air Navigation Act. Unlike the Maritime Code, legislation on aviation does not mention *clausula intabulandi*.

416. Similarly, rights incorporated in the dematerialized securities are acquired upon entry into the Central Register of Dematerialized Securities (Sl. *Centralni register nematerializiranih vrednostnih papirjev*) maintained by the Central Securities Clearing Corporation (Sl. *Centralna klirinško depotna družba*) as provided for in the Book Entry Securities Act.[899]

II. Immovables

417. According to Article 49 of the CPL, acquisition of ownership of an immovable by means of a legal transaction requires an entry in the land register on the basis of an obligatory contract and a document containing the land registry permission. The latter takes the form of a real agreement in case of immovables. Ownership on immovables is, therefore, transferred (with full effects) when the following prerequisites are met: conclusion of obligatory contract (e.g., sales contract), issuance of land registry permission on which the owner's signature is attested by the notary (although this is not expressly set out in the legislation, the acquirer's consent to the transfer is deemed given at the latest by taking possession of the transferor's land registry permission),[900] and registration in the land register on the basis of these documents. In case of derivative acquisition, ownership does not pass with full effects until registration. Entry in the land register is thus of a constitutive, and not merely of declarative nature. As has already been stressed,[901] in recent years, Slovenian legal theory and the courts have, however, started stressing that *inter partes*, i.e., between the parties, ownership passes already with the conclusion of the real agreement (i.e., by issuance and handing over of the land registry permission), while *erga omnes* effects take place with registration.[902] Theory and case law speak of 'expected ownership' and 'ownership in formation' (Sl. *pričakovana lastninska pravica*) and of 'expected owner' (Sl. *pričakovani lastnik*).[903] In some cases, possession of the land registry permission of the acquirer suffices even to preclude third

899. Zakon o nematerializiranih vrednostnih papirjih (ZNVP-1) [Book Entry Securities Act], Official Gazette RS, No. 75/15, with further amendments.

900. See, e.g., Plavšak, Vrenčur, *Pomen razpolagalnega upravičenja pri razpolaganju z lastninsko pravico na nepremičnini* [The Importance of the Disposal Right for Transactions with Ownership Right on Real Estate], in Podjetje in delo, 2016, pp. 595 ff.; Decision of the Constitutional Court of RS, No. Up-591/10 of 2 Dec. 2010.

901. See para. 399 of this monograph.

902. See, e.g., Juhart, *Nekaj dodatnih premislekov k stvarnopravnim izhodiščem pri prenosu lastninske pravice na nepremičninah* [Some Additional Thoughts on Property Law Principles of Transfer of Ownership on Immovables], in Pravna praksa, 17. jan. 2013, Y. 32, No. 2, pp. 6–9; cf. Hudej Jasna & Ščernjavič Iztok, *Ponovni premislek o nekaterih temeljnih izhodiščih stvarnega prava pri prenosu lastninske pravice na nepremičninah* [New Reflections on Some of the Basic Principles of Property Law Regarding the Transfer of Ownership on Immovable Property], in Pravna praksa No. 3/2012, p. 23; Plavšak, Vrenčur, *Pomen razpolagalnega upravičenja pri razpolaganju z lastninsko pravico na nepremičnini* [The Importance of the Disposal Right for Transactions with Ownership Right on Real Estate], in Podjetje in delo, 2016, pp. 595 ff.

903. See, e.g., the following judgments/decisions of the Supreme Court of RS: Nos II Ips 475/2008 of 5 Apr. 2012, Sklep II Ips 924/2008 5 Apr. 2012, II Ips 132/2009 of 12 Jul. 2012, II Ips 324/2011 of 26 Apr. 2012, II Ips 78/2010 z dne of 13 Sep. 2012. See also judgment of High Court in Koper, I Ips 243/2013 of 22 Jan. 2015.

persons (even if in good faith) from obtaining rights on such immovable.[904] The Constitutional Court of RS and the Supreme Court of RS have, for example, held that a creditor in enforcement proceedings, conducted against the registered owner, cannot rely on the registered data, if the real owner acquired his or her ownership in a non-derivative manner (via acquisitive prescription or the establishment of joint ownership of the spouses) or if the new (future) owner is already in possession of the land registry permission.[905] Such expected owner would be protected also against the transferor's creditors in case the transferor went bankrupt and the bankruptcy proceedings were initiated after the acquirer got hold of the land registry permission.[906]

§6. PRINCIPLE *NEMO PLUS*

418. Another important principle of Slovenian property law is the old Roman law *nemo plus* principle requiring the transferor to be entitled to dispose of the real right – for example, ownership (*nemo plus iuris ad alium transferre potest, quam ipse habet*). Unless possessing this power, the transferor[907] can, in principle, not transfer ownership or otherwise dispose of an asset. The so-called right or *entitlement to dispose* (Sl. *razpolagalno upravičenje*)[908] can thus be characterized as one of the transfer prerequisites. Although the CPL does not regulate the entitlement to dispose expressly, it can be inferred from its provisions.[909]

419. There are, however, important exceptions to this principle protecting bona fide acquirers in certain situations on behalf of real owners who put the Slovenian version of the *nemo plus* principle somewhat closer to those systems that favour the good faith acquirer than to systems that favour the owner with whose asset is being disposed of without his or her consent. Under Slovenian law, such *a non domino*

904. For a thorough presentation and evaluation of this case law, see Tratnik, *Lastninska pravica na nepremičnini v pričakovanju* [The Expectation of Ownership of an Immovable], in Pravna praksa, No. 2/2013, pp. II-VIII.

905. See, e.g., Judgment of High Court in Koper, No. I Cp 838/2014 of 10 Mar. 2015; Decision of the Constitutional Court of RS, No. Up-591/10 of 2 Dec. 2010; the following Judgments/Decisions of the Supreme Court of RS: Nos II Ips 475/2008 of 5 Apr. 2012, II Ips 924/2008 of 5 Apr. 2008, II Ips 132/2009 of 12 Jul. 2012, II Ips 324/2011 of 26 Apr. 2012, II Ips 78/2010 of 13 Sep. 2012, II Ips 60/2014 11 Dec. 2014; II Ips 166/2012 of 20 Feb. 2014.

906. See Plavšak, Vrenčur, *Pomen razpolagalnega upravičenja pri razpolaganju z lastninsko pravico na nepremičnini* [The Importance of the Disposal Right for Transactions with Ownership Right on Real Estate], in Podjetje in delo, 2016, p. 636. For further details on bankruptcy proceedings in Slovenia, see Part III, Ch. 11, §2 of this monograph.

907. Be it the owner, his or her representative, insolvency manager, etc.

908. Term 'the capacity to dispose' is usually being used but has started being replaced by 'the right to dispose' or 'the entitlement to dispose' in order to stress that it does not relate to the transferor's capacity but to the right of which he or she disposes of which such entitlement is part. For further details, see, e.g., Plavšak, Vrenčur, *Pomen razpolagalnega upravičenja pri razpolaganju z lastninsko pravico na nepremičnini* [The Importance of the Disposal Right for Transactions with Ownership Right on Real Estate], in Podjetje in delo, 2016, pp. 595 ff.; Juhart in Juhart, Tratnik, Vrenčur, *Property Law*, p. 240.

909. For example, Arts 61, 64, 133, 156 of CPL. Tratnik in *Property Law*, 224.

acquisition – where ownership is acquired from a non-owner and without the owner's consent – is, under specific circumstances, possible in case of immovables as well as movables.[910]

§7. Principle of Trust in the Land Register

420. In case of immovables, the exception to the *nemo plus* principle is reflected in the so-called principle of trust in the land register (Sl. *načelo zaupanja v zemljiško knjigo*) – that is, reliance on the data on rights on immovables registered in the land register. According to Article 10 of the CPL and Article 8/1 of the LRA, anyone acting in good faith in legal transactions (in *legal commerce* as put down in legislation) and relying on the data on rights registered in the land register cannot bear detrimental consequences because of that.[911] The principle of trust in the land register thus enables acquisition of ownership (or other rights in rem) of immovables from the registered, but not real, legal proprietor. This way the real, legal proprietor (e.g., the person who had acquired ownership out-of-register on the basis of acquisitive prescription at the moment the prescriptive period had lapsed) loses his or her right because a third person has in good faith relied upon the data registered in the land register. The principle, therefore, gives preference to legal transactions over the position of the real legal proprietor who has not provided for registration of his or her right[912] or has not provided for deletion of an invalid registration although he or she had the possibility of doing that.

421. According to Article 9 of the CPL, good faith is presumed unless proven otherwise. The burden of proving that the acquirer was operating in bad faith is, therefore, on the original owner. According to theory and case law analysing the issue in question in the first years after the enactment of the CPL and the LRA, the acquirer need not check the factual status of an immovable in order to be in good faith and could merely rely on the data registered in the land register (provided he or she is not proven knowing of the fact that someone else has acquired ownership on the immovable[913]).[914] More recent theory and case law have, however, departed from such position requiring the acquirer to check the actual status of an immovable in order to be able to rely on the principle of trust in the land register.[915] This is reasonable given the fact that the system of social ownership of land coupled with

910. For immovables, see Part III, Ch. 1, §7; for movables, see Part III, Ch. 1, §8.

911. Vlahek, *Odprta vprašanja načela zaupanja v zemljiško knjigo* [Issues Relating to the Principle of Trust in the Land Register], in *Izbrane teme civilnega prava II*, 111–129 (Ed. Ude, Institute of Comparative Law at the Faculty of Law in Ljubljana 2007).

912. Similarly, Art. 8/2 of LRA.

913. See the following Judgment of the High Court in Ljubljana: No. VSL I Cp 1198/2011 of 4 Apr. 2012.

914. See Vlahek, *Odprta vprašanja načela zaupanja v zemljiško knjigo* [Issues Relating to the Principle of Trust in the Land Register], in *Izbrane teme civilnega prava II*, 111–129 (Ed. Ude, Institute of Comparative Law at the Faculty of Law in Ljubljana 2007).

915. See, for example, Tratnik, *Pridobitev lastnine in drugih stvarnih pravic na nepremičnini na podlagi zaupanja v zemljiško knjigo* [Acquisition of Ownership and other Property Rights on Immovables on the Basis of Trust in the Land Register], 139 (Ed. Ude, Institute of Comparative Law at

decades of factual insignificant importance of the land register has had a detrimental effect on the regulation of relationships on immovables in Slovenia. Until land register problems originating in the previous regime that had turned the property law system upside down are resolved and the land register fully accords to the real status of property rights on immovables, following blindly the data registered in the land register without taking into account all the circumstances of the actual case would be unfair.

422. According to legal theory and case law as they stand now, only *derivative inter vivos transactions* (concluded by the registered person and a third person in good faith) can lead to *a non domino* acquisition of immovables by way of referring to the principle of trust in the land register. This is inferred from the wording of the CPL and the LRA, which use the term '*legal commerce*' (Sl. *pravni promet*) to denote the sphere of relationships in which *a non domino* acquisition can occur.[916] *Mortis causa* transactions, for example, do not qualify as transactions to which the principle of trust in the land register would apply. In these cases, preference is given to out-of-register owners (e.g., acquirers of immovables by acquisitive prescription) instead of heirs irrespective of the heirs' good faith in the decedent's registered ownership.[917] The question of whether applicability of principle of trust in the land register is limited to transactions made for consideration is not expressly settled in legislation. It is thus on legal theory and courts to interpret the term '*legal commerce*' accordingly.[918]

423. It must again be stressed that Slovenian courts have held that a creditor in enforcement proceedings conducted against the registered owner, cannot rely on the registered data (irrespective of his or her good faith), if the real owner acquired ownership in a non-derivative manner (via acquisitive prescription or the establishment of joint ownership of the spouses) or if the new (future) owner is already in

---

the Faculty of Law in Ljubljana 2007); Juhart, *Dobrovernost kot pogoj za učinkovanje načela zaupanja v zemljiško knjigo*, [Good Faith Prerequisite of the Principle of Trust in the Land Register], 156–157 (Ed. Ude, Institute of Comparative Law at the Faculty of Law in Ljubljana 2007). See also the following Judgment of the Supreme Court of RS: No. II Ips 397/2006 of 15 Jan. 2009.

916. See Vlahek, *Odprta vprašanja načela zaupanja v zemljiško knjigo* [Issues Relating to the Principle of Trust in the Land Register], in *Izbrane teme civilnega prava II*, 111–129 (Ed. Ude, Institute of Comparative Law at the Faculty of Law in Ljubljana 2007).

917. Vlahek, *Odprta vprašanja načela zaupanja v zemljiško knjigo* [Issues Relating to the Principle of Trust in the Land Register], in *Izbrane teme civilnega prava II*, 120 (Ed. Ude, Institute of Comparative Law at the Faculty of Law in Ljubljana 2007); Tratnik, *Pridobitev lastnine in drugih stvarnih pravic na nepremičnini na podlagi zaupanja v zemljiško knjigo* [Acquisition of Ownership and other Property Rights on Immovables on the Basis of Trust in the Land Register], 133 (Ed. Ude, Institute of Comparative Law at the Faculty of Law in Ljubljana 2007). See also the following Judgments of the Supreme Court of RS: Nos II Ips 622/2008 of 19 Jan. 2012, II Ips 1030/2008 of 16 Feb. 2012. See also the following Judgment of the High Court in Ljubljana: No. II Cp 2602/2010 of 10 Nov. 2010.

918. See Vlahek, *Odprta vprašanja načela zaupanja v zemljiško knjigo* [Issues Relating to the Principle of Trust in the Land Register], in *Izbrane teme civilnega prava II*, 122 (Ed. Ude, Institute of Comparative Law at the Faculty of Law in Ljubljana 2007); Tratnik in *CPL with Commentary 2016*, pp. 56–57.

possession of the permission to be registered in the land register.[919] Another exception has been recently introduced by the Supreme Court of RS stating that immovables having the status of a 'plot belonging to a building' cannot be validly transferred as individual immovables regardless of any good faith of the acquirer.[920]

§8. *A NON DOMINO* ACQUISITION OF MOVABLES

424. In case of (non-registered) movables, Article 64 of the CPL sets down the following prerequisites for obtaining ownership from a person lacking the right to dispose with the movable. First, the acquirer must – at the moment of obtaining possession of the movable – be in *good faith* regarding the transferor's right to dispose. Second, the legal transaction between the acquirer and the transferor must be made *for consideration.* Third, the underlying contract and the real agreement between the transferor and acquirer must be *valid.* Finally, the transfer must be performed in one of the following *circumstances that justify the protection of the third party*: (i) a movable is bought at a public auction,[921] (ii) a movable is purchased from a person that put it into circulation as part of his or her (registered) commercial activity, or (iii) the owner voluntarily put the movable into the transferor's possession (e.g., on a basis of a barter agreement, but also on a basis of a contract obliging the transfer of ownership, such as sales, that was null or invalidated).[922] Additionally, if delivery was accomplished by means of *constitutum possessorium*, the acquirer acquires ownership only at the moment the transferor delivers the thing into his or her direct possession, unless he or she is no longer in good faith at that time. Delivery in the form of possessory constitute does not, therefore, suffice for *a non domino* acquisition.

425. It is to be underscored that in contrast to many other legal systems, the Slovenian regulation of *a non domino* acquisition of movables does not preclude *a non domino* acquisition in cases of stolen or lost goods. Provided that the prerequisites set out in Article 64 are met, the acquirer obtains ownership irrespective of the fact that the goods were stolen or lost. The police, however, will seize stolen property (mostly cars) for the purposes of criminal proceedings (and in practice plausibly return it to the original owner) irrespective of the fact that the acquirer of such goods has become an owner on the basis of Article 64 of the CPL (i.e., mostly in cases

---

919. See, e.g., Judgment of High Court in Koper, No. I Cp 838/2014 of 10 Mar. 2015; Decision of the Constitutional Court of RS, No. Up-591/10 of 2 Dec. 2010; the following Judgments/Decisions of the Supreme Court of RS: Nos II Ips 475/2008 of 5 Apr. 2012, II Ips 924/2008 of 5 Apr. 2008, II Ips 132/2009 of 12 Jul. 2012, II Ips 324/2011 of 26 Apr. 2012, II Ips 78/2010 of 13 Sep. 2012, II Ips 60/2014 11 Dec. 2014; II Ips 166/2012 of 20 Feb. 2014.

920. See the following decisions taken by the Supreme Court of RS: Nos II Ips 420/2011 of 19 Sep. 2013 and II Ips 369/29 of 27 May 2013. For further details on the concept of 'plot belonging to a building', see paras. 65, 112, 115, 142 of this monograph.

921. Rules on *a non domino* acquisition apply only in case of a voluntary public auction because otherwise i.e., in case of an involuntary public auction carried out in enforcement proceedings, good faith of the acquirer of a movable is not a prerequisite for obtaining ownership. Tratnik in *Property Law*, 246. See Art. 96/7 of the CESA.

922. Tratnik in *Property Law*, 247.

where the car was bought from a car dealer). An important rule in case of acquisition *a non domino* is that ownership is acquired *free of encumbrances*. According to Article 64/5 of the CPL, all other rights with respect to the movable cease to exist under the proviso the acquirer believed in good faith that these rights did not exist.

426. Despite the general rule of *a non domino* acquisition (i.e., that a bona fide acquirer becomes a new owner), the original owner has a *claim to repurchase* his or her movable if the movable has a special importance for him or her (*pretium affectionis*). According to Article 64/5 of the CPL, the previous owner may in this case require (within one year after *a non domino* acquisition occurred) the acquirer to sell the movable to him or her at the market price.

427. Article 61 of the CPL enables *anticipatory transfer* of movables. If a movable was delivered at the time the transferor did not yet have the right to dispose of it but subsequently acquires this right, the transferee acquires ownership at the time when the transferor acquires the right to dispose (and not at the moment the delivery took place), which matches the *nemo plus* principle. If a movable was delivered this way to two or more transferees, ownership is acquired by the person to whom the movable was first delivered.

§9. Unitary Principle

428. The foregoing principles apply equally, regardless of the type of relationship between the transferor and the transferee. Slovenian law neither differentiates transfer rules based on the commercial, non-commercial, and consumer nature of a relationship nor as to the type of the underlying contract. The only difference ensues from the nature of the asset being the object of transfer – that is, movable, immovable, or registering movable.

§10. Payment of the Price

429. According to Article 37/2 of the CPL, transfer of ownership cannot be subject to a time limit or a condition unless provided otherwise by law. Transfer of ownership of a movable may, however, be subject to a resolutory or a suspensive condition. Article 63 of the CPL states that this is usually manifested as transfer of ownership as security or as reservation of title. The former is further regulated in Articles 201–206 of the CPL while the latter is regulated in Articles 520 and 521 of the CO. As in majority of other legal systems, payment of the price (or any other act representing a fulfilment of a condition) is therefore *not a transfer requirement* under Slovenian law *unless stipulated for in the contract*. To produce effects to third parties (e.g., transferee's creditors), the buyer's signature on the contract containing the reservation of title clause must be attested by the notary prior to the buyer's bankruptcy or attachment of the goods in enforcement proceedings.[923]

430. It should be stressed that, in contrast to movables, immovables cannot be transferred conditionally. A similar effect can, however, be attained by *prenotation* that enables the transferee to pre-note his or her future ownership in the land register and thereby protect his or her registration rank on the basis of a contract lacking the required *clausula intabulandi* that would enable the full registration. If the missing documents are provided in the prescribed time limit, then the full registration is deemed to be in effect on the day of the prenotation, and all subsequent (still pending) applications colliding with the prenotation are superfluous and are, therefore, removed from the land register.[924]

923. Article 520/2 of CO.
924. See Part I, Ch. 2.

Chapter 2. Transfer of Property by Death

431. According to Article 41 of the CPL and Article 132 of the IA, in case of inheritance (be it testamentary or statutory), the decedent's estate (as a whole or its aliquot part) is transferred to his or her heir or heirs at the moment of the decedent's death.[925] Derivative universal succession, therefore, takes place *ipso iure upon decedent's death* regardless of any other relevant moments – for example, delivery, registration (which is thus of a mere declaratory nature), judicial decision on inheritance (in which heirs and their shares in the estate as a whole are determined – but they are deemed to be heirs from the time of death on), heir's acceptance of the heritage before the probate court, etc.[926] Under Slovenian law, the moment of *delatio* thus coincides with the moment of *acquisitio*. In case of *immovables*, the final judicial decision on inheritance serves as a document on the basis of which heirs can be registered in the land register[927] as new joint owners of all the inherited immovables (without any shares registered), while after the division of the estate, the heirs are registered as individual owners or co-owners of the immovables according to the division of the estate. It is an official duty of the court to forward the decision to the land registry.[928]

432. In principle, every individual and every legal entity existent at the moment of the decedent's death is capable of inheriting and of receiving a legacy.[929] Unworthiness to inherit, however, renders inheritance and all other benefits from the decedent's estate impossible, except in cases where the decedent had pardoned the successor's conduct.[930] Specific rules on inheriting immovables located in Slovenia apply to foreign citizens and foreign legal persons who may (unless they fall into one of the privileged categories of foreigners)[931] inherit Slovenian immovables only

925. Or at the moment the court determines as the moment a missing person is deemed dead. If the court does not determine such moment in its decision, a person is deemed dead at the moment the court decision becomes final.
926. Acceptance of inherited assets is anticipated. Heirs may, of course, reject inheritance until the end of the probate proceedings (Arts 133/1, 205/3, and 214/2/3 of IA). They may also transfer their inheritance to another heir until the moment of division of inherited estate, or bind themselves to transfer to a third person the inherited property after the division of the heritage (Art. 146 of IA). In exceptional cases, an individual (descendant) may *ex ante* reject inheritance by concluding an agreement on it with his or her (still living) predecessor (Art. 137/2 of IA). Heirs may also expressly or impliedly accept inheritance and thereby eliminate uncertainty as to rejection/acceptance of inheritance.
927. Article 40/1/6 of LRA.
928. Article 46/1 of LRA. It must do so within fifteen days after the decision has become final, and must attach the decision in question (on which it must record that it is final).
929. An unborn child, who was already conceived at the moment of the decedent's death (*nasciturus*), is deemed to be already born under the proviso that it is born live (Art. 125/2 of IA). It is deemed to be conceived at the moment of death if it is born in 300 days after the decedent's death (Art. 113 of FC).
930. Grounds for unworthiness are listed in Art. 126 of the IA. Only the unworthy, and not his or her descendants, bears consequences of unworthiness in cases of statutory inheritance. In case of testamentary inheritance, statutory heirs inherit instead of the unworthy testamentary heir, unless the decedent determined something else for such cases (Art. 79 of IA).
931. See Part I, Ch. 3.

under the proviso of reciprocity[932] as set out in the Reciprocity Act of 1999. Reciprocity in these cases is assessed by the Ministry of Justice.[933]

433. Heirs may be *testamentary* (Sl. *oporočni dediči*) or *statutory (intestate*, Sl. *zakoniti dediči)*, while inheritance contracts are, in principle, unknown to Slovenian law.[934] Inheritance on the basis of a will takes precedence over statutory inheritance (on condition the so-called obligatory shares are guaranteed).

434. *Statutory heirs* form three categories or classes according to the degree to which they are related or otherwise close to the decedent, and among which no overlapping is possible. If at least one of the persons belonging to the first category is alive, those belonging to the second and third are, in principle, precluded from inheriting. The regulation of intestate succession follows the parentelic system with unlimited representation, but entails some minor deviations from it because not only relatives can be statutory heirs. The categories and heirs' shares are (in principle) as follows. The first category: decedent's spouse or heterosexual cohabiting partner or registered same-sex partner or cohabiting homosexual partner[935] and decedent's children (legitimate and illegitimate) and adoptees (the latter under the proviso that the right to inheritance was not excluded upon adoption) who take in equal shares; in case any of the children or adoptees should predecease the decedent (or are unworthy to inherit, or had rejected inheritance only for him- or herself, but not for his or her descendants), the child or an adoptee of the predeceased inherits the predeceased's share, and so on (Sl. *vstopna pravica*, Lat. *ius repraensentationis*). It should be stressed that the decedent's spouse or partner may not inherit in the first category if there are no descendants (be it natural or adopted); in such case, the spouse or partner inherits with persons from the second category. The second category (relevant only in case there is no descendant): decedent's spouse or partner and decedent's parents or adopters (the latter only in case of the so-called perfect adoption), whereby the spouse or partner takes one-half, and others the other half of the inherited assets (each parent/adopter one-half of the one-half). In case parent/ adopters are not alive, their descendants or adoptees inherit their share, and so on. If one of the deceased parents/adopters has no descendants or adoptees (or are unworthy of inheritance or had rejected it), his or her share goes to the other parent's/adopter's lineage (Sl. *prirast*, Lat. *ius accrescendi*). If the deceased parents/ adopters have no descendants or adoptees and their descendants at all, the spouse or partner is the sole heir. If the spouse or partner is deceased, his or her half comes

---

932. Art. 6 of IA.

933. See Part I, Ch. 3. For further details on acquisition of ownership on immovables in Slovenia by foreigners Vlahek, *Pridobivanje lastninske pravice na nepremičninah v Sloveniji s strani tujcev* [Acquisition of Ownership on Immovables in Slovenia by Foreign Citizens], in Pravnik (Ljubljana: 2008), y. 63, No. 1/3, pp. 7 ff.

934. Contract, obliging a party to will his or her estate to a co-contractor or another person, is prohibited under Art. 103 of the IA. Contract on the content of will is prohibited as well (Art. 105 of IA). Further, contract on alienation of expected inheritance or legacy is also invalid (Art. 104 of IA). Contract between a predecessor and his or her successor on the rejection of inheritance that would occur in case of predecessor's death is, however, permitted (Art. 137/2 of IA).

935. Inheritance of same-sex partners is explained in detail below.

down to the parents'/adopters' lineages. The third category (relevant only in case there is no heir from the second category): decedent's grandparents (or parents of decedent's adopters), who take in equal shares, one-half parents of the decedent's mother/adopter, and the other half parents of the decedent's father/adopter. If one of them is deceased, his or her descendants and adoptees inherit their share, and so on. If one of the deceased grandparents has no descendants, his or her share goes to the other grandparent or his or her descendants or adoptees or their descendants. If all grandparents and their descendants or adoptees and their descendants are deceased, the decedent's estate becomes ownership of the RS.[936]

435. In Slovenian law, the principle of testamentary freedom is combined with the concept of the so-called *obligatory heirs* (Sl. *nujni dediči*) – that is, statutory heirs who cannot be omitted as heirs by the testator. Obligatory heirs can be (all under the proviso that they would be actual heirs in case of statutory inheritance, and under the proviso they were not disinherited by the decedent[937]) decedent's descendants and adoptees or their natural or adopted descendant's (adoptees under the proviso that the right to inheritance was not excluded upon adoption); decedent's parents or his or her adopter (the latter only in case of the so-called perfect adoption); decedent's spouse or partner; or decedent's grandparents and brothers and sisters (or parents and children or adoptees of the decedent's adopters in case of perfect adoption) if they do not have enough subsistence and are permanently incapable of working. Decedent's descendants or adoptees and decedent's spouse or partner are entitled to one-half and others to one-third of what they would obtain had they been statutory heirs.[938]

436. In case of more heirs, they all obtain *joint ownership* on each of the inherited assets at the moment of the decedent's death and stay in such relationship until the division of the heritage.[939] From the time of death to the moment of division, they form a so-called *community* or *partnership of co-heirs*.[940] Each of the co-heirs may, at any time,[941] request division of the inherited estate.[942] Once the division is performed, the joint ownership turns to individual (co-ownership) of the heirs.[943]

437. Because inheritance is a form of derivative acquisition, the successors obtain ownership in the same substance as it existed before death – that is, with all

936. Articles 10–24 of IA.
937. Grounds for disinheritance as consequence of heirs' improper behaviour (*exhereditatio ob iusta causa*) are listed in Art. 42 of the IA, whereas disinheritance in favour of heir's descendants (*exhereditatio bona mente*) is regulated in Art. 45 of IA.
938. Articles 25–27 of IA.
939. For further details, see Part I, Ch. 5, §2, III.
940. Article 145/1 of IA. The testator may, however, will to obligatory heirs only specific things or rights, and not aliquote parts of his or her estate. In such cases, they do not take part in the community of co-heirs. For further details, see Part I, Ch. 5, §2, III.
941. Though not at an inappropriate time (Art. 144/1 of IA).
942. Because the IA does not entail rules on the division, rules of the CPL on division of a thing in joint ownership apply (Arts 69–71 of CPL).
943. For further details, see Part I, Ch. 5, §2, III.

those restraints, limited property rights (e.g., superficies, easements, etc.) and obligatory rights that can be effected against heirs and not only against the decedent.

438. All debts left by the deceased, too, are inherited. The heir is personally responsible for the debts of the deceased. He or she is liable with his or her whole, and not only inherited property, but only up to the value of the estate he or she inherited (the so-called *responsibility pro viribus hereditatis*).[944] Co-heirs are jointly and severally responsible for the debts of the estate up to the value of their part in estate, while, in their internal relationship, they are responsible for the debt in proportion to their part in estate. Interests of the creditors of the deceased may be protected by the separation of estate from the property of the heirs (Sl. *ločitev zapuščine*, Lat. *separatio bonorum*).[945] Within three months after introduction of inheritance, creditors may contact the responsible court with the request for the separation of the estate from the property of the heirs, and those creditors of the deceased who have requested separation are privileged with regard to the heirs' creditors, but may be repaid only from the separated estate, and not from other property of the heirs. Further, *estate insolvency proceedings* are regulated in the FOIPCDA setting out anew also specific rules for cases of *insolvency proceedings of estate without heirs* applicable as of 15 June 2013.[946]

439. Inheritance of *certain agricultural immovables* (the so-called protected farms, Sl. *zaščitene kmetije*)[947] is subject to specific legislation[948] aiming at preventing fragmentation of protected farms, and enabling their acquisition in the least burdensome way possible, thereby making subsistence of such farms feasible. To name a few solutions which serve these objectives: as a rule, only one, the most suitable person for running the farm (be it a testamentary or statutory heir), inherits it; testamentary freedom is thereby limited; the list of statutory heirs is shorter, their shares smaller and in the form of monetary sum only; etc.[949]

---

944. In some instances, legislation provides for responsibility *cum viribus hereditatis*, where debts can be paid only from the inherited property (e.g., in case of *separatio bonorum*), while absolute *ultra vires hereditatis* responsibility is unknown to Slovenian system. For further details, see Zupančič & Žnidaršič Skubic, *Dedno pravo* [Inheritance Law], 230–241 (GV Založba 2009).
945. Article 143 of IA.
946. Articles 414–418 of FOIPCDA. The rules on insolvency proceedings of estate without heirs are since 2016 laid down also in the IA. For further details, see Plavšak, *ZFPPIPP, Uvodna pojasnila* [FOIPCDA, Introductory remarks], 294–296 (GV Založba 2008); Plavšak, *ZFPPIPP-E, Uvodna pojasnila* [FOIPCDA-E, Introductory remarks], 68–73 (GV Založba 2013).
947. Two prerequisites must be met for a farm to be designated protected farm (administrative units decide on the status of protected farms, their status is then notated in the land register): first, it must be a so-called semi-large farm (the law sets down sizes (in ha) of specific types of such semi-large agricultural land (e.g., 5–100 ha of field or garden, 40–800 ha of forest), and second, it must have a specific ownership status (it must be owned by only one person; or by spouses (civil partners); or by a person and his or her descendant (or adoptee and his or her descendant)). For further details, see Zupančič & Žnidaršic Skubic, *Dedno pravo* [Inheritance Law], 293 ff. (GV Založba 2009).
948. Zakon o dedovanju kmetijskih gospodarstev (ZDKG) [Inheritance of Agricultural Holdings Act], Official Gazette RS, No. 70/95, with further amendments.
949. For further details, see Zupančič & Žnidaršic Skubic, *Dedno pravo* [Inheritance Law], 293 ff. (GV Založba 2009).

440. Inheritance of *denationalized assets* (Sl. *denacionalizirano premoženje*) is also subject to specific legislation. Probate procedure regarding denationalized assets may be carried out only after conclusion of the denationalization procedure and is unconnected to the probate procedure that had been performed regarding the decedent's non-nationalized property. According to Article 78 of the Denationalization Act, inheritance of denationalized assets is *introduced* at the moment the decision on inheritance of the decedent's non-nationalized assets is final, whereas inheritance of denationalized assets is *acquired* at the moment the decision on the denationalization is final.[950]

441. Since 2006, *same-sex partners* can register their partnership in Slovenia. Those who had done so in accordance with the Registration of a Same-Sex Civil Partnership Act,[951] were, among others, entitled to inherit his or her partner's estate. In July 2009, the Constitutional Court ascertained that Article 22 of the aforementioned act, which set down rules on inheritance between same-sex partners, was not in accordance with the Slovenian Constitution, and instructed the legislature to abolish the discordance in six months. Until then, general rules on inheritance between spouses were to apply to registered same-sex partners.[952] The unconstitutional provisions provided that same-sex partners could not, unless they were testamentary heirs, inherit their partner's separate property; only his or her community (joint) property (his or her part in it) could be inherited by his or her partner.[953] Further, Article 22 provided that same-sex partners were not obligatory heirs and deprived them of some further rights ensured to heterosexual partners. In March 2013, also non-registered same-sex partners (whose relationships were at the time otherwise not regulated in Slovenian legislation) who were in a longer lasting cohabitation (provided that no reasons existed why a registered partnership between them would be invalid), were recognized by the Constitutional Court of RS the right to inherit their partner's estate under the same rules as applied to inheritance between heterosexual cohabiting partners.[954] The Constitutional Court ascertained that by not regulating inheritance between non-registered same-sex partners who are in a longer lasting cohabitation, the IA was discriminatory and was not in line with the Slovenian Constitution. The court instructed the legislature to abolish the discordance in

---

950. Zakon o denacionalizaciji (ZDen) [Denationalization Act], Official Gazette RS, No. 27/91, with further amendments. In 1998, the Slovenian legislature amended such regulation by equating *delatio* and *aquisitio* to the moment of finality of the decision on denationalization, while in 2001 the Constitutional Court, despite strong critique between legal theory and case law, invalidated the amendment. For further details, see Zupančič & Žnidaršič Skubic, *Dedno pravo* [Inheritance Law], 317–336 (GV Založba 2009).
951. Zakon o registraciji istospolne partnerske skupnosti (ZRIPS) [Registration of a Same-Sex Civil Partnership Act], Official Gazette RS, No. 65/05, with further amendments.
952. Decision No. U-I-425/06-10, 2 Jul. 2009, Official Gazette RS, No. 55/09.
953. The unconstitutional Art. 22 set down the following rules: when a decedent has descendants, they take one-half, and the partner the other half of decedent's part in community property; when a decedent has no heirs, his or her partner inherits the whole part by him- or herself (legislature thus withdrew from the general rules on statutory inheritance where partner would inherit within the second category of heirs).
954. ECLI:SI:USRS:2013:U.I.212.10.

six months. Until then, general rules on inheritance between heterosexual cohabiting partners were to apply to non-registered same-sex partners in a longer lasting cohabitation. In 2016, the Registration of a Same-Sex Civil Partnership Act was repealed by the new Civil Union Act[955] that redefined the status of (registered or non-registered) same-sex partners leading to an improved inheritance regime for them.

442. If a decedent has no heirs, the RS becomes an owner of the decedent's assets (the so-called *estate without heirs*, Sl. *zapuščina brez dediča*) unless the deceased's creditors request that the assets are transferred into the insolvency assets within the so-called *insolvency proceedings of estate without heirs* (Sl. *stečaj zapuščine brez dedičev*).[956] If the RS becomes an owner of the decedent's assets, it is not responsible for the deceased's debts.

443. Decedent may, in his or her will, bequeath a certain thing or right (*legacy, bequest*, Sl. *volilo*) to a person or legal entity. Under Slovenian law, legatees are not heirs and do not obtain ownership on the bequeathed things directly; they merely obtain a claim towards the heirs to the transfer of the bequest.[957] Such claim is, in principle, obtained *ipso iure* upon testator's death (*dies legati cedens*) – that is, upon the transfer of the decedent's estate to the heirs – and is subject to prescription of one year from the moment the legatee found out about his or her right to legacy and could claim it.[958] Unlike the heirs, recipients of legacies are not responsible for any debts left by the deceased, unless the testator had determined otherwise.[959]

955. Zakon o partnerski zvezi (ZPZ), Official Gazette RS, No. 33/16.

956. Articles 9 and 142a of IA. Upon finding that there are no heirs to inherit the estate, the court publishes a call to unknown creditors to request in six months that the estate is transferred into the insolvency estate without heirs. This is done by filing the transfer request and by initiating insolvency proceedings of estate without heirs. Detailed rules on such proceedings are laid down in the IA and in the FOIPCDA.

957. Articles 80 and 85–94 of IA. Like heirs, legatees must, however, have capacity to inherit, must not be unworthy to inherit, and must be alive at the moment of the decedent's death.

958. Article 94 of IA.

959. In such case, the legatee is responsible up to the value of the bequest (Art. 92 of IA).

Chapter 3. Acquisitive Prescription

§1. General on Acquisitive Prescription

444. Acquisitive prescription of ownership (Sl. *priposestvovanje*, Lat. *usucapio*) as one of the *non-derivative (original)* ways of acquiring ownership is regulated in Articles 43–46 of the CPL.

445. According to Article 43 of the CPL, a proprietary possessor of a movable acquires ownership on the movable after three years of good faith possession, while a proprietary possessor of an immovable acquires ownership on it after ten years of good faith possession. If such possession is exercised on part of an immovable, that part is subject to independent acquisitive prescription.[960]

446. Prerequisites for acquisitive prescription can be denoted as *fides*, *possessio*, and *tempus*. First, the possessor must be a proprietary possessor, such that he or she possesses the asset as if it was his or her own. Second, the possessor believes that he or she is entitled to ownership, and he or she must, therefore, be in good faith as to his or her entitlement. Finally, a set time of continuous possession, the so-called prescriptive period (three or ten years respectively) must lapse – when this occurs, ownership is acquired *ipso iure*. As in case of inheritance, no delivery or registration is required for acquiring ownership.

447. There are some legislative restrictions to acquisitive prescription regarding the asset of such acquisition. According to Article 44 of the CPL, ownership of property in the public domain and of assets that are *extra commercium* cannot be acquired by prescription.

448. The moment the possessor acquires ownership under the rules of acquisitive prescription, all limited property and other rights that existed beforehand and were not respected by the acquirer during the prescriptive period cease to exist.[961] Further, the acquirer need not compensate the original owner for the loss of his or her property.[962]

§2. Proprietary Possession

449. Possession is of major importance for the concept of acquisitive prescription. Continuous possession as a factual state leads to ownership as a legal right. However, not any kind of possession suffices. The possessor must be the so-called

960. This is an exception to the general principle of speciality set down in Art. 7 of the CPL according to which only an asset as a whole and not its parts can be object of property rights.

961. Tratnik in *Property Law*, 264.

962. Vlahek, *Priposestvovanje lastninske pravice na nepremičninah* [Acquisitive Prescription of Ownership on Immovables], in Zbornik znanstvenih razprav, y. 66, 2007, 309 ff.); Rudolf, Rijavec & Lurger, *Schriften zur Europäischen Rechtswissenschaft*, Bd. 7, vol. 7, 608 (Sellier European Law Publishers 2008).

proprietary possessor, such that he or she possesses the asset *as if it was his or her own.*[963] According to theory, possession obtained under the rules of *constitutum possessorium* does not suffice as proprietary possession, while possession obtained under the rules of *longa manu traditio* does.[964]

§3. Good Faith

450. Slovenian legislation defines good faith of a possessor negatively. Article 28 of the CPL states that a possessor is in bad faith if he or she knew or should have known that he or she is not entitled to possession. Bona fide possessor is *a contrario* a possessor who did not know and could not have known that he or she is not entitled to possession. More recently, Slovenian courts and legal theory have been interpreting the good faith acquirer in cases of acquisitive prescription as someone who *has made an excusable mistake as to his or her ownership* regarding the possessed asset.[965] This definition is then applied to each individual dispute on acquisitive prescription leaving the parties somewhat uncertain as to the result.

451. The Slovenian legislature introduced the *mala fides superveniens nocet* rule that the possessor must be in good faith the entire duration of the prescriptive period, and not only at the moment of acquiring possession.[966] The CPL also provides that in case of co-ownership acquired by prescription, good faith of each co-owner is judged independently[967] and that good faith of the possessory successor is judged independently if a possessory predecessor was in bad faith (while otherwise, the predecessor's period is included in the prescriptive period of the successor).[968]

452. Article 46 of the CPL clarifies that *good faith of a legal entity* is judged according to good faith of its bodies (either director or board of directors, where good faith of all members of the board is required)[969] and other persons for whom, with regard to their area of work, it is important that an asset belongs to the entity (e.g., warehouseman, purchasing manager, and so forth).[970]

---

963. Article 27 of CPL.
964. In the first situation, the acquirer's possession cannot be perceived outwardly, whereas in the latter, notice to the third person is believed to serve as act of publicity. Tratnik in *Property Law*, 261. For further details on the types of tradition, see Part III, Ch. 1, §4.
965. Tratnik in *Property Law*, 256; Tratnik, *Pridobitev lastninske pravice s priposestvovanjem* [Acquisition of Ownership by Prescription], in Pravna Praksa, Priloga (2003) 42–43, p. III; Tratnik in *CPL with Commentary 2004*, 263. See also Judgments of the High Court of Ljubljana, Nos I Cp 2698/2010 of 20 Oct. 2010, II Cp 1317/2011 of 12 Oct. 2011, II Cp 3861/2011 of 30 May 2012, I Cp 3103/2013 of 29 Jan. 2014.
966. Article 45/1 of CPL.
967. Article 45/3 of CPL.
968. Article 45/4 of CPL.
969. Tratnik in *Property Law*, 259.
970. *Ibid.*, 260.

453. Under Slovenian law, obviously *immovables*, and not only movables, can be acquired under the rules of acquisitive prescription. This can also be deduced from the wording of Article 44/2 of the CPL, according to which a right (on an immovable) acquired by prescription may not be detrimental to a person who in good faith and trusting in the public records (e.g., land register) acquired a right before the right acquired by prescription was entered in the public record. There was, though, some uncertainty in theory and court practice as to full applicability of the concept of acquisitive prescription to immovables.[971] Uncertainty, which has fortunately already been clarified to some extent by the courts and legal theory, refers mostly to those cases of prescription in which the possessor obtained possession in a derivative way (e.g., on the basis of a sales contract) but has not yet become an owner because he or she has not yet registered in the land register. Because *good faith* as to entitlement to an asset is a prerequisite for acquisitive prescription, while at the same time everyone is deemed to be familiar with the registered data, including data on who the owner is of an immovable, the acquirer can – if the principle of publicity of the land register is interpreted strictly – in cases of derivative acquisition where ownership is acquired by registration, hardly be said to be in good faith regarding his or her ownership unless he or she is, at the same time, the registered owner. Some authors were, therefore, of an opinion that only a person registered as an owner (but not an owner in reality if, for example, the registration has been based on a null sales contract that has, because of the principle of causality, led to invalidity of the registration) can acquire ownership under the rules of acquisitive prescription, except those cases where registration is not of a constitutive nature and can therefore be acquired regardless of registration (statutory acquisition, acquisition on the basis of a judicial decision). According to such opinion, the so-called *out-of-register acquisitive prescription* (Sl. *zunajknjižno priposestvovanje*, *protiknjižno priposestvovanje*, Lat. *praescriptio contra tabulas*) is, in cases of possession obtained on a derivative ground, generally not possible, at least not in times of a functioning and efficient system of land registration.[972] Such harsh opinion was later softened by arguing that out-of-register acquisitive prescription should be allowed only in exceptional cases where non-registration and thus non-acquisition of ownership on the basis of a contract cannot be ascribed to the acquirer.[973] Analysis of Slovenian case law shows that Slovenian courts have been mostly acknowledging out-of-register acquisitive prescription.[974] In their judgment, the acquirer's good faith is to be based on his or her subjective understanding of the situation, regardless of what is registered in the land register. Transactions with

971. Vlahek, *Priposestvovanje lastninske pravice na nepremičninah* [Acquisitive Prescription of Ownership on Immovables], in Zbornik znanstvenih razprav, y. 66, 2007, pp. 309–332. See also Judgment of the District Court in Kranj, No. I P 486/2007 of 26 Jan. 2009 which was confirmed by the High Court in Ljubljana in its judgment No. I Cp 1782/09 on 26 Aug. 2009.

972. Vlahek, *Priposestvovanje lastninske pravice na nepremičninah* [Acquisitive Prescription of Ownership on Immovables], in Zbornik znanstvenih razprav, y. 66, 2007, pp. 309–332.

973. See, for example, Tratnik in *Property Law*, 259. See also the following Judgments of the High Court in Ljubljana: Nos I Cp 3671/2009 of 25 Nov. 2009, I Cp 112/2010 of 10 Feb. 2010.

974. For example, see Judgment of the District Court in Ljubljana, No. P 3631/2005-I of 21 May 2007, which was confirmed by the High Court in Ljubljana in its Judgment No. I Cp 3894/2007 of 5 Mar. 2008; Judgment No. P 55/2001 of the Local Court in Grosuplje of 21 Oct. 2008, which was confirmed by the High Court in Ljubljana in its Judgment No. II Cp 605/2009 of 17 Jun. 2009; see

numerous immovables – in particular, blocks of houses or apartments – were made in times when the land register did not operate effectively and was thus of little importance, and when buyers of immovables often obtained them from construction undertakings as investors (who were often not even registered as owners in the land register) or from municipalities who did not take care of the registration of the buyers as owners in the land register. The land on which the apartments or houses were built was usually not even properly parcelled. Especially in such cases, the actual relationships on immovables oftentimes still do not accord to the registered ones, what frequently leads to disputes. Contracts for harmonizing the registered state with the actual one on the basis of corresponding documents (sales contracts, contracts on transferring municipal land to investors, etc.) are usually concluded by all the involved persons and enable registration of the 'real' owner. Acquisitive prescription can serve as alternative. It is still to be seen how courts will interpret rules on acquisitive prescription in cases of more recent transactions. At least with regard to relationships arising during the times of the social property regime, improperly implemented spatial planning and overall low importance of the land register, it is only fair to take into account all the circumstances of the cases instead of blindly following the data registered in the land register as the only relevant data on the ownership of immovables.

454. Prior to enactment of the Slovenian CPL in 2003, acquisitive prescription of ownership was regulated somewhat differently. The Yugoslav BPLR of 1980 (following the rules of the ABGB) set out two types of acquisitive prescription of ownership: a so-called regular acquisitive prescription (Sl. *redno priposestvovanje*) requiring a title and good faith of the acquirer and setting down a ten-year prescriptive period; and a so-called irregular acquisitive prescription (Sl. *izredno priposestvovanje*) requiring only good faith of the acquirer and setting down a twenty-year prescriptive period.[975] As was stressed in the preceding paragraphs, the CPL regulates acquisitive prescription uniformly by requiring a ten-year possession of immovables in good faith, whereby the (valid) title listed as a prerequisite of the former regular acquisitive prescription will in fact be the most common proof of good faith.

455. It is to be underscored that according to the currently valid property law, i.e., the CPL, ownership may be acquired only in good faith, while real easements may (following the rules of the formerly valid BPLRA which were not fully aligned with the rules of the ABGB applied in Slovenia prior to the enactment of the federal Yugoslav BPLRA) also be acquired by acquisitive prescription regardless of good faith.[976]

---

also the following Judgments of the High Court in Ljubljana: Nos II Cp 21/2009 of 25 Mar. 2009, I Cp 808/2011 of 24 Aug. 2011. See also Judgment of the Supreme Court of RS, No. II Ips 796/2008 of 9 Feb. 2012.

975. For further details, see Vlahek, *Analiza sodne prakse glede priposestvovanja lastninske pravice na nepremičninah* [Analysis of case law on acquisitive prescription of ownership on immovables], in Zbornik, 13 ff. (GV založba 2011).

976. For further details, see Part I, Ch. 4, §1, II, A.

§4. Prescriptive Period

456. According to Article 45/1 of the CPL regulating calculation of the prescriptive period, the period (*three years for movables* and *ten for immovables*) begins to run on the day when the possessor obtained proprietary possession in good faith and ends on the last day of this period. The prescriptive period also includes the time when the predecessors of the current proprietary possessor had proprietary possession in good faith.[977] The prescriptive period also includes the time when the possessor was temporarily unable to exercise possession for reasons independent of his or her will – for example, when losing the movable he or she possessed or when the movable he or she possessed is stolen.[978]

977. Article 45/2 of CPL.
978. Article 45/5 of CPL, which neither specifies how long such *temporary* unwilling loss of possession may last nor whether the acquirer must acquire back proprietary possession afterwards, or if he or she may become an owner during such loss – regardless of the fact that the moment the period runs out, he or she does not have direct possession. See Tratnik in *Property Law*, 262.

Chapter 4. Accession

457. Acquisition of ownership by accession of a movable to immovable (Sl. *prirast*) is a type of *non-derivative statutory acquisition* of ownership that is based on the old Roman principle *accessio cedit principali*, according to which lateral things share the same fate as the principal thing, an element of which they become by accession. According to Article 54 of the CPL, ownership on an immovable extends to all movables that have become elements of the immovable. Land is always deemed to be the principal thing, regardless of the value of the land in comparison to the value of the accessed movable that accords to the *superficies solo cedit* rule set down in Article 8 of the CPL.

458. As, after accession, movables are not self-standing and individually determined objects, they cannot be objects of ownership according to the principle of speciality set down in Article 7 of the CPL. Upon accession, ownership of movables ceases to exist, while ownership of the principal thing – immovable – expands to its new elements.[979]

459. Property rights on such movables cease to exist as well, which can be of importance with regard to possible securities that had existed on the movables before they acceded to the immovable. After accession, the object of a security no longer exists, while, on the other hand, object of a security existing on an immovable becomes more valuable.

460. A special type of accession is regulated in Article 48 of the CPL regarding *the improvements of an existent building* by someone else with the consent of the owner of the building. This is frequent in Slovenian environment where children often stay at home after growing up and invest in the parents' building by erecting it, improving it, and so forth. Article 48/1 of the CPL states that if a person (builder) erects, adds to, or improves a building with the consent of the owner of an immovable, he or she does not acquire ownership of the immovable, but he or she may make a claim on the owner of the immovable for the amount by which the owner was enriched. Here, too, all movables used for such an increase become part of a building and thereby part of the immovable on which the building is raised. The owner of the immovable becomes an owner of all movables added to the building that had become its elements, whereas the builder is merely compensated for the improvements made.[980] Article 48/2 of the CPL, however, expressly states that the owner and the builder may agree on establishing co-ownership of the immovable that is acquired once registered in the land register on the basis of a contract with

979. According to Arts 95/6 and 96/6 of the CPL, a proprietary possessor has *ius tollendi* – that is, a right to separate and retain for him- or herself those elements that he or she had invested in another's thing for his or her own satisfaction or for embellishing the thing, before returning the thing to its owner under the proviso such elements can be separated without any damage.

980. According to Art. 48/3 of the CPL, the period of limitation for claims by the builder (i.e., five years according to Art. 346 of CO) begins to run on the day the builder lost possession of the immovable (and not at an earlier date, i.e., when the improvements were already finalized). General rules on unjustified enrichment are set down in Arts 190–198 of the CO.

which the owner of the immovable obliges to acknowledge co-ownership to the builder, and on the basis of a corresponding *clausula intabulandi*. Accession is, in such cases, the general rule, while formation of co-ownership must be specifically agreed.[981]

461. Article 47 of the CPL, regulating *constructions that extend over the boundary of an immovable*, sets down an exception to the rule on accession. Normally, a building or its part built on someone else's land would form part of the land it is built on according to Article 54 of the CPL. However, according to Article 47 of the CPL, in case a person (builder) builds a building, a part of which extends onto, over, or beneath another's immovable,[982] the owner of the immovable or the builder may (had they not reached an agreement as to it) request that the court[983] decide the arrangement of their mutual relationship. There are two possible solutions. The court may either order the builder to pull down the structure and restore the neighbour's immovable to its original condition which somehow accords to the *superficies solo cedit* rule and the rule on accession. However, if the consequences of restoring the immovable to its original condition would be clearly disproportionate to the damage suffered by the owner of the immovable as a result of the construction, the court may exceptionally set reasonable compensation for the owner of the immovable and issue a ruling establishing a new border between the neighbouring immovables.[984] When deciding on the case, the court must take into account all the circumstances – in particular, the justified interests of the participants, the question of the good faith of the builder, and the actions of the owner of the immovable after he or she had learned of the construction.[985]

981. For further details, see Tratnik in *Property Law*, 281–285.
982. Though not in cases in which the whole building is built on someone else's land.
983. In a non-contentious procedure.
984. Some authors (Tratnik in *Property Law*, 279) state that if such construction violates building legislation (what will most often be the case), the application of Art. 47 of the CPL is precluded. As building over a boundary will most often violate building legislation, it is hard to imagine in which cases Art. 47 would apply if such reasoning was adopted by the courts. The courts have so far only rarely applied Art. 47 of the CPL. The Supreme Court of RS has, however, recently issued a Decision (No. II Ips 112/2014 of 20 Nov. 2014) clarifying to some extent the application of Art. 47 of the CPL, in particular of the reasonable compensation to be set by the courts.
985. For further details, see Tratnik in *Property Law*, 279–281.

Chapter 5. Merger, Confusion, Commixture

462. If one of the movables that are being *merged* can be considered a *principal (dominant) movable*, the *subordinate movable* becomes constituent part of the principal movable. According to Article 55/2 of the CPL, the owner of the principal movable continues to be the owner of the movable to which a subordinate movable was attached. Ownership of other movables that have become elements of the principal movable ceases to exist. Article 55/3 of the CPL defines the principal movable as a thing that is, according to general perception, deemed to be principal.

463. If movables belonging to different owners are in a *non-hierarchical relationship*, Article 55/1 of the CPL states that they become elements of a merged movable, whereby previous owners of the contributing movables acquire co-ownership of the new movable in proportion to the value their movables had prior to the merger.

464. While merger results from merging of different movables, *confusion* arises from the mixing of liquids and *commixture* from the mixing of solids. According to Article 56 of the CPL, provisions of Article 55 of the CPL regulating merging of movables apply *mutatis mutandis* to confusion and commixture, if movables of different owners are mixed in such a way that they are incapable of being separated, or in such a way that their separation would incur disproportionate costs. Is this not the case, ownership of individual liquids or solids remains intact.

465. Because merger, confusion, and commixture lead to *original acquisition of ownership*, the new owner(s) acquire(s) ownership free of all encumbrances that might have existed prior to merging, confusing, and mixing, save those cases where the previous owner becomes (co-) owner of the new movable, because rights that encumbered the movable that belonged to him or her are resuscitated in respect of his or her (co-)ownership of the new movable.[986]

986. Article 58 of CPL.

Chapter 6. Making of a New Movable

466. Article 57 of the CPL states that anyone *creating a new movable*[987] *out of his or her own material* acquires ownership on the new movable. Further, if a person creates a new movable *out of another person's material*, the person creating the movable acquires ownership of the new movable if the value of the work is not substantially lower than the value of the material and regardless of whether he or she knew that the material belonged to someone else.[988] In both instances, ownership on the material ceases to exist and the ownership of the new product vests in the creator. Because creation of a new movable is an *original way of acquiring ownership*, the new owner acquires ownership free of all encumbrances that might have existed on the material prior to creating a new movable, except those cases where the owner of a material becomes the owner of the new movable because rights that encumbered the movable that belonged to him or her are resuscitated with respect to the new movable.[989]

467. Commercial importance of the rules on specification arises in cases of securing credits in industry. Producers often buy raw material on credit that has been secured by a reservation of title. However, applying the rules on specification, the goods that are produced from the sellers' material and that often become owned by the buyer, are free of all encumbrances, including reservation of title. Consequently, the so-called clause of remake is usually agreed in practice, protecting the seller from losing ownership of the material. According to such clause, the seller and the buyer become co-owners of the new movable in proportion of the value of the material and the production costs.[990]

987. Writing, drawing, painting, printing, or engraving on a surface or treating it in some other way are, according to CPL, also deemed as creating a new movable.
988. Tratnik in *Property Law*, 275.
989. Article 58 of CPL.
990. For further details, see Vrenčur in *Property Law*, 522; Vrenčur, *Moderne oblike zavarovanja plačil* [Modern Methods of Securing Payments] (GV Založba 2005).

Chapter 7. Appropriation

468. According to Article 50 of the CPL, ownership of a movable without an owner is acquired by the person who takes possession of the movable with the intention of appropriating it and thus becoming an owner, unless otherwise determined by law.

469. The main feature of appropriation (occupation, Sl. *prilastitev*, *okupacija*) is that the occupied *movable is without an owner* (*res nullius* – a thing belonging to no one, Sl. *nikogaršnja stvar*, *ničija stvar*). Such circumstances occur when the owner derelicts (abandons, Sl. *zavrže*) his or her movable, which is deemed to be the case when the owner undoubtedly expresses his or her will not to be the owner anymore.[991] By such an act, ownership ceases to exist. New ownership arises at the moment of occupation – that is, when the acquirer takes hold of the derelict thing (Sl. *zavržena stvar*, *dereliktirana stvar*, Lat. *res derelicta*) into proprietary possession. If he or she lacks the *intent to appropriate*, occupation does not occur, despite taking hold of the movable.

470. Movables that have merely been lost or mislaid, and not derelict, still have an owner and cannot, therefore, be appropriated. In these cases, rules on finding, and not on appropriation, apply. Rules on acquisitive prescription might apply, though, under the proviso that the acquirer occupied the movable in good faith. Special rules apply in cases of finding a treasure;[992] recreational gathering of wild fruit, mushrooms, chestnuts, moss, and other forest plants;[993] fishing and hunting;[994] and so forth.

471. It should be stressed that rules on appropriation apply to *movables only*, because immovables cannot, under Slovenian law, be derelict and cannot, therefore, be occupied. Appropriation of movables, though, is quite rare because, in practice, not many movables are derelict. Also, in cases where a decedent has no heirs, assets

991. Article 102 of CPL.
992. See Ch. 6 of this part of the monograph.
993. According to the Zakon o gozdovih (ZG) [Act on Forests], Official Gazette RS, No. 30/93, with further amendments, and according to the Pravilnik o varstvu gozdov [Rules on the Protection of Forests], Official Gazette RS, No. 114/09, with further amendments, an individual, except the owner of a forest, may pick for his or her personal use a maximum of 2 kg of non-protected mushrooms, chestnuts, fruits or moss) per day, and a maximum of 1 kg of non-protected herbaceous plants. If the owner of a forest cultivates trees for usage of fruits, the local municipality may prohibit gathering of fruits on the petition of the owner.
994. According to the Zakon o varstvu okolja (ZVO-1) [Environment Protection Act], Official Gazette RS, No. 41/04, with further amendments, the RS is the owner of wild game defined as such in the Zakon o divjadi in lovstvu (ZDLov-1) [Wild Game and Hunting Act], Official Gazette RS, No. 16/04, with further amendments.

are not ownerless and cannot be occupied because, in such cases, the RS becomes an owner of the decedent's assets.[995]

995. Article 9 of IA. Doctrine holds that such escheat assets are acquired at the moment of the decedent's death and that acquisition of ownership is not performed by occupation (at least not by occupation in the sense of property law), but by a *sui generis* universal succession *mortis causa*. See Zupančič & Žnidaršič Skubic, *Dedno pravo* [Inheritance Law], 66–69 (GV Založba 2009). For further details, see Part III, Ch. 2.

Chapter 8. Finding

§1. Lost Movables

472. Because immovables cannot be lost, rules on finding as set down in Articles 51 and 52 of the CPL, and detailed further in the Rules on the Procedure Involving Lost and Found Items,[996] are applicable to *movables only*. As has already been stressed in the previous chapter, rules on finding apply to cases where a movable has been lost and thus still has an owner, and not to cases where it has been derelict and is, therefore, ownerless.

473. If someone takes possession of the found movable (it is not obligatory to take hold of it, the finder may leave it as it is), he or she must *immediately notify* the owner of the movable or a person who the finder justifiably believes is entitled to take over the movable. If the finder does not know such a person or his or her address, the finder must *report the finding to the police* unless the movable is of insignificant value. The police must draw up the minutes regarding the finding and *announce* the finding with a description of the found movable on its website[997] and on the announcement board of the police station on whose territory the finding had occurred. The announcement must be available for one year (or less if the owner is determined before that). If the police ascertain who the owner might be, it invites him or her to identify the found movable at a fixed date, or to inform the police of the date on which he or she is willing to perform identification (if, of course, identification is performed within one year from the notification of the finding).

474. If the police had been notified of the finding, it may take *storage* of the movable (e.g., in cases of found firearms or drugs) or leave it in the safekeeping of the finder. In all other cases, the goods are handed to the Financial Administration of RS if the police does not find the owner in thirty days after it has been notified of the finding. In case the movable is kept by the finder, the police warns him or her that he or she may not use the thing or dispose of it, and that he or she must manage well with the thing.[998] If the movable may become damaged, or if disproportionate costs are associated with its maintenance, the police may sell it at a public auction or at the daily price, whereby the proceeds from the sale take the place of the found movable. In case of perishables that could not be sold at the daily price, the police offer them to the finder for free; if he or she does not want to accept them, then they are offered to humanitarian organizations or are ordered to be destroyed.

475. Under Slovenian law, it is impossible to acquire ownership of a movable by merely finding it. Titles of owners that have lost their movables are, in principle,

996. Pravilnik o postopku z najdenimi stvarmi [Rules on the Procedure Involving Lost and Found Items], Official Gazette RS, No. 90/15. In case the goods are found on one of the public carriers (train, bus, plane, ship, etc.), special legislation applies.

997. The website is in Slovene only, https://www.policija.si/apps/predmeti/index.php#/., accessed on 31 Jul. 2019.

998. The same goes for keepers other than finders that the Financial Administration of RS agrees with on the professional safekeeping of the found goods.

unaffected by the fact that the movables have been lost or that somebody else has found them. Acquisition by finding is merely an exception justified by the fact that the owner has not, for a certain period of time, claimed his or her movable from its finder or other person keeping it. A finder who has fulfilled his or her obligations regarding the finding acquires ownership of the movable *one year from the notification or reporting of the finding*,[999] provided an entitled person has not requested its handover, and provided the movable is still in safekeeping with the finder or the police or the Financial Administration of RS. If a thing is found by a state or municipality official during his or her working hours, the institution in which he or she is employed is deemed the finder.

476. The police hands over the thing, or the proceeds from the sale (sale is performed by the Financial Administration of RS in accordance with the rules of tax procedure[1000]), to the finder, provided he or she reimburses the expenses the thing has induced. Same goes for the owner, has he or she claimed the found movable. In case a movable is registered in a public register, the police issues a certificate that the finder has become an owner of the thing, which enables listing in the register.

477. The found thing is deemed abandoned if the finder declares undoubtedly that he or she does not want to become owner of the thing. In this case, the RS becomes the owner via occupation.[1001]

478. Legislation does not provide for any *reward for the finder*. The owner may, of course, decide to award the finder as he or she thinks fit.[1002]

§2. Treasure Trove

479. Article 53 of the CPL lays down special provisions on finding a treasure – that is, a thing of substantial value that has been hidden for so long that it is no longer possible to ascertain its owner. The finder of a treasure must *report the finding to the police*. A found treasure belongs *in equal parts to the finder and to the*

999. If the movable is of insignificant value and the owner or presumed owner or his or her address is unknown, the period runs from the time of the find.
1000. Zakon o davčnem postopku (ZDavP-2) [Tax Procedure Act], Official Gazette RS, No. 117/06, with further amendments.
1001. The thing is then sold on public auction or is offered free of charge to state agencies or humanitarian organizations. If the thing cannot be sold or taken over, or if the costs for its sale or maintenance are disproportionate, the thing is destroyed.
1002. Legislation prior to the CPL, however, provided for a reward in the amount of 15% of the value of the found thing in case the thing was of smaller value, and in the amount of maximum 10% in case it was of greater value, whereby the court decided on the entitlement to and the amount of the reward. If the owner did not present the finder with the reward, or did not claim the thing, or did not reimburse the expenses the found thing had induced, the thing was sold on public auction and money acquired thereby became revenue of a competent municipality.

owner of the movable or immovable in which it was found, unless otherwise determined by law (e.g., in cases of archaeological findings and remnants where ownership of the RS is presumed).[1003] In contrast to ordinary find, in cases of treasure trove, ownership is acquired at the moment of the trove and not only after certain lapse of time.

1003. Article 6 of the Zakon o varstvu kulturne dediščine (ZVKD-1) [Act on the Protection of Cultural Heritage], Official Gazette RS, No. 16/08, with further amendments.

Chapter 9. Acquisition of Fruits

480. Article 20/1 of the CPL defines 'fruits' as direct products of a thing that form its part until separation, whereas upon separation, they become independent movables. According to Article 59/1 of the CPL, the owner of the principal thing, in principle, becomes also the owner of the separated fruit.[1004] An exception is for example set down in Article 82 of the CPL in cases of fruits that fall on someone's land from a neighbour's tree. In such cases, the owner of the land on which fruits had fallen, and not the owner of the tree, acquires ownership of the fruits.[1005] Additionally, Article 51/3 of the CPL stresses that under conditions determined by law, anyone may acquire ownership of forest fruits, mushrooms, and other freely growing plants, regardless of the fact that someone else is the owner of the forest where these plants are growing.[1006]

1004. According to Art. 59/2 of the CPL, proprietary possessor in good faith acquires ownership of the fruits at the moment of their severance from the principal thing he or she possesses. The same applies to a person who has the right to the fruits on the basis of a legal relationship with the owner of the principal thing.

1005. If a tree grows on a boundary, then fruits are to be divided among neighbours equally, regardless of which side of the boundary they fall down on.

1006. See Part III, Ch. 7.

Chapter 10. Expropriation

§1. General on Expropriation

481. Expropriation (Sl. *razlastitev*) is regulated in Article 69 of the Slovenian Constitution, according to which ownership on immovables may be taken or limited in the public interest only with the provision of in kind or monetary compensation under conditions established by law. Expropriation is further regulated in the general rules of the SPA (Articles 192–215), and in some specific legislation, for example, in the Cultural Heritage Protection Act,[1007] Nature Conservation Act,[1008] Water Act,[1009] Environmental Protection Act,[1010] Mining Act,[1011] Public Roads Act[1012] and Roads Act,[1013] Electronic Communications Act,[1014] and Energy Act.[1015]

482. Expropriation may be *full* where an immovable is permanently taken from its owner, or *partial* where ownership on an immovable is merely limited. In theory and in practice, though, only full expropriation is meant when using the term 'expropriation'. Besides full expropriation,[1016] the SPA regulates two types of partial expropriation.[1017] First, a *temporary or permanent easement* may be established in public interest on someone's immovable (easement in the public interest, Sl. *služnost v javno korist*). And second, *temporary use of someone's immovable* (Sl. *začasna uporaba nepremičnine*) may be allowed for the purposes of constructing or reconstructing edifices in public interest, or for the purposes of renovating the degraded and other regions if renovation is financed from public funds. In addition to specific provisions regulating these two types of restrictions, rules on full expropriation apply to them *mutatis mutandis*.

483. The RS or Slovene municipalities are *beneficiaries* in case of full expropriation, while the RS, Slovene municipalities, providers of public services and

1007. Article 63 of the Act on the Protection of Cultural Heritage.
1008. Articles 88–90 of the Zakon o ohranjanju narave (ZON) [Nature Conservation Act], Official Gazette RS, No. 56/99, with further amendments.
1009. Articles 36 ff. of the Zakon o vodah (ZV-1) [Water Act], Official Gazette RS, No. 67/02, with further amendments.
1010. Article 100 of the Zakon o varstvu okolja (ZVO-1) [Environmental Protection Act], Official Gazette RS, No. 41/04, with further amendments.
1011. Articles 67–68 of the Zakon o rudarstvu (ZRud-1) [Mining Act], Official Gazette RS, No. 61/10, with further amendments.
1012. Articles 19 and 28 of the Zakon o javnih cestah (ZJC) [Public Roads Act], Official Gazette RS, No. 29/97, with further amendments.
1013. Articles 3a and 12 of the Zakon o cestah (ZCes-1) [Roads Act],, Official Gazette RS, No. 109/10, with further amendments.
1014. Articles 16–23 of the Zakon o elektronskih komunikacijah (ZEKom-1) [Electronic Communications Act], Official Gazette RS, No. 109/12, with further amendments.
1015. Articles 471–477 of the Energetski zakon (EZ-1) [Energy Act], Official Gazette RS, No. 17/14, with further amendments.
1016. Articles 192–209 of SPA.
1017. Articles 210, 211 and 214 of SPA.

holders of infrastructure activities may be beneficiaries of partial expropriation.[1018] *Expropriated persons* can be individuals as well as private or public entities, except the RS.[1019]

484. According to the Constitution, expropriation may be performed only on the following terms, which are regulated in detail in the SPA: first, expropriation is in public interest; second, due compensation is provided in exchange; and finally, expropriation is performed in accordance with the rules that must be regulated by laws, and not by subordinate legislation.

§2. PUBLIC INTEREST

485. The goal of expropriation as the most invasive interference with someone's property is evident from Article 192 of the SPA, which states that expropriation is permitted in the public interest only under the proviso that it is essential for attaining the public benefit and that the latter is proportionate to the encroachment upon the rights the expropriation induces. Additionally, expropriation is prohibited if the expropriator already disposes of an appropriate immovable.

486. Unless special legislation provides otherwise, expropriation may be accomplished only for the following reasons.[1020] First, to build or to obtain edifices or land for the purposes of public service infrastructure, state defence, state reserves, safety of civilians and their property, safety from natural and other catastrophes or to reconstruct or demolish such edifices, where it is deemed that the public interest exists if these purposes are foreseen in the state or municipal planning.[1021] And second, to build or to obtain edifices or land for the purposes of maintaining public services of health, education, culture, science, research, and social security; to build welfare and non-profit apartments; or to reconstruct or demolish edifices which serve such purposes, where the Slovenian government or municipal council must additionally make a decision that the foreseen activities are in public interest. After obtaining such decision, the beneficiary will initiate expropriation proceedings.

§3. EXPROPRIATION PROCEEDINGS

487. Unless provided otherwise (as in case of renovating regions where municipalities decide on the temporary use of an immovable) state *administrative units* (Sl. *upravne enote*) decide on expropriation in the first instance proceedings, while the

1018. Article 195 of SPA.
1019. *Ibid.*. If the immovable owned by a public entity is used for public purposes, expropriation is limited to cases where the expropriation purpose outweighs the public purpose the immovable already serves.
1020. Article 193 of SPA.
1021. It suffices that reconstructions and demolishments are in accordance with the existent municipal planning.

ministry responsible for spatial planning is the appeals body.[1022] Except for specific procedural provisions of the SPA and of specific legislation regulating expropriation, general rules on administrative procedure (Sl. *upravni postopek*)[1023] apply. *Judicial protection* in the form of administrative dispute (Sl. *upravni spor*)[1024] is also guaranteed.[1025]

488. Before initiating expropriation proceedings, the beneficiary must *offer* the owner of an immovable the option to acquire it by purchase.[1026] If the owner accepts the offer, ownership on the immovable is acquired according to the rules of derivative *inter vivos* acquisition. If, however, the sales contract is not concluded (and the land registry permission issued)[1027] within thirty days after the offer was made, the beneficiary may file the expropriation request.

489. The following documents must be enclosed with the *request*:[1028] a detailed list of immovables to be expropriated, an extract from the planning act that is the basis for expropriation, the expropriation plan with proof of the public interest the expropriation pursues, a statement on the time limits in which the purpose of the expropriation will be attained, and the offer made to the owner.

490. The administrative unit first *decides on the initiation of expropriation proceedings*. It will initiate the proceedings only if it finds that the public interest is demonstrated and that expropriation is essential for attaining its goal as well as that it is proportional to the negative effects it induces. In cases where a decision of the Slovenian government or of a municipal council on the public benefit of the foreseen activities is required, the administrative unit must also verify whether such decision exists. Appeal against the administrative unit's decision on initiation of expropriation proceedings and administrative dispute are the available legal remedies. Initiation of expropriation proceedings is denoted in the land register on the basis of the decision on initiation of expropriation proceedings forwarded to the registry by the competent administration unit within fifteen days from its finality.[1029] From initiation to conclusion of expropriation proceedings, transactions with the

1022. Articles 196–205of SPA.
1023. Zakon o splošnem upravnem postopku (ZUP) [General Administrative Procedure Act], Official Gazette RS, No. 80/99, with further amendments, applies.
1024. Zakon o upravnem sporu (ZUS-1) [Administrative Dispute Act], Official Gazette RS, No. 105/06, with further amendments, applies.
1025. For further details on administrative procedure and administrative dispute, see Androjna & Kerševan, *Upravno procesno pravo* [Law of Administrative Procedure] (GV Založba 2006).
1026. Article 197 of SPA. If the beneficiary cannot make the offer because residence of the owner is unknown and he or she does not have a representative to whom the offer could be made, the beneficiary may request for appointment of a trustee who will act on behalf of the owner.
1027. It is not clear from the wording of the SPA whether the beneficiary is precluded from filing the expropriation request into the moment the offer is accepted, the moment the land registry permission is issued by the owner, or the moment of registration. Because the beneficiary may initiate expropriation proceedings already after thirty days, conclusion of the contract accompanied by the land registry permission obviously suffices.
1028. Article 199 of SPA.
1029. Article 200/2 of SPA and Art. 46/2 of LRA.

immovable or its alterations are prohibited, except sales to the beneficiary or to a third person with the beneficiary's consent.[1030]

491. After assessing all relevant information, the administration unit issues a *decision on expropriation* – that is, decision on the suppression of ownership of the expropriated person.[1031] Appeal against the decision on expropriation as well as administrative dispute are available.

§4. Compensation

492. In exchange for the immovable, the expropriation beneficiary must provide the owner with due compensation in the form of an *equivalent substitutive immovable* or *monetary sum* and reimburse all costs incurred by the owner for the purposes of expropriation.[1032]

493. If the immovable is used as a residence or serves for maintaining essential agricultural or commercial activity, compensation must take the form of an equivalent substitute immovable, unless the owner requests monetary compensation. In these cases, the beneficiary cannot opt for the type of compensation.

494. Whether the beneficiary may do so in other cases is, however, not clear. Neither the Constitution nor the SPA settled this matter explicitly; the legislation merely enumerates in kind and monetary compensation as alternatives. It is therefore not clear who, and if at all, may opt for one of the alternatives in these cases. Case law is also not uniform. Courts have occasionally stressed that it is the beneficiary's right to decide on the type of compensation,[1033] while, on the contrary, they have noted that substitute immovable must be provided if the expropriated person shows legitimate interest in it.[1034] Further, some authors believe that compensation in kind must take precedence over monetary compensation if a substitute immovable is available, regardless of the parties' interest.[1035]

495. Fifteen days after the expropriation decision becomes final, the administrative unit invites the beneficiary and the owner to reach an agreement on all aspects of compensation – in particular, on the amount of monetary compensation or on the characteristics of the substitute immovable, as well as on deadlines for performing

1030. Article 200/3 of SPA.
1031. Article 203 of SPA.
1032. Article 206 of SPA.
1033. Judgment of the High Court in Ljubljana of 18 Sep. 2002 (No. II Cp 720/2002).
1034. Judgment of the High Court in Ljubljana of 17 Jun. 2009 (No. I Cp 751/2009).
1035. Čebulj in Čebulj et al., *Zakon o urejanju prostora s komentarjem pravo* [Spatial Planning Act with Commentary], 572 (GV Založba 2005); Tratnik & Vrenčur, *Omejitve lastninske pravice in posebni pravni režimi na nepremičninah* [Restrictions of Property and Special Legal Regimes on Immovables], 58 (GV Založba 2009). For further details, see Grižon, *Nadomestilo za razlaščeno nepremičnino* [Compensation for Expropriated Immovable], Master Thesis, University of Ljubljana, 2016.

the agreement. Notification of the agreement is provided to the administrative unit, which, after receiving the deposition of the agreement, issues an enforceable decision containing the contents of the agreement. The agreement is also enforceable if it is in the form of a notarial protocol. If, after two months from the invitation, such agreement is not concluded, each of the parties may start non-contentious court proceedings for determining compensation.[1036]

§5. Acquisition of Ownership

496. Expropriation is one example where ownership is acquired on the basis of a decision made by a state body. According to the general Article 42 of the CPL, ownership is acquired, unless otherwise provided by law, the moment a decision of an administrative body is final (Sl. *dokončna*) – that is, when appeal against it is no longer available. The SPA on the contrary stipulates that in cases of expropriation, ownership is acquired only when the decision is final in such a way that a judicial remedy against the decision, and not only appeal in administrative procedure, is no longer available (Sl. *pravnomočna*).[1037] Being *lex specialis*, the SPA prevails.[1038] In urgent cases, ownership on expropriated immovables may, by exception, be acquired and possession of the immovables obtained prior to the finality of the expropriation decision.[1039]

497. Expropriation decision has a constitutive effect. Ownership is therefore transferred regardless of delivery or registration, which thus only has declaratory effect. The expropriation beneficiary may not, however, take possession of the immovable before compensating the owner with a new immovable or a monetary sum, or before the date set in the expropriation decision.[1040] Because of the ambiguous wording of the SPA,[1041] some authors are of the opinion that payment of the monetary sum or handing over the substitute immovable is a prerequisite for transferring ownership on the immovable to the beneficiary, and not only for delivering the expropriated immovable into the beneficiary's possession.[1042]

1036. Article 207 of SPA.

1037. For further details on administrative procedure, see Androjna & Kerševan, *Upravno procesno pravo* [Law of Administrative Procedure] (GV Založba 2006).

1038. Tratnik in *Property Law*, 291; Juhart in *CPL with Commentary 2004*, 258..

1039. Article 205 of SPA.

1040. Article 204/2 of SPA, which stipulates that ownership is acquired at the moment the expropriation decision is final, or when the agreement on compensation is concluded, or when the decision containing such agreement becomes final.

1041. Article 204/1 of SPA.

1042. Čebulj in Čebulj et al., *Zakon o urejanju prostora s komentarjem pravo* [Spatial Planning Act with Commentary], 589–590 (GV Založba 2005). See also Tratnik & Vrenčur, *Omejitve lastninske pravice in posebni pravni režimi na nepremičninah* [Restrictions of Property and Special Legal Regimes on Immovables], 55–56 (GV Založba 2009), where the opinion of Čebulj is confirmed while at the same time finality of the expropriation decision is acknowledged as the moment of acquiring ownership on expropriated immovables.

498. Any property rights and leases on the expropriated immovable cease to exist to the extent set down in the expropriation decision. The administrative unit decides on the expiration of such rights on the expropriator's request only and under the proviso that the expiration is urgent and proportional to the public interest pursued by expropriation.[1043] Holders of such rights take part in expropriation proceedings and are entitled to compensation in case their rights cease to exist.[1044] It is to be underscored that such regulation is not appropriate and should address differently in particular the question of effects of expropriation on mortgages existing on expropriated immovables and thus on the relationships between the new owners and the creditors.

499. If the construction of the planned edifices is not initiated in the time fixed in the expropriation decision or in the contract, the expropriated person may *request the immovable be returned to him or her.*[1045] If ownership was acquired on the basis of a contract, the former owner may avoid the contract and consequently obtain back the immovable, while in case the immovable was acquired on the basis of an administrative decision, the former owner may request the administrative unit to annul the expropriation decision it had issued.[1046] Before filing such request, the former owner must try to reach an agreement with the beneficiary on the return of the immovable. Notification of the agreement may be given to the administrative unit, which, after receiving the deposition of the agreement, issues an enforceable decision containing the contents of the agreement. Agreement is also enforceable if it is established in the form of a notarial protocol.

500. The former owner may also request the administrative unit to annul the decision if compensation is not provided one year after the agreement on compensation was concluded before a notary, or after the administrative unit issued the decision containing the contents of the agreement, or after the unit decided on from the rules on the so-called simplified compulsory settlement procedure compensation on request and such decision became final.[1047]

1043. If the expropriated immovable is mortgaged, the beneficiary bears subsidiary liability for the secured claim. Such regulation has been rightfully criticized and should undoubtedly be amended. See Damjan, *Hipoteka na nepremičnini, ki je predmet razlastitve* [Mortgage on an Expropriated Immovable],in*Sodobno stvarno pravo*, 237 ff. (Eds Juhart, Plavšak, Vrenčur, Pravna fakulteta v Ljubljani, Planet GV, TaxFinLex, 2016).; Grižon, *Nadomestilo za razlaščeno nepremičnino* [Compensation for Expropriated Immovable], Master Thesis, University of Ljubljana, 2016.

1044. Article 209 of SPA.

1045. Article 212 of SPA; Art. 214 of the SPA similarly regulates annulment of easements established in the public interest.

1046. Art. 213 of SPA. The decision is annulled with *ex tunc* effects.

1047. Article 215 of SPA. It is unclear how provisions on the time limits for performing the agreement on compensation, which are essential parts of the agreement according to Art. 207 of the SPA, are to be applied in view of the one-year time limit set down in Art. 215 of the SPA.

Chapter 11. Insolvency

§1. Types of Procedures Following Insolvency

501. Procedures following insolvency (insolvency proceedings, Sl. *postopki zaradi insolventnosti*) are regulated in the Financial Operations, Insolvency Proceedings and Compulsory Dissolution Act (FOIPCDA) of 2007 (entering into force in 2008)[1048] and are classified as: (1) procedures of arrangement with the creditors called compulsory settlement procedures (Sl. *postopek prisilne poravnave*),[1049] and (2) bankruptcy procedures (Sl. *stečajni postopek*), the latter taking form of: (a) bankruptcy of a legal entity (Sl. *stečaj nad pravno osebo*),[1050] (b) personal bankruptcy (Sl. *osebni stečaj*),[1051] i.e., bankruptcy of: (i) a consumer within the meaning of the FOIPCDA (Sl. *potrošnik*, i.e., a person who is not a legal entity, a businessman (sole trader) or a person exercising a liberal profession), (ii) a businessman (sole trader, Sl. *podjetnik*), or (iii) a person exercising a liberal profession (Sl. *zasebnik*), or (c) bankruptcy of inherited estate (Sl. *stečaj zapuščine*).[1052] In cases of compulsory settlement, the company or the sole trader in question is merely restructured in order to cease being insolvent and to guarantee to the creditors better repayment as in the case of instituting bankruptcy proceedings. In cases of bankruptcy, on the contrary, the legal entity or a business of a sole trader or a person exercising a liberal profession ceases to exist.

1048. FOIPCDA was amended twice in 2009, once in 2010, twice in 2011, twice in 2013, once in 2015, and once in 2016. The last amendment has entered into force in April 2016, while in April and May 2016, the Constitutional Court of RS has ruled that parts of the FOIPCDA are unconstitutional and has requested the legislator to amend the provisions accordingly. Before FOIPCDA entered into force in 2008, bankruptcy (and other insolvency and liquidation) proceedings were regulated in the Compulsory Settlement, Bankruptcy and Liquidation Act of 1993 and in the Financial Transactions of Enterprises Act of 1999. Between 1991 and 1994, the former Yugoslav Compulsory Settlement, Bankruptcy and Liquidation Act of 1989 was in force in Slovenia.

1049. Articles 45–134 and 135–221.z of FOIPCDA. The fifth FOIPCDA amendment (FOIPCDA-E) applying as of 15 Aug. 2013 inserted a new chapter setting out specific rules on the so-called simplified compulsory settlement procedure (Sl. *poenostavljena prisilna pora*vnava), i.e., such regarding micro companies and businessmen (Arts 221.a–221.g of FOIPCDA; small-sized companies and businessmen were added by the next FOIPCDA amendment, i.e., the FOIPCDA-F), while the sixth FOIPCDA amendment (FOIPCDA-F) inserted anew a chapter on specific rules on compulsory settlement procedures regarding medium-sized and large companies (Arts 221.h–221.z of FOIPCDA). The last FOIPCDA amendment (i.e., FOIPCDA-G) has, however, excluded application of the rules on simplified compulsory settlement procedure to small-sized companies.

1050. Articles 45–134 and 222–380 of FOIPCDA.

1051. Articles 381–413 of FOIPCDA. The last FOIPCDA amendment (FOIPCDA-G) was drafted mainly to guarantee that proceedings of personal bankruptcy are no longer abused by the debtors.

1052. Articles 414–418 of FOIPCDA.

502. According to the FOIPCDA, insolvency arises in the following two cases: where for a longer period of time a debtor is not able to settle all his or her liabilities falling due within such a period of time (so-called continuous non-liquidity, Sl. *trajnejša nelikvidnost*),[1053] or is facing long-term payment inability (Sl. *dolgoročna plačilna nesposobnost*).[1054]

1053. Article 14/1,2,4 of FOIPCDA. Unless proven otherwise, continuous non-liquidity is deemed to arise in the following cases:

(1) for a debtor who is a legal entity, a sole trader or a person exercising a liberal profession: (a) if the debtor does not perform for more than two months one or more of his or her obligations in a total amount exceeding 20% of the amount of his or her obligations as set out in the debtor's annual report for the last business year before such obligations became due; (b) if for the last sixty days before a request to initiate insolvency proceedings is filed with the court (or for more than sixty days within the period of last ninety days before the request to initiate insolvency proceedings is filed with the court) the assets on the debtor's accounts do not suffice for enforcing a claim against the debtor; (c) if the debtor does not have an account in the RS and has not performed his or her obligations in sixty days after the enforcement decision became final;
(2) for a debtor that was in compulsory settlement procedure that had ended with a final approval of the compulsory settlement, if the debtor is late for more than two months: (a) with its obligations arising out of the settlement: (b) with its obligations towards the secured creditors that had arisen before the insolvency proceedings were initiated; (c) with other measures as are set out in the financial restructuring plan;
(3) for a debtor who is a consumer within the meaning of the FOIPCDA: (a) if he or she is delayed for more than two months in meeting one or more liabilities in the total amount exceeding the amount of three times the amount of his or her salary, compensation or other remunerations received in a regular manner in periods not longer than two months; (b) if he or she is unemployed and does not receive any other regular remunerations and is delayed in meeting his or her liabilities for more than two months, in the amount exceeding EUR 1,000.

Continuous non-liquidity is, however, always deemed to arise in the following cases (proving the opposite is not possible): if the legal entity, a businessman or a consumer is late for more than two months in paying its employees their salaries in the amount of the minimum salary, or is late in paying taxes and duties that are to be paid or charged when paying the salaries, if such state exists on the day before the proposition on the commencement of insolvency proceedings is filed.

1054. Article 14/1,3 of FOIPCDA. Unless proven otherwise, a debtor shall be considered facing long-term payment inability: (1) if the value of his or her assets is smaller than the sum of his liabilities (so-called over indebtedness, Sl. *prezadolženost*); (2) for a debtor who is a company (with excluded liability of its shareholders): also if the loss for the current year together with the transferred loss amounts to one-half of the share capital, and such loss cannot be deducted from the transferred profit or from reserves.

503. Besides procedures following insolvency,[1055] procedures of compulsory dissolution of legal persons – be they compulsory liquidation procedures (Sl. *postopek prisilne likvidacije*)[1056] or procedures of removal from the register of companies without liquidation (Sl. *izbris pravne osebe iz sodnega registra brez likvidacije*)[1057] – are regulated in the FOIPCDA, while procedures of voluntary liquidation of companies and some other legal persons are regulated in the Companies Act.[1058]

504. As of December 2013, pre-emptive restructuring of financial claims of companies is also regulated in the FOIPCDA[1059] enabling (court-controlled) restructuring of financial claims in cases where otherwise the company would become insolvent within one year.[1060] In practice, companies in Slovenia have also started performing out-of-court restructuring of claims in order to avoid any of the stigmatized regulated court-controlled restructuring proceedings or bankruptcy proceedings.

§2. General on Bankruptcy Procedure

505. As of 1 September 2010, district courts in Slovenia have jurisdiction in all proceedings following insolvency depending on the place of seat or residence or property of the debtor or the place of seat of the person paying salary or other permanent income to the debtor.[1061] Sole judges are appointed to hear bankruptcy cases

1055. For more details on all types of insolvency proceedings, see Plavšak, *Zakon o finančnem poslovanju, postopkih zaradi insolventnosti in prisilnem prenehanju, Razširjena uvodna pojasnila* [Financial Operations, Insolvency Proceedings and Compulsory Dissolution Act, Extended Introductory Remarks] (GV Založba 2008); Plavšak, *ZFPPIPP-A do D, Uvodna pojasnila* [FOIPCDA-A to E, Introductory remarks] (GV Založba 2011); Plavšak, *ZFPPIPP-E, Uvodna pojasnila* [FOIPCDA-E, Introductory remarks] (GV Založba 2013); Plavšak, *ZFPPIPP-F, Uvodna pojasnila* [FOIPCDA-F, Introductory remarks] (GV Založba 2014).
1056. Articles 419–423 of FOIPCDA. Various laws (e.g., the Companies Act, the Liability of Legal Persons for Criminal Offences Act, the Foundations Act) set out when compulsory dissolution is to be performed by the courts. The FOIPCDA sets out the compulsory liquidation procedure by mainly referring to relevant provisions of the Companies Act regulating liquidation procedures, and to relevant provisions of the FOIPCDA regulating bankruptcy procedures.
1057. Articles 424–444 of FOIPCDA.
1058. Zakon o gospodarskih družbah (ZGD-1) [Companies Act], Official Gazette RS, No. 42/06, with further amendments.
1059. Chapter on pre-emptive restructuring was inserted into the FOIPCDA by the sixth FOIPCDA amendment (FOIPCDA-F entering into force on 7 Dec. 2013) enabling pre-emptive restructuring of medium-sized and large companies. The seventh FOIPCDA amendment (i.e., FOIPCDA-G entering into force on 26 Apr. 2016) enabled pre-emptive restructuring also for small-sized companies leavingonly micro companies outside the application of these rules.
1060. Articles 44.b–44.z of FOIPCDA.
1061. Articles 51–52 of FOIPCDA. Before 1 Sep. 2010, district courts had jurisdiction in cases of insolvency of legal entities and businessmen, while local courts were vested with jurisdiction in cases of consumers' insolvency, insolvency of persons exercising a liberal profession, and insolvency of inherited estate.

and compulsory settlement cases.[1062] As of 1 January 2011, the appellate court having jurisdiction in insolvency proceedings is the High Court in Ljubljana that assesses appeals in a panel of three judges.[1063] An appeal must be lodged within fifteen days after the first instance court has issued the decision that has been served (or published depending on the person appealing).[1064] It must be stressed that according to the FOIPCDA, the court of first instance may, once having received a promptly lodged and allowed appeal, find on its own the appeal as founded and replace its first decision with a new decision without forwarding the appeal to the appellate court as would otherwise be the case.[1065] The FOIPCDA explicitly excludes the extraordinary remedies of revision and of opening of proceedings in insolvency proceedings enabling thus only the extraordinary remedy of 'petition for protection of legality' filed by state prosecutors.[1066] Reversion to the previous state of affairs (*restitutio in integrum*) is also not allowed.[1067] All questions of insolvency proceedings that are not covered by the FOIPCDA, are to be addressed by applying the CPA *mutatis mutandis*.[1068] As of 15 June 2013, mediation is obligatory in all insolvency proceedings if the judge is of the opinion that mediation is suitable for solving a disputed issue arising out of insolvency proceedings or being directly connected to the proceedings.[1069] The parties of a lawsuit in insolvency proceedings may opt for mediation on their own motion in order to solve their dispute amicably.[1070]

506. Bankruptcy proceedings may be initiated on the request of: (1) a debtor; (2) a personally liable shareholder of a company; (3) a creditor who demonstrates with probability his or her claim towards the debtor and that the debtor is late with the payment for more than two months; and (4) the Public Guarantee, Maintenance and Disability Fund of the Republic of Slovenia if it demonstrates with probability that employees have claims towards the debtor and that the debtor is late with these payments for more than two months.[1071] The court itself commences the proceedings only in exceptional cases set out in the FOIPCDA (e.g., if the court dismisses the debtor's request to commence the compulsory settlement procedure[1072]).[1073] The moment of filing with the court the request for the commencement of bankruptcy proceedings is called 'initiation of bankruptcy proceedings' (Sl. *uvedba stečajnega*

1062. Article 53 of FOIPCDA.
1063. Articles 52/4 and 128/4 of FOIPCDA.
1064. Article 127 of FOIPCDA.
1065. Article 128/1,2,3 of FOIPCDA.
1066. Article 121/2 of FOIPCDA.
1067. *Ibid.*
1068. Article 121/1 of FOIPCDA. According to Art. 125 of the FOIPCDA, the High Court is to decide on the appeal in one month, except in cases of appeals against the court's decision on the commencement of the proceedings where it is to decide in fifteen days.
1069. Article 48.a of FOIPCDA. The mediation is deemed unsuccessful if the issue in question is not solved within thirty days. In practice, mediation in insolvency proceedings is not performed.
1070. Article 48.b of FOIPCDA. The mediation is deemed unsuccessful if the dispute is not solved within thirty days.
1071. Article 231 of FOIPCDA.
1072. Article 141/3 of FOIPCDA.
1073. Article 230/2 of FOIPCDA.

postopka), while the moment when the court decides on the request and issues the decision on the commencement of bankruptcy proceedings is called 'commencement of bankruptcy proceedings' (Sl. *začetek stečajnega postopka*).[1074] The court must publish its decision the same day it is issued.[1075] It must at the same time inform the creditors of the commencement of bankruptcy proceedings by publishing information on the commencement of the proceedings.[1076] Decisions on commencement of bankruptcy proceedings and other procedural steps in bankruptcy proceedings are published by the court in the business register which is available on the web pages of Agency of the Republic of Slovenia for Public Legal Records and Related Services (Sl. *Agencija Republike Slovenije za javnopravne evidence in storitve – AJPES*).[1077]

507. From the day following the publication of the commencement of the bankruptcy proceedings of a legal entity, the debtor or its representatives lose the right to administer and dispose of the debtor's assets that are part of the insolvency estate and were acquired prior to or after the commencement of the bankruptcy proceedings. The administration of the estate and legal representation of the debtor are transferred to the bankruptcy administrator (Sl. *stečajni upravitelj*), who is appointed by the district court in charge of the proceedings.[1078] The bankruptcy administrator takes over the debtor's books, business as well as premises and other debtor's property.[1079] All debtor's existing orders and offers become invalid, and the debtor is prohibited from issuing payments from its account.[1080] After the commencement of bankruptcy proceedings, the bankruptcy administrator may enter into legal relationships only for the purposes of the management and realization of bankruptcy assets,[1081] except in court-approved cases of finalization of existent urgent transactions (Sl. *končanje nujnih poslov*) and in cases of reasonable continuation of the debtor's business warranting better repayment of creditors as would be the case otherwise (Sl. *nadaljevanje poslovanja stečajnega dolžnika*).[1082] Under specific conditions set out in the FOIPCDA that deviate from the general regulation of contracts of lease in the CO and the HA, the debtor may terminate all lease contracts it has entered into prior to its bankruptcy.[1083] Limitation periods of the creditors' claims towards the insolvency debtor are stayed once the creditors file them within

1074. The court is to issue the decision on the commencement of bankruptcy proceedings in three working days after the request had been filed by the debtor or by the debtor's personally liable shareholder, or – in other cases – in three working days after various procedural steps set out in Art. 241 of FOIPCDA take place.
1075. Article 242/3 of FOIPCDA.
1076. Article 243 of FOIPCDA.
1077. http://www.ajpes.si/?language=english, accessed on 31 Jul. 2019.
1078. Articles 245 and 251 of FOIPCDA. If an appeal is lodged against the decision on the commencement of insolvency proceedings, the legal representatives who are not the administrator represent the debtor in the appeals proceedings.
1079. Articles 290–295 of FOIPCDA.
1080. Articles 246–247 of FOIPCDA.
1081. For details on the management and the realization of the debtor's assets, see Arts 320–352 of the FOIPCDA.
1082. Articles 315–319 of FOIPCDA.
1083. Article 248 of FOIPCDA.

the insolvency proceedings,[1084] while limitation periods of the insolvency debtor's claims towards its debtors do not run for one year after the commencement of insolvency proceedings.[1085] The effect of bankruptcy proceedings on enforcement proceedings and proceedings for insurance of claims that were initiated prior to the commencement of bankruptcy proceedings, depends on various criteria, such as whether the creditor has already obtained the right of separation, whether the debtor's property has already been sold in enforcement proceedings, etc.[1086]

508. Management of the debtor's estate is consisted mainly of leasing the debtor's property and investing the debtor's funds.[1087] After the commencement of the bankruptcy proceedings, the debtor's property may be leased only if that does not prolong the selling of these assets and only for a maximum of one year (in practice, further leases for a maximum of one year may be granted by the courts if the required criteria is met). In agreement with the court, the bankruptcy administrator may in these cases establish a right of pre-emption in favour of the lease.[1088] The debtor's money may be invested only in: (1) bonds issued by the RS or other EU Member State or by the European Central Bank, bank of Slovenia or other EU Member State central bank; (2) bonds (except subordinated bonds) issued by a bank having its seat in the RS or a credit institution having its seat in another EU Member State; (3) bank money deposits with a bank having its seat in the RS or a credit institution having its seat in another EU Member State.[1089]

509. Assets in possession of the insolvent debtor that are owned by third persons do not form the insolvency estate. The law grants the owners (as well as the principals or trustees in the fiduciary relationships)[1090] the so-called *right of separation* (Sl. *izločitvena pravica*) – that is, a right to request separation of such assets from the debtor's estate.[1091] The right of separation may be referred to by the following persons: i) the owner of a movable in possession of the insolvency debtor requests the debtor to retransfer the possession of the movable back to him or her; ii) the owner of an immovable who obtained ownership on the immovable on the basis of acquisitive prescription but the immovable is still registered with the insolvency debtor to issue him or her a declaration that he or she is the owner of the immovable; iii) the principal or trustee in the fiduciary relationship with the insolvency debtor who is the legal owner of the movable in question to retransfer the ownership back to him or her; iv) the owner of the state commodity reserves that are in possession of the insolvent debtor to deliver the commodities. The commencement of bankruptcy proceedings does not, therefore, affect the ownership of

1084. Article 258 of FOIPCDA.
1085. Article 249 of FOIPCDA.
1086. Article 132 of FOIPCDA.
1087. Article 322 of FOIPCDA.
1088. *Ibid.*
1089. Article 324 of FOIPCDA.
1090. In case of retention of title, Art. 520/2 of the CO provides that the reservation of title has effect on the buyer's creditors only if the buyer's signature on the contract was certified by a notary before the buyer went bankrupt.
1091. Article 22 of FOIPCDA.

third persons. This right is not lost even if the creditor does not apply for the separation within three months from the day following the publication of the proclamation of the commencement of bankruptcy procedure (as is the case with other creditors).[1092] However, if the owner applies for the right of separation after the three-month deadline, he or she may only claim the amount obtained by the sale, reduced by the costs of the sale. The creditor, however, always loses the right of separation if he or she does not apply for it prior to publication of the plan of the first general distribution of the assets to the creditors.[1093] If the right of separation is acknowledged in the course of verification of claims, the court issues a decision on acknowledgment and enforcement of the right of separation. If it is not, then the parties are instructed to start litigation on the existence of the right of separation one month after the decision on verification of the claims was published.[1094]

510. Assets that do form the insolvency estate are divided into the so-called *special estate* and the so-called *general estate*, the former intended for repayment of *secured creditors*, i.e., those creditors of the insolvent debtor who have the so-called *right of separate satisfaction* (Sl. *ločitvena pravica*)[1095] and the latter for the equal repayment of the *unsecured creditors*.[1096] The right of separate satisfaction is the right to payment of the creditor's claims from the special insolvency estate prior to payment of claims of other, unsecured creditors from such estate. The secured creditors base their request on pledge and other instruments existent on the debtor's estate for securing their claim.

511. Unsecured creditors are grouped into three categories and are ranked as follows: (1) *preferential creditors* having preferential claims (Sl. *prednostne terjatve*), (2) *ordinary creditors* having ordinary claims (Sl. *navadne terjatve*), and (3) *subordinated creditors* having subordinated claims (Sl. *podrejene terjatve*).[1097] Within each of these groups, the *pari passu* principle is observed meaning that all the creditors in each of these categories are repaid in proportion to the size of their admitted claims. Ordinary creditors are repaid after preferential creditors while subordinated creditors are repaid only after preferential and ordinary creditors. All unsecured creditors are repaid from the special estate only after the secured creditors. If the special estate does not suffice for repayment of secured creditors, they are repaid the rest of their claim out of the available general estate together with other unsecured ordinary creditors. The so-called *bankruptcy estate creditors* (Sl. *upniki stečajne mase*), i.e., creditors with claims that have arisen only after bankruptcy

1092. Special provisions of Art. 299a of the FOIPCDA apply as of 26 Apr. 2016 in regard to application and assessment of rights of separation in cases where the alleged owners have initiated proceedings proving their ownership of immovables registered as ownership of the insolvency debtor. Final provisions of the 2016 FOIPCDA amendment (i.e., FOIPCDA-G) are also relevant in this regard (Art. 33 of FOIPCDA-G).
1093. Article 299 of FOIPCDA.
1094. Articles 309–312 of FOIPCDA. If litigation is not initiated, the right of separation ceases to exist.
1095. Articles 19 and 225 of FOIPCDA.
1096. Article 225 of FOIPCDA.
1097. Article 21 of FOIPCDA. In case of personal bankruptcy, additional claims are listed in Art. 390 of FOIPCDA as preferential.

proceedings had commenced, as well as some creditors put by the FOIPCDA in the same position as bankruptcy estate creditors, have preferential claims that are covered preferentially to all other creditors from the funds reserved for covering the costs of bankruptcy proceedings.[1098] A special position in bankruptcy proceedings is given also to certain *set-off creditors* (Sl. *pobotni upniki*)[1099] as well as to creditors from the so-called mutually non-performed contracts (Sl. *vzajemno neizpolnjena dvostranska pogodba*).[1100]

512. The insolvency administrator and creditors (both for the benefit of the insolvency estate) may make use of the *anti-deprivation claim* (Sl. *izpodbojna tožba*) – that is, the claim for annulment of legal transactions effected by the debtor in the period starting twelve months prior to initiation of insolvency proceedings and ending on the date of the commencement of bankruptcy proceedings, if the transaction caused unequal treatment of the creditors, and the benefited party knew or should have known of the insolvency of the debtor.[1101] It is presumed that the benefited party knew or should have known of the insolvency if the transaction was effected within three months prior to initiation of bankruptcy proceedings, or if the benefited party's claim was paid before it fell due, or if the contract was performed by the debtor in the form or in a way that does not match the usual business practice of the contracting parties.[1102] Knowledge of insolvency is, however, not a prerequisite for claiming annulment if the benefited party did not have to perform to the debtor in exchange.[1103] In such cases, however, the period starts already thirty-six months before the initiation of bankruptcy proceedings.[1104] Special rules applying even longer periods are laid down for cases of personal bankruptcy.[1105] If the anti-deprivation actin is brought in the set time limits[1106] and the claimants succeed (they must request annulment as well as the recovery), then the effects of the fraudulent transactions are annulled by the court (regular, not insolvency courts have jurisdiction) as far as the relationship between the parties to the transaction are concerned, and the assets forming the debtor's contractual performance recovered to the debtor for the benefit of the bankruptcy estate, while the creditors who were privileged by the fraudulent conveyance take part in the estate as unsecured creditors.

1098. Article 355 of FOIPCDA.
1099. Article 261 of FOIPCDA.
1100. Articles 24, 165–167 of FOIPCDA.
1101. Articles 224–226 of the FOIPCDA. General rules on *actio pauliana* as set out in the CO (that differ to some extent to those as set out in the FOIPCDA) do not apply.
1102. Articles 269–278 of FOIPCDA.
1103. Article 271/2 of FOIPCDA.
1104. Article 269 of FOIPCDA. This rule was set out in the FOIPCDA by one of the act's amendments. It applies in cases of bankruptcy proceedings commencing after 14 Jun. 2013.
1105. Article 391 of FOIPCDA.
1106. Within twelve months after the decision on the commencement of the insolvency proceedings becomes final (Art. 277/1 of FOIPCDA). Before 26 Apr. 2016, the action had to be filed within six months after the commencement of insolvency proceedings was published to the creditors.

513. In the case of personal bankruptcy, the debtor may – until the end of the bankruptcy proceedings – ask the court to discharge him or her of the debt (i.e. leaving the debtor with only natural obligations) that arose until the commencement of the personal bankruptcy proceedings and that has not been repaid within the bankruptcy proceedings.[1107] Preferential and some additionally listed claims may not be covered by the discharge.[1108] Discharge is available only to honest debtors who have to meet the discharge criteria listed in the FOIPCDA and only after a so-called discharge trial period of two to five years (in exceptional cases shortened to six months) has passed.[1109]

§3. Selling of Assets in Insolvency Procedure

514. Selling of the debtor's assets is one of the acts within the realization of the bankruptcy estate.[1110] Assets of the insolvent debtor that form the bankruptcy estate are eventually sold (tend to be sold)[1111] in order to cover the costs of the proceedings and to pay the creditors for their claims. After *preparatory work* (including estimation of the value of the estate)[1112] is performed by the bankruptcy administrator, the court starts the sale (on the request of the administrator and after receiving the opinion of the board of creditors if the board was established)[1113] by issuing a *decision on the sale* in which it determines the mode of the sale,[1114] the starting price to be paid for the assets, and the sum of the caution (Sl. *varščina*) to be deposited.[1115] The sale may in principle be performed via a public auction (Sl. *javna dražba*)[1116] or by giving a binding tender (Sl. *zavezujoče zbiranje ponudb*). If such mode is not successful, direct negotiations with a buyer (Sl. *neposredna pogajanja s kupcem*) may be performed if so determined by a new court decision on the sale.[1117] Specific rules allowing the administrator to sell certain goods in the most appropriate way

---

1107. Articles 408 ff. of the FOIPCDA.
1108. See Art. 408/2 of the FOIPCDA.
1109. Articles 397–413 of the FOPCDA.
1110. Articles 320 and 325–347 of FOIPCDA.
1111. Article 374 of the FOIPCDA sets out the rules for distributing the insolvency assets in the cases where sales are unsuccessful or would cause non-proportional expenses.
1112. For details as to estimation of the value, see Arts 327 and 328 of the FOIPCDA.
1113. Article 331 of FOIPCDA.
1114. First as a public auction or binding tenders. If such mode is not successful, then non-binding tenders may be determined by a new court decision on the sale (Arts 329 and 331 of FOIPCDA).
1115. Under certain conditions, consent of the creditors with the rights of separate satisfaction must also be obtained (Art. 345 of FOIPCDA).
1116. Public auction must be published by the court a day after the court receives a request by the administrator that the auction be published which must be filed with the court in eight days after the court's decision on performing the action becomes final. The publication of the action is to be made at least one month prior to the action if the initial price exceeds EUR 50,000, and at least eight days prior to the action in all other cases. The action is performed by the bankruptcy administrator or by another person authorized by the administrator. After the auction is performed, the successful auctioneer is pronounced and is informed of the date of conclusion of the sales contract which is to be held within three days after the action was finalized. If the auctioneer does not sign the contract, he or she must pay the contractual penalty in the amount of the advance payment which is kept by the bankruptcy debtor.
1117. Article 329 of FOIPCDA.

apply to: highly perishable goods; non-market stock provided the whole value of a certain type of stock is under EUR 15,000 eur; used equipment or used machines, retail and final products, and immovables provided their individual value is under EUR 15,000.[1118] Securities and goods sold on securities/goods market must be sold on an organized market for such securities/goods for a market price. After the decision on the sale is final, the bankruptcy administrator may proceed with the *sale* and *conclude a sales contract* with a buyer, who must make an advance payment (Sl. *ara*)[1119] followed by payment of the purchase price within the set time limit.[1120] If the estimated value of the sold assets amounts to or exceeds EUR 100,000, the court must consent to the sale.[1121] After paying the price, the administrator delivers the movable to the buyer, who thereby acquires ownership thereof.[1122] In case of immovables, however, the court issues, on the bankruptcy administrator's request, *a decision on delivering the immovable to the buyer* after he or she pays the price, by which the court decides that all the conditions for the entry of the buyer's ownership into the land register have been met.[1123] The moment such decision is final, the buyer acquires ownership,[1124] and entry into the land register, which is of a declaratory nature only, may be performed. It is to be stressed that the bankruptcy debtor is not liable for any defects on the goods or other property that was sold to the buyer.[1125]

515. The following rights on the assets sold terminate when the payment is made: pledge, mortgage, land debt, and the right to prohibition of alienation and encumbrance, regardless of when they were acquired; and personal easements, rights of encumbrance, or superficies if they were acquired after the commencement of insolvency proceedings.[1126] Real easements do not cease to exist

1118. Article 346 of FOIPCDA.
1119. The advance payment must be made in maximum five days after concluding the contract. The sales contract is concluded under the proviso that the advance payment is paid (Art. 338 of FOIPCDA).
1120. The time limit for paying the purchase price is maximum three months after the sales contract was concluded. If the buyer is late with the payment for more than fifteen days, the bankruptcy administrator may avoid the contract without giving the buyer additional time to perform his or her obligation (Art. 339 of FOIPCDA).
1121. Article 341 of FOIPCDA.
1122. Juhart in *CPL with Commentary 2004*, 257; Tratnik in *Property Law*, 290. When exactly the ownership is transferred is not expressly settled in legislation. Because FOIPCDA stipulates that some rights on the assets sold terminate the moment the purchase money is paid, one could also argue that the moment of payment is the moment of acquiring ownership. Such argumentation could also be deduced from the wording of Art. 343 of the FOIPCDA regulating cases of sale of a whole business entity.
1123. Article 342/2,3 of FOIPCDA, and Arts 89 and 96 of LRA.
1124. Juhart in *CPL with Commentary 2004*, 256–257.
1125. Article 340 of FOIPCDA.
1126. Article 342/1 of FOIPCDA. If personal easements, rights of encumbrance, or superficies were acquired on an immovable after a mortgage or land debt was established on such immovable, they also cease to exist. For further details, see Plavšak, *Pravna usoda služnosti in stavbne pravice v primeru prisilne prodaje nepremičnine v izvršbi in stečaju – pomen prednostnega načela* [Legal Destiny of Easements and Superficies in Cases of Forced Sale of an Immovable in Insolvency and Enforcement Proceedings – the Meaning of the Priority Principle], in *Sodobno stvarno pravo*, 287 ff. (Eds Juhart, Plavšak, Vrenčur, Pravna fakulteta v Ljubljani, Planet GV, TaxFinLex, 2016).

even if they were established after the commencement of insolvency proceedings.[1127]

516. To protect the buyer, other tenderers, creditors, holders of a right of pre-emption, or third persons may not claim that the sales contract or the real agreement is null or voidable, or request the contract be concluded with them under the same terms, or claim anything that would interfere with the rights the buyer had acquired.[1128] Creditors may, however, appeal against the court's decisions regarding the sale of the debtor's assets.[1129]

517. According to the FOIPCDA, a whole bankruptcy debtor's business entity (i.e., all things and other patrimonial rights that are required for performing certain type of business or businesses for making certain goods or performing certain services) may be sold instead of selling each individual debtor's thing separately.[1130] Apart from ownership on such things and rights, the buyer obtains also the debtor's concessions, licences, etc., and is deemed the debtor's universal successor with regard to these rights.[1131]

1127. *Ibid.* Plavšak explains (although this is not the wording of the FOIPCDA and can also not be deduced from its provisions) that this applies (only) to those real easements that have the character of the way of necessity or an easement in the public interest as here it would not be reasonable to set out their termination as in this case, they would most plausibly be established anew. Plavšak, *Pravna usoda služnosti in stavbne pravice v primeru prisilne prodaje nepremičnine v izvršbi in stečaju – pomen prednostnega načela* [Legal Destiny of Easements and Superficies in Cases of Forced Sale of an Immovable in Insolvency and Enforcement Proceedings – the Meaning of the Priority Principle in *Sodobno stvarno pravo*, 306 (Eds Juhart, Plavšak, Vrenčur, Pravna fakulteta v Ljubljani, Planet GV, TaxFinLex, 2016).

1128. Article 342/5 of FOIPCDA.

1129. Article 344 of FOIPCDA. If such appeal is lodged, performance of the court's decision by the administrator is stayed.

1130. Article 343 of FOIPCDA.

1131. *Ibid.*

Part IV. Fiduciary Mechanisms

Chapter 1. Security: Fiducia cum Creditore

518. Slovenian law regulates two fiduciary mechanisms for security purposes: fiduciary transfer of title and fiduciary assignment of a claim. Both of these mechanisms are regulated in the CPL and are instruments for securing creditor's claims by way of transferring the debtor's property or claims to the creditor.

§1. Fiduciary Transfer of Title

519. Under Slovenian law, conditional transfer of title is generally prohibited.[1132] Only those mechanisms of conditional transfer that are expressly regulated by law are allowed. These are the reservation of title and the fiduciary transfer of title that apply to movables, as well as fiduciary assignment that applies to claims, whereas transfer of immovables cannot be conditional.

520. Fiduciary transfer of title is based on the Roman law *fiducia cum creditore contracta*. It is a conditional non-possessory transfer of ownership on a movable from a debtor to his or her creditor.[1133] It is deemed that the acquirer (fiduciary) acquired title under the resolutory condition of payment of the secured claim (a so-called accessory *fiducia*). The parties may, however, agree otherwise – that is, they may agree that in case of payment of the secured claim, ownership on the movable will not be automatically transferred to the transferor but will serve as security for further fiduciary's claims (a so-called non-accessory *fiducia*).[1134]

521. Because the title is transferred to the creditor and the transfer need not be accessory to the secured claim, the fiduciary transfer of title represents an important security mechanism for the creditor, protecting him or her more intensively than a pledge, where ownership is not transferred to the creditor, and further, where the security is always accessory to the secured claim. On the other hand, the mechanism of fiduciary transfer is also of significance to the debtor because the movable

1132. Article 37 of CPL.

1133. Article 201 of CPL. Vrenčur is of the opinion that fiduciary transfer need not be non-possessory if the parties agree that the possession on the movable is transferred to the creditor; Vrenčur in *Property Law*, 563.

1134. Article 201/2 of CPL.

remains in his or her direct possession as opposed to 'pignus', where the debtor cannot use it because possession is transferred to the creditor.

522. An *agreement on the transfer of title as security* must be concluded in the form of a directly enforceable notarial protocol.[1135] It must contain a designation of the fiduciary and the transferor as well as the debtor of the secured claim if the debtor is not the transferor, the legal basis, a description of the movable (which serves as security), and the amount and maturity of the secured claim.[1136] In case of non-accessory *fiducia*, however, such agreement is valid even if it does not set the amount and maturity of the secured claim.[1137] The agreement may also regulate the mutual rights and obligations of the parties.[1138] For the duration of the fiduciary relationship, the provisions on non-possessory pledge of movable property apply *mutatis mutandis* with respect to the rights and obligations of the parties of fiduciary relationship unless provided otherwise in the agreement.[1139]

523. In order for the ownership to pass, constructive delivery in the form of a *constitutum possessorium* must be performed, besides concluding the obligatory and the real agreement – that is, the parties must agree that despite the transfer of ownership, the movable is to remain in the possession of the transferor.[1140]

524. If a secured claim is not paid at maturity, the transferor must deliver the movable property into the direct possession of the fiduciary.[1141] The fiduciary may retain the movable for a proper price or sell it in the manner provided for in the agreement. If the agreement does not determine the manner of the sale, then the provisions on non-possessory pledge of movable property apply *mutatis mutandis*.[1142] The fiduciary must always deliver to the transferor any surplus of the value of the movable over the secured claim.[1143]

525. The transferor may argue inadmissibility of enforcement against the fiduciary's creditors and exercise a right of separation in insolvency proceedings.[1144] Although the transferor is not the owner, the law treats him or her as such when the fiduciary is in insolvency as well as in enforcement proceedings. The fiduciary, on the other hand, has only limited protection in insolvency proceedings in the form of a right of separate satisfaction and not in the form of right of separation, notwithstanding that he or she is the owner of the movable.[1145] The fiduciary is, however,

1135. Article 202/1 of CPL. In case of non-accessory *fiducia* it will usually be in the form of a notarial protocol, and not in the form of a directly enforceable notarial protocol. Vrenčur in *Property Law*, 567.
1136. Article 202/2 of CPL.
1137. Article 201/2 of CPL.
1138. Article 203/1 of CPL.
1139. Article 203/2 of CPL.
1140. Vrenčur in *Property Law*, 567.
1141. Article 204/1 of CPL.
1142. For rules on non-possessory pledge, see Part V.
1143. Article 204/2 of CPL.
1144. Article 205 of CPL.
1145. Article 206/1 of CPL.

protected as the owner in cases of enforcement on the transferor's property, because he or she may argue inadmissibility of enforcement against the fiduciary's creditors.[1146]

526. Except special provisions on fiduciary transfer of title set down in Articles 201–206 of the CPL, the general provisions on the transfer of title apply *mutatis mutandis* to a fiduciary transfer.[1147]

§2. Fiduciary Assignment

527. Assignment of a claim as security (fiduciary assignment) is a form of security of the assignee's claim, where the assignor assigns his or her claim to an assignee.[1148] While in cases of fiduciary transfer, ownership on a movable is transferred, here a claim is assigned. Except special provisions on fiduciary assignment set down in Articles 207–209 of the CPL, the general provisions on the assignment of a claim apply *mutatis mutandis* to a fiduciary assignment,[1149] while rules of the CO apply to the obligatory agreement which is the basis of the fiduciary assignment.[1150]

528. As in cases of fiduciary transfer of ownership, it is deemed that the acquirer acquired the claim under the resolutory condition of payment of the secured claim, unless agreed otherwise.[1151]

529. If the same claim has been assigned as security more than once, the claim is to be acquired by the person to whom it was first assigned.[1152]

530. If the secured claim is not paid at maturity, the assignee may be repaid from the assigned claim. He or she must hand over any surplus to the assignor.[1153]

531. In the event of the assignee's insolvency or enforcement on his or her property, the assignor is protected as if he or she was the real holder of the assigned claim.[1154] In the event of the assignor's insolvency, the assignee is protected with the right of separate satisfaction only if an agreement on the fiduciary assignment is concluded in the form of a notarial protocol.[1155] In cases of enforcement, too, the assignee may argue inadmissibility of enforcement against the fiduciary's creditors

1146. Article 206/2 of CPL.
1147. Article 201/3 of CPL.
1148. Article 207/1 of CPL.
1149. Article 207/2 of CPL.
1150. Articles 417–426 of CO. Juhart, *Cesija – pogodbeni odstop terjatve* [Assignment – Contractual Transfer of a Claim], 205 (Gospodarski Vestnik 1996).
1151. Article 207/1 of CPL.
1152. Article 207/3 of CPL. In cases of ordinary assignments, notification of the debtor is the relevant moment for assessing priority of the assignments according to Art. 420 of the CO.
1153. Article 208 of CPL.
1154. Article 209/1 of CPL.
1155. Article 209/2 of CPL.

only if the agreement on the fiduciary assignment is concluded in the form of a notarial protocol.[1156]

1156. *Ibid.*

Chapter 2. Administration: *Fiducia cum Amico*

532. Apart from fiduciary relationships formed for security purposes, several fiduciary transfers based on a relationship of a mandate between a mandator and a mandatory can be traced in Slovenian law that apply to administering one's property. These relationships, some of which are presented here, are, however, only seldom described as *fiducia cum amico* and are, due to their particularities, hardly comparable to the Roman law institute.[1157]

§1. Commission Agent: Commissioner

533. A commission agent and a commissioner are in a fiduciary relationship regarding the goods the agent possesses (and owns) in order to supply them to the commissioner (i.e., in cases of the so-called purchasing commission) or to supply them to a third party on the commissioner's behalf (i.e., in cases of the so-called selling commission).[1158]

534. According to Article 805 of the CO, the commission agent's creditors may not – even in the event of the commission agent's bankruptcy – encroach upon the rights and things that the commission agent acquired in the commission agent's own name for the commissioner when fulfilling the mandate, unless their claims arose in connection with the acquisition of such rights and things. Further, Article 806 of the CO stipulates that, in the event of bankruptcy of the commission agent, the commissioner may request that the goods the commissioner delivered to the commission agent for the agent to sell, and the goods supplied for the commissioner by the commission agent, be removed from the bankruptcy estate. If the third-party seller has not yet delivered the goods, the commissioner may request the bankruptcy administrator to assign the claim to him or her. The commissioner may also request that a third person to whom the commission agent delivered the goods pays for the goods directly to the commissioner. However, in case the buyer has already paid the agent for the goods, the commissioner cannot request the money be transferred to him or her and is equated with other creditors of the agent.

§2. Tutelary Notary: Buyer

535. The Protection of Buyers of Apartments and Single Occupancy Buildings Act[1159] regulates a special relationship of commission between a notary and a buyer of an apartment or a single occupancy building in those cases where the so-called tutelary account is formed on the basis of an agreement concluded among the seller

1157. See also General Introduction, §3, VII.
1158. For further details on the relationship of commission, see Plavšak in *CO with Commentary*, 4th book, 275–328.
1159. Zakon o varstvu kupcev stanovanj in enostanovanjskih stavb (ZVKSES) [Protection of Buyers of Apartments and Single Occupancy Buildings Act], Official Gazette RS, No. 18/04.

of apartments or buildings, a tutelary bank, and a tutelary notary in order to protect the buyers who have already paid the price in cases of the sellers' non-performance of the sales contract. Thus, the buyers deposit the purchase money on the tutelary account under the administration of the tutelary bank. The tutelary notary is a holder of the account on the buyers' behalf and must always protect the buyers' interests. The notary has a monetary claim against the bank in the amount of the funds deposited on the tutelary account (the funds are owned by the bank according to the rules of *depositum irregulare*). Article 89/3 of the act provides that, in case of the notary's insolvency or death, his or her creditors cannot encroach upon such claim.[1160]

§3. Holder of an Account: Beneficiary

536. Another fiduciary relationship – between a holder of a fiduciary account of non-materialized securities (i.e., a notary, a solicitor, heritage guardian, or other person performing guardianship services within the sphere of his or her activity) and a beneficiary on whose behalf the account is administrated – is regulated in the Financial Instruments Market Act.[1161]

537. Similarly, the FOIPCDA requires that the bankruptcy administrator open a special fiduciary bank account in order to administer the estate of the bankrupt individual separately from his or her own assets.[1162]

1160. For further details on the tutelary account, see Plavšak, *Zakon o varstvu kupcev stanovanj in enostanovanjskih stavb, Uvodna pojasnila* [Protection of Buyers of Apartments and Single Occupancy Buildings Act, Introductory Remarks], 74–86 (GV Založba, 2004).

1161. Article 255 of the Zakon o trgu finančnih instrumentov (ZTFI) [Financial Instruments Market Act], Official Gazette RS, No. 67/07, with further amendments.

1162. Article 388 of FOIPCDA.

Part V. Security

538. In a state based on the rule of law, every creditor has the possibility of instituting court proceedings if a debtor is reluctant to fulfil his or her obligation, first a civil procedure and then, if necessary, enforcement proceedings. These proceedings, however, are usually costly and relatively long. The creditor also faces the danger of his or her debtor becoming insolvent and thus not able to (entirely) fulfil his or her obligation, even if it is determined by a court decision. The security mechanisms discussed in this part of the monograph offer more security to the creditor than the mere possibility of filing a law suit to demand that the debtor fulfil his or her obligation, especially in the event of the debtor's insolvency, and in case there exist other creditors of the same debtor.

539. Slovenian law distinguishes between securities under the law of obligations and those under the law of property. The latter are lien, reservation of title, fiduciary transfer of property, encumbrance, and retention. The land debt was abolished in 2013, via an amendment to the CPL.[1163] However, land debts created between 2003 when this security was enacted with the adoption of the CPL, and 2013, continue to produce effects. Compensation/offset is traditionally considered to be a mechanism under the law of obligations. Nevertheless, because of its property law nature in some other legal systems, it will also be discussed in this section.

1163. Official Gazette RS, No. 91/13.

Chapter 1. Securities Common to Movable and Immovable Property

§1. Lien: General Characteristics

540. The lien (Sl. *zastavna pravica*) is perhaps the most important and widely used security under the law of property.[1164] It can be established on movables (a pledge) as well as on immovables (a mortgage, Sl. *hipoteka*). Regulation of the lien differs according to the type of its object. The general regime of the lien is, however, common to both movables and immovables and is presented in this section. For details on mortgage, see Part I of this monograph. For details on pledge, see Chapter 3 later in this part.

I. General Definition

541. Lien is a *limited property right* to a specific *thing* (Sl. *stvar*), *right* (Sl. *pravica*), or *negotiable instrument/security* (Sl. *vrednostni papir*) belonging to another person, which serves as security for the lienor's (Sl. *zastavni upnik*) claim against the lienee (Sl. *zastavni dolžnik*) or against a third person.[1165] In the event of the non-payment of a secured claim upon maturity, the lienor has the right to receive payment together with interest and costs from the value of the object placed under lien prior to all other creditors of the lienee.[1166]

542. A lien can be established on things, rights, and negotiable instruments, provided they *can be alienated and encumbered* and *have a pecuniary value*.[1167] Only *pecuniary claims* can be secured by lien.[1168] Such nature of the lien object and of the secured claim is requested because the security provided by a lien lies mainly in the fact that the lien object can be sold and the lienor's claim repaid from the purchase money. A lien can also be established to secure *future* and *conditional claims*.[1169] An object can be under *more than one lien* at the same time, which can be of interest for the creditors if the value of the lien object is much higher than the value of the secured claims. In this case, the order in which the lienors are repaid in full is determined by the time when the lien was created.[1170]

1164. For detailed study of the lien in the Slovenian law, see Tratnik, *Zastavna pravica* [Lien] (GV Založba 2006).
1165. According to Art. 128/2 of the CPL, the lienee may establish a lien for security of his or her own debt or the debt of another.
1166. Article 128/1 of CPL.
1167. Article 128/3 of CPL.
1168. Tratnik in *Property Law*, 412.
1169. Article 129 of CPL. See, e.g., Judgment of the Supreme Court RS, No. II Ips 294/2013 of 15 May 2014, Judgment and Decision of the High Court in Koper, No. Cpg 27/2015 of 19 Mar. 2015, and Judgment of the High Court in Ljubljana, No. II Ip 4352/2011 of 21 Sep. 2011 (on the distinction between future and conditional claims).
1170. Article 136 of CPL. See, e.g., Decision of the Supreme Court RS, No. III Ips 64/2012 of 19 Nov. 2013.

543. In principle, the lienor cannot retain or sell the object under lien him- or herself. The *sale* must be demanded in *court*.[1171] In the event of the lienee's insolvency, the lienor has the so-called *right of separate satisfaction* (Sl. *ločitvena pravica*), which means that he or she will be able to ensure the repayment of the secured claim out of the purchase money obtained for the lien object before all other creditors.[1172] If this amount does not suffice, the rest of the claim will be treated as all the other unsecured debts of the insolvent debtor.

II. Principles Applicable to the Lien

544. General principles of the law of property, such as the principle of speciality, the principle of publicity, and the principle of priority, apply also to the lien.[1173] According to the *principle of speciality*, a lien can be established only on an individually specified thing or property right; it generally comprises the whole thing, with all its elements and, if not agreed otherwise, its appurtenances.[1174] The same applies for the secured claim, but with several exceptions (future and conditional claims, 'maximum mortgage').[1175] As to the *publicity* of the lien, it is usually expressed in terms of the lienor's possession of the lien thing in the case of movables and with entry in the land register in the case of immovables. According to the *principle of priority*, if there is more than one lien on the same lien object, the repayment of different lienors will follow the order of the establishment of each lien.[1176] The second lienor will only be repaid when the first one has received the full amount of his or her claim, and so on; the lienors will thus not be repaid in proportion to their claims – the deciding moment is the registration in the land register and not the conclusion of the contract.[1177] Until 2011, there was one exception to

1171. The legislation provides for several exceptions where an out-of-court sale is possible, e.g.,Art. 167 of CPL regarding pledge on movables, and Arts 15.a–15.t of the Zakon o finančnih zavarovanjih [Financial Collateral Act], Official Gazette RS, No. 47/04, with further amendments. The latter introduced the possibility of an out-of-court sale via an amendment adopted in 2013 for the cases of a mortgage established by a notarial deed. The Constitutional Court limited such possibility only to mortgages established after the entry into force of the mentioned amendment: Decision No. U-I-196/14–31 of 5 Nov. 2015. The case law of the Court of Justice of the EU in the case *Kušionová v SMART Capital* (C-34/13 of 10 Sep. 2014) must also be respected.

1172. Articles 19 and 225 of FOIPCDA. For more details, see Vrenčur, *Uveljavljanje stvarnopravnih zahtevkov v postopkih zaradi insolventnosti* [The Enforcement of Property Law Claims in the Insolvency Proceedings], in Podjetje in delo, 2014, No. 5, pp. 764–804.

1173. Tratnik in *Property Law*, 402–409. For more on these principles, see also Introduction to Property Law in the General Introduction of this monograph.

1174. Tratnik in *Property Law*, 402 and 410.

1175. *Ibid.*, 402.

1176. Article 198/2 of CESA. Keresteš in *CPL with Commentary 2004*, 616.

1177. Keresteš in *CPL with Commentary 2004*, 616; Tratnik in *Property Law*, 419. See, e.g., Decision of the High Court in Ljubljana, No. II Ip 2518/2015 of 8 Jul. 2015 (the court held that the priority of another creditor can only be challenged if the challenging creditor's claim would thus be repaid at least in part).

the principle of priority: the priority order of the mortgages could be changed on the basis of a cession of priority (previously regulated in Article 191 of the LRA).[1178]

545. Among the principles applicable especially to the lien, the *principle of accessority,* which originates in the broader principle of *accessio cedit principali,*[1179] is perhaps the most important. In relation to the secured claim, the lien is of an accessory nature. With the exception of future and conditional claims, the lien cannot exist if the secured claim has not yet come into existence.[1180] Article 137 of the CPL provides that, unless otherwise determined by the law, the lien extinguishes upon the extinguishment of the secured claim[1181] or the extinguishment of the object of the lien. However, 'if a new lienable object takes the place of the original object of the lien, the lienor acquires the same type of lien on the new object'.[1182] If the secured claim expires, it cannot be agreed that the lien will continue to exist and secure another claim; a new lien will have to be established.[1183] It is also not possible to establish a lien for a higher amount than the amount of the secured claim.[1184] The lienor is always the creditor of the secured claim (whereas the lienee is not necessarily the debtor of this claim), so that the debtor is protected against the possibility of two persons claiming the payment of the same claim.[1185] This means that the lien is always transferred together with the secured claim,[1186] unless the lienor and the new creditor have agreed that only the claim will be transferred – in this case, the lien expires.[1187] The principle of accessority also limits the creditor's right to repayment to the value of the secured claim, as well as the interests and costs related to this claim, even if the lien object is sold for a higher price.

546. The legal theory cites two other principles that apply to the lien. According to the *principle of indivisibility* of a lien, a lien expires only upon full repayment of the claim, so that any partial payments do not 'free' any part of the lien object or any of a greater number of lien objects.[1188] The *principle of the persistence of the debtor's personal liability* entails that the debtor is generally liable with all his or

1178. See Kuzma, *(Ne)spremenljivost vrstnega reda hipotek* [(Un)Changeability of the Priority Order of Mortgages], in Pravna praksa, 46/2011, pp. 8 ff. (the author argues that in certain cases it is still possible to change the priority order of mortgages, despite the eradication of Art. 191 of LRA).
1179. Tratnik in *Property Law*, 403.
1180. *Ibid.*, 404.
1181. See, e.g., Judgments of the Supreme Court RS, Nos II Ips 833/2009 of 20 May 2010 and II Ips 120/2007 of 14 Oct. 2009.
1182. Article 137/2 of CPL.
1183. Tratnik in *Property Law*, 406.
1184. *Ibid.*, 405. An exception to this rule is the 'maximum mortgage'. For details on maximum mortgage, see Part I.
1185. Tratnik in *Property Law*, 404.
1186. Article 418 of CO. See, e.g., Decision of the Supreme Court RS, No. II Ips 75/2009 of 11 May 2009 (the court held that the mortgage was transferred together with the claim, whereas the entry in the land register only serves the publicity of such transfer). For the exception concerning the maximal mortgage, see Judgment of the High Court in Ljubljana, No. I Cpg 1169/2014 of 18 Sep. 2014.
1187. Tratnik in *Property Law*, 406.
1188. *Ibid.*, 410. See, e.g., Decision of the High Court in Maribor, No. I Ip 1271/2013 of 6 Mar. 2014.

her assets for the whole amount of the claim, notwithstanding the value of the lien object.[1189] If the lienee is not the debtor of the secured claim, he or she is logically liable only up to the value of the lien object.[1190] If the claim is repaid from the lien thing, such lienee is subrogated into the rights of the creditor and can demand repayment from the debtor.[1191]

III. Establishment and Expiration of the Lien

547. A lien can be created on the basis of a legal transaction, a law (a statutory lien), or a court decision.[1192] A *statutory lien* is normally created at the moment when all the conditions laid down in law for the creation of a lien are met;[1193] it must, however, be stressed that a statutory mortgage is validly established the moment when the legal conditions are satisfied and not the moment of its registration in the land register.[1194] As a rule, a lien on the basis of a *court decision* is created when the decision becomes final.[1195] A mortgage created by a court decision is, however, established only upon its registration in the land register.[1196]

548. The court can create a lien by a decision in enforcement proceedings or proceedings for securing civil claims.[1197] Article 240 of the CESA provides for the possibility to secure claims determined in a final judgment by establishing a lien on a movable or on a share in a commercial company, or a mortgage on an immovable. Subject to conditions of the CESA, the court can also grant a preliminary measure (Sl. *predhodna odredba*) consisting of a prenotation in a land register of a mortgage on an immovable or a lien on a registered right, as well as a registration of a lien on movables registered in the Register of Non-Possessory Liens and Seized Movable Property, or of a registration in the court register of a lien on a share in a commercial company.[1198] A preliminary measure is granted on a basis of a domestic or foreign judgment which is not yet enforceable, if the creditor demonstrates the probable existence of a danger that the enforcement of the claim will otherwise be impossible or considerably more difficult.[1199]

1189. Tratnik in *Property Law*, 411.
1190. *Ibid.*, 415.
1191. Judgment of the High Court in Ljubljana, No. II Cp 3544/2011 of 23 May 2012. The court also held that such lienee cannot demand that the creditor first seeks repayment from the debtor of the secured claim.
1192. Article 130 of CPL.
1193. Article 134 of CPL.
1194. Article 144 of CPL.
1195. Article 135 of CPL.
1196. Article 143 of CPL. See, e.g., Judgment of the High Court in Ljubljana, No. II Cp 1465/2013 of 11 Dec. 2013 (the court explained that the permission to register can only be requested when the mortgage is established by a contract or by a court decision; the statutory mortgage, however, is established when the necessary legal conditions are met).
1197. Tratnik in *Property Law*, 420.
1198. Article 260 of CESA.
1199. Article 257 of CESA. Art. 258 of the CESA determines the cases where the existence of such danger is presumed (e.g., the judgment will have to be enforced in a foreign country which is not a EU Member State).

549. The acquisition of a lien on the basis of a *legal transaction* requires a valid legal transaction from which the obligation to establish a lien derives, as well as the fulfilment of the other conditions laid down by the CPL.[1200] For the acquisition of a lien on the basis of a legal transaction, the lienee must have the right to alienate and encumber the lien property.[1201] This means that the lienee must be the owner of the object, he or she must not be the subject of an insolvency procedure, and there must be no valid prohibition regarding his or her capacity to alienate or encumber the object.[1202] The legal transaction that serves as the basis for the establishment of the lien is a contract under the law of obligations and must fulfil the general conditions provided by the CO.[1203] Since the CPL entered into force, this transaction is no longer regulated as a specific contract in the Special Part of the CO.[1204] The CPL, however, only regulates the so-called prohibited agreements, which cannot be included in the contract or otherwise are considered null and void,[1205] and the necessity that the lienee has the capacity to dispose of the lien object.[1206]

550. Apart from the *expiration of the secured claim*, the lien expires also upon the *expiration of the object* of the lien. However, if a new lienable object takes the place of the original object of the lien, the lienor acquires the same type of lien on the new object.[1207] The secured claim usually expires upon its payment or upon the invalidation of the contract on the basis of which it was created. The lien also expires if the secured claim is transferred with the express agreement that the lien will not be transferred (otherwise, the lien is transferred automatically[1208]).[1209] A mortgage expires upon its *removal from the land register* and not at the moment of the expiration of the secured claim.[1210] Apart from the expiration of the claim or of the pledged object, a pledge also expires if the *pledgee voluntarily returns the pledged property* into the possession of the pledgor.[1211]

1200. Article 131 of CPL. For the other conditions, see the chapters in this monograph dealing with the specific forms of a lien.
1201. Article 133 of CPL.
1202. Tratnik in *Property Law*, 418. Regarding the money on a bank account, the debtor can dispose of the amount which was on his/her account before the initiation of the insolvency proceedings; regarding the sums which were transferred to the debtor's bank account after that moment, the debtor does not have the right of disposal: Judgment of the Supreme Court RS, No. III Ips 101/2013 of 11 Nov. 2014.
1203. Tratnik in *Property Law*, 417.
1204. Article 274 of CPL.
1205. Article 132 of CPL.
1206. Article 133 of CPL.
1207. Article 137 of CPL.
1208. Article 418 of CO.
1209. Tratnik in *Property Law*, 423.
1210. Article 154/1 of CPL.
1211. Article 168 of CPL. See, e.g., Judgment of the Supreme Court RS, No. II Ips 50/2012 of 20 Nov. 2014 (the court held that in the case when the pledgee returns the pledged thing to the pledgor on the basis of a court decision on a temporary measure, the lien does not extinguish upon such return, because the pledgee did not return the thing voluntarily and definitely).

IV. Prohibited Agreements

551. For the protection of the lienee, who is usually the economically weaker party to the contract and can thus become the victim of the lienor's unjust conditions, the law expressly forbids the conclusion of certain types of agreements. Generally speaking, all agreements that contradict the nature of the lien are forbidden.[1212] Furthermore, the CPL specifically forbids the so-called *lex commissoria* for liens on both movables and immovables. Article 132 of the CPL thus provides that contractual provisions stipulating that the ownership of lien property transfer to the lienor if his or her claim is not paid at maturity, as well as those stipulating that the lien property can be sold at a predetermined price, are null and void unless they are concluded after the secured claim has matured. According to the legal theory, such contractual provisions do not cause the nullity of the lien as such; the provisions of Article 88 of the CO on partial nullity must be applied.[1213] A *lex commissoria* agreement is forbidden because the lien object normally has a higher value than the secured claim and/or the secured claim is often already partly repaid when the consequences of such agreement would take place.[1214] Its fulfilment would thus put the lienor in an unjustly better position. Nevertheless, a *lex commissoria* agreement is possible when the debtor is already in arrears. If he or she concedes to such agreement, it is his or her free will and the *lex commissoria* agreement represents a way of repaying the debt, which is perhaps of more interest to the debtor than a public sale with an uncertain outcome.[1215] Under special legislative provisions, a *lex commissoria* agreement is, under certain conditions, possible regarding financial securities.[1216]

§2. Right of Retention

552. In Slovenian law, the right of retention (Sl. *pridržna pravica*) is regulated in Articles 261–264 of the CO. The legal theory is not unanimous as to the question of whether this right is a security under the law of obligations or under the law of property. Being that it presents the characteristics of both legal branches, it is considered to be some kind of a right *sui generis*, conferring on creditor both relative (*inter partes*) and absolute (*erga omnes*) effects.[1217]

1212. By analogy to Art. 1371 of the ABGB. Keresteš in *CPL with Commentary 2004*, 685.

1213. Tratnik in *Property Law*, 421. The High Court in Maribor held that a contract on sale and lease-back is null and void if its provisions are not sufficiently clear to exclude the *lex commissoria*: Judgment No. I Cp 1352/2013 of 15 Apr. 2014.

1214. Tratnik in *Property Law.*, 421.

1215. *Ibid.*, 421.

1216. Article 8 of the Zakon o finančnih zavarovanjih (ZFZ) [Financial Collateral Act], Official Gazette RS, No. 47/04, with further amendments. See, e.g., Decision of the High Court in Koper, No. Cpg 293/2015 of 11 Nov. 2015.

1217. See, e.g., Sajovic, *Osnove civilnega prava, Splošni del* [Bases of Civil law, General Part], 63 (Uradni list 1994).

553. According to the CO, the creditor of a claim that has fallen due has the right to *retain any asset of the debtor that is 'in his or her hands'*[1218] *until the claim is paid thereto*. If the debtor becomes insolvent, the creditor has the right of retention, even if the claim has not yet fallen due.[1219] According to the legal theory, the creditor does not have the right of retention if he or she was or should have been aware of the debtor's insolvency at the moment of the establishment of the claim.[1220] It is not necessary that the creditor has possession of the asset at the very moment when the claim falls due; he or she can obtain it any time later – according to some authors, until the claim becomes prescribed,[1221] whereas others suggest that the right of retention exists also for the so-called natural obligations, typically the prescribed claims.[1222]

554. The *retained asset* can be either movable (including negotiable instruments[1223]) or immovable.[1224] The retained object must not necessarily be 'in connection' with the secured claim (e.g., the retention of the maintained thing because of the non-payment of the costs of the maintaining); the creditor can in principle retain any asset belonging to the debtor.[1225] The value of the retained object must not be proportionate to the claim.[1226]

555. The primary goal of this right is to force the debtor to fulfil his or her obligation, under the assumption that he or she will want to regain the retained thing as soon as possible. However, the debtor will not necessarily prefer to fulfil the obligation specified in the contract to leaving the thing in the creditor's possession. The other important consequence of this right is thus the fact that the creditor will be able, after informing the debtor of this intention, to *sell the asset and repay the debtor's claim out of the acquired proceeds from the sale*, same as the lienor.[1227] If the secured claim arises from a non-commercial private contract, the creditor must secure a court decision ordering the sale of the retained asset. If the contract is defined as commercial, the creditor can sell the asset by him- or herself, after informing the debtor.[1228] So, the effect of the right of retention is mostly analogous to that of a (statutory) lien. That is why legal theory holds that the legal provisions

1218. Meaning in the direct non-proprietary possession. See, e.g., Cigoj, *Teorija obligacij* [The Theory of Obligations], 385 (Uradni list RS 2003).
1219. Article 261/2 of CO.
1220. Juhart in *CO with Commentary*, 2nd book, 274; Cigoj, *Komentar obligacijskih razmerij*, Books I–IV, 1000 (ČZ Uradni list SRS 1984–1986).
1221. Juhart in *CO with Commentary*, 2nd book, 274.
1222. Cigoj, *Teorija obligacij* [The Theory of Obligations], 384 (Uradni list RS 2003).
1223. *Ibid.*
1224. Decision of the High Court in Koper, No. Cp 826/2011 of 29 Feb. 2012, and Judgment of the Supreme Court RS, No. II Ips 112/97 of 4 Jun. 1998. Vrenčur, on the other hand, argues that retention of immovables is not possible: Vrenčur, *Retencijska pravica in pridržek lastninske pravice na nepremičninah?* [Right of Retention and Reservation of Title on Immovables?], in Pravna praksa, No. 9/2002, p. 7.
1225. Cigoj, *Teorija obligacij* [The Theory of Obligations], 384 (Uradni list RS 2003). See, e.g., Judgment of the High Court in Ljubljana, No. I Cpg 564/2010 of 15 Jun. 2010.
1226. Judgment of the High Court in Ljubljana, No. I Cpg 1270/2014 of 1 Oct. 2014.
1227. Article 264 of CO.
1228. Juhart in *CO with Commentary*, 2nd book, 282; Arts 162, 166, and 167 of CPL.

regulating a lien must analogically be applied to the right of retention if the law does not provide otherwise.[1229] Contrary to the lien, however, the debtor must be the owner of the retained asset, at least at the moment of retention; it is not possible to retain someone else's asset as security for the debtor's obligation.[1230]

556. The holder of the retention right does not have the *right to use* the retained asset.[1231] He or she is not liable for accidental destruction or damage to the property.[1232]

557. According to legal theory, the creditor of a *non-pecuniary claim* also has the right of retention.[1233] However, he or she will only be able to profit from the first effect of the retention right, which is that the debtor is urged to fulfil his or her obligation; because their claim is not pecuniary, the possibility of sale and repayment is irrelevant.[1234] Repayment from the proceeds from the sale of such property nevertheless becomes possible if the original claim changes its nature – for example, if the creditor annuls the contract and claims the return of his or her earlier payment to the debtor.[1235] The right of retention will have a similarly limited effect if the *retained asset does not have pecuniary value* (but, for example, has an emotional value for the debtor). In such cases, the creditor will not be able to ensure that his or her claim is repaid by selling the asset, but will nevertheless be able to count on the effect of the retention as such – that is, of the fact that the debtor cannot use the retained asset until the repayment of the claim.[1236]

558. The right of retention usually *expires* upon the debtor's payment of the claim;[1237] however, it also expires and the creditor must return the asset if the debtor offers another adequate security for the claim.[1238] Any other manner of expiration of the secured claim also causes the expiration of the right of retention, because of

1229. Juhart in *CO with Commentary*, 2nd book, 273.
1230. *Ibid.*, 274–275. In 2013, the Supreme Court RS accepted to decide on the question whether the right of retention can be exercised if the debtor is a lessee of the retained thing (Decision of the Supreme Court RS, No. III DoR 47/2013 of 13 Sep. 2013), however, the claimant later failed to satisfy all procedural requirements and the procedure ended without a court decision on the substance (Decision No. III Ips 8/2014 of 25 Feb. 2014).. The High Court in Celje decided that this was not possible, as one of the conditions for the possibility of retention was the existence of a creditor's claim against the owner of the retained thing: Judgment No. Cpg 14/2013 of 5 Apr. 2013.
1231. By analogy to Art. 158/1 of the CPL.
1232. Juhart in *CO with Commentary*, 2nd book, 273.
1233. *Ibid.*, 272, and Judgment of the High Court in Ljubljana, No. I Cpg 1270/2014 of 1 Oct. 2014. Previously, the case law did not allow retention for securing non-pecuniary claims: Judgment of the High Court in Koper, No. Cp 103/99 of 23 Nov. 1999.
1234. Juhart in *CO with Commentary*, 2nd book, 272.
1235. *Ibid.*, 271.
1236. *Ibid.*, 276.
1237. When the plaintiff demanded the return of a thing and the defendant objected on the basis of his or her right of retention, the plaintiff must prove not only that he or she is the owner of the thing and that the defendant is the possessor of this thing, but also, that he or she already repaid the debt of which the defendant was the creditor at the moment of the expiration of the contract of rent: Judgment of the High Court in Ljubljana, No. II Cp 2563/2010 of 8 Dec. 2012.
1238. Article 263 of CO.

its accessory nature.[1239] Furthermore, the retention right ceases if the creditor loses possession of the asset.[1240] Naturally, the retention right also expires upon expiration of the retained asset. After the expiration of the retention right, the creditor must return the asset and its fruits.[1241] He or she has the right to claim the repayment of the expenses he or she encountered by the retention.[1242]

559. The logic of the regulation of the right of retention lies in the fact that, in most cases, it would be inappropriate to oblige the creditor to return the debtor's asset if the latter refuses to fulfil his or her obligation to the creditor or if the fulfilment of the obligation is obviously not to be expected when the claim is due. The law thus offers a means for the creditor to urge the debtor to fulfil his or her obligations and allows another option to resolve this situation before entering long and costly legal proceedings. The success of this security nevertheless depends, above all, on the nature and value of the retained asset.

560. The CO regulates many *exceptions* to the right of retention, based on the creditor's manner of acquiring possession of the debtor's asset or based on the characteristics of the asset. Article 262 provides that '[t]he creditor shall not have the right of retention if the debtor demands the return of an asset that, against the debtor's will, is no longer in the debtor's possession or if the debtor demands the return of an asset that was delivered to the creditor for safekeeping or for loan use'. This provision seeks to prevent situations where the creditor would, for example, alienate a debtor's asset without the consent of the latter, with the goal of exercising the right of retention. This right cannot be established by force, deception, or abuse of trust.[1243] The creditor need not, however, be the person to whom the debtor has directly transferred the possession of the asset, but can gain possession of the debtor's asset from another person (who him- or herself acquired it legally).[1244] Also, '[t]he creditor may not retain an authorisation obtained from the debtor, other documents, cards, letters, or similar things belonging to the debtor, or other things that cannot be placed on sale'.[1245]

561. The right of retention is often *compared to the lien*. These two instruments have many similarities, but mainly with regard to their legal consequences. The right of retention is usually established on the basis of the CO and not on the basis of an agreement of the parties;[1246] furthermore, it is not established in advance as is the case with the lien. It is the creditor's 'way out' of a situation where the debtor is already late in fulfilling his or her obligation or it is obvious that the debtor will

1239. Juhart in *CO with Commentary*, 2nd book, 276.
1240. *Ibid.*
1241. Analogy with Art. 159 of the CPL.
1242. Analogy with Art. 157 of the CPL.
1243. Juhart in *CO with Commentary*, 2nd book, 278.
1244. *Ibid.*, 278–279.
1245. Article 262/2 of CO.
1246. The majority of the legal theory is of the opinion that the right of retention can be established on the basis of an agreement between the parties, however not in advance, but only as security for the claim already due. Juhart in *CO with Commentary*, 2nd book, 271.

not be able to fulfil. As there is no prior agreement, it will, in reality, rarely happen that the creditor will possess a debtor's asset he or she could retain and even rarer that the value of the retained asset will correspond to the amount of the claim. If it is much higher, retention can be prohibited on grounds of immorality;[1247] if it is much lower, it does not offer proper security. Because it is a form of self-help of the creditor, its use is subject to many legal restrictions, which further narrow this option even in cases where the creditor is in possession of a debtor's asset. Furthermore, contrary to the lien, the right of retention is not a limited property right; its holder can only seek legal protection on the basis of his or her possession of the asset.[1248] For all these reasons, we can conclude that the right of retention is a considerably weaker security for the creditor than the lien.

1247. This prohibition can be deduced from Art. 3 of CO, which establishes the principle of free regulation of obligational relationships: '[p]articipants shall be free to regulate obligational relationships, but may not act in contravention of the Constitution, compulsory regulations or moral principles'. See also Cigoj, *Teorija obligacij* [The Theory of Obligations], 384 (Uradni list RS 2003).

1248. Juhart in *CO with Commentary*, 2nd book, 271.

Chapter 2. Securities in Immovable Property

§1. Mortgage: Lien on Immovable Property

562. A mortgage is a lien on an immovable.[1249,1250] A lien established on immovable property is characterized by many specifics that upgrade the already presented general regime of the lien. For details, see Part I.

§2. Land Debt

563. A land debt is the right to demand repayment of a specified money sum from the value of an immovable prior to other creditors with an inferior ranking.[1251] The land debt was first regulated in the Slovenian legal system with the adoption of the CPL in 2003. Due to some cases of alleged abuse, in which the debtors supposedly established land debts securing very high claims, but without a real creditor, in order to prevent the real creditors' enforcement by means of the sale of the immovable, the legislature decided to abolish this security in 2013. Land debts established in the meantime are, however, still effective. In order to prevent the mentioned abuse, an amendment to the CESA was adopted in 2014[1252] which provides for a procedure of establishing the identity of the land debt creditor, and, if this is not possible, the enforcement to the benefit of the other creditors.[1253] For details on the land debt, see Part I.

§3. Encumbrance

564. An encumbrance is a right on the basis of which the owner of an encumbered immovable is bound to a future charge or service.[1254] It is one of the limited property rights that can exist only with regard to immovables. In contrast to easements, where only inactivity is required, an encumbrance consists of the obligation of a debtor to perform some action. For details on encumbrance, see Part I.

1249. See also Part I and Part IV.
1250. Article 138 of CPL.
1251. Article 192 of CPL.
1252. Official Gazette RS, No. 53/14.
1253. Article 172a of CESA.
1254. Article 249 of CPL.

Chapter 3. Securities in Movable Property

§1. PLEDGE (LIEN ON MOVABLE PROPERTY)

565. In Slovenian law, a pledge can be possessory or non-possessory.[1255] A possessory pledge implies direct possession of the pledged object by the pledgee or a third person. Nevertheless, the pledgor does not fully lose the possession – he or she becomes the indirect possessor of the object.[1256] In the case of a non-possessory pledge, direct possession of the object rests with the pledgor.

I. Possessory Pledge

566. A pledge (Sl. *ročna zastava,* Lat. *pignus*) is *created* on the basis of a valid contract of pledge when a pledgor delivers the pledged movable into the direct possession of the pledgee[1257] or if the pledged movable is delivered into the direct possession of a third person under the condition that only the pledgee can demand its delivery.[1258] The key element of the possessory pledge is the pledgor's lack of possession, rather than the pledgee having possession.[1259] The elements required for the creation of a possessory pledge are thus: a valid contract of pledge, an agreement on the creation of a pledge, the delivery of the pledged object in the direct possession of the pledgee or a third person (Lat. *traditio*),[1260] and the pledgor's right to encumber[1261] the pledged object.[1262] The possessory pledge is traditionally the rule, but its practical importance has to this day diminished considerably in favour of the non-possessory pledge and the fiduciary transfer of ownership.[1263] The possessory pledge has many similarities with the right of retention.[1264]

567. By analogy to acquiring ownership,[1265] a possessory pledge can also be created on the basis of a law (a *statutory pledge*). The CO established several statutory pledges, such as the pledge of the contractor under a contract for work, of the carrier under a contract of carriage, of the warehouseman under a contract of storage,

1255. See also Part II and Part IV.
1256. Tratnik in *Property Law*, 456. For definitions of direct and indirect possession, see General Introduction, §3.
1257. Article 155/1 of CPL.
1258. Article 155/2 of CPL.
1259. Juhart in Juhart et al., *Zavarovanje in utrditev obveznosti* [Security and Consolidation of Obligations], 99 (Gospodarski Vestnik 1995); Berden in *CPL with Commentary 2004*, 711.
1260. The delivery of the pledged object can be performed in any of the manners determined in Art. 60 of the CPL, which regulates delivery in the case of a transfer of ownership, apart from the so-called *constitutum possessorium*. Berden in *CPL with Commentary 2004*, 710.
1261. The right to alienate and encumber the pledged object means that the pledgor must be the owner of the pledged object and must not be the subject of an insolvency procedure. Tratnik in *Property Law*, 461.
1262. Tratnik in *Property Law*, 459.
1263. *Ibid.*, 456.
1264. See Ch. 1 of this part of the monograph.
1265. Article 139 of the CPL, which regulates the establishment of a lien, is analogous to Art. 39 of the CPL, which refers to acquiring ownership.

of the mandate recipient under a contract of mandate, of the commission agent under a contract of commission, of the agent under a commercial agency contract, of the freight-forwarding agent under a contract of forwarding, and of the inspector under a goods and services inspection contract.[1266] A statutory pledge is also determined by Articles 169/2 of the CPL[1267] and 147/2 of the IA.[1268] As was already explained in the section dealing with the establishment of the lien, a pledge can also be *created by a court decision* in an enforcement procedure or in a security of claims procedure under the CESA.

568. The *object* of a pledge can be any specifically determined (individualized)[1269] movable object that is in legal commerce (Lat. *res in commercio*) and has a commercial value.[1270] Fungible movables (Lat. *genus*) cannot generally be the subject of a pledge.[1271] This is, however, possible if they are individualized – for example, by means of the place where they are kept.[1272] The pledge also stretches to the elements of the pledged object.[1273] As to the appurtenances, they are encompassed by the pledge only if possession of such was also transferred to the pledgee or a third person.[1274]

569. For the duration of a pledge, the pledgee has the same *legal protection* as an owner and may, under the same conditions, demand the return of the pledged property, the cessation of interference, and the protection of possession.[1275] A pledgor who needs the pledged object for his or her own needs while the pledge is still in force may request that the court order the pledgee to return it, under the condition that the pledgor provides other appropriate security.[1276]

570. The possessory pledge *expires* by the cessation of the secured claim, by a renouncement of the pledgee (the pledgee voluntarily returns the pledged object into

1266. Articles 647, 697, 753, 780, 803, 829, 870, and 877 of CO.
1267. 'If the secured claim of a pledgee who has possession of an object is paid in full, he or she must deliver the pledged property to the next pledgee. […] It shall be considered that this pledge is created on the same day as the pledge which expired as a result of the payment of the secured claim.'
1268. If the court decides that a certain movable or immovable is left to one of the heirs who in return must compensate the other heirs in money, the latter obtain a lien on these movables or immovables until their claims are repaid.
1269. It is not possible to establish a pledge on the whole movable property of the pledgor without specifying each individual object. Tratnik in *Property Law*, 457.
1270. Berden in *CPL with Commentary 2004*, 707, 708.
1271. Such movables can, however, be the subject of a *pignus irregulare*, where the pledgee acquires ownership of the object(s) and must, upon the expiration of the pledge, return the same amount of objects of the same kind. Tratnik in *Property Law*, 458; Berden in *CPL with Commentary 2004*, 708.
1272. An often cited example is an amount of money kept in a sealed envelope. Berden in *CPL with Commentary 2004*, 707.
1273. Tratnik in *Property Law*, 457.
1274. *Ibid.*.
1275. Article 164 of CPL.
1276. Article 163/2 of CPL.

the possession of the pledgor),[1277] if the same person becomes the pledgor and the pledgee, by cessation of the pledged object, by alienation of the pledged object to a third person in good faith, and by compulsory sale of the pledged object.[1278] A possessory pledge does not extinguish if the pledgee loses possession of the pledged object.[1279]

571. An object that is owned by more than one person (*co-ownership* or *joint ownership*) can be pledged only by all the owners together.[1280] Only one co-owner cannot perform a valid *traditio*[1281] (delivery with effect of transfer of possession for the purpose of the establishment of a possessory pledge). A pledge can, however, be established on the individual co-owner's share of the movable object.[1282]

572. To the benefit of a *pledgee in good faith*, Article 156/1 of the CPL (and, by analogy Article 64 of the CPL concerning ownership) establishes an exception to the rule that an object can only be pledged by its owner. A bona fide acquirer usually acquires a pledge even if the pledgor did not have the right to encumber the movable, if the pledgor has the movable in his or her possession by the will of its owner. A pledgee can be in good faith not only as to the ownership of the thing but also as to the non-existence of other pledges. In this case, he or she acquires a pledge with the highest ranking if he or she has the movable in his or her possession.[1283] The most common situations involving acquiring a pledge from a pledgee without the capacity to encumber the pledged object are the pledging of someone else's asset (where the 'pledgor' has the object in his or her possession – e.g., on the basis of a lease or a leasing), the pledging of an object in co-ownership or joint ownership by one of the owners, and the pledging of an already pledged object.[1284]

573. It is possible to place the same object under *more than one pledge*. The second and subsequent pledgees acquire a pledge at the moment when the pledgor notifies the pledgee who has direct possession of the object or for whom a third person has direct possession of the object.[1285] If the secured claim of a pledgee who has possession of a thing is paid in full, he or she must deliver the pledged property to the next pledgee.[1286]

1277. Article 168 of CPL. See, e.g., Judgment of the Supreme Court RS, No. II Ips 50/2012 of 20 Nov. 2014 (the court held that in the case when the pledgee returns the pledged thing to the pledgor on the basis of a court decision on a temporary measure, the lien does not extinguish upon such return, because the pledgee did not return the thing voluntarily and definitely).
1278. Tratnik in *Property Law*, 473–474. For more on the expiration of the possessory pledge, see Tratnik, *Zastavna pravica* [Lien], 196–199 (GV Založba 2006). For the alienation to a third person in good faith, see Art. 64 of the CPL.
1279. Tratnik in *Property Law*, 474.
1280. *Ibid.*, 458. For the exception of the pledgee in good faith, see Art. 156/1 of the CPL.
1281. Tratnik in *Property Law*, 458.
1282. *Ibid.*.
1283. Article 156/2 of CPL.
1284. Tratnik in *Property Law*, 462.
1285. Article 169/1 of CPL.
1286. Article 169/2 of CPL.

574. A pledgee must *store* the pledged object diligently.[1287] The level of the required diligence depends on whether the pledgee is a professional taking part in commercial legal transactions (thus a higher level of diligence is required) or not.[1288] If the pledgee incurs any costs by storing the pledged object, his or her claim is increased by the amount of these costs.[1289] A pledgee does not have the right to use the pledged property or to deliver it to another person for use or in pledge (a secondary pledge) unless the pledgor allows him or her to do so.[1290] A pledgee who acts contrary to this rule is liable also for accidental perishing or damage to the pledged object caused by such actions.[1291] It is in the pledgor's interest that a pledged object of which he or she will normally regain possession after repayment of the secured claim maintains its value. The CPL, therefore, provides that if the pledgee fails to store the pledged movable property properly, if without the pledgor's permission he or she uses it or gives it to another person to use, or if he or she uses it contrary to such permission, and generally if he or she uses it contrary to a contract or a statute, the pledgor can request the court order that the pledged property be taken from the pledgee and delivered to a third person, who will possess the object for the pledgee.[1292]

575. Special provisions of the CPL regulate the situation when the pledged object provides *fruits* while the pledge is in force. The ownership of these fruits is acquired by the pledgor, unless otherwise provided in the contract of pledge.[1293] If the parties agreed that the ownership of the fruits is acquired by the pledgee (Lat. *pactum antichreticum*), the value of the secured claim is reduced by the value of the fruits.[1294] The same rule applies if the pledgee achieves other benefits by using the pledged object.[1295]

576. The CPL also envisages the possibility that after the establishment of the pledge, the pledgee discovers a factual or a legal *defect regarding the pledged object* or that the pledgor, contrary to the agreement between the parties, did not remedy such defect. If such defect causes an insufficiency of the security provided by the pledge, the pledgee has the right to demand that the pledgor provide some other appropriate security.[1296] Thus, there are two conditions under which the pledgee can demand the replacement of the pledged object: first, that at the moment

1287. Article 157 of CPL.
1288. *Ibid.*.
1289. Article 157 of CPL. See, e.g., Judgment of the High Court in Ljubljana, No. I Cpg 288/2012 of 29 Apr. 2013.
1290. Article 158/1 of CPL.
1291. Article 158/2 of CPL. The limitation period for a pledgor's claim against a pledgee for reimbursement for damage as a result of the impairment of the property expires one year from the day on which the property was returned (Art. 158/3 of CPL).
1292. Article 160 of CPL.
1293. Article 159/1 of CPL. See, e.g., Decision of the High Court in Ljubljana, No. Cst 205/2015 of 21 Apr. 2015 (the court held that rents are fruits of the lien thing (an apartment), and that they do not belong to the creditor).
1294. Article 159/2 of CPL.
1295. Article 159/3 of CPL.
1296. Article 161 of CPL.

of the conclusion of the contract of pledge the pledgee was not aware of the defect or that the known defect was agreed to be remedied before the delivery into the pledgee's possession; second, that because of the defect, the pledged object no longer sufficiently secures the repayment of the secured claim.[1297] If the pledged object accidentally perishes or is damaged or its market value drops after the pledging, the pledgor is not liable on the basis of the contract on the establishment of the lien.[1298]

577. The CPL further regulates the *legal consequences of a pledge* in case of the repayment or non-repayment of the secured claim. In the first case, the pledgee must return the pledged property to the pledgor or enable the pledgor to take direct possession of it from a third person as soon as the secured claim is paid off in full.[1299] If, however, the secured claim is not settled upon maturity, the pledgee may ask the court to order that the pledged property be sold and the payment be made.[1300]

578. Exceptionally, the pledged object can be sold before the claim falls due if the *pledged object is losing its value* and there is a risk of it becoming insufficient to secure the creditor's claim. Such sale can be ordered by the court, upon a request from the pledgee or the pledgor (because they are both interested in obtaining the highest value from the pledged object) and after hearing the other party.[1301] The sale is conducted by the court, at a public auction, and the proceeds from such sale are delivered to the pledgee as repayment of the secured claim (after deduction of the costs of the sale and the interests for premature payment).[1302] The pledgor can prevent such sale if he or she offers to provide other appropriate security.[1303]

579. As a rule, the *sale of the pledged object* is conducted by the *court.* On the basis of the judgment (or other enforcement title)[1304] against the debtor ordering him or her to pay the debt, the creditor can institute enforcement proceedings and request that the court order the sale of the pledged object in an enforcement procedure. The manner of selling the object is determined by the bailiff.[1305]

580. The object is normally sold to the highest bidder and only in the event of the debtor's failure to repay the secured claim. However, Article 163 of the CPL provides for an exception to this rule. At the request of the pledgor, the court may permit the pledged property to be sold to a specific person at a set price if it establishes that the price is reasonable and if the justified interests of the pledgee are thereby

1297. Tratnik in *Property Law*, 469.
1298. Berden in *CPL with Commentary 2004*, 721.
1299. Article 165 of CPL.
1300. Article 166 of CPL.
1301. Article 162/1 of CPL. For the possibility of sale of immaterialized (book entry) securities before the maturity of the claim, see, e.g., Judgment of the High Court in Ljubljana, No. I Cp 592/2014 of 1 Oct. 2014.
1302. Berden in *CPL with Commentary 2004*, 723–724; Tratnik in *Property Law*, 470.
1303. Article 162/2 of CPL.
1304. A court transaction, an arbitral award or a land letter: Tratnik in *Property Law*, 422, 423.
1305. Article 93 of CESA.

protected. The pledgor will be interested in such premature sale if, in any case, he or she prefers the sale of the pledged object to the repayment of the claim or if he or she knows in advance that the repayment will not be possible upon maturity of the claim.[1306]

581. An *out-of-court sale* is possible only upon a written agreement between the parties.[1307] So-called commercial contracts (contracts concluded between parties carrying out a commercial activity)[1308] are an exception to this rule, because the existence of an agreement on an out-of-court sale is presumed.[1309] In the case of an out-of-court sale, the pledgee may sell the pledged property at a public auction or at an exchange price or the market price if there is one, if the secured claim is not settled upon maturity. The pledgee must inform the debtor (and the pledgor, if he or she is not the debtor) of his or her intention to sell the pledged object. The sale can be carried out no less than eight days from this notification. The pledgee must inform the debtor (and the pledgor) of the place and time of the sale. After the sale is carried out, the pledgee receives payment of his or her entire claim from the proceeds of the sale, together with interest and costs, and must deliver any surplus to the pledgor.[1310] This regulation of an out-of-court sale is mandatory: any provisions of a contract of pledge providing for a different method of out-of-court sale are null and void.[1311] As a special type of out-of-court realization of the security provided by the pledge, the legal theory[1312] cites an agreement between the parties that enables the creditor to keep the pledged object for him- or herself (and thus gain ownership of the object) or to sell it at a price set in advance. Such agreement, the so-called *lex commissoria*, is, however, possible only after the claim has fallen due.[1313]

582. The creditor can *alienate the claim* secured by a pledge. In this case, according to the principle of accessority, the new creditor also obtains the pledge, without any special agreement necessary. For the purpose of protecting the pledgor's interests, the new creditor, however, does not automatically obtain the right to possess the pledged object. The pledgor must give his or her consent to the transfer of possession; otherwise, the possession of the pledged object remains with the original creditor, who thus possesses it for the new creditor.[1314] The 'old' and the 'new' creditor can also reach an agreement that the claim is transferred without the pledge. In this case, the pledge expires, because it cannot exist without the secured claim.[1315]

1306. Tratnik in *Property Law*, 470.
1307. Article 167 of CPL. In this case, such pledge does not have to be declared in insolvency proceedings: Decision of the Supreme Court RS, No. III Ips 52/2011 of 20 Mar. 2012.
1308. For the exact definition of the commercial contracts, see Art. 13 of the CO.
1309. Article 167/1 of CPL.
1310. Article 167/2 of CPL.
1311. Article 167/3 of CPL.
1312. Tratnik in *Property Law*, 473.
1313. Article 132/2 of CPL.
1314. Article 418/2 of CO.
1315. Tratnik in *Property Law*, 470–471.

II. Non-possessory Pledge

583. According to Article 170 of the CPL, a non-possessory pledge (Sl. *neposestna zastavna pravica*) is a pledge on a movable, where the pledged object is neither delivered into the direct possession of the pledgee nor into the direct possession of a third person on behalf of the pledgee but remains in the possession of the pledgor or a third person on his or her behalf. The movable can thus represent a security for the creditor's claim and simultaneously be used by the pledgor. This can be in the interest of both the pledgor, who can continue to use the object, and the creditor, who need not store the object.[1316] A non-possessory pledge can be either 'ordinary' or 'registered'. A registered non-possessory pledge is possible only with regard to movables expressly enumerated in a decree adopted by the Slovenian government,[1317] which will be presented below. Regarding such movables, only a registered non-possessory pledge can be established.[1318] It is, however, possible to encumber them with a possessory pledge or, if they are appurtenances of an immovable, with a mortgage.[1319]

584. A non-possessory pledge has the same purpose as the fiduciary transfer of property,[1320] but it does not affect the ownership status of the movable. Also, the pledge is accessory to the secured claim, whereas the fiduciary transfer of ownership persists even if the secured claim ceases.[1321] A non-possessory pledge is also similar to a mortgage, because the pledgor keeps direct possession and use of the pledged object. The register of certain non-possessory pledges has similar function as the land register regarding mortgages: avoiding the disadvantages (possibly enabling abuse) of the lack of the creditor's possession of the pledged object.[1322]

585. Being that the pledged object remains in direct possession and thus under the control of the pledgor, the pledgee is less protected by a non-possessory pledge than he or she would be by a possessory one. The conditions regarding the *establishment* of a non-possessory pledge are thus more severe: until 30 June 2020, an agreement in the form of a directly enforceable notarial protocol[1323] is required.[1324] From 1 July 2020, an amendment of the CPL enters into force, which reduced the formality requirement so as to demand a notarial protocol, but not necessarily a

1316. *Ibid.*, 474.

1317. Uredba o registru neposestnih zastavnih pravic in zarubljenih premičnin [Decree on the Register of Non-possessory Liens and Seized Movable Property], Official Gazette RS, No. 23/04, with further amendments.

1318. Tratnik, *Neposestna zastavna pravica na premičninah, 1. del* [Non-possessory Pledge on Movable Property, 1st part], in Pravna praksa, 2012, Nos 39–40, Supplement, p. III.

1319. *Ibid.*

1320. Articles 201–206 of CPL. Tratnik in *Property Law*, 475. For details, see General Introduction, §3, and Part IV.

1321. *Ibid.*

1322. Tratnik, *Neposestna zastavna pravica na premičninah, 1. del* [Non-possessory Pledge on Movable Property, 1st part], in Pravna praksa, 2012, Nos 39–40, Supplement, p. II.

1323. Article 4 of Zakon o notariatu (ZN) [Notary Act], Official Gazette RS, No. 13/94, with further amendments.

1324. Article 171/1 of CPL.

directly enforceable one.[1325] The CPL further specifies the mandatory contents of such protocol regarding the pledgor, the pledgee, the secured claim (its amount and the due date), and the pledged object.[1326] Concluding this protocol in the form of a directly enforceable notarial protocol has the effect of a seizure of movable property in an enforcement procedure,[1327] which would otherwise have to be performed by a bailiff.[1328] In an enforcement procedure, the creditor can demand either the delivery of the movable into his or her possession or the sale of the movable if the debtor agreed to the direct enforceability of the notarial protocol.[1329] The requirement of a notarial protocol brings another benefit: there cannot be any doubt about the real date of the establishment of the pledge, which can be important, for example, in the case of multiple pledging or in the case of a challenge of the debtor's legal actions by a so-called *actio pauliana*.[1330,1331] If the object of the non-possessory pledge is movable property for which a register of non-possessory pledges is kept, the pledge is created with its entry in this register on the basis of the notarial protocol. Before requesting the entry in the register of a non-possessory pledge, the notary must verify whether the pledgor is really the owner of the pledged movable or if he or she has the right to access the premises where the movables are located, whether the movable is already registered as being pledged and the pledgees have not consented to the subsequent pledge, whether the movable is already registered as seized, and whether the registered non-possessory pledge is impossible because of the pledgor's insolvency; if any of the conditions for the establishment of the pledge are not met, the notary must not request the entry in the register.[1332] The creditor does not have any legal remedy against the decision of the notary not to request such entry.[1333]

586. In contrast to a possessory pledge,[1334] a non-possessory pledge cannot normally be established if *the pledgor is not the owner* of the pledged object, notwithstanding the eventual good faith of the pledgee.[1335] This can, however, happen in the case of a registered non-possessory pledge. According to the principle of trust in the register, if a non-existing pledge is registered and the 'secured' claim is transferred to a new creditor who is in good faith, the latter will acquire the pledge.[1336] The pledge is also created if the pledgor subsequently acquires the right to alienate

1325. Article 171/1 and 171/3 of the amended CPL (SPZ-B), Official Gazette RS, No. 23/20.
1326. Articles 171/2 and 177/2 of CPL.
1327. Article 171/3 of CPL.
1328. See also Rijavec, *Civilno izvršilno pravo* [Civil Enforcement Law], 246 (GV Založba 2003).
1329. Article 175/3 of CPL.
1330. *Actio pauliana* or a challenge of the debtor's legal actions in the event of a detriment of creditors is regulated in Arts 255–260 of the CO.
1331. Tratnik in *Property Law*, 480.
1332. Article 24 of the Decree.
1333. Tratnik, *Neposestna zastavna pravica na premičninah, 1. del* [Non-possessory Pledge on Movable Property, 1st part], in Pravna praksa, 2012, Nos 39–40, Supplement, p. VIII; Tratnik in *Property Law*, 484.
1334. See Art. 156 of the CPL.
1335. Tratnik in *Property Law*, 485.
1336. *Ibid.* On the basis of Art. 24 of the Decree, it is the notary's obligation to verify the pledgor's ownership of the movable.

and encumber the pledged object or if the object is delivered into the possession of the pledgee in good faith; in both of these cases, the pledge is created *ex tunc*.[1337]

587. The pledgor may *use the pledged property* in accordance with its economic purpose or in accordance with an agreement with the pledgee. He or she can alienate or further encumber the object, but only with the consent of the pledgee.[1338] If the pledgor, through his or her actions or omissions, reduces the value of the pledged object, the pledgee may demand that the property be delivered into his or her direct possession or that of a third person on his or her behalf.[1339] The pledge thus becomes possessory, and an out-of-court sale agreement is presumed as additional protection of the pledgee.[1340]

588. Article 175 of the CPL regulates the *consequences* of a non-possessory pledge if the debtor fails to settle the secured claim when it falls due. If this occurs, the pledgor must deliver the pledged movable into the direct possession of the pledgee, who thus acquires a possessory pledge, whereby an agreement on an out-of-court sale is presumed to exist. If the pledgor, who agreed to the direct enforceability of the notarial protocol, fails to deliver the pledged movable to the pledgee, the latter may start an enforcement procedure demanding the delivery of the object or its sale. Problems can arise if the pledgor abuses the fact that the pledged object remained in his or her possession in that he or she alienates the object to a purchaser who is not aware of the pledge. Such purchaser is protected by Article 64 of the CPL and will acquire unencumbered ownership of the pledged object.[1341] The pledgor can also hide the object or encumber it by a possessory pledge, in which case the (new) pledgee is protected by Article 156 of the CPL.[1342] These problems are mainly avoided in the case of a registered non-possessory pledge because of the principle of publicity, which prevents the pledgor from alienating and encumbering the object to the benefit of third persons in good faith.[1343]

589. The *multiple pledging* of the same movable is possible also in the case of a non-possessory pledge. In the case of registered non-possessory pledges, the order of precedence is established on the basis of the date of the request of the notary to enter the pledge into the register.[1344] The pledgor must inform all the previous pledgees of each subsequent non-possessory pledge.[1345] In the case of the debtor's failure to fulfil the first secured claim, the pledged object can be sold and the proceeds from the sale are then divided among the pledgees, taking into account the

1337. Tratnik in *Property Law*, 485.
1338. Article 172 of CPL, Art. 24/1/2 of the Decree.
1339. Article 174/1 of CPL.
1340. Article 174/2 of CPL.
1341. If the conditions of Art. 64 of the CPL are not met, the purchaser will acquire ownership of the object, encumbered with the pledge. Tratnik, *Zastavna pravica* [Lien], 181 (GV Založba 2006).
1342. Tratnik in *Property Law*, 494. Art. 156/2 of the CPL provides: 'A pledgee who is in good faith as to the non-existence of other pledges acquires a pledge with the highest ranking if the pledgor has the movable in his possession.'
1343. Tratnik in *Property Law*, 494.
1344. Article 31/1 of the Decree.
1345. Article 176/1 of CPL.

order in which the non-possessory pledges were acquired (the second pledgee will get the repayment of his or her claim only when the first one is fully repaid, etc.) and the due dates of the secured claims (for the claims that are not yet due, the bank interest rate, specified in the CPL, will be taken into account).[1346] A movable placed under a non-possessory pledge can also be the subject of a possessory pledge and a fiduciary transfer of property, as well as a reservation of title.[1347]

590. A non-possessory pledge *expires* by the cessation of the secured claim (the principle of accessority); by a renouncement of the pledge by the pledgee; if the same person becomes both the pledgor and the pledgee; by the cessation of the pledged object, by the alienation of the pledged object to a third person in good faith; and in the event of the compulsory sale of the pledged object.[1348] A registered non-possessory pledge expires only upon its removal from the register – by analogy to a mortgage, the principle of publicity prevails over the principle of accessority.[1349]

591. Article 177 of the CPL lays the foundation for the establishment of a *Register of Non-possessory Liens*. The legislature thus delegated the more specific regulation of the register of non-possessory pledges to the executive branch. In 2004, the Slovenian government adopted the Decree on the Register of Non-possessory Liens and Seized Movable Property (hereinafter 'Decree'),[1350] which regulates 'the types of movables that are entered in the register; their identification; the procedure and the contents of the entries in the register and in other official records and documents; the manner of keeping, linking, and searching the data in the register; and the tariff regarding the costs of making the entries and the enabling access to the register'.[1351] The register is maintained by the Agency of the RS for Public Legal Records and Related Services.[1352]

592. This register is intended to have a similar function as the land register regarding mortgages.[1353] In both cases, the fact that an object is encumbered by a lien is not visible, because the pledged object remains in the direct possession of the pledgor. The mentioned registers thus ensure the possibility of persons having legal interest to verify if an object is encumbered by a pledge or not, because the data in these registers are public. In the case of the movables, these data comprise the identification of the movable property, the details about the secured claim and the pledge, and the details about the documents which are the basis for the entry, as

1346. Article 176/2 and 176/3 of CPL.
1347. Tratnik in *Property Law*, 487.
1348. *Ibid.*, 495–496.
1349. *Ibid.*, 496.
1350. Uredba o registru neposestnih zastavnih pravic in zarubljenih premičnin [Decree on the Register of Non-possessory Liens and Seized Movable Property], Official Gazette RS, No. 23/04, with further amendments.
1351. Article 1 of the Decree.
1352. Agencija Republike Slovenije za javnopravne evidence in storitve. The Internet site of the agency is available also in English, www.ajpes.si/?language=english, accessed on 31 Jul. 2019.
1353. That is why the provisions of the CPL regarding the registry of mortgages apply *mutatis mutandis* to the registry of non-possessory pledges (Art. 177/1 of CPL).

well as information regarding the creditor, the debtor, and the pledgor, if the pledgor is not also the debtor.[1354] The register of non-possessory pledges exists for movables that can be 'uniformly identified', as is the case for immovables. According to Article 8 of the Decree, these include stored material, equipment, motor and track vehicles, motorcycles, trailers, semi-trailers, and certain animals. The uniform identification mark for the stored material and the business equipment is the identification of the place where they are situated.[1355] The stored material is usually destined for subsequent sale or remaking by the debtor and must, therefore, remain in his or her possession.[1356] The pledgor must ensure the normal renewal of the stored material and must enable the pledgee to have regular supervision of this renewal.[1357] For vehicles, motorcycles, and trailers, the uniform identification mark is the number of the chassis,[1358] while for animals it is the number of the animal in the reference register, its sex, breed, and date of birth.[1359]

593. The movables listed in the decree can only be the subject of a 'registered non-possessory pledge' – an 'ordinary' non-possessory pledge cannot be validly established on such movables.[1360] The entry of the pledge into the register is of a constitutive nature, which means that the pledge is validly established only upon its entry into the register and not just upon the formation of the notarial protocol.[1361]

594. The principles that apply regarding this register are similar to the ones regarding the land register: the principle of publicity,[1362] the principle of the constitutive nature of the entry in the register, and the principle of trust in the register.[1363] If a pledge is entered in the register of non-possessory pledges, no one may rely on the argument that he or she was unaware of the details of this pledge.[1364] On the contrary, anyone who relies on the information in the register and who acts conscientiously in legal transactions cannot suffer detrimental legal consequences as a result.[1365] Nevertheless, the Register of Non-possessory Liens and Seized Movable Property differs from the land register in several essential characteristics; above all is the fact that, contrary to the land register, this is not a register of ownership and not all movables are registered in it.[1366] A movable is only entered into the register if it is seized in an enforcement procedure or if a non-possessory pledge is established on it. That is why it is not generally possible to obtain an extract from the register with information about the 'legal state' of a movable, as is possible in the

1354. Article 177/2 of CPL, Art. 7 of the Decree.
1355. Articles 10 and 11 of the Decree, and Article 173 of the CPL as amended by SPZ-B.
1356. Tratnik in *Property Law*, 458.
1357. Article 173/2 of CPL.
1358. Article 12 of the Decree.
1359. Article 13 of the Decree.
1360. Tratnik in *Property Law*, 477.
1361. *Ibid.*, 476.
1362. Article 6 of the Decree.
1363. Tratnik in *Property Law*, 477.
1364. The pledgee thus does not lose the registered non-possessory pledge if the pledged thing is sold to a third party: Decision of the High Court in Ljubljana, No. Cst 205/2015 of 21 Apr. 2015.
1365. Article 177/4 of CPL.
1366. Tratnik in *Property Law*, 476.

land register regarding immovables; it is only possible to obtain either a certificate stating that the movable is not entered in the register (from which it can be concluded that it is not encumbered with a non-possessory pledge and that it has not been seized) or a certificate regarding the pledge(s) established on the movable.[1367] Anyone can obtain information regarding the movable, the documents on the basis of which the movable was registered, the seizure and the secured claim on the Internet site of the agency; one must, however, prove his or her legal interest to obtain information on the creditor, debtor, or pledgor.[1368]

§2. Conditional Sale/Reservation of Title

595. Reservation of title (Sl. *pridržek lastninske pravice*, Lat. *pactum reservati dominii*) is regulated in Articles 520 and 521 of the CO, among the special types of contracts of sale.[1369] Article 520 provides that the seller of a specific movable may, via a special contractual provision, reserve title to the object once delivered to the buyer until the buyer pays the purchase money. The classification in the CO is, however, not entirely fortunate, because the reservation of title is in fact a non-possessory property law security[1370] and has no impact on the sale as the obligational relationship between the parties.

596. Reservation of title is a *very efficient security* for the seller: until the buyer pays the whole price, he or she does not become the owner of the thing. In the event of any problems in paying, the seller will be able to gain his or her thing back, and the buyer will only be able to demand the return of the paid instalments.[1371] Nevertheless, the buyer can often be interested in such an agreement, because it gives him or her the opportunity to use the object being sold as its owner before paying the whole purchase money. It must also be noted that the seller's position is strong only if the buyer respects the reservation of title. If the buyer alienates the object in favour of a bona fide third party, who was misled by the buyer's possession of the object, this party might be protected by Article 64 of the CPL. In this case, the seller cannot demand the return of the object from the third party, but only compensation from the buyer. The security can thus entirely lose its effect.

1367. *Ibid.*, 477.

1368. Vratanar, *Register neposestnih zastavnih pravic in zarubljenih premičnin* [The Register of Non-possessory Liens and Seized Movable Property], in Podjetje in delo, Nos 6–7/2005, p. 1394; Tratnik, *Neposestna zastavna pravica na premičninah, 1. del* [Non-possessory Pledge on Movable Property, 1st part], in Pravna praksa, 2012, Nos 39–40, Supplement, p. III.

1369. Commentators mention the possibility of a similar clause in other contracts involving the transfer of ownership – for example, in a contract of exchange. Juhart in *CO with Commentary*, 3rd book, 352–354.

1370. Vrenčur, *Pridržek lastninske pravice* [Reservation of Title], in Podjetje in delo, No. 6/2005, p. 1365.

1371. 'The reservation of title protects the seller and not the buyer, therefore the seller can decide whether he or she will demand the fulfilment of the obligation (payment of the purchase money) or the return of the thing': Judgment of the Supreme Court RS, No. II Ips 1135/2008 of 29 Mar. 2012.

597. The reservation of title is an exception to the basic rule of the transfer of the ownership of movables by way of the transfer of possession (Lat. *traditio*) and can, therefore, lead to misinterpretation and damage to the buyer's creditors in insolvency and enforcement proceedings. Therefore, the CO provides that the reservation has *effects against the buyer's creditors* only if the buyer's signature on the contract containing the provision on the reservation of title has been attested by the notary prior to the aforementioned events. Thus, in the case of a conflict of interests between the seller and the buyer's creditors, the CO does not fully protect the seller, but searches for a compromise. Apart from this special regulation regarding insolvency and enforcement proceedings, there is no special *form* required for the valid conclusion of a reservation of title agreement.[1372]

598. Article 521 of the CO regulates the *transfer of the risk* of the accidental perishing or damage of the object. According to this article, the risk is transferred to the buyer at the moment of delivery of the sold object, even if the seller remains the owner of the object.[1373] This is an exception to the general rule that all risks are borne by the owner (Lat. *res perit domino*). If the thing is destroyed or damaged while already in the buyer's possession, the owner can still demand the payment of the purchase money.[1374] The legal theory holds that if the contract of sale is rescinded for a reason in the seller's sphere (e.g., the sold object has a defect), the risk is considered not to have been transferred.[1375]

599. The commercial practice has developed several special forms of the reservation of title, more appropriate for the securing of commercial obligations. The most common are the *prolonged reservation of title* and the reservation of title with clause of remake. The first is a combination of the classical reservation of title and the fiduciary assignment of a claim so as to ensure the security of a claim also after the buyer has sold the thing to further buyers.[1376] The second one targets situations where the buyer intends to remake the purchased thing, in which case the seller would normally lose ownership on the thing that has become the element of another thing (Articles 55 and 57 of the CPL). By the *reservation of title with clause of remake*, this rule is excluded so as to enable the seller to acquire ownership or co-ownership on the new thing.[1377] The legal theory also cites the so-called *extended reservation of title* (where the reservation of title secures not only the claim for the purchase money for the thing on which the title is reserved, but also other claims the seller has against the buyer) and the so-called *transferred reservation of title*.[1378]

1372. See, e.g., Judgment and Decision of the High Court in Ljubljana, No. I Cp 2784/2013 of 2 Apr. 2014.
1373. See, e.g., Judgment of the High Court in Ljubljana, No. II Cpg 222/2010 of 11 Mar. 2010.
1374. Juhart in *CO with Commentary*, 3rd book, 364.
1375. *Ibid.*, 365.
1376. Vrenčur, *Pridržek lastninske pravice* [Reservation of Title], in Podjetje in delo, No. 6/2005, pp. 1365 ff.
1377. *Ibid.*
1378. For more on these forms of the reservation of title, see Juhart in *CO with Commentary*, 3rd book, 361–362.

600. The reservation of title can be established also on the basis of a law, in the case of a division of a movable in co-ownership by the court (*statutory reservation of title*). The co-owners are the holders of the reservation of title up to the amount of their shares until the co-owner who acquires the movable pays them out.[1379]

§3. COMPENSATION/OFFSET

601. Offset (Sl. *pobot*) is a mode of expiration of two or more obligations between the same parties, but arising from different legal relations.[1380] In Slovenian law, an offset is usually not considered to be a security under the law of property. It is regulated in the CO and studied within the law of obligations. It is, by far, most common in the case of two reciprocal money claims, but it can also come into existence in the case of reciprocal claims of any other fungible things (Lat. *genus*). Above all, the offset simplifies the execution of these obligations (instead of active behaviour for the purpose of executing the obligation, a mere statement of offset suffices for the obligations to be executed, at least to the extent of the smaller claim), which is its principal purpose.[1381] But it can also be regarded as a form of ad hoc security instrument, because it ensures the execution of the reciprocal obligation by practically empowering one party to execute the reciprocal obligations of both parties.

602. Article 311 of the CO lays down the *general conditions* for a valid offset: '[t]he debtor may offset his or her claim against the creditor against the creditor's claim against him or her if the two claims are declared in money or in other replaceable things of the same type and the same quality and if both claims have fallen due'. Apart from these three conditions, the legal theory and the case law add a fourth one (which can also be deduced from Article 314 of CO, which regulates the offset of prescribed claims): both claims must be actionable.[1382]

603. For the offset to come into existence, one of the parties must issue a *declaration of offset*. After that, the offset is, however, reputed to exist *ex tunc* – that is, from the moment when all the required conditions were fulfilled.[1383]

604. The condition of *reciprocity* could raise some questions as to its interpretation in certain cases – for example, in the event a claim is secured by a surety or a pledge. Article 313 of the CO thus provides that if a debtor's debt is secured by a surety and this surety has a claim against the creditor, the debtor cannot offset the surety's claim with the creditor's claim against him or her. However, the surety can offset the debtor's claim against the creditor if the creditor demands the fulfilment of the debtor's obligation from the surety. This regulation is logical, because the

1379. Article 71/4 of CPL.
1380. Juhart in *CO with Commentary*, 2nd book, 389.
1381. *Ibid.*
1382. *Ibid.*, 392.
1383. Article 312 of CO.

burden of the obligation should primarily lie on the debtor and the surety should come to the rescue only if necessary. The law also protects a pledgor who is not a debtor. He or she can demand the return of the pledged object from the creditor if the latter could have obtained repayment from the debtor by way of an offset, even though the creditor has not used this option.

605. Questions could arise also as to the *prescribed claims*. These still exist and can be validly fulfilled, but they no longer enjoy legal protection by the court if the debtor raises the objection of prescription. Article 314 of the CO provides that such claim can be offset against a debt if at the moment of the fulfilment of the conditions for an offset, the claim was not yet prescribed. If one of the claims was already prescribed at that moment, the debtor of the prescribed claim must raise an objection to prevent the coming into existence of the offset.

606. The institution of offset can present difficulties in cases of a *change of one of the parties in a civil relation*. In the case of the transfer/assignment (Lat. *cessio*) of a claim,[1384] the debtor of the transferred claim may exercise, with the assignee, an offset of the debtor's claims that could have been offset with the assignor prior to notification of transfer.[1385] The debtor may also offset, with the assignee, those of his or her claims against the assignor that were acquired prior to the notification of assignment but that had not yet fallen due when the debtor was notified of the assignment – but only if they fall due before the assigned claim or simultaneously with it.[1386] However, if the debtor declares to the assignee that he or she consents to the assignment without any reservation, he or she loses the right to offset against the assignee any of his or her claims against the assignor.[1387] Article 315 of the CO thus protects the status of a debtor who is not a party to the contract of transfer of the claim and must accept the change of creditor, with the exception of a prior agreement between the debtor and the creditor forbidding the transfer of the claim (Lat. *pactum de non cedendo*).[1388] The CO, however, also protects the assignee, but only when the assigned claim is entered into a public register. The debtor can only exercise an offset of his or her claim with the assignee if this claim is entered into the register besides the assigned claim or if the assignee was informed of its existence at the moment of the assignment.[1389] Trust in the state of the claim discernible from the registers thus prevails over the debtor's protection.

607. Third persons entering into the relation between the creditor and the debtor on the basis of enforcement proceedings are protected by Article 317 of the CO, which provides that the debtor may not exercise an offset of his or her claim against the creditor if it only fell due after a third person obtained the seizure (attachment) of the creditor's claim against the debtor. The legal theory holds that Article 317 of

1384. Articles 417 ff. of CO.
1385. Articles 315/1 and 421/2 of CO.
1386. Article 315/2 of CO.
1387. Article 315/3 of CO. See, e.g., Judgment of the High Court in Maribor, No. I Cpg 482/2013 of 6 Feb. 2014.
1388. Article 417/2 of CO.
1389. Article 315/4 of CO.

the CO should be interpreted broadly and applied also to situations where a claim has been pledged, due to the protection of third parties (in this case the pledgee); for appropriate protection of the debtor of the pledged claim, this is, however, possible only if the reciprocal claim came into existence after the establishment of the pledge.[1390]

608. Article 316 of the CO further determines the *claims that cannot extinguish by way of an offset:* claims that cannot be attached in enforcement proceedings; claims for objects or the value of objects that were placed in the debtor's safekeeping or lent to the debtor, or that the debtor unlawfully took or retained; claims arising through the intentional infliction of damage; compensation claims for damage to health or damage for causing death; and claims deriving from a legal obligation of maintenance. Further exceptions to the possibility of offset are envisaged in insolvency proceedings.[1391] The legal theory holds that the parties can also conclude an agreement regarding the limitations or the prohibition of an offset (Lat. *pactum de non compensando*).[1392]

609. In Slovenian law, the offset is also an *institution of procedural law*, since it can also come into existence by way of a court judgment. The defendant in civil proceedings can raise an objection of offset in that he or she admits that the claim of the plaintiff against him or her really exists but that it ceases to exist (in part or fully) because of the existence of the defendant's claim of the same kind against the plaintiff.[1393] This 'procedural offset' is possible if, by analogy to the CO, the claims are reciprocal, of the same kind, mature, and actionable. The court will issue a judgment with an operative part consisting of three parts. The court will first establish the existence of the plaintiff's claim; second, it will establish the existence of the defendant's claim (up to a maximum of the amount of the plaintiff's claim); and third, the court will pronounce the offset and dismiss the plaintiff's claim (up to the value of the defendant's claim if the latter is smaller).[1394] The 'procedural offset' comes into existence only with the finality of the judgment.[1395] It must be stressed that, naturally, the offset under the law of obligations also has effects in civil proceedings: if the offset was declared and came into existence before the dispute, the defendant can raise the objection that the obligation has been fulfilled and the plaintiff's claim will be dismissed. In this case, the operative part of the judgment will only contain the decision of the court on the plaintiff's claim and not on the existence of the reciprocal claims.

610. The offset is also an important instrument in *insolvency proceedings*. In comparison to the basic regulation in the CO, the offset in insolvency proceedings presents some important differences for the purpose of facilitating the repayment of

1390. Juhart in *CO with Commentary*, 2nd book, 410.
1391. Articles 263 and 264 of FOIPCDA.
1392. Juhart in *CO with Commentary*, 2nd book, 409.
1393. Ude, *Civilno procesno pravo* [Civil Procedure Law], 226 (Uradni list 2002).
1394. Article 324/3 of CPA. Ude, *Civilno procesno pravo* [Civil Procedure Law], 227 (Uradni list 2002).
1395. Ude, *Civilno procesno pravo* [Civil Procedure Law], 228 (Uradni list 2002).

the creditors as much as possible. Article 261 of the FOIPCDA regulates the offset in insolvency proceedings.[1396] All reciprocal claims between the insolvent debtor and his or her creditors are declared to be offset from the moment of the beginning of the insolvency proceedings, even if the claims have not yet fallen due; if they are not of the same kind (the subject of the obligation is converted into money);[1397] and if, under certain conditions, they are conditional.[1398]

§4. Fiduciary Transfer of Ownership

611. The fiduciary transfer of ownership is regulated in Article 63 of the CPL: '[t]ransfer of ownership of a movable may be tied to a resolutory condition or a suspensive condition, in particular as transfer of ownership as security … ', and especially in Articles 201–206 of the CPL. For more about this mechanism, see the General Introduction, and especially Part IV.

1396. Articles 164, 261–264 of FOIPCDA.
1397. Article 161 of FOIPCDA.
1398. Article 262 of FOIPCDA.

Chapter 4. Lien on Patrimonial Rights

612. Patrimonial rights are rights that are transferable, and the value of such rights can be expressed in money.[1399] On the basis of the explicit provision of Article 3/2 of the CPL, a lien can also be created regarding property law rights, although these are not 'things' according to Article 15 of the CPL. Apart from the general regulation common to all liens, a 'lien on rights' is specifically regulated in Chapter 5 of Part VI of the CPL. This chapter is further divided into three sections: the first one regulating the lien on a claim, the second one the lien on a negotiable instrument (a security), and the third one the lien on other property law rights.

§1. Lien on a Claim

613. Article 178 of the CPL provides that for the purpose of securing a claim, a lien may be established on another claim whose subject is an active obligation (a charge, *datio*) – typically, the payment of an amount of money. It is thus not possible to put under lien a claim whose subject is a service or an omission. Also future claims, which do not yet belong to the lienee (because they do not yet exist or they still belong to another person), can be placed under lien; by analogy to Article 61/1 of the CPL, the lien will be effective when the lienee acquires the right to encumber the lien claim.[1400] The debtor of the future claim must, however, be known at the moment of the establishment of the lien, because his or her notification is a constitutive element of a lien.[1401] If the debtor is still unknown, a fiduciary assignment of the claim (Lat. *fiducia cum creditore contracta*)[1402] is a possibility.[1403]

614. A lien on a claim is widely used as a security, although the existence and the quality of this security depend on the legal relationship, which serves as a basis for the lien claim, as well as on the solvency of the debtor of the lien claim.[1404] Nevertheless, the risk of the creditors becomes more acceptable if the debtor places under lien a bigger number of claims against different debtors, which is normally the case.[1405]

1399. Article 22 of CPL.
1400. Tratnik in *Property Law*, 497. If a lien is established on future deposits on the debtor's bank account and insolvency proceedings are started against such debtor, the lien covers only the claims concerning the money which was actually deposited in the debtor's account before the beginning of the insolvency proceedings. The debtor namely lost his ability to dispose of his patrimony with the beginning of the insolvency proceedings; therefore, the condition for the effectiveness of a lien on future claims which is that the lienee acquires the right to encumber the claim, will never be fulfilled. Supreme Court RS, Judgment No. III Ips 101/2013 of 11 Nov. 2014.
1401. Tratnik in *Property Law*, 498.
1402. Article 426 of CO, Arts 207–209 of CPL. For further details, see Tratnik in Tratnik et al., *Stvarnopravna zavarovanja*, 201–208 (IARS 2001); Tratnik, *Zastavna pravica* [Lien], 267–272 (GV Založba 2006); Tratnik in *CPL with Commentary 2004*, 854–870. See also Part IV.
1403. Tratnik in *Property Law*, 498.
1404. *Ibid.*, 497.
1405. *Ibid.*

615. According to the general rule,[1406] a lien on a claim can be *established* on the basis of an agreement between the lienee and the lienor (which can be concluded in the form of a directly enforceable notarial protocol),[1407] on the basis of a law, and on the basis of a court decision. Regarding the establishment *by way of an agreement*, a lien on a claim is created at the moment when the debtor of the lien claim receives notification from the lienee that the claim has been placed under lien.[1408] The obligation to inform the debtor is the reason many prefer a fiduciary transfer of a claim to a lien on a claim.[1409] The assignor in a fiduciary transfer is not usually required to inform the debtor of the assignment for the claim to be transferred into the property of the recipient.[1410] Nevertheless, some warn that exactly this 'discreet' nature of the fiduciary assignment of a claim causes its relative unreliability.[1411] Another reason for the preference for fiduciary assignment is the very formal manner of obtaining the repayment from the lien claim.[1412] The lienee must deliver to the lienor a document and other proof of the lien claim,[1413] but this obligation of the lienee is not of a constitutive nature regarding the creation of the lien.[1414] The establishment of a lien on a claim *on the basis of a law* is very rare; one example thereof is Article 264/2 of the CPL.[1415] The establishment of a lien on a claim *on the basis of a court decision* is possible in enforcement and security proceedings, by way of seizure of the claim[1416] or by way of a preliminary injunction.[1417]

616. After receiving the notification of the lien, the debtor of the lien claim may only make valid fulfilment to the lienor and no longer to the creditor.[1418] The consequence of this provision is the requirement of a certain *diligence of the lienor*

1406. Article 130 of CPL.
1407. Rijavec, *Civilno izvršilno pravo* [Civil Enforcement Law], 249 (GV Založba 2003).
1408. Article 179/1 of CPL.
1409. Tratnik in *Property Law*, 497.
1410. Juhart in *CO with Commentary*, 2nd book, 604; Rijavec, *Civilno izvršilno pravo* [Civil Enforcement Law] (GV Založba, 2003).
1411. Vrenčur, *Novosti na področju cesije* [Novelties Regarding the Assignment of a Claim], in Pravna Praksa, No. 5/2003, pp. 9 ff.
1412. Sajovic, *Osnove civilnega prava, Stvarno pravo I* [Bases of Civil Law, Property Law I], 143 (Uradni list 1994); Rijavec, *Civilno izvršilno pravo* [Civil Enforcement Law], 248 (GV Založba 2003).
1413. Article 179/2 of CPL.
1414. Rijavec, *Civilno izvršilno pravo* [Civil Enforcement Law] (GV Založba 2003).
1415. Tratnik in *Property Law*, 499. Art. 264 of the CPL provides that a building that is built on an immovable encumbered with a right of superficies may be put under lien (actually the right of superficies is put under lien). Upon expiration of the right of superficies, the lienor acquires a lien on the claim of the holder of the right of superficies for payment of compensation, which has to be paid by the owner of the land that has a higher value due to the building that has been built on it.
1416. Article 107/3 of CESA.
1417. Articles 257 and 260/1/2 of CESA.
1418. Article 180 of CPL.

regarding the claim. He or she is obliged to take all necessary steps to preserve the lien claim and collect the possible interest or other periodic claims arising from the lien claim.[1419]

617. When a lien claim falls due, the lienor must collect it.[1420] If the object of the lien claim is the delivery of an object, a lien is created on this object at the moment of the fulfilment of the claim.[1421] If the secured claim has fallen due, the lienor can proceed to the sale of the lien object. For the protection of the debtor of the secured claim in cases where the object of the lien claim is money, which could be spent by the lienor, the lienor must, at the request of the lienee, deposit the amount collected with the court.[1422] The money collected by the lienor namely does not become his or her property, but the lienor acquires a lien thereupon.[1423] If the object of the lien and of the secured claim is money, which is most often the case, the lienor may retain as much as is owed to him or her and must deliver the remainder to the lienee.[1424] The reciprocal claims of the lienor and the lienee thus become offset.

618. As to the *expiration* of the lien, Article 183 of the CPL provides that if a secured claim expires (most commonly because of its repayment by the lienee), the lienor must notify the debtor of the lien claim that the claim is no longer under lien.[1425] After receiving this notification, the debtor of the lien claim can validly fulfil his or her obligation only to the 'original' creditor (the former lienee). The lien expires also upon expiration of the lien claim or in the event of the same person becoming the lienee and the lienor.[1426]

619. Article 186 of the CPL regulates the *objections* that can be raised by the debtor of a lien claim against the lienor. The debtor can raise the objections he or she holds against the lienor, as well as, by analogy to an assignment, the objections that the debtor could have raised against the lienee until the notification of the lien.[1427] These objections can originate in the invalidity of the lien claim, in the invalidity of the lien, or in the offset of the debtor's claim by the claims of either the lienee or the lienor.[1428]

620. If the conditions for the repayment of the lien claim to the lienor are met and the debtor of the lien claim opposes the lienor's right to repayment, the latter can (on the basis of an appropriate enforceable title, e.g., a directly enforceable

1419. Articles 181 and 182 of CPL.
1420. Article 184/1 of CPL.
1421. Article 184/2 of CPL.
1422. Article 184/3 of CPL.
1423. Cigoj, *Komentar obligacijskih razmerij* [Commentary of the Obligational Relationships], 4th book, 2630 (ČZ Uradni list SRS1986), cited by Tratnik in *Property Law*, 501.
1424. Article 185/1 of CPL.
1425. Judgment of the High Court in Ljubljana, No. I Cpg 962/2014 of 12 Jun. 2014.
1426. Tratnik in *Property Law*, 503.
1427. Article 421/2 of CO.
1428. Cigoj, *Komentar obligacijskih razmerij*, Books I–IV, 2631 (ČZ Uradni list SRS 1984–1986).

notarial protocol) institute *enforcement proceedings* and demand the court order that the lien claim be seized and transferred to him or her, either instead of performance or for collection.[1429] If the claim is transferred only for collection, the lienor will be able to demand the fulfilment of the claim and the secured claim will be considered satisfied up to the amount of the collected money. If the claim is transferred instead of performance, the lien claim will be considered fulfilled up to the amount of the transferred claim (even if the lienor will finally not be able to collect the whole amount of the claim); such transfer is analogous to the assignment of a claim under the law of obligations.[1430]

621. In the enforcement procedure, the court will not repeat the notification to the debtor, because he or she has already been notified, and will order the transfer of the claim, as well as prohibit all lienee's disposal of the claim.[1431] If the lienee delivered the documentation regarding the claim to the lienor, the court will note on the documents that the claim has been transferred to the lienor; if the documentation has not been delivered, the court will force the lienee to deliver.[1432] The seizure and the transfer of the claim are performed only up to the amount of the secured claim.[1433] If only a part of the lien claim has been transferred to the lienor, the lienee can demand that the lienor deposits caution money to ensure that the documents regarding the claim will be returned to the lienee after the collection of the transferred part of the claim.[1434] If the claim is indivisible (e.g., a claim arising from a negotiable instrument which is transferred by way of endorsement), then the seizure and the transfer of the whole claim is performed, if the creditor deposits caution money to ensure that the remainder of the collected money will be delivered to the court.[1435]

622. If another creditor of the lienee demands the repayment of his or her claim out of the lien claim, the lienor who acquired the lien on the basis of an agreement with the lienee before such enforcement procedure, will preserve his or her priority;[1436] i.e., his or her claim will be fulfilled out of the lien claim and the creditor who started the enforcement proceedings will obtain the remainder.

1429. Article 114 of CESA. See also Rijavec, *Civilno izvršilno pravo* [Civil Enforcement Law], 250 (GV Založba 2003). For the regulation of the transfer of a claim instead of performance or for collection, see Art. 425 of the CO.
1430. Article 127 of CESA.
1431. Rijavec, *Civilno izvršilno pravo* [Civil Enforcement Law], 250 (GV Založba, 2003).
1432. Articles 118/3 and 118/5 of CESA. See also Rijavec, *Civilno izvršilno pravo* [Civil Enforcement Law], 250 (GV Založba 2003).
1433. Article 105 of CESA.
1434. Article 118/2 of CESA.
1435. Article 116 of CESA, Rijavec, *Civilno izvršilno pravo* [Civil Enforcement Law] (GV Založba 2003).
1436. Rijavec, *Civilno izvršilno pravo* [Civil Enforcement Law], 290 (GV Založba 2003).

§2. Lien on a Negotiable Instrument (Security)

623. According to Article 187 of the CPL, a lien may also be established on a negotiable instrument. Such instrument must be transferable, and it must be possible to express its value in money.[1437] The basis for the creation of a lien is a valid contract of lien, but as to the actual creation of the lien, the CPL distinguishes among negotiable instruments issued to the bearer, negotiable instruments issued by order, and negotiable instruments registered to a name.

624. If a *negotiable instrument* under lien is *issued to the bearer*, a lien is created when the negotiable instrument is delivered to the lienor.[1438] Such a negotiable instrument is usually similar to a movable object, and the lien on it is usually similar to the possessory lien on a movable. If it is issued *by order* (or *to a name*, but in accordance with the law, it can be transferred by endorsement), a lien is created by an endorsement in which it is stated that the negotiable instrument is delivered in lien (endorsement in lien) and with the delivery of the negotiable instrument.[1439] If a negotiable instrument under lien is *registered to a name*, a lien is created the moment the debtor under the negotiable instrument receives notification from the lienee that the claim arising from the security has been placed under lien.[1440] This kind of negotiable instruments is usually transferred by assignment; therefore, the creation of a lien on such negotiable instruments is analogous to that on claims.[1441] The creation of a lien on a negotiable instrument that is *issued in non-materialized form* is regulated by the Book Entry Securities Act.[1442] The regulation of the latter is similar to the one applying to the mortgage because of the existence of a public register.[1443]

625. According to Article 189 of the CPL, the provisions of the CPL regulating the lien on a claim apply *mutatis mutandis* to the lien on a negotiable instrument. These do not, however, regulate the option of the lienor to sell the negotiable instrument under lien (because the claims are normally not sold as a consequence of the non-payment by the lienee); in this case, the provisions applying to the selling of a movable object under lien should apply.[1444]

626. As to the *expiration* of a lien on negotiable instruments, it must be stressed that, contrary to the general rule, this does not occur with the expiration of the secured claim, but only when the lienor undertakes all the necessary acts for the

1437. Tratnik in *Property Law*, 505.
1438. Article 188/1 of CPL.
1439. Article 188/2 of CPL. This endorsement is regulated in Art. 222 of the CO.
1440. Article 188/3 of CPL.
1441. Tratnik in *Property Law*, 506.
1442. Zakon o nematerializiranih vrednostnih papirjih (ZNVP-1) [Book Entry Securities Act], Official Gazette RS, No. 75/15.
1443. Tratnik in *Property Law*, 504.
1444. *Ibid.*, 507–508.

transfer of the negotiable instrument back to the lienee.[1445] What these acts are depends on the nature of the negotiable instrument.[1446]

§3. Lien on a Share in a Commercial Company

627. A share in a commercial company is composed of patrimonial (right to participate at the profit of the company, right to withdrawal, etc.) and non-patrimonial (right to vote, right of representation, etc.) entitlements, but it is nevertheless considered to be a patrimonial right.[1447] A partner can only dispose of the share as a whole and not of the single entitlements thereof.[1448] The share can also be put under lien. Such lien is not explicitly regulated by the CPL; thus, the general provisions on 'a lien on other patrimonial rights' apply. According to Article 190 of the CPL, the lien on such rights is generally established according to the method that applies to the transfer of such rights. The legal act necessary for the transfer of a share and thus also for the *establishment* of a lien, is a notarial protocol.[1449] Nevertheless, because the lien is not a transfer of a share, but its encumbrance, the other partners in the company, who have a statutory right of pre-emption, must not necessarily be informed of the placement of the share under lien.[1450] If the lien is to have effect regarding the company, the company must be notified thereof.[1451] A lien on a share in a commercial company is entered in the register of commercial companies,[1452] held by district courts. Such entry has a declaratory effect, i.e., the effect of publicity, and is not of a constitutive nature.[1453]

§4. Lien on Other Patrimonial Rights

628. A lien can also be created on other patrimonial rights, according to the method that applies to the transfer of such rights, unless the law provides otherwise.[1454] The CPL contains general provisions applicable to liens on patrimonial rights other than those for which the lien is expressly regulated in the CPL or in some other act. Such are, for example, patrimonial intellectual property rights.[1455]

1445. *Ibid.*, 508.
1446. *Ibid.*
1447. Rijavec, *Civilno izvršilno pravo* [Civil Enforcement Law], 251 (GV Založba 2003).
1448. *Ibid.*
1449. Article 481/3 of the Zakon o gospodarskih družbah (ZGD-1) [Companies Act], Official Gazette RS, No. 42/06, with further amendments.
1450. Rijavec, *Civilno izvršilno pravo* [Civil Enforcement Law], 251–252 (GV Založba 2003).
1451. *Ibid.*, 252.
1452. Podpečan, *Zastavna pravica na poslovnem deležu v družbi z omejeno odgovornostjo* [Lien on a Share in a Limited Liability Company], in Pravna praksa, 2009, No. 18, p. 22.
1453. Supreme Court RS, Judgment, No. III Ips 63/2003 of 17 Feb. 2004.
1454. Article 190 of CPL.
1455. Tratnik in *Property Law*, 508; Tratnik, *Zastavna pravica* [Lien], 281 (GV Založba 2006).

629. As a general rule, the provisions on liens on movable property also apply to liens on other patrimonial rights[1456] and so do, naturally, all the general provisions regarding liens.

1456. Article 191 of CPL.

Chapter 5. Delegation, Direct Claim

630. In Slovenian law, a possibility to claim the payment directly from the debtor of one's debtor does not exist as such. The legal relationships based on the law of obligations strictly oblige only the parties to the relationship – that is, the creditor can only demand the fulfilment of the claim from his or her debtor and not from other persons, notwithstanding their eventual relationship with the debtor. This is only possible when the creditor legally replaces the debtor in the relationship with the latter's debtor (Lat. *subrogatio*), which can happen on the basis of an agreement among the parties (usually between two of the three parties involved in the operation) or on the basis of a law. Such possibilities are, for example, the assignment of a claim,[1457] the takeover of a debt,[1458] the takeover of performance,[1459] or the surety contract.[1460] The term 'direct claim' is used in Slovenian legal language mainly to describe the possibility of the victim to claim damages directly from the insurer of the person liable for causing the harm.[1461]

1457. Articles 417 ff. of CO.
1458. Articles 427 ff. of CO.
1459. Article 434 of CO.
1460. Articles 1012 ff. of CO.
1461. Article 965 of CO.

Selected Bibliography

Books and parts therein

In English:

Ekey Friedrich L. et al. *Heidelberger Kommentar zum Wettbewerbsrecht*, 2., neu bearbeit. Aufl. Heidelberg: C. F. Müller, cop. 2005.

Fatur Andrej & Podobnik Klemen. *Slovenia/Commentary: SI/C*. In Ymke Hofhuis (ed.), *Competition Law in Western Europe and the USA, Competition Law*, suppl. 412 (November 2018). Alphen aan den Rijn: Kluwer Law International, 2018.

Fatur Andrej & Podobnik Klemen & Vlahek Ana. *Slovenia*. International Encyclopaedia of Laws, Competition Law. Alphen aan den Rijn: Kluwer Law International, 2016.

Galič Aleš. *Slovenia*. International Encyclopaedia of Laws, Civil Procedure. Alphen aan den Rijn: Kluwer Law International, 2008.

Galič Aleš. *Slovenia*. International Encyclopaedia of Laws, Civil Procedure. Alphen aan den Rijn: Kluwer Law International, 2014.

Galič Aleš. 'From Kudla to Lukenda: Legal Remedies against Undue Delay in Civil Proceedings in Slovenia'. In Gudowski Jacek & Weitz Karol (eds), *Aurea praxis aurea theoria: księga pamiątkowa ku czci profesora Tadeusza Erecińskiego*. Tom 1. Warszawa: LexisNexis, 2011, 1453 ff.

Galič Aleš. 'Slovenian National Report: Current Status of Civil Procedure in Slovenia'. In Maleshin Dmitry (ed.), *Civil Procedure in Cross-Cultural Dialogue: Eurasia Context: Conference Book*, Moscow, Statut, 2012, 386 ff.

Grilc Peter & Juhart Miha. 'Slovenia'. In *International Privatization*. London, The Hague; Boston, Kluwer Law International, 1996, 199 ff.

Grilc Peter & Podobnik Klemen. 'Slovenia'. In Cahill Dermot & Cooke John D. & Wils Wouter (eds), *The Modernisation of EU Competition Law Enforcement in the European Union*: FIDE 2004 National Reports. Cambridge: Cambridge University Press, 2004, 517 ff.

Hess Burkhard et al., *European Insolvency Law: The Heidelberg-Luxembourg-Vienna Report on the Application of Regulation no. 1346/2000/EC on Insolvency Proceedings* (external evaluation JUST/2011/JCIV/PR/0049/A4). München, C. H. Beck; Oxford, Portland, Hart; Baden-Baden, Nomos, 2014, XXXII.

Možina Damjan & Vlahek Ana. *Contract Law in Slovenia*. International Encyclopaedia of Laws, Contracts. Alphen aan den Rijn: Wolters Kluwer, cop. 2019.

Selected Bibliography

Podobnik Klemen & Vlahek Ana. 'Chronology of Development of Private Law in Slovenia'. In Lavický Petr et al., *Private Law Reform*, Acta Universitatis Brunensis, Iuridica, Editio Scientia, No 501, Brno, Masaryk University, 2014, 283 ff.

Rudolf Claudia, Rijavec Vesna & Keresteš Tomaž. 'National Report on the Transfer of Movables in Slovenia'. In Faber Wolfgang & Lurger Brigitta (eds), *National Reports on the Transfer of Movables Europe: Volume I: Austria, Estonia, Italy, Slovenia*. Schriften zur Europäischen Rechtswissenschaft, Bd. 7, vol. 7. München, Sellier European Law Publishers, 2008.

Vlahek Ana & Damjan Matija. 'Slovenian Regulation of Short-Term Apartment Rentals via Digital Platforms'. In Hojnik Janja (ed.), *Sharing Economy in Europe: Opportunities and Challenges*, Zavod 14, Ljubljana, European Liberal Forum, Brussels, 2018, 119 ff.

In German:

Juhart Miha. 'Die Eigentumsübertragung im Recht der Republik Slowenien'. In Rainer & Filip-Fröschl (eds), *Transfer of Title Concerning Movables, Part 1*. Salzburger Studien zum europäischen Privatrecht, Bd. 18. Frankfurt am Main, Peter Lang, 2006.

Juhart Miha. 'Die Bedeutung des österreichischen Allgemeinen Bürgerlichen Gesetzbuchs (ABGB) für die Entwicklung des slowenischen bürgerlichen Rechts'. In Geistlinger (ed.). *200 Jahre ABGB - Ausstrahlungen: die Bedeutung der Kodifikation für andere Staaten und andere Rechtskulturen*. Wien, MANZ'sche Wien, 2011, 89 ff.

Galič Aleš. 'Die Entwicklung des Zivilprozessrechts in Slowenien'. In Sutter-Somm & Harsági (eds), *Die Entwicklung des Zivilprozessrechts in Mitteleuropa um die Jahrtausendwende: Reform und Kodifikation – Tradition und Erneuerung*. Zürich, Schulthess, 2012, 87 ff.

In Croatian:

Gavella Nikola et al. *Stvarno pravo* [Property Law]. Zagreb, Narodne Novine, 2007.

Klarić Petar & Vedriš Martin. *Građansko pravo* [Civil Law]. 12th edn. Zagreb, Narodne Novine, 2009.

In Slovene:

Androjna Vilko & Kerševan Erik. *Upravno procesno pravo* [Law of Administrative Procedure]. Ljubljana, GV Založba, 2006.

Berden Andrej et al. *Novo stvarno pravo* [New Property Law]. Maribor, Studio Linea, Zavod Codex Iuris, 2002.

Cigoj Stojan. *Teorija obligacij* [The Theory of Obligations]. Ljubljana, Uradni list RS, 2003.

Cigoj Stojan. *Komentar obligacijskih razmerij* [Commentary of Obligatiory Relationships]. Books I–IV. Ljubljana, ČZ Uradni list SRS, 1984–1986.

Čebulj Janez et al. *Zakon o urejanju prostora s komentarjem* [Spatial Planning Act with Commentary]. Ljubljana, GV Založba, 2005.

Damjan Matija. *Hipoteka na nepremičnini, ki je predmet razlastitve* [Mortgage on an Expropriated Immovable]. In Juhart, Plavšak, Vrenčur (eds), Sodobno stvarno pravo. Ljubljana, Pravna fakulteta v Ljubljani, Planet GV, TaxFinLex, 2016, 237 ff.

Damjan Matija. *Služnost v javno korist* [Easement in the Public Interest]. In Zbornik. Ljubljana, GV Založba, 2016, pp. 89–113.

Damjan Matija, Ude Lojze, Vlahek Ana. *Strokovno mnenje o predlogu Zakona o vzpostavitvi etažne lastnine na določenih stavbah in o ugotavljanju pripadajočega zemljišča* [Professional Opinion on the Draft ZVEtL]. Ljubljana, Inštitut za primerjalno pravo pri Pravni fakulteti v Ljubljani, 2016.

Galič Aleš. *Ustavno civilno procesno pravo* [Constitutional Civil Procedure Law]. Ljubljana, GV Založba, 2004.

Grižon Maja. *Nadomestilo za razlaščeno nepremičnino* [Compensation for Expropriated Immovable], Master Thesis. Ljubljana, University of Ljubljana, 2016.

Hudej Jasna, Ščernjavič Iztok. *Aktualna vprašanja izbrisne tožbe* [Current Issues of Action for Deletion]. In Zbornik. Ljubljana, GV Založba, 2016, 15–26.

Juhart Miha & Plavšak Nina (eds). *Obligacijski zakonik s komentarjem, 1.–3. knjiga* [Code of Obligations with Commentary 1st – 3rd Book]. Ljubljana, GV Založba, 2003.

Juhart Miha et al. *Stvarno pravo* [Property Law]. Ljubljana, GV Založba, 2007.

Juhart Miha et al. *Zavarovanje in utrditev obveznosti* [Security and Consolidation of Obligations]. Ljubljana, Gospodarski Vestnik, 1995.

Juhart Miha et al. *Stvarnopravni zakonik s komentarjem* [Code of Property Law with Commentary]. Ljubljana, GV Založba, 2004.

Juhart Miha et al. *Stvarnopravni zakonik (SPZ) s komentarjem* [Code of Property Law with Commentary]. Ljubljana, Uradni list RS, Pravna fakulteta v Ljubljani, Pravna fakulteta v Mariboru, 2016.

Juhart Miha. *Cesija – pogodbeni odstop terjatve* [Assignment – Contractual Transfer of a Claim]. Ljubljana, Gospodarski Vestnik, 1996.

Juhart Miha. *Dobrovernost kot pogoj za učinkovanje načela zaupanja v zemljiško knjigo.* [Good Faith Prerequisite of the Principle of Trust in the Land Register]. In Lojze Ude (ed.). Izbrane teme civilnega prava II. Ljubljana, Inštitut za primerjalno pravo pri Pravni fakulteti v Ljubljani, 2007, 153 ff.

Kranjc Janez. *Rimsko pravo* [Roman Law]. 2nd ed. Ljubljana, GV Založba, 2010.

Novak Barbara. *Družinsko pravo* [Family Law]. Ljubljana, Uradni list, 2014.

Novak Barbara (ed). *Komentar Družinskega zakonika* [Commentary of the Family Code]. Ljubljana, Uradni list, 2019.

Pavčnik Tomaž. *Usklajenost sodne prakse glede priposestvovanja služnosti v javno korist* [Harmony of Judicial Decisions on Acquisition of Easements in the Public Interest]. In Juhart, Plavšak, Vrenčur (eds), Sodobno stvarno pravo. Ljubljana: Pravna fakulteta v Ljubljani, Planet GV, TaxFinLex, 2016, 271 ff.

Plavšak Nina. *Pravna usoda služnosti in stavbne pravice v primeru prisilne prodaje nepremičnine v izvršbi in stečaju – pomen prednostnega načela* [Legal Destiny of Easements and Superficies in Cases of Forced Sale of an Immovable in Insolvency and Enforcement Proceedings – the Meaning of the Priority Principle]. In Juhart, Plavšak, Vrenčur (eds), Sodobno stvarno pravo. Ljubljana, Pravna fakulteta v Ljubljani, Planet GV, TaxFinLex, 2016, 287 ff.

Plavšak Nina. *Izbrisna tožba* [Action for Cancellation]. In Zbornik, 2. Dnevi stvarnega in zemljiškoknjižnega prava. Ljubljana, GV Založba, 2010, 41–49.

Plavšak Nina. *Zakon o varstvu kupcev stanovanj in enostanovanjskih stavb, Uvodna pojasnila* [Protection of Buyers of Apartments and Single Occupancy Buildings Act, Introductory Remarks]. Ljubljana, GV Založba, 2004.

Plavšak Nina. *ZFPPIPP, Uvodna pojasnila* [FOIPCDA, Introductory remarks]. Ljubljana, GV Založba, 2008.

Plavšak Nina. *ZFPPIPP-A do D, Uvodna pojasnila* [FOIPCDA-E, Introductory remarks]. Ljubljana: GV Založba, 2011.

Plavšak Nina. *ZFPPIPP-E, Uvodna pojasnila* [FOIPCDA-E, Introductory remarks]. Ljubljana, GV Založba, 2013.

Plavšak Nina. *ZFPPIPP-F, Uvodna pojasnila* [FOIPCDA-E, Introductory remarks]. Ljubljana, GV Založba, 2014.

Rijavec Vesna et al. *Pravna ureditev nepremičnin* [Legal Regulation of Immovables]. Ljubljana, GV Založba, 2006.

Rijavec Vesna. *Civilno izvršilno pravo* [Civil Enforcement Law]. Ljubljana, GV Založba, 2003.

Rijavec Vesna & Ekart Andrej. *Zakon o nepravdnem postopku (ZNP) z uvodnimi pojasnili* [Non-Contentious Civil Procedure Act (NCCPA) with introductory Remarks]. Ljubljana, Uradni list RS, 2009.

Sajovic Bogomir. *Osnove civilnega prava, Splošni del* [Basics of Civil Law, General Part]. Ljubljana, Uradni list, 1994.

Šinkovec Janez & Tratar Boštjan. *Zakon o nepravdnem postopku s komentarjem, vzorci in sodno prakso* [Non-Contentious Civil Procedure Act with Commentary, Forms and Case-law]. Ljubljana, Primath, 2003.

Toplak Ludvik. *Civilno pravo, Splošni del civilnega prava* [Civil Law, General Part of the Civil Law]. Maribor, Univerza v Mariboru, Pravna fakulteta, 2002.

Tratnik Matjaž. *Zastavna pravica* [Lien]. Ljubljana, GV Založba, 2006.

Tratnik Matjaž. *Stvarnopravni zakonik z uvodnimi pojasnili* [Property Code with Introductory Remarks]. Ljubljana, Uradni list, 2002.

Tratnik Matjaž. *Pridobitev lastnine in drugih stvarnih pravic na nepremičnini na podlagi zaupanja v zemljiško knjigo* [Acquisition of Ownership and other Property Rights on Immovables on the Basis of Trust in the Land Register]. In Lojze Ude (ed.). Izbrane teme civilnega prava II. Ljubljana, Inštitut za primerjalno pravo pri Pravni fakulteti v Ljubljani, 2007, 131 ff.

Tratnik Matjaž & Vrenčur Renato. *Zemljiškoknjižno pravo* [Land Registry Law]. Maribor, Codex Iuris, 2008.

Tratnik Matjaž & Vrenčur Renato. *Omejitve lastninske pravice in posebni pravni režimi na nepremičninah* [Restrictions of Property and Special Legal Regimes on Immovables]. Ljubljana, GV Založba, 2009.

Tratnik Matjaž et al. *Stavbna pravica in služnosti* [The Right of Superficies and Easements]. Maribor, Inštitut za nepremičninsko pravo Maribor, 2007.

Tratnik Matjaž et al. *Stvarnopravna zavarovanja* [Securities under Property Law]. Maribor, IARS, 2001.

Ude Lojze. *Civilno procesno pravo* [Civil Procedure Law]. Ljubljana, Uradni list, 2002.

Verčko Miha. *Uporaba pravil stvarnega prava pri varstvu vknjižene, resnične in pričakovane lastninske pravice* [Application og the Rules of Property Law in the Protection of Registered, real and expected ownership]. In Juhart, Plavšak, Vrenčur (eds), *Sodobno stvarno pravo*. Ljubljana, Pravna fakulteta v Ljubljani, Planet GV, Tax-Fin-Lex, 2016, 81 ff.

Vlačič Patrick et al. *Pomorsko pravo* [Maritime Law]. Ljubljana, Uradni list, 2008.

Vlahek Ana. *Pogodbeni prenos lastninske pravice na premičninah v evropskem pravnem prostoru* [Contractual Transfer of Ownership on Movables in European Legal Environment]. Ljubljana, GV Založba, 2010.

Vlahek Ana. 'Odprta vprašanja načela zaupanja v zemljiško knjigo' [Issues Relating to the Principle of Trust in the Land Register]. In Ude (ed.), *Izbrane teme civilnega prava II*,' Ljubljana, Institute of Comparative Law at the Faculty of Law in Ljubljana, 2007, 111 ff.

Vlahek Ana. 'Avstrijski prenosni sistem kavzalne tradicije' [Austrian Transfer System of Causal Tradition]. In Polajnar-Pavčnik (ed.), *Izročilo Občnega državljanskega zakonika*, Zbirka Pravna obzorja, 46, Ljubljana, GV založba, 2013, 191 ff.

Vlahek Ana. *Problematika skupnih površin in skupnosti lastnikov v vzorčnih soseskah* [Problems of Common Immovables and the Community of Owners in Sample Housing Estates]. In Zbornik. Ljubljana, GV Založba, 2016, pp. 104–105.

Vrenčur Renato. *Moderne oblike zavarovanja plačil* [Modern Methods of Securing Payments]. Ljubljana, GV Založba, 2005.

Vrenčur Renato. *Pravni temelji pridobitve služnosti v javno korist s komentarjem najnovejše sodne prakse* [Legal Basis of Acquisition of Easements in the Public Interest with Commentary of the Novel Case-Law]. In Juhart, Plavšak, Vrenčur (eds), Sodobno stvarno pravo. Ljubljana, Pravna fakulteta v Ljubljani, Planet GV, TaxFinLex, 2016, 253 ff.

Zidar Sambolec Alenka. *Stavbna pravica in posebnosti njene ureditve ter uporabe v javnem sektorju* [The Right of Superficies - Special Features of Regulation and Use in the Public Sector], Master Thesis. Ljubljana, University of Ljubljana, 2016.

Zupančič Karel. *Družinsko pravo* [Family Law]. Ljubljana, ČZ Uradni list RS, 1999.

Zupančič Karel. *Zakonska zveza in družinska razmerja* [Marriage and Family Relations]. Ljubljana, Časopisni zavod Uradni list SR Slovenije, 1989.

Zupančič Karel & Žnidaršič Skubic Viktorija. *Dedno pravo* [Inheritance Law]. Ljubljana, GV Založba, 2009.

Žnidaršič Skubic Viktorija. *Zasebna ustanova, trust, fiduciarni posli in njihov vpliv na dedovanje* [Private Foundation, Trust, Fiduciary Transactions and their Impact on the Law of Succession]. Ljubljana, Uradni list RS, 2015.

Articles

In English:

Podobnik Klemen. *Framing a New Competition Law for Slovenia*. In Global Competition Review, Aug./Sep. 1999, pp. 20 ff.

Selected Bibliography

Galič Aleš. *The Human Rights Dimension of the Argument of Precedent in the Case Law of the Slovenian Constitutional Court*. In Slovenian Law Review, Dec. 2005, vol. 2, no. 1/2, pp. 41 ff.

Galič Aleš. *Alternative Dispute Resolution in SLOVENIA*. In Slovenian Law Review, May 2004, vol. 1, no. 1/2, pp. 41 ff.

Galič Aleš. *Access to the Supreme Court in Slovenian Civil Procedure*. In ConferinŢa internaŢional bienal: Timişoara, 23–25 octombrie 2008. Bucureşti, Wolters Kluwer România, 2010, pp. 165 ff.

In German:

Galič Aleš. *Das slowenische Zivilprozessrecht zwischen Transmission, Kontinuität und Transformation*. In Ritsumeikan Law Review. International ed., March 2010, no. 27, pp. 117 ff.

Pogorelčnik Vogrinc Neža. *Der Zivilprozess in Slowenien*. In Jahrbuch für Ostrecht, bd. 59, hb. 1, 2018, pp. 25–68.

In Slovene:

Berden Andrej. *Reforma stvarnega prava: Načela stvarnega prava* [Reform of Property Law: The Principles of Property Law]. In Podjetje in delo, No. 6/2000, pp. 1447 ff.

Berden Andrej. *Načela stvarnega prava* [Principles of Property Law]. In Pravna Praksa, No. 6/2003, 9, No. 8/2003, 9, No. 9/2003, 13, No. 10/2003, 7, No. 12/2003, 11, No. 13/2003, p. 9.

Damjan Matija. *Služnost v javno korist* [Easement in the Public Interest]. In Pravosodni bilten,Y. 37, No. 1, 2016, pp. 69 ff.

Damjan Matija. *Pravne podlage za ureditev položaja infrastrukturnih omrežij na tujih zemljiščih* [Legal Basis for Regulating the Position of Infrastructure Networks on Others' Property]. In Pravni letopis 2013, pp. 85 ff.

Damjan Matija. *Zapleti pri lastninjenju nekdanjih nepremičnin v družbeni lastnini in urejanju sedanjega (neurejenega) stanja na zemljiščih* [Complications in the Privatization of the Former Socially Owned Real Property and Solving of the Current (Disorderly) Situation]. In Pravosodni bilten, 2011, Y. 32, No. 1, pp. 119 ff.

Damjan Matija. *Idealne imisije industrijskih in infrastrukturnih objektov*. [The Ideal Immissions of Industrial and Infrastructural Facilities]. In Pravnik, 2010, Y. 65, No. 9/10, pp. 573 ff.

Damjan Matija & Bergant Rakočević Vesna. *Dobra vera pri priposestvovanju služnosti: vidik pridobitelja služeče nepremičnine* [Good Faith in Acquisitve Prescription of Easements on Immovables: Position of the Acquirer of Encumbered Immovable]. In Pravnik, 2015, Y. 70, No. 5/6 (2015), pp. 307 ff.

Damjan Matija & Vlahek Ana. *Priposestvovanje služnosti v javno korist* [Acquisitive Prescription of an Easement in Public Interest]. In Pravnik, Nos 3–4/2014, pp. 149 ff.

Fajs Tamara Mateja. *ZVEtL in ovire za njegovo izvajanje v praksi* [ZVEtL and the Obstacles for its Application in Practice], In Pravna praksa, Y. 30, No.28/29, pp. 9–11.

Hudej Jasna. *Izbrisna tožba – analiza aktualne sodne prakse s komentarjem* [Deletion Claim – Analysis and Commentary of Case-law]. In Podjetje in delo, 2014, Y. 40, No. 8, pp. 1445 ff.

Hudej Jasna & Ščernjavič Iztok. *Ponovni premislek o nekaterih temeljnih izhodiščih stvarnega prava pri prenosu lastninske pravice na nepremičninah* [New Reflections on Some of the Basic Principles of Property Law Regarding the Transfer of Ownership on Immovable Property]. In Pravna praksa No. 3/2012, p. 23.

Juhart Miha. *Nekaj dodatnih premislekov k stvarnopravnim izhodiščem pri prenosu lastninske pravice na nepremičninah* [Some Additional Thoughts on Property Law Principles of Transfer of Ownership on Immovables]. In Pravna praksa, 17. jan. 2013, Y. 32, No. 2, pp. 6–9.

Juhart Miha. *Prenos lastninske pravice v zavarovanje* [Fiduciary Transfer of Property]. In Pravnik, Nos 1–3/1995, pp. 43 ff.

Juhart Miha. *Zavezovalni in razpolagalni pravni posli – med kavzalnostjo in abstraktnostjo* [Obligatory and Real Legal Transactions – Between Causality and Abstraction]. In Zbornik znanstvenih razprav, Pravna fakulteta v Ljubljani (Ljubljana: 1995), y. 55, pp. 129 ff.

Krševan Erik. *Morsko javno dobro: slabo* [Sea as Property in Public Domain: Insufficient]. In Podjetje in delo, 6–7/2007, pp. 1430–1438.

Kramberger Škerl Jerca. *(Ne)razumevanje pridržka javnega reda in posvojitev s strani istospolnih partnerjev* [The (Non)Understanding of the Public Policy Defense and the Adoption by Same-Sex Partners]. In Pravna Praksa, Y. 29, No. 29/30, Supplement, pp. II-VII.

Kuzma Dominik. *(Ne)spremenljivost vrstnega reda hipotek* [(Un)Changeability of the Priority Order of Mortgages]. In Pravna praksa, 46/2011, pp. 8 ff.

Pavčnik Tomaž. *Izbrisna tožba: (analiza prakse višjih sodišč)* [Deletion Claim: (Analysis of High Courts' Case-Law]. In Pravosodni bilten, 2012, Y. 33, No. 1, pp. 165 ff.

Plavšak Nina, Vrenčur Renato. *Pomen razpolagalnega upravičenja pri razpolaganju z lastninsko pravico na nepremičnini* [The Importance of the Disposal Right for Transactions with Ownership Right on Real Estate]. In Pravnik. Ljubljana: Zveza društev pravnikov Slovenije, 2016, pp. 595 ff.

Podpečan Mitja. *Zastavna pravica na poslovnem deležu v družbi z omejeno odgovornostjo* [Lien on a Share in a Limited Liability Company]. In Pravna praksa, 2009, No. 18, p. 22.

Pogorelčnik Vogrinc Neža. *Začasne odredbe v postopkih v pravdah zaradi motenja posesti* [Provisional Measures in Proceedings in Disputes for Disturbance of Possession]. In Pravnik. Ljubljana: Zveza društev pravnikov Slovenije, 2016, pp. 303–325, 421–422.

Skubic Zoran. *Premoženje* [Patrimony]. In Pravna Praksa, No. 12/2007, p. 34.

Šuler, *Pomen vpisa obligacijskih pravic v zemljiško knjigo* [The Importance of the Registration of Obligational Rights in the Land Register]. In Pravna praksa, No. 18/2013, pp. 14 ff.

Tratnik Matjaž. *Lastninska pravica na nepremičnini v pričakovanju* [The Expectation of Ownership of an Immovable]. In Pravna praksa, No. 2/2013, p. VIII.

Selected Bibliography

Tratnik Matjaž, Berden Andrej. *Javno dobro* [Property in Public Domain]. In Pravna praksa, No. 38/2010, pp. II-VIII.

Tratnik Matjaž. *Neposestna zastavna pravica na premičninah, 1. del* [Non-Possessory Pledge on Movable Property, Part One]. In Pravna Praksa, Nos 39–40/ 2012, Supplement, pp. I ff.

Tratnik Matjaž. *Neposestna zastavna pravica na premičninah, 2. del* [Non-Possessory Pledge on Movable Property, Part Two]. In Pravna Praksa, Nos 41–42/2012, Supplement, pp. I ff.

Tratnik Matjaž. *Pridobitev lastninske pravice s priposestvovanjem* [Acquisition of Ownership by Prescription]. In Pravna Praksa, Priloga (2003) 42–43, pp. 19 ff.

Tratnik Matjaž. *Stvarno pravo: Pojem stvari, njenih sestavnih delov in pritiklin* [Property Law: The Notion of Things, their Elements and Appurtenances]. In Pravna Praksa, No. 45/1999, pp. 4 ff.

Tratnik Matjaž. *Stvarno pravo: O problemih definicije nepremičnine in premičnine* [Property Law: About the Problems of the Definition of an Immovable and a Movable]. In Pravna Praksa, No. 46/1999, pp. 8 ff.

Tratnik Matjaž. *Stvarnopravni zakonik in obligacijsko pravo* [Code of Property Law and the Law of Obligations]. In Podjetje in delo, No. 6/2002, pp. 1392 ff.

Tratnik Matjaž & Vrenčur Renato. *O sistemu abstraktne ter kavzalne tradicije v stvarnem pravu* [On the System of Abstract and Causal Tradition in Property Law]. In Pravnik, y. 54, No. 6/8, Ljubljana, 1999, pp. 333 ff.

Vlahek Ana. *Priposestvovanje lastninske pravice na nepremičninah* [Acquisitive Prescription of Ownership on Immovables]. In Zbornik znanstvenih razprav, y. 66. Ljubljana: Pravna fakulteta v Ljubljani, 2007, pp. 309 ff.

Vlahek Ana. *Pridobivanje lastninske pravice na nepremičninah v Sloveniji s strani tujcev* [Acquisition of Ownership on Immovables in Slovenia by Foreign Citizens]. In Pravnik, Ljubljana, 2008, y. 63, No. 1/3, pp. 7 ff.

Vlahek Ana. *Prestavitev služnostne poti* [Alteration of Easements]. In Pravna Praksa, No. 8/2008, pp. 21 ff.

Vlahek Ana. *Stavbna pravica - sedem let po njeni uveljavitvi* [The Right of Superficies – Seven Years of its Regulation]. In Pravni letopis 2010, Ljubljana, pp. 165 ff.

Vlahek Ana. *Solastnina skupnih delov v etažni lastnini* [Co-ownership of Common Parts in Relationship of Divided Co-ownership]. In Zbornik stvarnega in zemljiškoknjižnega prava. Ljubljana: GV založba, 2010, pp. 26 ff.

Vlahek Ana. *Analiza sodne prakse glede priposestvovanja lastninske pravice na nepremičninah* [Analysis of Case Law on Acquisitive Prescription of Ownership on Immovables]. In Zbornik. Ljubljana: GV založba, 2011, pp. 13 ff.

Vlahek Ana. *Pravnoposlovni prenos lastninske pravice na premičninah v francoskem pravnem sistemu* [Derivative Inter Vivos Transfer of Movables in the French Legal System]. In Pravnik. Ljubljana: Zveza društev pravnikov Slovenije, 2010, pp. 171 ff.

Vratanar Nevenka. *Register neposestnih zastavnih pravic in zarubljenih premičnin* [The Register of Non-possessory Liens and Seized Movable Property]. In Podjetje in delo, Nos 6–7/2005, p. 1394.

Vrenčur Renato. *Vpisovanje obligacijskih pravic v zemljiško knjigo* [Entry of the Obligational Rights in the Land Register]. In Pravna Praksa, No. 26/2006, pp. 16 ff.

Vrenčur Renato. *Novosti na področju cesije* [Novelties Regarding the Assignment of a Claim]. In Pravna Praksa, No. 5/2003, pp. I ff.

Vrenčur Renato. *Omejitev razpolaganja po volji lastnika na področju nepremičnin* [Restriction of Disposal at the Will of the Owner Regarding Immovables]. In Pravna Praksa, No. 26/2003, pp. 5 ff.

Vrenčur Renato. *Pridržek lastninske pravice* [Reservation of Title]. In Podjetje in delo, No. 6/2005, pp. 1365 ff.

Vrenčur Renato. *Posest: Posredna in neposredna posest stvari* [Possession: Indirect and Direct Possession of a Thing]. In Podjetje in delo, No. 6/1999, pp. 1040 ff.

Vrenčur Renato. *Reforma stvarnega prava: Lastniška posest* [Reform of the Property Law: Proprietary Possession]. In Podjetje in delo, No. 6/2000, pp. 1454 ff.

Vrenčur Renato. *Ureditev fiduciarnega prenosa lastninske pravice v zavarovanje v novem slovenskem pravu* [Regulation of the Fiduciary Transfer of Ownership in the New Slovenian Law]. In Pravna Praksa, No. 42/2003, pp. 37 ff.

Vrenčur Renato. *Prenovljena ureditev izbrisne tožbe* [The Amended Regulation of the Action for Cancellation]. In Podjetje in delo, 6–7/2010, pp. 1387 ff.

Vrenčur Renato. *Retencijska pravica in pridržek lastninske pravice na nepremičninah?* [Right of Retention and Reservation of Title on Immovables?]. In Pravna praksa, No. 9/2002, pp. 7 ff

Žgavec Simon. *Univerzalno pravno nasledstvo pri statusnih preoblikovanjih gospodarskih družb* [Universal Legal Succession in the Change of Status of Commercial Companies]. In Pravna praksa, Nos 24–25/2010, pp. 8 ff.

Selected Bibliography

Index

The numbers here refer to paragraph numbers.

Index

Index

www.ingramcontent.com/pod-product-compliance
Lightning Source LLC
Chambersburg PA
CBHW071432230926
51846CB00001B/195